APPLIED OPERATIONS RESEARCH:
A SURVEY

Board of Advisors, Engineering

APPLIED OPERATIONS RESEARCH:
A SURVEY

GARY E. WHITEHOUSE
Department of Industrial Engineering
Lehigh University

BEN L. WECHSLER
Department of Industrial Engineering
Lehigh University

John Wiley & Sons,
New York Santa Barbara London Sydney Toronto

To our wives, Marian and
Bonnie, who eagerly
accepted a share of the
load that was more than
we had any right to ask of
them—an act for which we
shall be eternally grateful.

Library of Congress Cataloging in Publication Data:

Whitehouse, Gary E   1938–
   Applied operations research.

   Includes bibliographical references and index.
   1. Operations research. I. Wechsler, Ben L.,
1921–   joint author. II. Title.
T57.6.W6   658.4'034   76-16545
ISBN 0-471-94077-1

Printed in the United States of America

10 9 8 7 6 5 4 3 2 1

preface

This textbook provides the advanced undergraduate and first-year graduate students, regardless of their major discipline, with an understandable text that covers the fundamental operations research/management science techniques and their computational aspects. The trend toward increased use of these techniques in business and the social services, as evidenced for example by the CPA examination that requires a knowledge of linear programming, must be satisfied. In achieving this objective we feel that the text does three things.

First, it presents the techniques and their computational aspects within a broad, real-world applications environment. In short, the book whets the students' appetite with application, application, and more application through demonstrated usefulness. Each chapter explains the techniques using illustrative examples, numerous application cases used and usable in the real world, and a generous helping of progressively difficult problems that build a student's confidence early. We feel we have succeeded in alleviating the need for supplemental texts or readings, which should delight instructors as well as students.

Second, the text covers a very significant number of the available operations research techniques, at least those that are generally considered fundamental to an introductory understanding of the discipline. We have presented as much as we could in this survey, but the broad topical coverage of the eight chapters presents more material than can be dealt with normally in a single, three-credit-hour course. However, selecting topics of primary interest to the student for a three-hour course will pose no problem to the instructor if such a limitation exists. Adequate coverage of all the topics in an extended course is desirable and feasible.

Last, but not least, the text departs from the heavy mathematical orientation frequently encountered in the treatment of the subject matter. The average student who has completed algebra, introductory probability and statistics, and has a general facility with numbers has an adequate background for handling our treatment of the topics covered. Only a touch of calculus is used in a few selected topics where we felt it was indispensable. One of our colleagues, in reviewing the mathematical treatment, observed that it may distress those who are mathematically oriented but that it would be a joy to the average student.

No preface is complete without an acknowledgment. We would be remiss if we did not mention our colleagues, too numerous to name, both inside and outside of our discipline as well as our many students without whose encouragement we probably would not have been able to complete this book. Nor can we fail to acknowledge the understanding, encouragement, and assistance we were given by Professor George E. Kane, our department chairman. If the book achieves its objective, primary credit rests with their reinforcement of the spirit; if it falls short in any respect, primary responsibility rests with us.

Lehigh University   **Gary E. Whitehouse**
Bethlehem, Pennsylvania   **Ben L. Wechsler**

contents

3 Linear Programming

4 Specialized Mathematical Programming Topics

5 Network Techniques

6 Inventory Models

Appendices

Index

introduction 1

Operations research is a relatively new field of study. It first surfaced in Britain during World War II. The British were initially interested in the use of quantitative methods in the employment of radar. They named the approach *operational research* because they had used scientists to analyze *operational* problems. During the war the approach was very successful in dealing with problems in convoy operations, antisubmarine operations, strategic bombing operations, and mining operations. This application of *operational research* leads to our favorite definition of the approach:

"The art of winning wars without actually fighting."

After the war early practitioners of operations research concentrated on formalizing the approaches that they had developed during the war and seeking uses for these techniques in the industrial sector. Actually some work had been started in the industrial sector by such men as Frederick W. Taylor and his successors, which had led to the new discipline of industrial engineering. Taylor realized that before the Industrial Revolution most businesses were small one-man operations. But, with mechanization and growth, management and specializations developed. Automation and decentralization of operations caused further management problems. Many new disciplines developed in addition to industrial engineering such as marketing research, finance, various branches of engineering, and the like. With these specializations splitting of objectives developed. The various branches of the organization began solving problems in a way that was not necessarily in the interest of overall organization. Consider the production-inventory decision facing most organizations; the various elements of the organization would like to handle this problem differently:

1.1 WHAT IS OPERATIONS RESEARCH AND WHERE IS IT USED?*

---

* Material in this section is adapted from *Careers in Operations Research*, Operations Research Society, 1975, and is used with the permission of ORSA.

PRODUCTION wants long uninterrupted runs to reduce setup costs that would lead to high inventories.

MARKETING wants a high inventory of lots of products so customers can receive whatever they want immediately.

FINANCE wants no inventory.

PERSONNEL wants to stabilize employment throughout the year, which would lead to high inventory at times to smooth out the cyclic demands.

The executive must decide "What is the best policy for the whole organization?" The executive must find the overall optimum solution. The individual optimum solutions are generally easy to find but the overall optimum is difficult. The role of *operations research* or *management science* (the popular names for operational research used in business and industry) is to help management solve these problems involving interactions of objectives. Operations research tries to find the best decisions relative to as large a portion of the *total system* as possible. The Operations Research Society of America has suggested the following definition of operations research [5] which is probably more appropriate to the industrial sector:

"Operations Research is concerned with scientifically deciding how to best design and operate man-machine systems usually under conditions requiring the allocation of scarce resources."

The goals of Taylor's industrial engineering and those of operations research do not differ. Operations research just adds mathematical sophistication and "tools" that didn't exist previously. Some industrial decisions such as inventory, maintenance, and scheduling are similar to those encountered by the military, so these were the first industrial problems analyzed after World War II. Major acceptance of operations research in the industrial sector did not develop until the late 1950s with advent of computers and specialized techniques to handle problems such as marketing and capital budgeting. As knowledge of operations research increased in management, operations research groups were formed in hundreds of companies, especially large corporations such as oil companies.

Some of the industrial problems analyzed by operations research analysts are:

Finance, Budgeting, and Investments

1. Cash flow analysis, long range capital requirements, dividend policies, investment portfolios.
2. Credit policies, credit risks, and delinquent account procedures.
3. Claim and complaint procedures.

Purchasing, Procurement, and Exploration

1. Rules for buying supplies with stable or varying prices.
2. Determination of quantities and timing of purchases.

3. Bidding policies.

4. Strategies for exploration and exploitation of raw material sources.

5. Replacement policies.

Physical Distribution

1. Location and size of warehouses, distribution centers, and retail outlets.

2. Distribution policy.

3. Company-owned outlets versus franchised outlets.

4. Worldwide logistics and supply systems (military and industrial).

Facilities Planning

1. Numbers and location of factories, warehouses, hospitals, and the like, sizes and interactions.

2. Loading and unloading facilities for railroads, trucks, and boats.

Manufacturing

1. Production scheduling.

2. Stabilization of production and employment, the effects of instability, and the cost of hiring, training, lay-offs, and firing.

Construction Maintenance, Project Scheduling

1. Maintenance policies, preventive maintenance.

2. Maintenance crew sizes.

3. Project scheduling, allocation of resources.

Marketing

1. Product selection, timing, competitive actions.

2. Number of salesmen, frequency of calling on accounts, percent of time spent on prospectus.

3. Advertising strategies.

Personnel

1. Selection of personnel, mixes of age and skills.

2. Recruiting policies, assignments of jobs.

Research and Development

1. Determination of areas of concentration.

2. Reliability.

3. Control of development projects.

The applications of operations research have also had a strong impact in the study of societal problems and public affairs. Public administrators and government officials have become increasingly aware of how operations research can assist in the everyday decision-making activities. Significant applications have been made in the study of public health, city and regional planning, and educational systems. Recent advances in areas such as criminal justice, population control, meteorology, and ecological systems makes us aware that this is just the beginning.

Consider the following applications suggested by the Operations Research Society of America in their excellent booklet *Careers in Operations Research* [5]:

EXAMPLE

Operations Research Management
Emergency Energy Capacity Study
The objective of this study is to determine feasibility, costs, and benefits associated with alternative methods of assuring energy supplies to meet essential needs in an emergency due to a cutoff of imports. The methodology is a critical review of U.S. ability (using a regional refining, storage, and distribution model) to withstand future disruptions in foreign supply in relation to surplus producing capacity, stored crude and products available for emergency use, and transportation capacity and refinery capacity. The model consists of a linear programming transportation storage, distribution model with sub-models representing refinery operation flexibility.

EXAMPLE

Operations Research in Society
Operations Research and the Drug Abuse Problem
Current evaluation and operations research activities within the federal and state government are discussed. Practicality of applying operations research techniques to this problem is considered. Ongoing efforts in determining treatment effectiveness, treatment costs, ancillary support requirements, population descriptions, and patient flows are described. A model is developed that optimizes treatment and rehabilitation cost-effectiveness from a total system viewpoint. Model utilization is illustrated with select data gathered by Johns Hopkins University. Various measures of effectiveness, such as pre- versus posttreatment arrest rates, median time of client retention versus programmed treatment cycle time, and the like, are examined in detail. A scheduling model, using queueing concepts, is developed and manipulated with representative data.

EXAMPLE

Medical Manpower Modeling
Modeling Physician Career Disposition
The problem to be solved by a comprehensive model of medical manpower supply and demand is how to match the geographic, speciality, and worksetting distributions of needs for health care personnel with corresponding multivariate distributions of graduates from health science institutions. The supply side of such a model requires social-psychological submodels that represent a number of application/selection and career disposition modification processes. The structure of such a submodel for physician manpower, currently being developed, will be presented, and preliminary insights from longitudinal data being collected to fit the model will be discussed.

Advanced Concepts for Highway Systems   EXAMPLE

The Effects of Driver Control and Display Aids on Simulated Platoon Traffic

One approach to improving the current transportation system is through augmentation of the driver's sensory, decision-making, and control capabilities. Various control and display aids were developed and tested under highway conditions for their effects on the individual driver. The effects of driver aiding in a series of closely following cars were also investigated through simulation experiments. Previously developed experimental display and control aids were tested in this simulation by altering the number of cars possessing the aid and finding subsequent effects on platoon safety and flow. Driver aiding resulted in improved traffic safety and flow and was significantly more important than altering vehicle or road characteristics.

The distinguishing feature of a system is the interaction among its various components. The structure of the system is determined by this interaction. The analyst must be concerned with these interactions when analyzing a given system. Insight into the cause-and-effect relationships and into the performance of the system as a whole can be gained through this knowledge. Quantitative analysis of systems is dependent on the structure of the system.

1.2 SYSTEMS MODELING AND THE TOOLS OF OPERATIONS RESEARCH*

Morris[3] has suggested the following steps for constructing models of systems:

1. Identify and formulate the manager's decision in writing.
2. Identify the constants, parameters, and variables involved. Define them verbally and then introduce symbols to represent each one.
3. Select the variables that appear to be most influential so that the model may be kept as simple as possible. Distinguish between those that are controllable by the manager and those that are not.
4. State verbal relationships among the variables based on known principles, specially gathered data, intuition, and reflection. Make assumptions or predictions concerning the behavior of the noncontrollable variables.
5. Construct the model by combining all relationships into a system of symbolic relationships.
6. Perform symbolic manipulations.
7. Derive solutions from the model.

---

* Material in this section is adapted from W. T. Morris, *The Analysis of Management Decisions*, Homewood, Ill., Richard D. Irwin, Inc., 1964. Used with the permission of Richard D. Irwin, Inc.

8. Test the model by making predictions from it and checking against real-world data.

9. Revise the model as necessary.

In this text we are concerned with a number of techniques that have become useful to the operations research analyst. We will also emphasize the applications of these techniques through the use of numerous examples and the use of *Application Studies* in each chapter. The Application Studies will demonstrate how people have used and misused the techniques discussed in business, government, and society.

We discuss what might be considered the basic tools of operations research. These are the ones that are being used the most by operations research analysts. There are, however, a number of "newer" techniques that, as you become more proficient in operations research, you may wish to consider. These techniques are reported in the more advanced texts of operations research and journals in the operations research area.

1.3 MANAGEMENT'S PERSPECTIVE OF QUANTITATIVE METHODS *

Managers over the years have had reservations about using operations research techniques because quantitative methods were not their "style" of management. Morris[2] has attempted through interviews with 320 middle managers and through his own extensive experience to assess 25 years of quantitative methods in decision making. Morris developed the following seven propositions that describe the majority views of the managers that he interviewed. We hope that Morris's discussion will give you a good feel for how management views the area you are about to study. It also should give you a feel for the environment within which the operations research analyst must work.

Morris's propositions are as follows:

1. *"Quantitative" is probably too narrow a word for the efficient development of one's management style. Better to think of a broad range of approaches that have in common three basic attributes: they are explicit; they involve data, whether quantitative or qualitative; and they are to some degree analytical.*

This seemed to be a way of saying that the original questions about the role of quantitative methods in management were not very usefully stated. The numbers, measurements, and equations ordinarily associated with "quantitative" are *really only surface manifestations.* One should consider a broader class of techniques that goes beyond such things as mathematical programming and simulation. It might be useful, for example, to consider whatever fundamental similarities there may be

---

* Adapted with permission from June, 1975 *Industrial Engineering.* Copyright © American Institute of Industrial Engineers, Inc., 25 Technology Park/Atlanta, Norcross, Ga. 30071.

among such approaches as management by objectives, organizational development, job enrichment, various participative strategies, sensitivity groups, T groups, risk analysis, zero defects programs, value analysis, cost-effectiveness analysis, and so on. All of these, in varying degrees, involve an explicit statement of a policy, an hypothesis, an objective, or a program statement. They all tend toward the generation of data on performance, effectiveness, progress, or output. Data generation involves all sorts of scaling and measurement problems employing judgments, ratings, evaluations, classifications, and so on. Yet, data are produced by some sort of measurement process. Also, all of these approaches tend to be analytical, if not in a formal mathematical sense, then in terms of some less rigorous logic. They tend to encourage a look into the structures or models that might be helpful in analyzing management phenomena.

The relevant question then for many of these managers seemed to be the degree to which approaches involving explicitness, measurement, and analysis were to become a part of their management styles.

2. *Management can be usefully viewed as an experimental undertaking in much the same sense that science is so regarded.*

To suggest that the ongoing operations of an organization be regarded as a series of experiments is to suggest a rather important management concept. This is the proposition that a firm should be run so as not only to produce its products or services at a profit but also to produce information on how to improve its own operations. Organizations ought deliberately to produce, among their various outputs, information relevant for moving further toward their objectives. In less general terms, a production manager should seek to produce not only the products but also information on how the products and the production operations themselves may be improved. Each management action should be treated as a test of the decision conceptualization on which it is based, a test of a hypothesis that has been produced out of assumptions and simplifications, the truth of which is necessarily a matter of doubt and uncertainty. Ideally, the setting in which managers decide and act should be something like that of a laboratory.

Based on the very casual evidence available from these discussions one could plausibly raise the hypothesis that the greater the tendency of a manager to view management as an experimental undertaking, the greater the tendency for him to incorporate quantitative methods in his personal style of managing. The use of explicit, analytical approaches to management problems appears to be, logically enough, consistent with the viewpoint that there is much in common between good management and good science.

3. *"Quantitative" methods (in the large sense) sometimes have life cycles that can be roughly modeled as a series of phases:*

- *Reformulation and renaming of some basic ideas.*

- *Application to a particular management situation.*

- *Enthusiasm bred by specific success.*

- *Generalization and institutionalization.*

- *Emergence of vested interests.*

- *Marketing and the creation of high expectations.*

- *Implementation and recession.*

In making judgments about quantitative methods, it seems helpful to be aware of the almost fadlike nature of their comings and goings. To emphasize the faddish aspect of many of these methods is not to be unnecessarily cynical about them. Many such methods seem to behave as do other types of fads, and this is a very useful observation to have in mind when considering one of the currently popular ones. If one considers the evolution, progress, application, and decline of these methods in relation to the following model, it may be clear that there is a kind of life cycle through which some have already passed, and various stages to which others have just recently progressed.

We might take as an illustrative example, PERT—program evaluation and review technique—a graphical and analytical method of project planning and control. In the first stage there is a reformulation and renaming of some basic ideas. PERT had many direct ancestors including the Gantt chart, for example.

These newly named ideas are then applied to a particular production situation. It is important to build atomic submarines in a hurry, and PERT is applied to help increase the productivity of this program. In the next stage the specific program succeeds and some of the credit, some of the glory, goes to the method. PERT gets some of the credit for the successful ship construction program. At this point, three types of persons enter the picture, stimulated by the publicity that the method has received. The academics enter, generalizing the method, making it more sophisticated, enriching it and publishing articles laying out their results. They are not articles about application, but about the sophistication of the technique itself, a sophistication that may even lead to a whole new body of applied mathematics, where the word "applied" refers only to imagined possibilities. The second group to enter are the consultants who see the favorable publicity as a sound basis for a marketing effort. They begin to market the technique, emphasizing its newness, the "revolutionary" character of the method, and its great and universal potential for productivity improvement. The third group consists of people in organizations whose careers are not progressing to their own satisfaction. They decide that it might be possible to build a career on the new method so they become resident advocates and local spokesmen for it. They become leaders and marketers of in-house programs to apply the method, hoping that its success will result also in their own advancement. At this point extensive marketing effort has built up expectations that simply cannot all be realized. A lot of people, however, now have vested interests in the technique, so it is pushed to the point of actual application in a variety of situations. Its implementation produces mixed results, a few successes, but quite a few failures. The technique has been oversold, disappointments are inevitable, reevaluations and "second thoughts" begin to appear in the management literature. The technique generally passes into decline, although it does remain and makes a useful contribution in a few places where it turns out to be appropriate.

4. *Probability of sustained, successful use is roughly proportional to the degree of client involvement in the creation and development of the method.*

This hypothesis, and that which follows, recognize that up to this point in the development of quantitative methods they are almost invariably introduced into an operating organization by some "outside" agency such as a staff group, a consultant, or an expert. They also recognize the distinction between a "one shot" trial of a method and the establishment of it as a routine aspect of organizational life, the former being considerably more common than the latter. Just what is meant by "successful" was far from clear in these discussions. In part it seemed to be a synonym for "sustained," implying that survival was a kind of operational definition of success. While it represents something of an oversimplification, it seemed useful to consider three types of strategies: those that emphasized persuasion, those that emphasized politics, and those that emphasized participation.

"Persuasion," or "selling," in its extreme form implies "solving" the client's problem on the basis of his rather brief definition of that problem, and then presenting him with the solution at a final briefing session. These sessions almost inevitably produce the conclusions that the solution is inappropriate, that many significant considerations have been left out, that many concerned people have not been consulted, and so on.

"Politics" is the strategy that is emphasized in many textbooks. Get top management behind the effort, have the staff group report at a very high level in the organization, and the result will be that the group will be listened to. Such evidence as there is suggests that this type of approach may be helpful, but by itself may lead to a tendency on the part of the operating people to implement studies in such a way as to subtly insure their failure.

"Participation," or "involvement," is the strategy that appears to have the most favorable record of success. Client groups are brought into the process of selecting and defining problems and projects. Client personnel actually participate with the staff professionals in the conduct of the project, designing experiments, constructing models, interpreting data, or whatever, right along with the staff analysis. Involvement, of course, has the disadvantage of using client personnel and removing them from their other duties. It also has the disadvantage that the staff can no longer claim quite as much credit for whatever successes may result.

5. *The probability of sustained successful use is roughly proportional to the degree of congruence with the client's personal and organizational style.*

Some difficulty is involved here in trying to be clear about the meanings of personal style and organizational style. In the case of personal style, it appeared that the following characteristics were thought to be negatively correlated with the use of quantitative methods:

- Tolerance for ambiguity.

- Tendency toward intuitive thinking and decision making.

- Tolerance for uncertainty.

- Self-confidence.

- Achievement orientation.

- Reluctance to delegate.

- Willingness to go beyond policy and precedent.

There is clearly a major problem in making these concepts operational, but they may begin to suggest a kind of distinction between those who are less likely to use quantitative methods and those more likely to do so.

A second rough, but perhaps useful, hypothesis suggests that the payoff from any method applied to any particular organization depends on where the organization has been, what its present state of development is, and what its style is. Some methods are more likely to work than others, depending on the history of the organization. It suggests rather crudely that organizations grow up, mature, and live through stages that predispose them toward succeeding stages. Changes in the organization that are compatible with its maturation or consistent with its pattern of evolution are more likely to be effective than are changes for which it is not yet "ready."

This hypothesis suggests, for example, that an organization is not ready for sophisticated computerized production scheduling until it has lived through first putting billing and accounts receivable on the computer, then putting some inventory control on the computer, and finally, putting purchasing and the customer order book on. After the organization has lived through these experiences it is "ready" for sophisticated computerized production scheduling. This strategy greatly increases the probability of success.

6. *To be explicit is not, a priori, better as a management style than to be implicit and intuitive in one's decision making.*

This hypothesis seemed to stem from several somewhat different considerations. In the first instance, it was a recognition that there have been a considerable number of "failures" in the use of quantitative methods, and one cannot reasonably assume that these methods are certain to be better than the use of intuition, hunch, unverbalized experience, and "gut feelings." Quantitative methods are not *the* answer; management remains, importantly, an art, and how one manages is, in a sense, an unsolved problem.

It was recognized further that the decision to become involved with quantitative methods is a risky one, and that there is some resentment among managers of any implied superiority of quantitative methods. The attitude among those who have advocated these methods in the past has sometimes been that as soon as analysis can be substituted for intuition, things will clearly begin to improve. As this attitude has moderated, the risks associated with quantitative methods have become somewhat easier to appraise.

The basic problem with intuitive decision makers seemed to be that some were consistently good, some consistently not very good, and most somewhere in between. While it was easy to identify those at the extremes, there was a large middle ground where it was not especially clear how good the intuitive decisions actually were. There was thus some interest in the concept of establishing the "track record" of an intuitive decision maker as a basis for deciding whether quantitative methods might or might not have some potential for improvement.

Finally, there was the general insistence that where quantitative methods were used, there must always be the opportunity for the final application of a management override, the final application of management judgment.

7. *The most favorable cost-effectiveness relationships are associated with the simple, basic, quantitative methods, rather than with those that are complex, exotic, and sophisticated.*

This again was an hypothesis about which it was difficult to be precise and operational. "Simple" and "sophisticated" seemed very much subjectively determined. Methods that gave basic structure to management decisions, that helped with the expression of uncertainty, that clarified value conflicts, and that tended to remove the bias from predictions were generally regarded as "simple." Things like quadratic programming, T groups, and multivariable simulations were generally seen as complex and sophisticated. There was some tendency to feel that those things that "worked" were also those things that one could readily "understand." Much else was regarded as "theoretical," "unproven," or simply far more costly than was warranted by the benefits to be expected.

**1.4
APPLICATION
STUDIES**

1.4.1
What is an
Application
Study?

Most operations research texts either present a highly "quantitative" approach excluding discussions of how the techniques might be used or present a more "applied" approach but deal in trivial examples. We have attempted to collect some examples of how people actually used (and in some cases misused) the techniques we will discuss in later chapters. At the end of each chapter we have presented some examples of our findings which we hope will give you better insight into the application of operations research techniques.

If you wish to find other examples of the use of operations research we suggest that you consult the following journals that we found useful:

Journal of Operations Research
Management Science
I.E. Transactions
Industrial Engineering
Journal of Industrial Engineering
Operational Research Quarterly
Naval Research Logistics Quarterly
C.O.R.S. Journal

We also found the *International Abstracts of Operations Research* to be a helpful index for finding appropriate applications.

We hope you find our application studies interesting and useful. Why not try to develop some of your own?

1.4.2
Human Decision
versus Math
Model: an
Experiment*

Pegels [4] developed an experiment that tried to answer the question, "Are mathematical models really any more effective than the intuitive decisions of experienced managers?" Pegels used his students at the State University of New York at Buffalo in an experiment where their intuitive feel for a decision situation was pitted against an operations research model.

Application Study

The firm studied in this experiment produces prefabricated houses on an assembly line. Each home, in unassembled form, is loaded directly on to a large, covered highway van at the end of the production line. Homes are only produced in response to specific orders and are never produced for inventory. Since each home is essentially unique in the sense that a large number of styles and options are available, the whole production process is considered to be of a job-shop nature.

---

* Adapted with permission from *Industrial Engineering*, December 1970. Copyright © American Institute of Industrial Engineers, Inc., 25 Technology Park/Atlanta, Norcross, Ga. 30071.

Management often has to adjust the level of production activity rather sharply. Changes in the production level may be accomplished in various ways. The labor force may be held constant or nearly constant, and overtime and idle time may be the means used to vary the level of production. Alternatively, the work force may be changed in direct proportion to the level of production. The problem is to find which method incurs the least cost.

The students were given a detailed explanation of the additional costs incurred if units were produced on overtime, if workers were hired or laid off, and if workers were idle because of lack of production. In addition, the detailed cost listing shown in Table 1.1 was presented to the group.

Table 1.1 Cost Tables Provided to Participants

Hiring and Layoff Costs		Overtime and Idle-Time Costs	
Number of Men Hired or Laid Off	Cost in Dollars Per Man Hired or Laid Off	Number of Units Produced on Overtime or Not Produced on Idle Time	Cost in Dollars Per Unit Produced on Overtime or Not Produced on Idle Time
1	5	1	50
2	20	2	200
3	45	3	450
4	80	4	800
5	125	5	1,250
6	180	6	1,800
7	245	7	2,450
8	320	8	3,200
9	405	9	4,050
10	500	10	5,000
20	2,000	20	20,000
30	4,500	30	45,000
40	8,000	40	80,000
50	12,500	50	125,000
60	18,000	60	180,000
70	24,500	70	245,000
80	32,000	80	320,000
90	40,500	90	405,000
100	50,000	100	500,000
200	200,000	200	2,000,000
300	450,000	300	4,500,000

Cost per man-month on regular time: $500.
Cost per unit built on regular time: $350.

The group was told to make their decisions with the aim of minimizing the combined cost of payroll, overtime, idle time, hiring, and layoffs. They were told that they would be expected to make about 24 decisions for an equal number of months. However, at the end of 15 months the experiment was stopped to eliminate end-play.

The group was reminded that their decisions would be compared with a mathematical model that could determine the minimum cost work-force level for each month. In addition, the group was exhorted to make the best possible decision, because obviously poor results would be reflected in their final grade. Information for each succeeding month was provided after everyone had completed the previous month's decision.

Before each monthly decision, the group was provided with a planned (actual) production level for the next month. In addition, they were provided with monthly sales forecasts for the next three months. Prior to the first monthly decision, the group was also provided with the work-force level in the previous month (270 employees). Table 1.2 lists

Table 1.2 Actual and Forecasted Sales Levels and Derived Work-Force Levels

Current Month	Actual Production Level for Current Month	Forecasted Unit Sales Levels for Future Months			Derived Work-Force Levels	
t	S_t	S_{t+1}	S_{t+2}	S_{t+3}	Minimum cost (Model)	Rule-of-thumb
0					270	270
1	236	200	367	654	169	165
2	160	295	589	791	119	112
3	224	669	844	747	169	157
4	685	771	755	896	468	479
5	782	718	870	838	542	547
6	668	797	758	640	475	468
7	788	751	642	694	547	551
8	709	570	618	489	494	496
9	553	635	488	378	394	387
10	685	540	418	258	471	479
11	538	407	250	197	377	377
12	391	246	195	292	274	274
13	243	244	314	544	175	170
14	273	366	567	661	193	191
15	400	623	722	756	283	280

the actual production levels and sales forecasts the students were given each month.

Important factors pointed out to the students and expressed in Table 1.1 were these: (1) the number of workers needed to build x houses is $.7x$ workers; (2) the cost of hiring or laying off workers increases exponentially with the number of men laid off or hired each month; and (3) the overtime and idle-time costs increase exponentially with the monthly number of units built on overtime or the monthly number of units not built, although the labor force was available.

The minimum-cost work-force level derived with the math model and a work-force level derived from a rather simple rule-of-thumb are also shown in Table 1.2. The rule of thumb used exactly tailors the work force to the planned production level and ignores overtime and idle time charges.

The results of 15 participants in the group of 32 were eliminated because their performance indicated that they were either very poor decision makers or that they did not understand the problem. The results of the remaining 17 are presented in Table 1.3, and are compared with

Table 1.3 Comparison of Work-Force Level-Decisions

Work-Force Rule	Total cost (000)	Deviation from optimal cost (000)
Optimal rule	$3512	$ 0
Rule of thumb	$3573	$ 61
Participant 1	$3564	$ 52
2	3572	60
3	3573	61
4	3573	61
5	3574	62
6	3581	69
7	3600	88
8	3747	235
9	3776	264
10	3883	371
11	3887	375
12	3890	378
13	3963	451
14	4034	522
15	4221	709
16	4374	862
17	4382	870

the total cost of the best work-force level and the rule-of-thumb work-force level. The rule-of-thumb work-force level is shown because it is an easy rule to follow for a participant. However, note that only two participants were able to come up with a lower total cost than the rule-of-thumb approach. Two others did well, and a fifth did nearly as well.

The experiment clearly points out that some decisions will be more effective from a cost point of view if they are based on a mathematical model. Unfortunately, mathematical models are usually unavailable, are costly to develop, and, in some instances, are impractical or impossible to develop for the specific situation. On the other hand, there are also many situations where models have been developed or can be developed at a reasonable cost.

The data on which the decisions were based in the experiment, although uncertain, were relatively clear and straightforward. Hence, only a rather simple mathematical model had to be developed, as opposed to a model having to cope with several sets of variables. The decision-making task of a human would be much more heavily taxed with a set of more complicated data, and good decisions would undoubtedly be extremely difficult to make.

1.4.3
When should you
trade your car?*

In 1969 Everett Beals [1] reported on his quantitative approach to the decision of whether to replace a car with a new one. While one may find fault with Beals' approach to the problem, it is a good example of the use of quantitative methods in a decision making situation which we are all familiar with and have probably made. This decision is seldom based on quantitative methods. Note that his analysis did not foresee the sky-rocketing costs of gas and cars.

Application Study

The author performed his study on his 1963 Dodge Polara. The evaluation considered total car costs including original cost, gas and oil, tires, and all maintenance costs from fan belts to complete engine overhauls. It was assumed that the cost per mile would eventually go up due to increased maintenance and gasoline and oil consumption. It was originally decided arbitrarily that once this cost went above 18 ¢ a mile, the car would be replaced. At replacement, the dollars received from selling the car would be subtracted from the accumulated cost to establish a total overall cost per mile figure.

Regression analysis was applied to the first 22 months of data to establish a projected cost curve. Since costs per mile were expected to

* Adapted with permission from *Industrial Engineering*, November 1969. Copyright © American Institute of Industrial Engineers, Inc., 25 Technology Park/Atlanta, Norcross, Ga. 30071.

increase at a faster and faster rate, the equation initially used for projecting costs was:

$$Y = \frac{1}{A + BX + CX^2}$$

The projected cost curve was calculated according to the hypothesis established and the replacement time indicated. This is shown in Figure 1.1. The equation selected develops a large "U." The calculated curve indicated that a cost of approximately 18 ¢ per mile would be reached in the one-hundred-and-first month. The vehicle would then be nearly 8.5 years old.

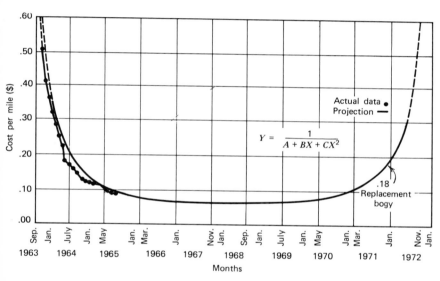

Figure 1.1 The original projected cost curve made a large U shape. Cumulative cost per mile figures were plotted on the same grid as they were calculated.

The data used in the calculation were plotted against the curve and as additional data was accumulated it was also plotted by the month. The actual data produced a cost per mile below the curve for all of the first 26 months. It then fell consistently above the calculated curve for over two years as shown in Figure 1.2. At this point, concern grew as to whether or not the appropriate equation had been chosen. A chart was made showing the cumulative cost per mile per month and also the individual cost per mile per month. The results are shown in Figure 1.3. This plotting shows that, even as early as the twenty-seventh month, a high fluctuation in specific monthly cost did not particularly affect the cumulative monthly

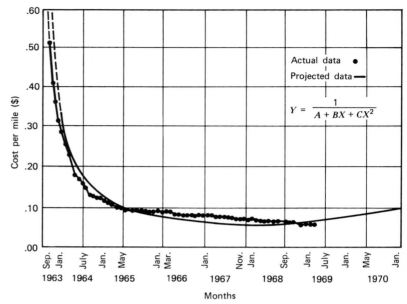

Figure 1.2 Actual cumulative cost per mile figures did not appear to follow projected curve.

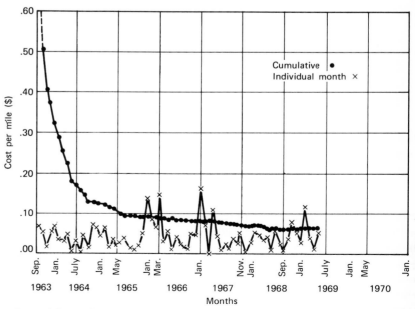

Figure 1.3 Individual cost per mile per month figures are plotted as well as cumulative cost per mile figures. Note that a high monthly cost does not apparently affect the cumulative cost.

cost per mile. Since this month was a low-mileage month with high per mile cost, it tended to confirm the suspicion that the equation chosen was not the best for cost projection. In fact, it appears that the actual cumulative dollar cost per mile per month will not increase significantly with considerably increased maintenance, gasoline, and oil costs.

Now a new equation needed to be found. Several of the more common expressions either turned negative or did not give a sharp enough bend in the curve. An expression that approached a desirable fit is shown in Figure 1.4.

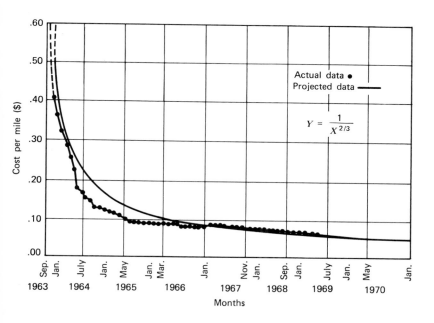

Figure 1.4 This expression approached a better fit. It now appears that costs per mile do not increase faster as the car gets older.

A projection of this curve indicates that there is no strictly economic point at which a vehicle should be replaced. At some age, of course, the vehicle will suffer from NORS (not operationally ready-supply), which means that you just can't get parts for it. An extension of the curve shows that the vehicle cost would approach fuel cost at approximately 350 months or over 29 years. At an average of 18,000 miles per year, as driven on this car, the 29 years would accumulate an enormous total mileage. Of course, these are unrealistic age and mileage figures and fuel cost would never actually be realized.

So it seems that if you can forget about keeping up with the Joneses there is no point, within realistic mileage accumulation, when you need to replace your car. Just keep paying for the repairs and maintenance as they occur. Even a sizable repair bill will not significantly affect the total mileage cost of the vehicle.

One might question Beals' choice of basing his decision on the cumulative cost curve (See chapter 2). This is the reason for his result (keep the car 29 years). You might wish to consider how you would quantitatively approach this decision. Maybe the author should have chosen a "life" that would give him a minimum cumulative cost.

REFERENCES
1. Beals, E., "When Should You Trade Your Car?" *Industrial Engineering*, Vol. 1; No. 11, November 1969.
2. Morris, W. T., "Quantitative methods—a management perspective," *Industrial Engineering*, Vol. 7, No. 6, June 1975.
3. Morris, W. T., *The Analysis of Management Decisions*, Homewood, Ill., Richard D. Irwin, Inc., 1964.
4. Pegels, C., "Human decision vs math model: an experiment," *Industrial Engineering*, Vol. 2, No. 12, December 1970.
5. *Careers in Operations Research*, Operations Research Society of America, 1975.

decision
analysis 2

The nature of quantitative decision making is as follows:
1. There are two or more courses of action possible but only one can be taken.
2. The decision process will select from these alternative actions, a single course of action.
3. The selection of a course of action is made to accomplish some designated purpose. The purpose is generally to choose an action that will lead to a desirable situation in the future.

The general process of decision making is to:
1. Predict the outcomes of each action that can be taken.
2. Evaluate the outcome in terms of some scale of desirability.
3. Select a criterion for decision making that will be used to make the actual selection.

EXAMPLE

Consider the decision facing your father each night with respect to his transportation to work the next day. He must decide tonight whether to:
1. Drive his car.
2. Take a bus.

The scales of desirability that he might consider are:
1. Save money.
2. Save time.
3. Be home by 6 P.M. to watch the news.

This decision situation is shown in Figure 2.1 assuming that your father has decided that being home by 6 P.M. is most important to him. Notice, however, that he is only considering the most likely outcomes, that is, if he takes the bus he will most likely be walking home from the bus stop while if he drives he will most likely be home. Your father would obviously decide to drive under these circumstances. But your father has

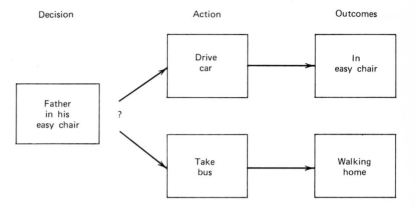

Figure 2.1   Sample decision-making environment.

probably made a mistake by not considering other possible outcomes from his decisions. Figure 2.2 reflects some of these outcomes for the decision to drive.

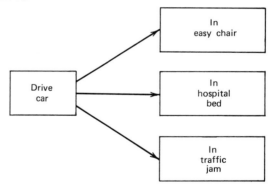

Figure 2.2   Consideration of alternative futures in the decision-making environment.

One of the typical ways of reflecting the decision making environment is to develop a decision matrix as shown in Table 2.1.

EXAMPLE   For example, consider the decision to bet $5 on a horse race. If we expect to win $20 if our horse wins then the decision matrix would appear as shown in Table 2.2.

There are many ways of classifying decisions; we will use the following definitions that are the most common:

Table 2.1 Decision Matrix

$$S_j$$

	S_1	S_2		$\ldots$	S_n
D_1	O_{11}	O_{12}		$\ldots$	O_{1n}
D_2	O_{21}	O_{22}		$\ldots$	O_{2n}
D_m	O_{m1}	O_{m2}		$\ldots$	O_{mn}

where
  D_i = decisions available to the decision maker.
  S_j = possible uncontrollable futures.
  O_{ij} = outcome given that D_i is chosen and S_j occurs.

Table 2.2 Decision Matrix for a Horse-Betting Example

	Horse wins	Horse loses
Bet	20	−5
Don't Bet	0	0

Decisions Under Assumed Certainty.   For some decisions it is convenient to assume that we have complete information and that there is no uncertainty connected with analysis of the decision. Such a case will be called a decision under assumed certainty. For example, the decision to purchase a U.S. government bond is one in which it is reasonable to assume complete information about the future. For practical decision-making purposes, most people will agree that there is no doubt that the federal government will, in fact, pay the interest as it falls due and the principal at maturity. Thus, in predicting the outcome of such an action, certainty is a reasonable assumption.

In terms of our decision model, assumed certainty means that only one possible future exists and has probability 1. The outcome for each alternative can be stated definitely. In matrix form a decision under assumed certainty would appear as shown in Table 2.3.

Decisions Under Risk.   A decision problem in which the analyst elects to consider several possible futures, the probabilities of which can, in his view, be stated, is called a decision under risk. The roulette player's decision is a typical example of a decision under risk. Less information is

Table 2.3 Decision Matrix for a Decision Under Assumed Certainty

$$S_j$$

$$S_1$$

		S_1
	D_1	O_{11}
D_i	D_2	O_{21}
	$\vdots$	$\vdots$
	D_m	O_{m1}

available than in a decision under certainty, since it is not definitely known what the outcome will be. However, it is possible to estimate the probabilities of the various possible futures, in the view of the analyst.

Decisions Under Uncertainty.   A decision for which the analyst elects to consider several possible futures, the probabilities of which *cannot*, in his judgment, be stated is called a decision under uncertainty. In matrix form a decision under uncertainty looks much like a decision under risk, except that the probabilities of the various possible futures are missing. Thus, decisions under uncertainty contain even less information than decisions under risk, and both contain less information than decisions under certainty.

**2.2
DECISION
MAKING
UNDER
ASSUMED
CERTAINTY**
Traditionally many decisions in the areas of economics, engineering, psychology, and operations research have been based on assumed certainty. Morris [9] feels that considerations for choosing this approach to decision making are as follows:*

1. The amount of risk involved in the decision may appear to be so small that the analyst feels safe in neglecting it.
2. Risk may be importantly involved, but the difficulty or expense of including it in the analysis of the decision may suggest that it had better be left to the managerial judgment that will be applied after the analysis has been completed.
3. The decision may be such that, even if the risk were explicitly included, the choice would depend only on average values of the outcomes. For example, in estimating the cost of using a particular

---

* Some material in this section is adapted from W. T. Morris, *The Analysis of Management Decisions*, Richard D. Irwin, Inc., Homewood, Ill., 1964. Used with the permission of Richard D. Irwin, Inc.

machine, its salvage value at some future time may be important. While the salvage value may not be exactly known, the analysis can be carried out by using the average salvage value for such machines.

Clearly, all of these reasons include the judgment or common sense of the analyst to a great extent.

The principles of choice for decisions under assumed certainty are very simple and straightforward. Examples of such principles are:

1. Everything else being equal, pick the alternative that maximizes profit.
2. Everything else being equal, pick the alternative that minimizes cost.
3. Everything else being equal, pick the alternative that minimizes the distance traveled.

EXAMPLE

Consider the problem of laying out a planned community, which has four facilities (pool, apartments, factory, and a shopping center) to be located on a plot of land. The planner wishes to lay out the community in such a way that the travel of residents will be minimized. The alternative courses of action are quite easy in this case because we would just consider all the possible ways of placing the four facilities in the four areas of the community. The total number of alternatives, which is four factorial or 24, could be enumerated as shown in Table 2.4. The next step

Table 2.4 Alternative Arrangements of Facilities in a Planned Community

	Location			
	1	2	3	4
Facility	P	A	F	S
arrangement	P	A	S	F
	P	F	A	S
	P	F	S	A
	.	.	.	.
	.	.	.	.
	.	.	.	.

P for pool.
A for apartments.
F for factory.
S for shopping mall.

in the analysis is to determine the daily distance traveled under each arrangement.

To determine the daily distance traveled we will need information on the distance between the locations, as shown in Table 2.5, and the number of daily trips anticipated between each facility, as shown in Table 2.6. The next step is to determine the distance traveled under each arrangement, for example, consider the arrangement of assigning the pool to location 1, the apartments to location 2, the factory to location 3, and the shopping mall to location 4. The analysis would proceed as shown in Table 2.7. In order to calculate the distance per day between the factory and the shopping mall we enter Table 2.6 and find that there are approximately 200 trips per day. Next realizing that the factory is in location 3 and the shopping mall is in location 4 we can enter Table 2.5 and find that the average distance per trip is 300 meters. Table 2.7 tells us that the total distance traveled under this arrangement is 445,000 meters. In order to find the best arrangement we would have to perform similar calculations for the other 23 possible arrangements of the community and pick the one with the lowest distance traveled.

As you can see even though the decision rule is quite simple in decisions under assumed certainty the calculations can become quite cumbersome. Sometimes the calculations become impossible and some form of approximation must be used.

Table 2.5 Distance Between Locations in a Planned Community in Meters

Location	Location			
	1	2	3	4
1	0	100	200	200
2	100	0	50	100
3	200	50	0	300
4	200	100	300	0

Table 2.6 Number of Trips Between Facilities Each Day

To	From			
	Pool	Apartments	Factory	Shopping Mall
Pool	—	400	200	100
Apartments	600	—	700	500
Factory	0	1000	—	100
Shopping Mall	100	400	200	—

Table 2.7 Calculation of the Distance Traveled for a Particular Arrangement of Facilities in a Planned Community

| | | Meters | |
| | | | |
Movement	Number of Trips	Distance Per Trip	Distance Per Day
Pool to apartments	600	100	60,000
Pool to factory	0	200	0
Pool to shopping mall	100	200	20,000
Apartments to pool	400	100	40,000
Apartments to factory	1000	50	50,000
Apartments to shopping mall	400	100	40,000
Factory to pool	200	200	40,000
Factory to apartments	700	50	35,000
Factory to shopping mall	200	300	60,000
Shopping mall to pool	100	200	20,000
Shopping mall to apartments	500	100	50,000
Shopping mall to factory	100	300	30,000
		Total distance	445,000

Suppose that our planned community had 20 facilities to be located, then there would be "only" 20! different ways of locating the facilities. This means we would be comparing 2.4329×10^{18} different alternatives, which is, of course, impossible to do.

In decisions under assumed certainty the choice of a decision rule is not always obvious; consider the following hypothetical problem:

EXAMPLE

The Groman Bakery of Bethlehem, Pennsylvania has been approached by a manufacturer who has developed a machine that can produce Moravian Sugar Cake much cheaper than the present system being used by the bakery. The company will lease the equipment to Groman's for $10,000 per year. The price includes all maintenance and repairs. At present the sugar cakes sell for a dollar and cost $.80 to make. The new process will lower the variable cost per cake to $.72. If the bakery sells 250,000 cakes per year should Groman's lease the equipment? The two alternatives could be compared on a total cost basis.

ALTERNATIVE 1: don't lease

Total cost = (number of cakes)(cost/cake) = (250,000)($.80) = $200,000

ALTERNATIVE 2: lease

Total cost = lease cost + (number of cakes)(cost/cake) = $10,000 + (250,000)($.72) = $190,000

Thus the bakery would save $10,000 per year by leasing the equipment. Since Groman's will have excess capacity when they lease the equipment, they approach a local discount store and offer to sell them sugar cakes at a reduced rate. Groman's feel that their business will not be affected by the discount store's selling sugar cakes under another brand name. The discount store offers to buy 100,000 cakes per year for $.75 per cake. What should Groman's do?

One member of management suggests that Gromans should not enter the agreement because the average cost of making sugar cakes is $.76 ($190,000/250,000); therefore the bakery would lose a penny per cake. Another member of management says that Groman's should sign the contract because each additional cake is only costing $.72 and the company will make $.03 on each cake sold to the discount store. Thus both managers have attempted to make a decision under assumed certainty and have come up with different conclusions. In this case, because each alternative represents a different volume of sales, comparing on a cost basis is difficult. Therefore comparing the alternatives on a total profit basis is suggested.

ALTERNATIVE 1: don't sell to the discount store

Total profit = revenue for Groman's − lease cost − (number of cakes made)(cost/cake) = (250,000)($1.00) − 10,000 − (250,000)($.72) = $60,000

ALTERNATIVE 2: sell to the discount store

Total profit = revenue from Groman's + revenue from the discount store − lease cost − (number of cakes made)(cost/cake) = (250,000) ($1.00) + (100,000) ($.75) − $10,000 − (350,000)($.72) = $63,000

Therefore Groman's should sell the Moravian sugar cake to the discount store and realize an additional profit of $3000.

We will consider a number of models in this book that are based on assumed certainty.

All the material dealing with linear programming and its extensions are models under assumed certainty. Some of the models presented in the chapters on networks, inventory, and dynamic programming are also examples of decisions under assumed certainty.

**2.3
DECISIONS
UNDER
RISK**

Most operations research models that are not assumed certainty models rely on decision making under risk. The waiting-line models, the simulation models, some network models, some dynamic programming models, and some inventory models will be developed as decisions under risk in this book. In this section we consider various decision-making principles used in decision making under risk.

In order to discuss the decision criteria consider the following decision situation:

A city government is trying to decide whether it should have a celebration for its one-hundredth anniversary. The financial success of the project will be strongly dependent on the weather. The alternatives available to the city are (1) have large celebration; (2) have a small celebration or (3) have no celebration. The payoff matrix for this decision is shown in Table 2.8. We will introduce the various decision criteria and apply them to this problem.

Table 2.8 Payoff Matrix for City Celebration Problem

		.5 S_1 Sun	.2 S_2 Cloudy	.3 S_3 Rain
D_1	Large celebration	350,000	80,000	−150,000
D_2	Small celebration	150,000	100,000	−50,000
D_3	No celebration	0	0	0

Maximize-Expected-Return Principle. In this criterion, the decision maker chooses the alternative that maximizes expected return.

D_1: large celebration
$E(D_1)$ = expected return from D_1 = .50(350,000) + .20(80,000) + .30(−150,000) = \$146,000
D_2: small celebration
$E(D_2)$ = expected return from D_2 = .50(150,000) + .20(100,000) + .30(−50,000) = \$80,000
D_3: no celebration
$E(D_3)$ = expected return from D_3 = .50(0) + .20(0) + .30(0) = \$0

Therefore the decision maker would choose to hold a large celebration.

Maximizing expected return is probably the most popular decision criterion used in decision making under risk. It does, however, have some weaknesses. The criterion assumes the decision in question or similar decisions will be repeated and that, in the long run, the decision maker will receive the expected value as his average return if he applies this criterion. The criterion also assumes stability of the probability over the time span of a long series of repeated decisions. If you are making a one-time decision, such as the decision to hold a centennial celebration, then other criteria might be more appropriate. As an example of some problems with decisions under risk, consider the following game:

EXAMPLE   A fair coin is tossed until a head appears at which time the gambler gets 2^N dollars where N is the number of the toss on which the first head appears. How much should the gambler be willing to pay to get into the game? If the gambler bases his decision on maximizing expected return he will pay an amount less than the expected value of the game.

Expected Value of the Game =
(payoff if the game ends on the first flip) × (probability of the game ending on the first flip) + (payoff if the game ends on the second flip) × (probability of the game ending on the second flip) + etc. =
$2(1/2) + 4(1/4) + \ldots + 2^N(1/2)^n + \ldots = 1 + 1 + \ldots + 1 + \ldots = \infty$

The gambler, of course, would not pay an infinite number of dollars to play this game, yet the maximize-expected-return criterion suggested this decision. (This famous example is known as the St. Petersburg paradox.)

The Most-Probable-Future Principle.   Another popular criterion overlooks all but the most likely return (the one with the highest probability of occurrence) and chooses the alternative which has the maximum most probable future.

EXAMPLE   The most probable futures for our example are:

Alternative	Most Probable Future	Probability
D_1	350,000	.5
D_2	150,000	.5
D_3	0	.5

The decision maker using the most-probable-future principle would choose to have a large celebration. The decision maker that chooses to make his decisions under most probable future principle is behaving as if the decision was one under assumed certainty.

The Aspiration-Level Principle. Often a manager will base his decision on such thoughts as "I don't care which alternative is selected as long as it doesn't lose money," or "Let's choose the alternative that has the best chance of having a 'respectable' return."

A manager of this type is using a criterion called the aspiration-level principle. He wants to choose the alternative that maximizes the probability of obtaining a level of return, for example, A. For our example:

EXAMPLE

If $A = \$100,000$
    Probability $(D_1 > \$100,000) = .50$
    Probability $(D_2 > \$100,000) = .70$
    Probability $(D_3 > \$100,000) = .00$

Choose a small celebration.

If $A = \$0$
    Probability $(D_1 > \$0) = .70$
    Probability $(D_2 > \$0) = .70$
    Probability $(D_3 > \$0) = 1.00$
Choose no celebration.

The obvious question at this point is, "Which criteria should be used?" Unfortunately, there is no easy answer to this question. These techniques are merely attempts to model the individual decision maker's behavior. They can be viewed as attempts at approximating a decision maker's utility curve. The concept of utility curves will now be investigated.

Which would you prefer: a tax-free gift of $10,000 or a 5 percent chance of getting $250,000 and 95 percent chance of getting nothing? Most people would take the first alternative even though its expected payoff is $10,000 compared to $12,500 for the second alternative. This apparent paradox is explained by *utility theory*. Basically, it states that every dollar is not equally valuable to an individual. For example, one dollar is worth much less to an individual who has lots of money than it is to a poor man. The utility theory approach attempts to determine a utility curve for a decision maker. This curve converts dollars to an arbitrary utility measure. The choice between alternatives is then made based on maximizing expected utility instead of maximizing expected return.

2.3.2
Utility
Theory

Some typical forms of utility curves are shown in Figure 2.3. Figure 2.3*a* shows a typical utility curve where the slope decreases as money values increase. Figure 2.3*b* shows the utility curve for a decision maker who says that every dollar amount is equally valuable. In this case, expected utility would give the same result as expected return analysis. This may be a realistic form of the curve for large companies and the

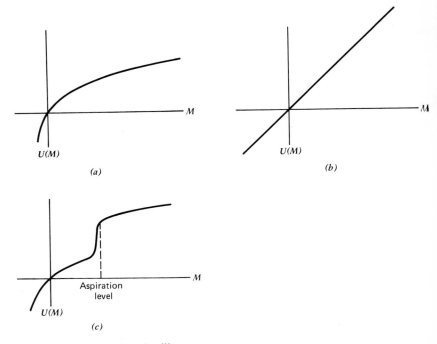

Figure 2.3 Examples of utility curves.

government. This is why large companies practice self-insurance and individuals do not. An individual with an aspiration level would have a curve similar to that in Figure 2.3c.

To choose between alternatives, the expected utility should be calculated and the alternative with maximum expected utility selected. For example, if the city's utility curve is shown in Table 2.9, the analysis proceeds as follows:

EXAMPLE

D_1: large celebration

Expected utility $= .5[U(350,000)] + .2[U(80,000)]$
$+ .3[U(-150,000)]$
$= .5(2.5) + .2(1.0) + .3(-7.0)$
$= -.65$

D_2: small celebration

Expected utility $= .5[U(150,000)] + .2[U(100,000)]$
$+ .3[U(-50,000)]$
$= .5(2.0) + .2(1.5) + .3(-2.0)$
$= .70$

Table 2.9 Utility Values for the City Making a Decision on a Centennial Celebration

Dollars	Utility Value
1,000,000	3.0
350,000	2.5
150,000	2.0
100,000	1.5
80,000	1.0
0	0
−50,000	−2.0
−150,000	−7.0
−500,000	−30.0

D_3: no celebration

Expected utility $= .5[U(0)] + .3[U(0)] + .2[U(0)]$

$= 0$

Therefore the city should choose to have a small celebration. This analysis is not meaningful unless the decision maker's utility curve is known. Consider the following approach to the construction of a utility curve:

EXAMPLE

1. Formulate an alternative (D_1) that promises two rewards with equal probability (e.g., $0, $10,000).
2. Assign arbitrary utility values to the two dollar values [maybe $U($0$) = 0$, $U($10,000$) = 1$].

$$U(D_1) = \tfrac{1}{2}U(0) + U(10,000)$$

$$= \tfrac{1}{2}(0) + \tfrac{1}{2}(1) = .5$$

3. Try to find an alternative (D_2) to which the decision maker is indifferent when compared to D_1 (suppose a guarantee of $3000 would be equivalent to D_1).

$$U(3000) = U(D_1) = .5$$

4. Find additional points by constructing alternatives composed of points with known utilities; then find alternatives to these for which the decision maker is indifferent.

$$U(5500) = \tfrac{1}{2}U(3000) + \tfrac{1}{2}U($10,000$)$$

$$= \tfrac{1}{2}(.5) + \tfrac{1}{2}(1) = .75$$

5. What if we need utilities for dollar values outside the range considered in step 1? We might ask:

$$U(5500) = \tfrac{1}{2}U(0) + \tfrac{1}{2}U(?)$$

Maybe

$$U(5500) = \tfrac{1}{2}U(0) + \tfrac{1}{2}U(100{,}000)$$

and

$$U(100{,}000) = 1.50$$

Or we might ask

$$U(3000) = pU(-1000) + (1-p)U(10{,}000)$$

Maybe

$$U(3000) = 1/3\,U(-1000) + 2/3\,U(10{,}000)$$
$$\therefore U(-1000) = -.5$$

6. Construct the utility curve, for example,

Money	Utility Index
$100,000	1.50
10,000	1.00
5,500	.75
3,000	.50
900	.25
0	.00
−1,000	−.50
−2,000	−1.50

7. Base the decisions on expected utility. For example, should the decision maker bet $1000 to get a 5 percent chance of winning $100,000?

$$U(\text{bet}) = .95[U(-1000)] + .05[U(100{,}000)]$$
$$= .95(-.50) + .05(1.50) = -.40$$
$$U(\text{don't bet}) = 0$$

DON'T BET

Raiffa [11] and Schlaifer [13] give detailed discussions of utility theory.

Often it is difficult to assign the probability of various futures accurately but we have found sensitivity analysis a very useful technique for finding the range of probabilities that will yield the same decision. Knowing this range it is often unnecessary to refine our estimate of the probabilities of the various futures.

2.3.3
Sensitivity
Analysis

Consider the decision matrix shown in Table 2.10. If we were using the maximum-expected-return principle D_1 would be preferred.

EXAMPLE

$$E(D_1) = .2(160) + .8(80) = 96$$

$$E(D_2) = .2(170) + .8(50) = 74$$

$$E(D_3) = .2(40) + .8(81) = 72.8$$

Table 2.10 Sample Decision Matrix

	.2 S_1	.8 S_2
D_1	160	80
D_2	170	50
D_3	40	81

Now let's assume that we are unsure of the probabilities of S_1 and S_2, we might ask the question, "How big does the probability of S_1 have to get before D_2 would be superior to D_1?"

Let the probability of S_1 be p and the probability of S_2 be $(1-p)$, then D_1 will be preferred to D_2 if $E(D_1) > E(D_2)$.

$$160p + 80(1-p) > 170p + 50(1-p)$$

which is equivalent to

$$80p + 80 > 120p + 50$$

$$\text{or } 30 > 40p$$

$$\frac{3}{4} > p$$

Therefore, if the probability of S_1 is less than $3/4$, D_1 will be superior to D_2.

How small does the probability of S_1 have to become before D_3 is superior to D_1? This can be found in a similar manner by observing that

$$E(D_1) > E(D_3)$$

$$160p + 80(1-p) > 40p + 81(1-p)$$

which is equivalent to

$$80p + 80 > -41p + 81$$

$$\text{or } 121p > 1$$

$$p > \frac{1}{121}$$

Therefore, if the probability of S_1 is greater than $1/121$, D_1 will be preferred to D_3.

The sensitivity analysis tells us that D_1 will be superior to D_2 and D_3 as long as the probability of S_1 is between $1/121$ and $3/4$. This approach should give the decision maker greater confidence in his analysis. Section 2.7.3 gives an excellent example of three-dimensional sensitivity analysis.

2.4 DECISIONS UNDER UNCERTAINTY

Describing how to make decisions under uncertainty is very difficult in the short space available in this section. The interested reader is encouraged to read other authors' descriptions of the process of making decisions under uncertainty [9, 13]. Some consideration about decisions under uncertainty are:

1. They are more complicated than decisions under risk.
2. We have no knowledge of the probabilities of the various states of nature.
3. There is no one best way of determining a strategy.
4. There are a number of different criteria each of which has a perfectly good rationale to justify it. The choice among these criteria is determined by one's policy and/or attitude.

In order to demonstrate the various criteria proposed consider the decision of how to invest one's money over the next five years. The alternatives are:

D_1 Invest in a speculative stock
D_2 Invest in a growth mutual fund
D_3 Buy a certificate of deposit

The various futures are:

S_1 Depression
S_2 Moderate growth in the economy
S_3 Rapid growth in the economy

The decision matrix for this investment decision is shown in Table 2.11 where the entries represent the annual rate of return on one's investment. Now let's consider some of the decision criteria that have been suggested to analyze this type of decision.

Table 2.11 Decision Matrix for an Investment Decision Under Uncertainty (percent)

		S_1 Depression	S_2 Modern Growth	S_3 Rapid Growth
D_1	Stock	-25	0	35
D_2	Mutual fund	-10	5	15
D_3	C.O.D.	8	8	8

Criterion of Pessimism (*Maximin or Wald's criterion*).   Wald has said that the decision maker should always be completely pessimistic. He should act as if nature would be a malevolent opponent.
Considering our example:

EXAMPLE

Strategy	Worst Payoff (percent)
D_1	-25
D_2	-10
D_3	8

Therefore Wald tells us to invest in certificates of deposit because the 8 percent return is the best of the pessimistic return.

Criterion of Optimism (*Maximax*).   Suppose we always assume that nature will be kind. Then we should choose the strategy that will maximize our best payoff.
Considering our example:

EXAMPLE

Strategy	Best Payoff (percent)
D_1	35
D_2	15
D_3	8

Thus the Maximax criterion suggests that we invest in speculative stocks because the 35 percent return is the best of optimistic payoffs.

Hurwicz Criterion. Hurwicz said that a rational decision maker should be neither completely optimistic nor pessimistic. He introduced the idea of a coefficient of optimism. Suppose your coefficient of optimism is C_{OPT} $(0 \leq C_{OPT} \leq 1)$. Then Hurwicz tells us to pick the strategy that maximizes

$$H = C_{OPT} (\text{max payoff}) + (1 - C_{OPT}) (\text{min payoff})$$

Suppose that our coefficient of optimism is .4, then Hurwicz tells us to pick the strategy that maximizes

$$H = .4 (\text{best payoff}) + .6 (\text{worst payoff})$$

EXAMPLE

Strategy	Best Payoff (percent)	Worst Payoff (percent)	H
D_1	35	−25	−1.0
D_2	15	−10	0.0
D_3	8	8	8.0

Therefore the individual with coefficient of optimism of .4 should buy certificates of deposit.

An estimate of someone's coefficient of optimism can be found in manner similar to that used to determine a utility curve in Section 2.3.2. First consider the simple decision matrix shown in Table 2.12. D_2 is a

Table 2.12 Decision Matrix to Help Determine Someone's Coefficient of Optimism

	S_1	S_2
D_1	20	−15
D_2	X	X

strategy that will have the same payoff no matter what future occurs. We ask the decision maker "What value of X will make you feel indifferent in the choice between D_1 and D_2?" Let's assume that it is 5. Then we assume that the value of H should be the same for each decision at the point of indifference.

Strategy	Best Payoff	Worst Payoff	H
D_1	20	-15	$20(C_{OPT})+(-15)(1-C_{OPT})$
D_2	5	5	$5(C_{OPT})+(5)(1-C_{OPT})$
			$=5$

Therefore

$$5 = 20(C_{OPT})+(-15)(1-C_{OPT})$$

$$35C_{OPT} = 20$$

$$C_{OPT} = .57$$

Therefore the decision maker's coefficient of optimism is approximately .57.

Criterion of Rationality (Bayes or Laplace Criterion). Since we don't know the probabilities of the future states of nature, why not assume that they are equal? Then maximize expected return.

For our example we would assume that each future has a probability of occurrence of $1/3$, therefore:

Strategy	Expected Return (percent)
D_1	$\frac{1}{3}(-25+0+35)=3\frac{1}{3}$
D_2	$\frac{1}{3}(-10+5+15)=3\frac{1}{3}$
D_3	$\frac{1}{3}(8+8+8)=8$

Thus the Bayes Criterion also suggests certificates of deposit are a good investment because its expected return is maximum at 8 percent.

Criterion of Regret (Savage criterion). Savage says that often after the decision has been made and the state of nature is known, the decision maker experiences regret because he chose the wrong strategy. Savage says we should minimize this regret.

The usual method for applying this criterion is to create a regret matrix by finding the best payoff in each column of the decision matrix and then determining how much other entries in the column deviate from the best value. After the regret matrix has been determined a Minimax analysis is performed to determine the best strategy according to Savage.

EXAMPLE   The regret matrix for our investment decision is shown in Table 2.13. The entries in the S_1 column are determined by observing the maximum

Table 2.13 Regret Matrix for the Investment Decision Under Uncertainty Shown in Table 2.11 (percent)

	S_1	S_2	S_3
D_1	33	8	0
D_2	18	3	20
D_3	0	0	27

payoff in column S_1 of Table 2.11. is 8 percent. Thus the regret of choosing a speculative stock given we have a depression is 33 percent [(8 percent)–(−25 percent)]. Next we apply a Minimax analysis to the regret matrix

Strategy	Max Regret (percent)
D_1	33
D_2	20
D_3	27

Thus Savage would tell us to buy the mutual fund because its maximum regret is 20 percent.

EXAMPLE   Very few models in the remainder of this text are handled as decisions under uncertainty so let's consider one more example before we move to new material. A company is trying to decide if they should install an expensive safety device on a machine. They know that they will have to install the device if an accident ever occurs and they also know the piece of safety equipment is 100 percent effective. The piece of equipment costs $2500. The alternatives available to the company are:

D_1 Install the safety device.
D_2 Wait to install the safety device until after an accident occurs.

The possible futures for this decision are:
S_1 No accident situation.
S_2 At least one accident situation.
The decision matrix for this decision situation is shown in Table 2.14.

Table 2.14 Decision Matrix for the Decision on Whether to Install a Safety Device

		S_1 No Accidents	S_2 At Least One Potential Accident
D_1	Install	2500	2500
D_2	Wait	0	2500+cost of an accident

If an accident occurs after we have decided not to install the device we will have a penalty of $2500 for installing the device after the accident plus the cost of the accident that occurred. We will now apply the various decision criteria that we have discussed. Note that the numbers in Table 2.14 are costs therefore selecting low values will maximize returns.

Wald's Criterion

Strategy	Worst Payoff
D_1	2500
D_2	2500 + cost of an accident

Install the equipment!

Maximax Criterion

Strategy	Best Payoff
D_1	2500
D_2	0

Don't install the equipment now!

Hurwicz's Criterion

Strategy	Best Payoff	Worst Payoff	H
D_1	2500	2500	$C_{OPT}(2500) + (1 - C_{OPT})(2500)$
D_2	0	2500 + cost of an accident	$C_{OPT}(0) + (1 - C_{OPT})(2500 + \text{cost}$ of an accident$)$

Thus we would prefer to install the safety device if

$$2500 < (1 - C_{OPT})(2500 + \text{cost of an accident})$$

or

$$\text{Cost of an accident} > \frac{C_{OPT}}{1 - C_{OPT}}(2500)$$

Bayes' Criterion

Strategy	Expected Cost
D_1	$\frac{1}{2}(2500) + \frac{1}{2}(2500)$
D_2	$\frac{1}{2}(0) + \frac{1}{2}(2500 + \text{cost of an accident})$

Thus we would prefer to install the device if the $E(D_1) < E(D_2)$.

$$2500 < \tfrac{1}{2}(2500) + \tfrac{1}{2}(\text{cost of an accident})$$

or

$$2500 < \text{cost of an accident}$$

Savage's Criterion

The regret matrix for this decision is shown in Table 2.15. Applying a minimax criterion to the regret matrix yields

Strategy	Maximum Regret
D_1	2500
D_2	Cost of an accident

Thus we would prefer to install the equipment if the (cost of an accident) > 2500.

**Table 2.15 Regret Matrix for the Decision on Whether to
Install a Safety Device**

	S_1	S_2
D_1	2500	0
D_2	0	Cost of an accident

All of the decisions discussed so far have been one-time decisions. Often, however, we are faced with a number of sequential interdependent decisions. One very popular approach to this problem is the use of decision trees. The decision tree approach is one in which the decision is made under risk and the decision criterion is to maximize expected return. There are a number of good references [2, 11, 15, 16] for decision tree analysis that the reader might consult.

Now let's consider an example to demonstrate the procedure [16].

**2.5
DECISION
TREE
ANALYSIS**

2.5.1
An
Introduction
To Decision
Tree
Analysis*

A company has decided to introduce a new product, but there has been no determination of whether to introduce the product regionally or nationally. The decision process is modeled by the decision tree shown in Figure 2.4. Each "square" is called a decision node. These nodes represent places where a decision maker must make a decision. Each branch leading away from a decision node represents one of several possible alternative choices available to the decision maker. For example, node 1 represents the decision to introduce the product regionally or nationally. If the former is chosen, this means that the path leading to node A is followed. Node A is a "circle" node and thus represents a chance node. The chance node represents a point at which the decision maker will discover the response to his decision. Each branch leading away from a chance node represents the outcome of a set of chance factors. For example, 30 percent of the time a "small regional demand" will be realized at node A while 70 percent of the time a "large regional demand" is experienced. If a large regional demand is experienced, the decision tree leads us to decision node 2. Hence, at this point another decision must be made, "go national" or "remain regional." If we decide to "go national," chance node D is encountered. Node D leads to a set of terminal branches. A terminal branch represents the amount received as a result of a particular sequence of decisions and chance occurrences that

EXAMPLE

* Adapted with permission from *Industrial Engineering*, July, 1974. Copyright © American Institute of Industrial Engineers, Inc., 25 Technology Park/Atlanta, Norcross, Ga. 30071.

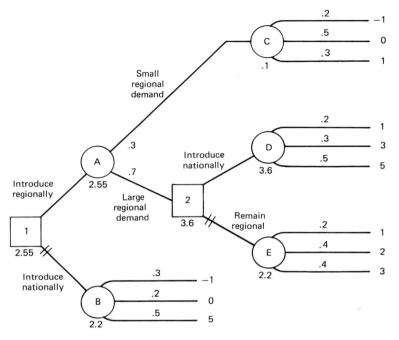

Figure 2.4 Decision-tree analysis of a marketing model. The square nodes are "decision nodes," the round ones are "chance nodes."

lead to the particular branch. Node D will lead to a return of 1, 20 percent of the time; 3, 30 percent of the time; and 5, 50 percent of the time. The remainder of Figure 2.4 can now be understood. Node B represents the outcome of deciding to go national immediately. Node C represents the result of marketing regionally, which yielded a "small regional demand," and node E results from a decision to "remain regional" after a "large regional demand" following the initial decision to "introduce region-ally."

The optimal sequence of decisions in a decision tree is found by starting at the right-hand side and "rolling backward." The goal of the "rolling backward" operation is to *maximize the return* from the decision situation. At each node, an expected return is calculated, the so-called position value. If the node is a chance node, the position value is calculated as the sum of the products of the probabilities on the branches emanating from the node and their respective position values. If the node is a decision point, the expected return is computed for each of its branches and the highest is selected. This is consistent with the desire to maximize return in the tree. Figure 2.4 shows the "position values" for the example. For node D the value is found as follows:

$$\text{Expected return} = 1(.2) + 3(.3) + 5(.5) = 3.6$$

The value for node 2 is equal to 3.6, which is the maximum of 3.6 and 2.2. The double lines on the diagram indicate those paths not chosen by the decision rule. Continuing with this analysis, it is found that the expected return for node 1 is 2.55, which is interpreted as saying that the maximum expected return from introducing a new product is 2.55 units. This return will be achieved by introducing the product regionally and then, if it is successful, by going national.

The decision tree approach exemplified in the preceding example can be conveniently summarized in the following manner:

2.5.2
Summary of
The Decision
Tree
Approach

The decision tree approach is a convenient method for representing and analyzing a series of investment decisions to be made over time (Figure 2.5). Each branch extending from a decision point represents one

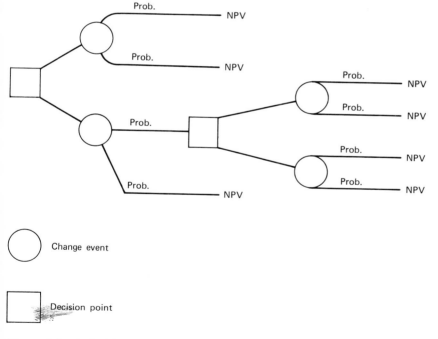

Figure 2.5 A decision tree.

of the alternatives that can be chosen at this decision point. The chance event represents the various levels of values of a decision parameter. It has a probability associated with each of the branches emanating from it.

This probability is the likelihood that the chance event will assume the value assigned to the particular branch.

The optimal sequence of decisions in a decision tree is found by starting at the right side and rolling backward. At each node, an expected return must be calculated, the so-called position value. If the node is a chance event node, the expected return is calculated as the sum of the products of the probability and the expected return for all paths leaving the node. If the node is a decision point, the expected return is computed for each of its branches, and the highest is selected. The procedure continues until the initial node is reached. The position values for this node correspond to the maximum expected return obtainable from the decision sequence.

2.5.3
Decision
Tree
Applications

Decision tree networks can be applied to many sequential decision situations. Raiffa [11] and Magee [8] concentrated on the use of decision trees for analyzing the value of additional information in suggesting the following areas for consideration.

EXAMPLE
Oil Drilling Problem.   An oil company must decide whether or not to drill at a given location before its option expires. There are many uncertainties: the cost of drilling, the value of the deposit and so on. There are records available for similar and not-so-similar drillings in the area. They could obtain more information about the geophysical structure at the site by conducting a seismic sounding. Soundings are very expensive. The problem: Should the company collect more information before making their final decision to drill or not to drill?

EXAMPLE
Introduction of a New Product.   A chemical firm must decide whether or not to market a new, long-lasting house paint. The decision must be whether or not to manufacture the product themselves and, if so, what size plant to build. Or, should they sell or lease their patents and technical know-how to a firm that deals exclusively in house paints? The uncertainty lies in the proportion of the market they will get at a given price, advertising expenditure if they manufacture the product themselves, and the time before a competitor introduces a similar product. Expensive market surveys could be run, but they might be misleading. The problem: How should the company proceed?

EXAMPLE
Treatment of Illness.   A doctor does not know whether his patient's sore throat is caused by strep or by a virus. If he knew it was strep, he would prescribe penicillin. If it was a virus, he would prescribe rest,

gargle, and aspirin. Failure to treat strep might result in serious disease. However, pencillin cannot be used indiscriminately, since it may result in a penicillin reaction.

The physician can take a throat culture, which will indicate the presence of strep. The test is not 100 percent accurate. The problem: What should the doctor do?

Plant Modernization.   A company management is faced with a deci-   **EXAMPLE**
sion on a proposal by its engineering staff to install a computer-based system in the company's major plant. The cost of the control system is $30 million. The benefits of the program depend on the level of production during the next decade. The project, according to the engineers, will yield 20 percent return on investment. There are many questions to be considered in the construction of the decision tree for this example. Will the process work? Will it achieve the economies expected? Will competitors follow the lead if you are successful? Will new products or processes make the new facility obsolete? Will the controls last 10 years? The alternatives considered were:

● To install the new control system.

● Postpone action until trends in the market and/or competition become clearer.

● Initiate more investigation or an independent evaluation.

Each alternative was followed by various other decisions depending on the outcomes of the other alternatives.

New Facility.   The choice of alternatives in building a new plant   **EXAMPLE**
depends on market forecasts. A company has won a contract to produce a new type of military engine suitable for army transport vehicles. The company has a contract to build productive capacity and to produce at a specified level over a period of three years. The company is not sure whether the contract will be continued at a relatively high rate after the third year. There is a possibility that a large commercial market might develop for the engine; this possibility is largely dependent on the cost of the item. Three alternative approaches are evaluated with the tree:

● Subcontract all fabrication and set up a simple assembly line.

● Undertake the major part of the fabrication but use general purpose machine tools.

● Build a highly mechanized plant with specialized fabrication and assembly equipment.

Either of the first two alternatives would be better adapted to low-volume production than would the third.

Now let's consider an adoption of the oil drilling problem that was suggested by Canada [2].*

EXAMPLE

An oil wildcatter must decide whether to drill or not to drill at a given site before his option expires. He is uncertain whether the hole will turn out to be dry, wet, or a gusher. The net payoffs (in present worths) for each state are −$70,000, $50,000, and $200,000, respectively. The initially estimated probabilities that each state will occur are .5, .3, and .2, respectively. Figure 2.6 is a decision tree depicting this simple situation.

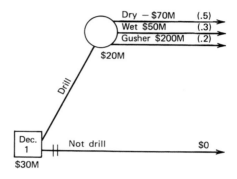

Figure 2.6 Oil wildcatter problem diagram, before consideration of seismic soundings.

Table 2.16 shows calculations to determine that the best choice for the wildcatter is to drill based on an expected monetary value of $20,000 versus $0 if he does not drill. Nevertheless, this may not be a clear-cut decision because of the risk of a $70,000 loss and because he might reduce the risk by obtaining further information.

Suppose it is possible for the wildcatter to take seismic soundings at the cost of $1000. The soundings will disclose whether the terrain below

Table 2.16 Expected Monetary Calculations for the Oil Wildcatter Problem Before Consideration of Seismic Soundings

Drill: −$70,000(.5) + $50,000(.3) + $200,000(.2) = $20,000
Not drill: = $0

---

* Adapted with permission from *Industrial Engineering*, June 1974. Copyright © American Institute of Industrial Engineers, Inc., 25 Technology Park/Atlanta, Norcross, Ga. 30071.

has no structure (outcome NS), or open structure (outcome OS), or closed structure (outcome CS). Table 2.17 provides the best assessment of the joint probabilities of outcome states for each combination of seismic sounding outcome and well state. From this, Table 2.18 shows calculations to determine the probabilities of each well state given each of the three seismic outcomes. The probabilities in Table 2.18 are calculated using Bayes' theorem, which says that the probability of A given B occurring, $P(A|B)$, is equal to the probability of *both A and B* occurring, $P(A, B)$, divided by the probability that B occurs, $P(B)$. In the situation at hand we want

$$P(W|S) = \frac{P(W, S)}{P(S)}$$

where W is the well state

S is the sounding outcome

For example the probability of a dry well given that no structure is found in .73.

Table 2.17 Joint and Marginal Probabilities for the Oil Wildcatter Seismic Soundings

State: (W)	Seismic Outcomes			Marginal Probability of Well State: [$P(W)$]
	NS	OS	CS	
Dry	.30	.15	.05	.50
Wet	.09	.12	.09	.30
Gusher	.02	.08	.10	.20
Marginal probability of seismic outcome: [$P(S)$]	.41	.35	.24	1.00

Table 2.18 Conditional Probabilities of the Oil-Well State, Given the Marginal Probabilities of the Seismic Soundings

Probability of Well State (W)	Seismic Outcomes		
	NS	OS	CS
Dry	.30/.41 = .73	.15/.35 = .43	.05/.24 = .21
Wet	.09/.41 = .22	.12/.35 = .34	.09/.24 = .37
Gusher	.02/.41 = .05	.08/.35 = .23	.10/.24 = .42

Figure 2.7 depicts the decision flow diagram with the alternative of taking seismic soundings. Table 2.19 shows calculations to determine the best choice for the wildcatter based on expected monetary value. Note

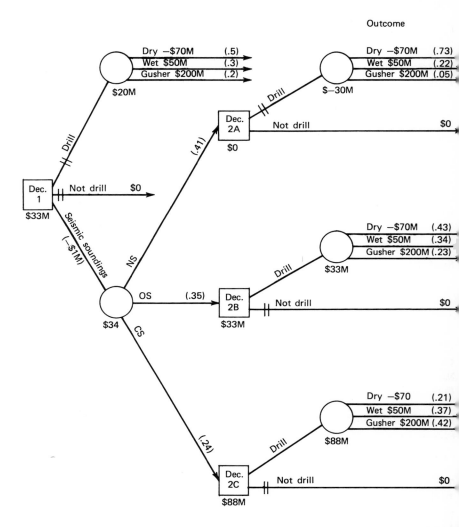

Figure 2.7 Oil wildcatter diagram when the seismic soundings are taken into consideration.

that even though the seismic soundings cost $1000, the wildcatter can increase his expected monetary return to $33,000 by having the soundings made before making the decision to drill or not drill.

Table 2.19 Expected Monetary Calculations for the Oil Wildcatter Problem with Consideration of the Seismic Soundings

Decision Point	Alternative	Expected Monetary Outcome	Choice
2A	Drill	$-\$70M(.73) + \$50M(.22)$ $+ \$200M(.05) = -\$30M$	
	Not drill	$0	Not drill
2B	Drill	$-\$70M(.43) + \$50M(.34)$ $+ \$200M(.23) = \$33M$	Drill
	Not drill	$0	
2C	Drill	$-\$70M(.21) + \$50M(.37)$ $+ \$200M(.42) = \$88M$	Drill
	Not drill	$0	
1	Drill	$20M	
	Not drill	$0	
	Seismic soundings	$\$0(.41) + \$33M(.35)$ $+ \$88M(.24) - \$1M$ $= \$33M$	Seismic soundings

The last topic to be covered in the decision-making area is game theory. The area of game theory is one of the first techniques of operations research that was applied to practical decision making. The British used this technique to aid in planning military and naval strategy. Unfortunately although much has been written about game theory [6, 10, 14, 17] the number of practical applications of the technique are very limited.

Game theory involves systems in which two or more decision makers are in competition. The games are repetitive with each trial being a "play." The average payoff per play is called the value of the game. All players make their decisions at the same time. Complete information is available to all players. The players are rational, that is, they like to win.

Some definitions that will be useful in our discussion can be stated as follows:

Players: The decision makers in the game.
Strategies: The alternatives available to a player.
Optimal strategy: Strategy such that the player is doing the best he can.
Payoff: The outcome of playing the game.
Zero-sum games: The total payoffs to all players at the end of each play is zero.
Payoff matrix: The tabular display of the payoffs to players under various alternatives.

Pure strategy: The player chooses the same alternative at every play.

Mixed strategy: The player chooses different alternatives from time to time.

N-person games: Game in which N players take part.

Our discussions will be limited to two person zero-sum games (often called rectangular or matrix games). The characteristics of such games are:

1. Only two players participate.

2. Each player has a finite number of alternatives.

3. Total payoffs to both players is zero.

The two-person game can be expressed in the form of a rectangular payoff matrix (thus the name rectangular game) as shown in Table 2.20. This matrix shows the payoffs from player A's standpoint. For example a_{ij} is the payoff to player A if he chooses his ith alternative and player B chooses his jth alternative.

Table 2.20 Payoff Matrix for a Rectangular Game

		Player B			
		Y_1	Y_2	$\ldots$	Y_n
	X_1	a_{11}	a_{12}	$\ldots$	a_{1n}
Player A	X_2	a_{21}	a_{22}	$\cdots$	a_{2n}
	$\vdots$	$\vdots$	$\vdots$	$\ldots$	$\vdots$
	X_m	a_{m1}	a_{m2}	$\ldots$	a_{mn}

$X = (X_1, X_2, \ldots, X_m)$ are the relative frequencies that player A chooses his alternatives, and $Y = (Y_1, Y_2 \ldots Y_n)$ are the relative frequencies that player B chooses his alternatives. The expected payoff of a game is

$$E(X, Y) = \sum_{i=1}^{m} \sum_{j=1}^{n} a_{ij} X_i Y_j$$

Let's consider the following competitive game.

EXAMPLE   Gail is sitting in the University Center thinking that she should be back in the dormitory studying when a handsome stranger approaches.

He asks her if she would like to play a game of chance. They decide that they will flip coins and if they match Gail will pay the stranger $1. If Gail has a head and the stranger a tail he will pay her $2 and if the stranger has a head and Gail has a tail no money will be exchanged. Since neither player has coins they decide to just call out heads or tails.

Table 2.21 Payoff Matrix for Gail's Game

		Stranger	
		Y_1 Call Heads	Y_2 Call Tails
X_1	Call heads	−1	2
Gail			
X_2	Call tails	0	−1

The payoff matrix for this game is shown in Table 2.21. If Gail calls heads 75 percent of the time and the stranger calls heads 50 percent of the time then the expected payoff of the game could be found as follows:

$$X = (.75, .25)$$

$$Y = (.50, .50)$$

$$E(X, Y) = (-1)(.75)(.50) + 2(.75)(.50) + (0)(.25)(.50)$$
$$+ (-1)(.25)(.50) = \$.25$$

This says that Gail will have an average winning of $.25 per play if they both adopt the strategies discussed. But what is the solution to a rectangular game?

The solution from player A's point of view is the value of X^* such that $E(X^*, Y)$ is as great as possible and similarly for B; Y^* that minimizes $E(X, Y^*)$.

Assuming a rational approach

$$E(X, Y^*) \leq E(X^*, Y^*) = V^* \leq E(X^*, Y)$$

Where $E(X^*, Y^*)$ is the value of the game.

Von Neumann and Morgenstern [14] suggested the following two theorems that should aid in the solution of rectangular games.

Every rectangular game has a value: a player of a rectangular game   THEOREM 1.
always has an optimal strategy.

THEOREM 2. V^*, X^*, and Y^* are, respectively, the value of a rectangular game, and optimal strategies of players A and B only if for every pure strategy X_p of A and Y_p of B.

$$E(X_p, Y^*) \leq V^* \text{ for every pure strategy } X_p \text{ of } A$$

$$E(X^*, Y_p) \geq V^* \text{ for every pure strategy } Y_p \text{ of } B$$

Theorem 1 says every rectangular game has a solution and that each game has a unique value. There may however be a number of alternative strategies giving this value.

Theorem 2 helps check proposed solutions of rectangular games. If the equations hold for some V^*, X^*, Y^* then it is a solution.

EXAMPLE   Applying Theorem 2 to Gail's problem we get:

$(-1)X_1^* + (0) X_2^* \geq V^*$ if the stranger always calls heads

$(2)X_1^* + (-1) X_2^* \geq V^*$ if the stranger always calls tails

We also know that $X_1^* + X_2^* = 1$, so we can substitute $X_2^* = 1 - X_1^*$, which yields:

$$-X_1^* \geq V^*$$

$$3X_1^* - 1 \geq V^*$$

Similar equations can be developed for the stranger:

$(-1) Y_1^* + (2) Y_2^* \leq V^*$ if Gail always calls heads

$(0) Y_1^* + (-1) Y_2^* \leq V^*$ if Gail always calls tails

Similarly we know that $Y_1^* + Y_2^* = 1$ so we can substitute $Y_2^* = 1 - Y_1^*$ which yields:

$$-3 Y_1^* + 2 \leq V^*$$

$$-1 + Y_1^* \leq V^*$$

These equations can be solved and the following optimum results are found:

$$X_1^* = \frac{1}{4}$$

$$X_2^* = 1 - X_1^* = \frac{3}{4}$$

$$Y_1^* = \frac{3}{4}$$

$$Y_2^* = 1 - Y_1^* = \frac{1}{4}$$

$$V^* = -\frac{1}{4}$$

Thus Gail would lose an average of $.25 per game if she calls heads 25 percent of the time and tails 75 percent of the time. The stranger's optimum strategy is to call heads 75 percent of the time and tails 25 percent of the time. If Gail deviates from her optimum policy while the stranger adheres to his, she will lose more on the average than $.25 per play. Similarly if the stranger deviates from his optimum policy and Gail adheres to hers, his average payoff per play will be less than $.25.

The solution procedure suggested is obviously awkward as the number of alternatives increases. The normal way of solving a large rectangular game is convert it into a linear programming model. This procedure is discussed in Section 3.8.7.

Before you resort to linear programming, one should check to see if the game has a "saddle point." The procedure for finding a saddle point is demonstrated by Table 2.22.

Table 2.22 Determination of a Saddle Point in a Rectangular Game

	B_1	B_2	B_3	Row Min
A_1	3	1	20	1
A_2	5	4	6	4 ← Maximin
Col. max	5	4	20	
		↑ Minimax		

Player A seeks to maximize his minimum gain and player B seeks to minimize his maximum loss. Therefore, player A selects A_2 as a pure strategy and player B selects B_2 as a pure strategy. If the minimax and maximin points are the same we have a *saddle point.* The value of this game is 4 and is achieved when player A adopts pure strategy A_2 and player B adopts pure strategy B_2.

Even if this procedure doesn't yield a saddle point it does give a range on the value of the game because

$$\text{Maximin} \le V^* \le \text{Minimax}$$

2.7
APPLICATION
STUDIES

2.7.1
Insurance
Decisions

Application Study

There are a number of decisions that take the same form often called the insurance decision. Should a person or an organization pay a fixed fee, F, to avoid a large loss, L, which has a probability, p, of occurrence?

Some problems of the form are:

1. Purchase of spare parts or equipment.
2. Purchase of any kind of insurance.
3. Installation of a safety device.
4. Development of redundant systems.
5. Building of flood control dams.

The basic decision format for all of these decisions is the decision between two alternatives:

D_1: insure.
D_2: don't insure.

considering two futures:

S_1: catastrophe occurs.
S_2: catastrophe does not occur.

The decision matrix for this situation is shown in Table 2.23. The decision maker who bases his decisions on the expectation principle will decide to insure only if

$$F < pL.$$

Table 2.23 Insurance-Type Decision Matrix

		p S_1 Catastrophe	$1-p$ S_2 No Catastrophe
D_1	Insure	F	F
D_2	Don't insure	L	0

It is interesting to note that in most cases this is not true. In fact, insurance companies usually set their rates by estimating pL and adding a sufficient amount so that they will make a profit. Therefore most people would decide not to insure if they base decisions on the expectation principle. Yet almost everyone has insurance. Clearly the insurance decision must be based on the aspiration level principle or maximizing expected utility. The logic for buying insurance is that we are willing to accept a small but certain loss in order to be protected against the possibility of a large loss. If we assume that the decision is made according to the aspiration level principle, we would assume that we have an aspiration level, A, which lies in the interval

$$F < A < L$$

and thus the decision to insure minimizes the probability of our loss exceeding the level A. If we view the decision criterion as a maximizing utility we would conclude that the decision maker would insure because

$$U(F) < pU(L).$$

Many large companies and governments do not insure because their utility curves are a straight line and thus the utility decision is basically the same as the expectation decision.

There are a number of situations in which a contractor is asked to submit a sealed bid in order to obtain a contract. After all interested contractors have submitted bids, they are opened and the contractor who has submitted the lowest bid wins the contract. A number of analysts [4, 9] have proposed decision models for this situation. We consider a simplistic approach to this problem.

2.7.2
A
Competitive
Bidding
Model

Application Study

First the contractor asks his estimator to estimate the cost of the job, C. It is probably wise to evaluate your estimator's skills. On jobs won we can compare actual costs with estimates.

Define

$$e = \frac{C}{\text{Actual cost}}$$

where e is a random variable.

Compute

$$\bar{e} = \int ef(e) \, de$$

Ideally $\bar{e}$ should equal 1. If it doesn't there is bias and all estimates should be revised as follows:

$$C' = \frac{C}{\bar{e}}$$

Given the choice between having an estimator with strong bias but low variability in his estimates, and one with no bias but high variability in his estimates, the contractor should prefer the former because it is possible to remove bias but not variability.

The expected profit from a bid B equals $(B - C')P(B)$ where $P(B)$ is the probability of winning with a bid of B. But how do we estimate $P(B)$?

For a competitor we can observe the size of his past bids relative to our estimate.

$$x = \frac{b}{C'}$$

and $g(x) =$ the probability distribution of x.

The probability of winning a contract from competitor X with a bid B is

$$W(X) = \int_{x=B/C'}^{\infty} g(x)\, dx$$

Of course we have to beat all competitors, say X, Y, and Z, to win the bid

$$P(B) = W(X) \cdot W(Y) \cdot W(Z)$$

Now let's consider an example in which we are competing against two competitors:

$$X;\ g(x) \text{ is uniform } (1.03 \le x \le 1.23)$$
$$Y;\ g(y) \text{ is uniform } (1.00 \le y \le 1.15)$$
$$f(e) \text{ is uniform } (.95 \le e \le 1.05)\ \bar{e} = 1.00$$

Our goal is to find the bid B that maximizes

$$E(B) = (B - C')P(B) = (B - C')W(X)W(Y)$$

The calulation is carried out in Table 2.24. For a bid of $1.05C'$, $W(X)$ is found as follows:

The frequency function for X's bid can be expressed in probabilistic terms as

$$g(x) = \begin{cases} 5 & \text{for } 1.03 \le x \le 1.23 \\ 0 & \text{elsewhere} \end{cases}$$

Therefore

$$W(X) = \int_{1.05C'/C'}^{1.23} 5\, dx$$

and

$$W(X) = \int_{1.05}^{1.23} 5\, dx = 5x \Big|_{1.05}^{1.23} = .90$$

Table 2.24 Evaluation of the Expected Profit from a Sealed Bid on a Contract

B	C'	$B - C'$	$W(X)$	$W(Y)$	$P(b)$	$E(B)$
$1.04C'$	C'	$.04C'$	.95	.73	.69	$.027C'$
$1.05C'$	C'	$.05C'$	.90	.67	.60	$.030C'$
$1.06C'$	C'	$.06C'$	.85	.60	.51	$.031C'$
$1.07C'$	C'	$.07C'$	.80	.53	.42	$.030C'$

From Table 2.24, we see that bidding 6 percent above revised cost will maximize profit yielding $.031C'$ per bid. An aspiration principle decision maker might wish to be successful 60 percent of the time on bids, in which case he would bid 5 percent above revised cost because $P(B)$ equals .60 for a bid equal to $1.05C'$.

Isaac [5] has suggested an interesting example of an equipment purchase situation in which sensitivity analysis is very appropriate. A company is trying to decide whether to buy some equipment from supplier A or supplier B. Supplier A is dependable but charges a high price. It is felt that supplier B might be able to deliver on time at a much lower price than Supplier A. There is however the possibility supplier B will deliver late or will not be able to deliver at all. The company feels that if it waited several months they would be in a much better position to estimate supplier B's capabilities. The company wants to consider three possible courses of action:

2.7.3
Equipment
Purchase
(An Example
of Three-
Dimensional
Sensitivity
Analysis)*

Application Study

D_1: order from A. If it later becomes clear that B could deliver, this order can be canceled on payment of certain cancellation charges. Further delay would be encountered while B produces the equipment.

D_2: order from B. If it later becomes clear that B cannot deliver, the order can be switched at a cost for cancellation and additional delay.

D_3: wait until B's capabilities are known. This would involve delay in any case.

The firm uses the present worths of profit over a six-year study period as a measure of value for each outcome. The results are shown in Table 2.25.

Let's assume that the probabilities of each future are unknown to the decisions maker, but he does have a feel for these probabilities. The

Table 2.25 Decision Matrix for an Equipment Purchase Model

	B Fails to Deliver	B Delivers late	B Delivers on time
D_1	142	142	160
D_2	43	49	250
D_3	83	106	177

* Material in this section is adapted from E. J. Isaac, "Note on Selection of Capital Equipment with Uncertain Delivery Date," *Operations Research*, Vol. 4, No. 3, June 1956. Used with the permission of ORSA.

probabilities will be defined as follows:

$$S \rightarrow \text{Probability that B delivers on time.}$$
$$R \rightarrow \text{Probability that B delivers late.}$$
$$1 - R - S \rightarrow \text{Probability that B doesn't deliver.}$$

We know that

$$S > 0 \qquad R > 0 \qquad \text{and } R + S \leq 1$$

therefore, assuming that the decision maker wishes to maximize expected profit, the alternatives can be compared using a two-dimensional space bounded by these constraints.

Considering alternatives D_1 and D_2
we know that D_2 is preferred if

$$E(D_1) \leq E(D_2)$$

$$142(1 - R - S) + 142R + 160S \leq 43(1 - R - S) + 49R + 250S$$

or

$$.06R + 1.91S > 1$$

This can be graphically displayed as shown in Figure 2.8a
Considering D_1 versus D_3

we know D_3 is preferred if

$$E(D_1) \leq E(D_3)$$

$$142(1 - R - S) + 142R + 160S \leq 83(1 - R - S) + 106R + 177S$$

or

$$.39R + 1.29S \geq 1$$

This is graphically displayed in Figure 2.8b and, finally, considering the comparison between D_2 to D_3, we know that D_3 is preferred if

$$E(D_2) \leq E(D_3)$$

$$43(1 - R - S) + 49R + 250S \leq 83(1 - R - S) + 106R + 177S$$

or

$$-.42R + 2.83S \geq 1$$

This comparison is shown in Figure 2.8c.

The final step in our analysis is to combine Figures 2.8a, b, and c into one figure so that all the alternatives can be compared. This step yields Figure 2.8d. We see that D_3 is never preferred. Furthermore, the decision seems to be insensitive to R. It would appear that D_1 should be preferred if the probability of S is less than .5. That is if the decision maker feels that there is less than a 50 percent chance that supplier B will deliver on time

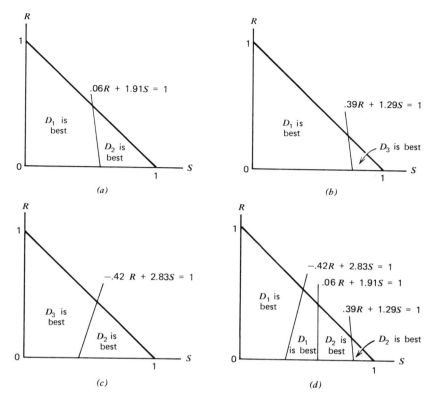

R
1

.06R + 1.91S = 1

D_1 is
best

D_2 is
best

0
1
S

(a)

R
1

.39R + 1.29S = 1

D_1 is
best

D_3 is best

0
1
S

(b)

R
1

−.42 R + 2.83S = 1

D_3 is
best

D_2 is
best

0
1
S

(c)

R
1

−.42R + 2.83S = 1

.06 R + 1.91S = 1

D_1 is
best

.39R + 1.29S = 1

D_1
is best

D_2 is
best

D_2 is best

0
1
S

(d)

Figure 2.8 Graphical representation of the sensitivity analysis for a purchasing
decision.

he should order from supplier A, otherwise he should order from supplier
B now.

Berger and Gerstenfeld [1] have suggested an interesting decision
tree model that considers the case of sequencing several tests of varying
cost, any one of which can fail the person or product under test.

Consider a pilot's physical examination. For simplicity let us
examine the sequence of three basic tests. Assume that the candidate
must pass a heart electrocardiogram, a lung X-ray test, and a series of eye
examinations. Which test should be performed first? Clearly if one test
eliminates 90 percent of all applicants, while another test eliminates 20
percent of all applicants, then, with costs equal, the more stringent test

2.7.4
The
Determination
of an
Optimal
Testing
Sequence*

Application Study

* Adapted with permission from *Industrial Engineering*, July 1972. Copyright © American
Institute of Industrial Engineers, Inc., 25 Technology Park/Atlanta, Norcross, Ga. 30071.

should be performed first. The more usual case is where the costs are not equal, and that is when a complicated sequencing problem exists and needs to be resolved.

Returning to the example of the pilot's test sequence, suppose the eye examination has least cost and also eliminates a high percentage of applicants. The decision to perform this test first is quite obvious. Then suppose that the heart electrocardiogram test costs twice as much as the lung X-ray test. The heart test should be sequenced ahead of the X-ray test only when the probability of rejects from the heart test far exceeds the probability of rejects from the X-ray test. We are now beginning to suspect how Bayesian analysis may be used to aid the decision-maker in determining the optimum sequencing strategy.

A classic example of this type of sequencing problem exists in a company where each finished product must be tested on each of three different machines. The product is rejected if it fails any one of them. Here again the trade-offs on costs and probabilities determine how to sequence tests.

Now let's consider a specific example.

A large manufacturing firm produces components in high volume. Each component must be inspected by subjecting it to a series of three tests (T_1, T_2, T_3). If the component passes *all three tests*, it is shipped to the customer. As soon as a component fails *any one test*, it is sent back to be reworked. The component must then be submitted again to all three tests. The volume is high, and it is an important decision for the firm to determine the optimal sequencing of the three tests. The cost per component to conduct each test is: test 1, $1.10; test 2, $1.20; test 3, $1.30. With no other information, it seems reasonable to order the tests by ascending cost. In this case, the result would be to eliminate the items that are going to fail before reaching the more expensive tests.

In order to estimate the relative frequencies with which a component passes and fails each test, 1000 components were submitted to all three tests. The results are shown in Table 2.26.

From this table we can observe that:

$$P(\text{failing } T_1) = (a_{13} + a_{14} + a_{23} + a_{24})/1000 = .31$$

$$P(\text{failing } T_2) = (a_{12} + a_{22} + a_{14} + a_{24})/1000 = .35$$

$$P(\text{failing } T_3) = (a_{21} + a_{22} + a_{23} + a_{24})/1000 = .29$$

If we consider probabilities *alone*, we should consider the tests: T_2, T_1, T_3. In the absence of other information, it is reasonable that the tests be sequenced so that a test, which has a higher probability of failing the components, is administered prior to a test with not as high a probability. On a purely cost basis, the ordering is different: cost, T_1, T_2, T_3; failure probability, T_2, T_1, T_3.

Table 2.26 Test Results (to nearest 10) of 1000 Components. Each Element is Labeled a_{ij} Where i Refers to the Row, j to the Column

	Pass Test 1		Fail Test 1	
	Pass Test 2	Fail Test 2	Pass Test 2	Fail Test 2
Pass Test 3	580 (a_{11})	10 (a_{12})	10 (a_{13})	110 (a_{14})
Fail Test 3	20 (a_{21})	80 (a_{22})	40 (a_{23})	150 (a_{24})

The best way to determine the optimal sequencing of the tests is to use a combination of probability considerations and cost considerations by representing the problem on a decision tree diagram and incorporating the use of conditional probabilities that can be determined from Table 2.26.

Since items can only pass or fail, it follows from the failure probabilities above that one can compute the pass probabilities as:

$$P(\text{pass } T_1) = .69$$
$$P(\text{pass } T_2) = .65$$
$$P(\text{pass } T_3) = .71$$

Bayes' rule is used to calculate the other probabilities required, as shown in Table 2.27.

Using the data in Table 2.26

$$P(\text{pass } T_1 | \text{ passed } T_2) = P(\text{pass } T_1 \text{ and } T_2)/P(\text{pass } T_2)$$

$$= \left(\frac{a_{11} + a_{21}}{1000}\right) \Big/ \left(\frac{a_{11} + a_{21} + a_{13} + a_{23}}{1000}\right)$$

$$= \frac{a_{11} + a_{21}}{a_{11} + a_{21} + a_{13} + a_{23}} = \frac{600}{650}$$

We now draw the appropriate decision tree (Figure 2.9), label the probabilities on the branches of the diagram, and assign the costs on the end of the branches as the sum of the costs of the tests performed along the path. Note that each component must go through all tests, or until it fails a test. Thus, the only costs relevant are the costs of conducting the tests. If we are performing the third in the series of tests, the result of the

Table 2.27 Conditional Probabilities are Found by Bayes' Rule

Conditional event	Probability via Bayes' Rule	
Passes T_1 given already passed T_2	$\dfrac{a_{11} + a_{21}}{a_{11} + a_{21} + a_{13} + a_{23}}$	$\dfrac{600}{650}$
Passes T_1 given already passed T_3	$\dfrac{a_{11} + a_{12}}{a_{11} + a_{12} + a_{13} + a_{14}}$	$\dfrac{590}{710}$
Passes T_2 given already passed T_1	$\dfrac{a_{11} + a_{21}}{a_{11} + a_{12} + a_{21} + a_{22}}$	$\dfrac{600}{690}$
Passes T_2 given already passed T_3	$\dfrac{a_{11} + a_{13}}{a_{11} + a_{12} + a_{13} + a_{14}}$	$\dfrac{590}{710}$
Passes T_3 given already passed T_1	$\dfrac{a_{11} + a_{12}}{a_{11} + a_{12} + a_{21} + a_{22}}$	$\dfrac{590}{690}$
Passes T_3 given already passed T_2	$\dfrac{a_{11} + a_{12}}{a_{11} + a_{21} + a_{13} + a_{23}}$	$\dfrac{590}{650}$

third test is not relevant to the sequencing decision and, therefore, the results of the third test are not shown on the diagram.

We next "roll back" the decision tree to determine the optimal sequencing, using a criterion of *minimum expected cost per component.* (At each decision node we choose the minimum expected cost.)

It can be seen from the diagram that the optimal strategy is this: perform T_2; if passed, perform T_3; if passed, perform T_1. Again, note that our optimal sequence differs from that found by utilizing cost considerations alone or probability considerations alone. The expected cost per component using the best sequencing is $2.694. Although not completely evident from the diagram, it can be determined that the *least effective* sequence would be T_3, T_2, T_1, at a cost per component of $2.801.

The amount of money involved *per component* is small, but the cost reduction applies to over one hundred thousand components per year.

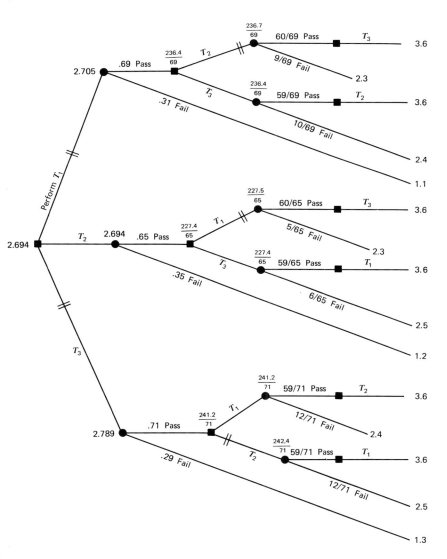

Figure 2.9 Decision-tree diagram for example application. Squares mark decision points; circles represent chance events.

2.7.5
Decision
Analysis in
the National
Football
League*

Application Study

Virgil Carter and Robert Machol [3] have applied decision analysis in an attempt to aid coaches of a professional football team. It is interesting to note that Virgil Carter is a well-known professional football player.

In order to perform such a study, they obtained data on the 56 games played during the first half of the 1969 National Football League schedule. Each of the 8373 individual plays in these games was coded, punched, and entered into a computer, and all analyses were made on this data base.

One analysis concerned the expected value of possession of the football, with first down and 10 yards to go, at any particular point on the playing field. The basic formula for expected value is, of course $E(X) = \sum X_i P(X_i)$. The number of possible outcomes is 103, the first four being touchdown ($X = +7$), field goal ($X = +3$), safety ($X = -2$), and an opponent's touchdown (due to a fumble or an interception) ($X = -7$). The remaining possible outcomes consist of eventually turning over the ball to the opponents at one of the 99 possible points on the field. It is then assumed that the appropriate value of X here is $-E(X)$. This led to a system of 99 equations in 99 unknowns. Since not enough data were available to determine these 99 probabilities with adequate accuracy, the field was divided into 10 strips, that is, 99 to 91 yards to go, 90 to 81 yards to go, 80 to 71 yards to go, and so on. These data sets are identified by their midpoints in Table 2.28. This condensation led to a system of 10 equations in 10 unknowns.

The results are presented in Table 2.28. The analysis was based on a study of 2852 first-and-ten plays. There are some obvious inadequacies in the analysis. In the first place, the several hundred situations starting on the 20 yard line should probably have been separated into an eleventh category. Apparently, first and ten on one's own 20 has an expected value very close to zero, which indicates wisdom on the part of the rule makers.

The numbers in Table 2.28, which are given to three decimal places, are obviously in error by perhaps several tenths of a point. Nonetheless, they have some obvious qualitative value. In basketball, a good deal of strategy is built about the accepted fact that the rebound is worth about one point. There is a similar qualitative value here in having an approximate knowledge of the value of having the ball at a particular point on the field. More significantly, it appears to us that one technical decision is regularly being made incorrectly in professional football. Specifically, the negative value of having the ball with first and ten very close to one's own

* Material in this section is adapted from V. Carter and R. E. Machol, "Operations Research on Football," *Operations Research*, Vol. 19, no. 2, March–April 1971. Used with the permission of ORSA.

Table 2.28 The Expected Point Values of Possession of the Football with First Down and Ten Yards to go for Various Ten-Yard Strips

Center of the Ten-Yard Strip (yards from the target goal line): X	Expected Point Value: $E(X)$
95	-1.245
85	$-.637$
75	$+.236$
65	.923
55	1.538
45	2.392
35	3.167
25	3.681
15	4.572
5	6.041

goal line has been ignored. We are referring to the type of situation where a team has the ball, fourth, and goal, in which case a field goal is routinely attempted. Even in desperate situations (e.g., six points behind in the fourth quarter, when a field goal is considered rather worthless), the usual tactic under a fourth and goal situation would be an attempt to pass. The rules of professional football, if a pass is incomplete in the end zone, require that the ball be brought out to the 20. We would recommend that the ball be rushed under these circumstances. The formal analysis is as follows: if the decision is to kick, there can be two possible outcomes. Three points will be made with probability varying from about .98 if the ball is well centered and the team has a good kicker to perhaps .6 if the angle is very bad and the kicker is poor. From this expected value must be subtracted the negative expected value of the ensuing kickoff. If the kick is missed, the ball is brought out to the 20 where the expected value is approximately zero. On the other hand if the ball is run, there is a probability of perhaps .2 or .3 of making virtually seven points; and if this run fails to make a touchdown, the ball is turned over so close to the enemy goal line that there is something between one and two points of negative value for the opposition. Unfortunately, there is insufficient data to pin down the exact variation in this negative value within the last few yards of the field. But even if the negative value is only the one and a quarter points, which appears to be the average for the one- to nine-yard lines, it seems clear that the analysis on a fourth-and-goal situation is very different from the situation where one has fourth and four on the 20-yard line, for example. In the latter case, the kick seems well justified. A similar analysis is pertinent in evaluating the "coffin-corner" punt.

2.7.6
Labor
Negotiations

Application Study

As discussed in Section 2.6, the applications of game theory have been limited in the area of government and industry. It was, however, useful in war gaming. One industrial application, which some feel is very close to war gaming, is the area of labor negotiations. The problem is usually viewed as both sides having three or four negotiating strategies.

1. Hard-aggressive bargaining.
2. Reasoning, logical approach.
3. Legalistic strategy.
4. Conciliatory approach.

The game theory approach to this problem would be to first set up a payoff matrix as shown in Table 2.29. The payoffs represent hourly increases for the union members. The U_i strategy is the union adopting its ith strategy and the C_j strategy is the company adopting its jth strategy. For example, if the union takes a conciliatory approach (U_4) and the company adopts a legalistic approach (C_3) the union members will get a 25¢ increase.

Analysing the payoff matrix as shown in Table 2.29 we find that there is a saddle point of 35¢ when the union adopts an aggressive strategy and the company adopts a legalistic strategy. If there was no saddle point, linear programming as discussed in Section 3.8.7 would have to be used to analyze the payoff matrix.

Table 2.29 Payoff Matrix for a Labor Negotiations Example (in cents)

	C_1	C_2	C_3	C_4	Row Min	
U_1	40	50	35	95	35	← Maximin
U_2	50	45	30	70	30	
U_3	80	15	25	40	15	
U_4	0	20	25	15	0	
Col. Max	80	50	35	95		

Minimax (↑ under C_3)

1. A series of holes must be drilled in a casting that forms the housing for a motor. The holes may be located and drilled without the aid of a jig by a skilled machinist whose wage rate is $6.50 per hour. His production time will be 1.5 minutes per plate. A jig could be built at a cost of $750 permitting the holes to be drilled by a machinist at a lower skill level. In this case the wage rate would be $5.20 and the production rate would be two housings per minute. Which alternative would you suggest for various production levels.

2. From your own experience select a personal or management decision that you feel is an example of each of the following types:

(a) A decision under assumed certainty.

(b) A decision under risk.

(c) A decision under uncertainty.

For each example identify the elements of the decision (e.g., the alternatives, possible futures, outcomes, etc.)

3. Assuming the decisions involved to be decisions in the face of risk, and using the principles of choice we have studied, explain briefly each of the following behaviors suggested by Morris [9];

(a) The board of directors that states that it is company policy never to run out of finished goods inventory.

(b) The plant manager in the same company who is more than satisfied if he runs out of finished goods inventory no more than once a week, on the average.

(c) The steel user who is carrying no more than his usual steel inventories in spite of the talk about a possible steel strike.

(d) The big company that conducts an elaborate market research program before launching a new product and their small competitor that does no formal market research at all before bringing out a new product.

(e) The man who regularly bets $2 a week on the horses but keeps his personal savings in government bonds.

(f) The manager who assigns two groups of engineers to work separately and independently to solve the same important technical problem.

(g) The big company that lets a computer decide whether or not a customer is a good credit risk, while a smaller company spends more money per customer to have an experienced credit manager make the same decision.

4. For the following decision matrix:

	$P_1 = .20$ S_1	$P_2 = .70$ S_2	$P_3 = .10$ S_3
D_1	20	100	1200
D_2	190	190	190
D_3	500	120	100

show how the following principles of choice would be applied:
(a) Expected profit.
(b) Most probable future.
(c) Aspiration level given $A = \$150$.
5. Consider the following decision matrix:

	$\begin{array}{c} p \\ S_1 \end{array}$	$\begin{array}{c} 1-p \\ S_2 \end{array}$
D_1	100,000	−10,000
D_2	0	0

(a) For what values of p would the expected dollar returns be equal for the two actions?
(b) Given that the expected dollar returns were equal, show the utility curves for individuals that would
(i) Prefer D_1.
(ii) Prefer D_2.
(iii) Be indifferent.
6. Develop a utility curve for two individuals. One being a classmate and one who doesn't know what a utility curve is. Predict their reaction to the following situation:
Would they pay $200 to enter a game that has the following payoffs?

$$\$ \quad 0 \quad \text{with probability of .50}$$

$$\$1000 \quad \text{with probability of .50}$$

7. A stock market speculator was interviewed to determine his attitudes toward investments. The following utility information was developed.

Dollars	Utility
−100,000	.000
−50,000	.167
−10,000	.300
0	.333
10,000	.367
25,000	.417
50,000	.500
100,000	.667
200,000	1.000

(a) Based on the above information, what conclusions can you draw about his investment attitudes?

(b) The speculator is considering one of two investment alternatives. Alternative A promises a profit of $50,000 with a probability of .60 and a loss of $20,000 otherwise. Alternative B offers a profit of $100,000 with a probability of .50 and a loss of −$100,000 otherwise. Which alternative should he choose? Support your answer with an analysis.

8. Suppose an individual gives us the following information about his feelings concerning changes in his money:

$13,000 is equivalent to [(.95, 15,000), (.05, −15,000)]
    5,000 is equivalent to [(.75, 15,000), (.25, −15,000)]
        0 is equivalent to [(.55, 15,000), (.45, −15,000)]
 − 5,000 is equivalent to [(.20, 15,000), (.80, −15,000)]
−10,000 is equivalent to [(.08, 15,000), (.92, −15,000)]

(a) Plot the utility curve.

(b) Consider a game in which he wins $2000 with probability 1/3 and loses $1000 with probability 2/3. Would he play?

9. A manufacturing firm is considering the purchase of a spare machine for standby service at a crucial point in the production process. The machine will cost $20,000 and will have a salvage value of $5000 after 10 years of standby service. The machine will be called into service whenever a breakdown occurs. The number of breakdowns occurring per year is defined by a Poisson distribution with a mean of two breakdowns.

When a breakdown does occur the costs that would result from lost production and enforced idleness would be a random variable y if no standby equipment were available. It is estimated that y is equally likely to fall anywhere in the range from $300 up to $1100 (neglect interest).

(a) On the basis of the expectation principle, does the standby machine appear to be a good investment?

(b) If the firm wishes to maximize the probability that the annual cost of dealing with breakdowns will be below a level A, show which alternative will be preferred as a function of A.

10. A machine is designed and built to special order for a manufacturing firm. The machine builder offers to furnish a spare for a major part at the time the machine is built for an additional cost of $1200. He also indicates that, if the spare is ordered later on, it will cost approximately $14,000 because of special setups and delays. Let the probability that a spare will be required during the life of the machine be p. The probability that more than one spare will be needed is so small that it may be neglected. For what value of p will the two alternatives be equally costly? Would you suggest an aspiration level principle for such a decision?

11. Consider the following decision under risk. The matrix values are dollar losses.

	$p_1 = .999$ S_1	$p_2 = .001$ S_2
D_1	-1	-1
D_2	0	-500

What could be said about the utility function of a subject who
(a) prefers D_1?
(b) prefers D_2?

12. Management of your company is faced with the following dilemma. At a crucial point in your production process there is a machine that breaks down in the following manner:

Breakdowns occur on the average of three per year and are distributed according to a Poisson distribution.

The cost per shutdown is a random variable and is distributed uniformly between $500 and $1500.

Considering the next five-year horizon there are three proposals being considered:

(a) Buy a backup machine for $20,000 which will last five years. The salvage value of the machine will be $0 after five years. This will eliminate all shutdown costs.

(b) Buy a $15,000-deductible insurance policy for $7500. (This policy covers the five-year period in question. You will be responsible only for paying for the first $15,000 of expenses during the five years.)

(c) Let the breakdowns occur and absorb the expenses.

What do you suggest that the company do? (Hint: Var. of $\sum_{i=1}^{y} x = $ (Var. $x)(\bar{y}) + ($Var. $y)(\bar{x})^2$.)

13. You have been hired as a consultant to a designer of a two-stage electronic device. This device will be fired three times when completed and the designer will be paid depending on the number of times it fails.

Number of Failures	Designer's Pay
0	$150,000
1	$ 70,000
2	0
3	$-250,000

Each stage can be made up of up to three components in parallel. These components cost $10,000 each and have a reliability of $\frac{1}{2}$ for each component. As a consultant you will be paid 10 percent of the designer's gross profit or will be penalized 10 percent of the designer's gross loss with a maximum penalty of $10,000.

(a) What is your recommendation if your major concern is your own fee?

(b) What is the basis for your decision? Compare other principles of choice.

(c) What would you suggest if all the designer was interested in was minimizing the probability of incurring a net loss?

(d) Would you suggest the use of a component with a reliability of 2/3 if it cost $20,000?

14. In September I had the honor of being elected "Wampum Bear" for the Comanche Tribe of the Shawnee nation of the Y Indian Guides. The tribe is saving its money for a spring camp-out in our "Wampum Pot." My "little brave," Sitting Bear, told me that he thought that there must be a million dollars in the pot, but I think a more reasonable estimate is between $10 and $25. Estimate the amount of money in the "Wampum Pot" using the various decision rules under uncertainty. What is the best decision if there is a penalty of $1 for each dollar underestimated and $3 for each dollar overestimated?

15. A firm engaged in bidding finds that very limited historical data on behavior of competitors is available. Management is willing to assume that the ratio of the lowest competing bid to their own cost estimate will be not less than 1.00 nor greater than 1.40. The evidence seems insufficient to say anything about the probabilities, however. They are willing to suppress the risk associated with estimating errors in performance costs. Show how various principles of choice for decisions under uncertainty might be applied.

16. Suppose you know that the instructor of this course gives only three grades, A, B, or C. He makes you the following offer: if you can guess the grade that he has already assigned you, he will raise it by one letter (except in the case of A); if you guess wrong he will lower it by one letter grade and if you choose not to guess you will of course receive the assigned grade. Use the various decision rules under uncertainty to analyze this problem.

17. Two bettors at a race track both believe in using the Bayes principle. They are considering a bet on a horse that carries the number 1 and wondering whether to bet $2 on this horse or not to bet on the race at all. If number 1 wins he is expected to pay $6, yielding a profit of $6 - $2 = $4. One bettor argues that there are two possible futures, the horse either wins or loses. The other bettor feels that there are six possible futures since one of the six horses in the race will win. What conclusions will they reach? If the bettors believed in other principles of choice under uncertainty would the argument be meaningful?

18. Construct an example where there are four actions and the Savage regret criterion selects action D_3 and where, in addition if action D_1 is made unavailable, that only actions D_2, D_3, D_4 remain, then Savage regret selects action D_2. Explain why this could be considered an undesirable characteristic of a decision rule.

19. A manufacturer is considering the possibility of introducing a new product and the advisability of a test marketing prior to making the final decision. His alternatives are:

D_1: market the product.

D_2: do not market the product.

For simplicity, only two possible futures are considered which are shown below together with his *a priori* probabilities associated with them.

		Profit	A Priori Probability
S_1	Product is a success	$10,000,000	.70
S_2	Product fails	−$5,000,000	.30

If the test marketing is made, two possible results are considered:

Z_1: test sales of more than 10 percent of the market.

Z_2: test sales of less than 10 percent of the market.

The conditional probabilities of the test results are given in the table below.

	Z_1	Z_2
$P(Z|S_1)$	.85	.15
$P(Z|S_2)$	.15	.85

(a) What is his best alternative before the test?

(b) What action is best for each possible result of the test marketing?

20. Use decision trees to model and analyze the following problem an oil company is trying to decide whether to:

D_1: drill for oil.

D_2: sound then decide to drill.

D_3: don't drill.

The following information is available: drilling that costs $1,000,000 might lead to payloads that can be classed as

Big	$2,000,000
Moderate	$1,000,000
Small	$ 250,000

Before soundings, it is guessed that the probability of a big payoff is .30, a moderate payoff is .50 and a small payoff is .20. The sounding costs $150,000 and yields the following:

Sounding Result	Actual Results Big	Moderate	Small
Big	.60	.20	.20
Moderate	.20	.60	.20
Small	.20	.20	.60

21. The probability of success of a new beer is indicated by past experience to be .7. Our company is about to introduce this product and it estimates the following:

	Product Successful	Product Unsuccessful
Introduce	$150,000	−$50,000
Do not introduce	0	0

A market survey firm has offered to conduct a survey for us at a cost of $40,000. If the firm's record is as follows:

Survey Indication of Success	Actual Degree of Success Successful	Unsuccessful
Successful	.75	.25
Unsuccessful	.25	.75

Should we hire the market survey firm?

22. Consider a game in which you and I are throwing 0, 1, or 2 fingers. If the sum on the fingers showing is even you pay me a dollar amount equal to number of fingers showing, otherwise I'll pay you two dollars. Is there a saddle point for this game?

23. Two ruthless but modern underworld gangs are competing in the same city. Once a month they must make a decision as to where to set up illegal gambling operations to minimize police interference. Some locations are more profitable than others. The outcomes of the competing

alternatives are as follows (payoffs to the Angels):

	Devils		
Angels	B1	B2	B3
A1	$-5M	$8M	$6M
A2	4M	-3M	2M
A3	-10M	7M	-2M

Is there a saddle point for this game?

24. Consider the well-known Colonel Blotto game where Colonel Blotto and his enemy are trying to take over two strategic locations. The regiments available for Blotto and his enemy are 2 and 3, respectively. Both sides will distribute their regiments among the two locations. Let n_1 and n_2 be the number of regiments allocated by Colonel Blotto to locations 1 and 2, respectively. Also, let m_1 and m_2 be his enemy's allocations to the respective locations. The payoff to Blotto is computed as follows:

If $n_1 > m_1$, he receives $m_1 + 2$ and if $n_2 > m_2$ he receives $m_2 + 3$. On the other hand if $n_1 < m_1$, he loses $n_1 + 2$ and if $n_2 < m_2$, he loses $n_2 + 1$. Finally, if the number of regiments from both sides are the same each side gets zero.

Formulate the problem as a two-person zero-sum game. Is there a saddle point?

25. You are owner of a company located in Wilkes-Barre, Pennsylvania. You have a factory along the Susquehanna River.

The probability of the number of floods per year is:

No. Floods	Probability
0	.60
1	.20
2	.15
3	.05

The expected damage per flood is:

$	Probability
10,000	.30
30,000	.40
100,000	.15
300,000	.15

I'll offer you three flood-insurance policies:

$60,000 per year for complete protection
$40,000 per year for $20,000 deductible flood protection
$22,000 per year for $60,000 deductible flood protection

Should you buy insurance? (Consider the various decision criteria.)

26. The United States has been offered a chance to purchase the formulae for a new rocket fuel. Through channels known only to the CIA, it has been learned that two Communist countries will be bidding for the plans. The United States has assigned world-renowned lover and part-time statesman, Hen Ri Smooch En Gey (an Hawaiian resident) to handle their bidding. The competitors, all being good Marxists, are assumed to be stereotyped bidders with bidding behavior described by the density function $f(t) = $ uniform over the range $100,000 < t < 1,000,000$.

Although the United States is close to discovering its own solid fuel, it is estimated that buying the formulae could save $1.5 million in research. Find the bidding policy that will minimize expected costs.

27. Your plant has four chemical tanks that have linings that fail according to the following probability distribution:

Failure Occurs in Month	1	2	3	4	5 or more
Probability	.05	.10	.35	.40	.10

If the tank fails in service the tank must be drained immediately, causing a variety of losses and interruptions in the production process. The tank remains idle until the end of the month. The costs of interruptions are estimated to be $10,000. On the other hand, the production schedule provides for emptying the tank at the end of each month and relining may be done at that time. Relining the tank at the end of the month costs $2000. In no case may the tank run more than four months without relining. This process is expected to run unchanged for the next 10 years.

(a) Develop a relining policy. Justify your choice of decision criteria.
(b) If you were dealing with one tank and one year, would your decision criteria and policy change?

28. Assume the Student AIIE Chapter is planning its annual picnic for Monday April 16. The success of these plans depends heavily on the weather.

Let S_1 be the outcome if the weather is nice
S_2 be the outcome if the weather is threatening
S_3 be the outcome if the weather is raining

AIIE's fearless president, John What's-his-name, on April 13, must decide how much to invest in the annual bash. The payoff matrix for various weather conditions is

		$S1$	$S2$	$S3$
D_1	Cancel	-100	0	0
D_2	Modest	0	50	-30
D_3	All out	100	0	-100

What course of action should John take? (Use three-dimensional sensitivity analysis to help you solve this problem.)

29. You are the managing director of a fairly large company. Your executive committee is considering these policies:

(A) Projected 200 percent expansion of the company's operations in two years, including new products and markets.

(B) Maintenance of present size of company with emphasis on models of existing products.

(C) Maintenance of present size of company with emphasis on replacement of less profitable products with new products.

The company's objective is to maximize long-term cash flows, and you are aware that one of three mutually exclusive events can occur. The rates of return for the three policies are:

	1 Cost of Capital Up Approx. 40 Percent	2 Period of Rapid Economic Expansion	3 New Competition Moves In
A	-10	15	10
B	8	10	-2
C	4	6	3

Perform a sensitivity analysis to determine which alternative seems attractive.

REFERENCES

1. Berger, P. D. and A. Gerstenfeld, "Decision Analysis for Optimal Test Sequencing," *Industrial Engineering,* Vol. 4, No. 7, July 1972.

2. Canada, J. R., "Decision Flow Networks," *Industrial Engineering,* Vol. 6, No. 6, June 1974.

3. Carter, V. and R. E. Machol, "Operations Research on Football," *Operations Research,* Vol. 19, No. 2, March–April 1971.

4. Friedman, L., "A Competitive Bidding Strategy," *Operations Research*, Vol. 4, No. 1, February 1956.
5. Isaac, E. J., "Note on Selection of Capital Equipment with Uncertain Delivery Date" (letter to Editor), *Operations Research*, Vol. 4, No. 3, June 1956.
6. Luce, R. D. and H. Raiffa, *Games and Decisions*, Wiley, New York, 1957.
7. Magee, J. F., "Decision Trees for Decision Making," *Harvard Business Review*, July–August 1964.
8. Magee, J. F., "How to Use Decision Trees on Capital Investment," *Harvard Business Review*, September–October 1964.
9. Morris, W. T., *The Analysis of Management Decisions*, Richard D. Irwin, Inc., Homewood, Ill., 1964.
10. Owen, G., *Game Theory*, W. B. Saunders Co., Philadelphia, 1968.
11. Raiffa, M., *Decision Analysis—Introductory Lectures on Choices under Uncertainty*, Addison-Wesley, Reading, Mass., 1968.
12. Raiffa, H. and R. Schlaifer, *Applied Statistical Decision Theory*, M.I.T. Press, Cambridge Press, 1961.
13. Schlaifer, R., *Analysis of Decisions Under Uncertainty*, McGraw-Hill, New York, 1969.
14. Von Neumann, J. and O. Morgenstern, *Theory of Games and Economic Behavior*, Princeton University Press, Princeton, N.J., 1944.
15. Whitehouse, G. E., *Systems Analysis and Design Using Network Techniques*, Prentice-Hall, Englewood Cliffs, N.J., 1973.
16. Whitehouse, G. E., "Using Decision Flow Networks," *Industrial Engineering*, Vol. 6, No. 7, July 1974.
17. Williams, J. D., *The Compleat Strategyst*, rev. ed., McGraw-Hill, New York, 1966.

linear
3 programming

3.1
INTRODUCTION

Linear programming is a methodology for solving problems where we:

- Seek to attain some objective (e.g., the maximization of profit or the minimization of costs).

- Which is a function of the system's outputs (e.g., the product being produced).

- Which result from inputs of resources into the system (e.g., raw materials and/or machine time).

- All of which are linearly related or at least their relationship can be so approximated.

Although we live in a largely nonlinear world, there are, nevertheless, significant numbers of instances in day-to-day endeavors that are linear in nature so that an understanding of linear programming and its application in solving problems is more than a matter of academic interest. Numerous successful applications in such fields as blending operations, machine scheduling, and transportation activities (to name just a few) indicate to us that knowledge of this basic operations research technique is essential for today's management practitioner.

3.2
GRAPHICAL
TECHNIQUE

EXAMPLE

The solution of linear programming problems by means of a graphical technique is severely limited in that we are not able to graph more than three-dimensional space. Nevertheless, examining a simple linear programming problem graphically is of significant value in that it provides us with a pictorial representation of the solution process and thus with an understanding not readily available by other means. For the purpose of such an examination, let us assume a problem where we are concerned with maximizing the profit (Z) realized from two products (X_1 and X_2)

that yield 2 and 3 units of profit per unit of product manufactured, respectively, and that we can sell all of the products we can make. This type of problem is often referred to as a Product-Mix problem. Thus the objective we are seeking to attain may be expressed as:

$$\text{Maximize } Z = 2X_1 + 3X_2 \qquad (3.1)$$

The problem is trivial as stated thus far because maximization of our profit is simply a matter of increasing X_1 and X_2 without limit. Normally, in a linear programming problem, constraints exist that preclude such a trivial solution. In our problem let us assume that it requires 3 units of labor to manufacture X_1 and 6 units of labor to manufacture X_2 and all we have available are 24 units of labor. Thus we could say:

$$3X_1 + 6X_2 \leq 24 \qquad (3.2)$$

Let us further assume that it requires 2 units of raw material to manufacture X_1 and 1 unit of raw material to manufacture X_2 and all we have available are 10 units of raw material. Thus we could also say:

$$2X_1 + X_2 \leq 10 \qquad (3.3)$$

Since we know that we cannot violate the constraint in Equation 3.2 we could plot the line expressed by $3X_1 + 6X_2 = 24$ as shown in Figure 3.1. Then any point in the cross-hatched area under the plotted line, or on the plotted line for that matter, would represent a feasible solution insofar as (3.2) is concerned. Note also that the plotted line and the shaded area stop at the intersection with the X_1 and X_2 axis since negative quantities of the items we are manufacturing have no meaning in the context of this problem.

Because (3.3) operates as a constraint simultaneously with (3.2) in our assumed problem, we must plot (3.3) in a similar fashion to that described above. Doing so would provide us with the graphics portrayed in Figure 3.2. Notice now that the cross hatching is restricted to that area that is simultaneously under both lines and that any point in that new area would be a feasible solution insofar as both (3.2) and (3.3) are concerned. Of course we are not just seeking any feasible solution but the solution that maximizes the value of (3.1).

We can plot a series of profit lines, that is, those profit lines that have a constant value for all combinations of X_1 and X_2, in order to see where in the shaded area the maximum profit occurs. This plot is shown in Figure 3.3 from which it can be seen that the maximum profit is 14 units at $X_1 = 4$ and $X_2 = 2$. It is no coincidence that this optimum solution is at a corner point of the polygon shown in the figures; it can be shown

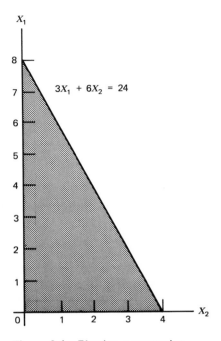

Figure 3.1   Plotting a constraint.

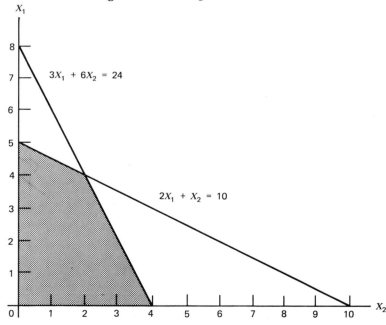

Figure 3.2   Plotting another constraint.

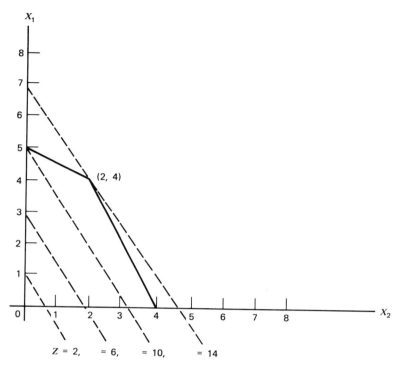

Figure 3.3 Plotting profit lines.

mathematically that the optimum solution will always occur at a corner point.* This should suggest that it would be more efficient to solve for values of the objective function only at corner points rather than to evaluate the objective function at all feasible solutions in order to select the optimal feasible solution. While this is certainly a true statement, a moment's reflection will also suggest that a search procedure that moves from one corner point toward another only in the direction of optimality and stops once optimality is achieved would be even more efficient. Before moving on to the treatment of more complex linear programming problems it would be well to solve our simple assumed problem via an efficient search pattern and algebra to gain a better understanding of the manipulative techniques we will use later.

* If the profit lines in the example had been parallel to either of the lines bounding (3.2) or (3.3), more than one optimal solution would have existed. These solutions would have consisted of the two corner points and all the points along the side of the polygon that coincided with the optimal profit line.

In order to start our algebraic solution, we need a corner point to start from. Certainly an obvious one is the intersection of the X_1 and X_2 axes. At that point $X_1 = X_2 = 0$ and if we evaluate our objective function (3.1) there we see that our profit is zero. While we have a solution at a corner point, the profit is not very appealing. In which direction should we move now? Examination of (3.1) shows that our profit will increase by 3 units for every unit of X_2 that we produce and this appears to be more desirable than producing X_1, which only yields 2 units of profit per article produced. We shall make as many units of X_2 as possible while ignoring X_1 for the moment. Then from (3.2) and (3.3) we see that

$$3(0) + 6X_2 \le 24 \qquad \text{or} \qquad X_2 \le 4$$
$$2(0) + X_2 \le 10 \qquad \text{or} \qquad X_2 \le 10$$

Since we cannot violate either constraint we elect to produce 4 units of X_2 and our profit from (3.1) now becomes

$$Z = 2X_1 + 3X_2 = 2(0) + 3(4) = 12 \text{ units}$$

which is certainly an improvement over the profit at the preceding corner point. Can we improve this profit further?

Remember that it only required 1 unit of raw material to produce 1 unit of X_2 and since no X_1 is to be produced at this corner point we must have 6 units of raw material left over. Three facts about our problem are now important.

First, we have raw material from which we can make X_1.

Second, we have no labor left with which to make X_1 but if we do not make as much X_2 as we had planned some labor would become available for making X_1. Incidentally a reduction in the amount of X_2 to be produced would generate additional raw material availability as well as the labor already mentioned.

Third, by looking at our objective function (3.1), we can see that it would be to our advantage to produce X_1 provided we could hold concomitant reductions in X_2 to somewhat less than two thirds of X_1 production.

Inspection of (3.3) indicates that for every unit of X_1 produced we would be required to reduce the production of X_2 by 1/2 unit. This is well within the 2/3 requirement which is to our advantage. We also note that such a reduction will provide 1/2 unit of raw material and, from (3.2), 3 units of labor for the production of X_1.

How much of X_1 can we produce? From (3.3) we know that it requires 2 units of raw material to produce a unit of X_1. And we also know that for each unit of X_1 we produce, we will generate 1/2 unit of raw material availability as a result of the required reduction in X_2. Since we have 6 units of raw material available at our present corner point we must be able to produce

$$\frac{6 \text{ units raw material available}}{\frac{2 \text{ units raw material required}}{\text{per unit } X_1} - \frac{1/2 \text{ unit raw material generated}}{\text{per unit } X_1}}$$

$$= 4 \text{ units of } X_1$$

The production of 4 units of X_1 will require the reduction of 2 units in the production of X_2; thus our new corner point is $X_1 = 4$, $X_2 = 2$ at which our profit is

$$Z = 2X_1 + 3X_2 = 2(4) + 3(2) = 14 \text{ units}$$

Can we obtain an increase over this profit by moving to another corner point?

Look at (3.2). We have no surplus of labor, and if we were to attempt to increase production of X_1 we would be required to reduce production of X_2 by 2 units. This is not within the 2/3 limit, which is where our profit advantage ceases. There is, in fact, no way to move that would increase our profits, and we have found that corner point at which our profit is maximized. You may wish to check the profit at the remaining corner point ($X_1 = 5$, $X_2 = 0$) but you will find that our profit would drop to 10 units.

Solving a complex linear programming problem as we have just done would be difficult and very time consuming and it is not necessary to do so. In 1947, Dr. G. B. Dantzig published a paper on a method for handling linear programming, called the simplex method, which since then has been elaborated and routinized into an easy to use but extremely powerful technique. We shall look at this technique without a rigid proof and instead rely on our examination of the graphical and algebraic techniques to provide us with an understanding of what the simplex method is doing.

In general, a linear programming problem is defined by a standard form as follows:

3.4 THE SIMPLEX ALGORITHM

Find the values of $X_1, X_2, \ldots X_n$ that maximizes

$$Z = C_1 X_1 + C_2 X_2 + \ldots C_n X_n \tag{3.4}$$

subject to a set of constraints that may be expressed as

$$a_{11}X_1 + a_{12}X_2 + \ldots a_{1n}X_n = b_1$$
$$a_{21}X_1 + a_{22}X_2 + \ldots a_{2n}X_n = b_2 \tag{3.5}$$
$$\vdots \qquad \vdots \qquad \vdots$$
$$a_{m1}X_1 + a_{m2}X_2 + \ldots a_{mn}X_n = b_m$$

and where $X_j \geq 0$ for $j = 1, 2, \ldots n$. $\tag{3.6}$

It is absolutely mandatory that the problem be placed in this form in order to utilize the simplex algorithm. Doing so may be considered as the first step in solving a problem, and we shall use it as such in describing the simplex algorithm that follows below:

STEP 1. Set up the problem in the standard form.

STEP 2. Find an initial corner point solution. In common simplex language this would be an initial basic feasible solution.

STEP 3. Determine whether a better feasible solution is possible. If not the optimal solution has been found. If a better feasible solution is possible proceed to step 4.

STEP 4. Identify the variable whose incremental contribution to the objective function is greatest.

STEP 5. Identify the variable to be removed from the basic feasible solution when the variable identified in step 4 is introduced into the solution.

STEP 6. Perform the necessary computations to introduce the entering variable (identified in step 4) and remove the departing variable (identified in step 5).

STEP 7. Return to step 3.

This is essentially the simplex algorithm and only one more device is necessary before we can start using it in a routinized fashion. That device is called the simplex tableau shown in Figure 3.4. The C_j data to be entered across the top of the tableau comes from (3.4) and remains fixed throughout the problem solution. The first column is a listing of the X_j in the basic feasible solution (the variables in the solution) being considered in the tableau and there will always be m (the number of constraints) of them. The next column contains the particular C_j corresponding to the X_j in the solution. Each of the next n columns contains the a_{ij} corresponding to the X_j shown at the column heading for the ith row (constraint) of the tableau. The b column contains the value of the variable in the solution, and we shall use the last column for computations in connection with the algorithm. Finally the bottom portion of the tableau contains spaces for contributions to the objective function total in the Z_j row and incremental increases possible in the objective function per X_j as shown in the $C_j - Z_j$ row. Now let us proceed through the algorithm solving our illustrative problem as shown by (3.1), (3.2), and (3.3), which are repeated here for easier reference.

	c_j						
Variables in Solution	Var c_j	X_1	X_2	X_3	...	X_n	b
$i = 1$							
2							
3							
. . .							
m							
z_j							
$c_j - z_j$							

Figure 3.4 A simplex tableau.

$$\text{Maximize } Z = 2X_1 + 3X_2 \qquad \text{(profit)} \qquad (3.1)$$

$$\text{subject to } 3X_1 + 6X_2 \le 24 \qquad \text{(labor)} \qquad (3.2)$$

$$2X_1 + X_2 \le 10 \qquad \text{(raw materials)} \qquad (3.3)$$

EXAMPLE

Step 1. Set up the problem in the standard form.
We see immediately that the constraints, (3.2) and (3.3), are not in proper form since they are not expressed as equalities. We can remedy this shortcoming in (3.2) by introducing a new variable to represent that portion of the labor that may be unused whenever the inequality in the constraint is operative. Calling the new variable X_3, (3.2) becomes

$$3X_1 + 6X_2 + X_3 = 24$$

Similarly, (3.3) becomes

$$2X_1 + X_2 + X_4 = 10$$

Notice also that in the standard form each equation must contain each variable and we can do this by proper placement of a zero coefficient. Now our problem looks like this

$$\text{Maximize } Z = 2X_1 + 3X_2 + 0X_3 + 0X_4$$
$$\text{subject to} \quad 3X_1 + 6X_2 + X_3 + 0X_4 = 24$$
$$2X_1 + X_2 + 0X_3 + X_4 = 10$$

and the only missing element to make it match the standard form precisely is the condition that all our variables must be equal to or greater than zero. In our problem we can neither produce negative products nor use more labor or raw materials than we have. The condition therefore exists and it only remains to state it:

$$X_j \geq 0 \qquad j = 1, 2, 3, 4$$

to complete step 1.

Step 2. Find an initial basic feasible solution.

We shall now introduce the simplex tableau into the problem to facilitate this work. Figure 3.5 illustrates the partially completed initial tableau with the data displayed taken directly from the standard form of the problem. The C_j values are the coefficients in the objective function.

	C_j	2	3	0	0	
Variables in Solution	Var. C_j	X_1	X_2	X_3	X_4	b
X_3	0	3	6	1	0	24
X_4	0	2	1	0	1	10
Z_j						
$C_j - Z_j$						

Figure 3.5 Developing the initial tableau.

The variables in our initial basic feasible solution, X_3 and X_4, stem from the fact that we are letting $X_1 = X_2 = 0$ so that the first constraint is used to solve for X_3 and the second constraint is used to solve for X_4. The C_j associated with the variables X_3 and X_4 are both zero and provide for the data in the second column. The values under the next four columns come from the coefficients in the two constraints and correspond row wise with the constraint from which the solutions to X_3 and X_4 are to be obtained. In a similar fashion the values in the b column are placed in the tableau. We have now completed step 2. If we permit $X_1 = X_2 = 0$ as we have done, the values of X_3 and X_4 are 24 and 10, respectively. Note that these are the precise values in the b column in the X_3 and X_4 rows. The values of the variables in our basic feasible solution will always be displayed in the b column. Furthermore, any variables in our problem not displayed in the solution column of the tableau will always be equal to zero. In effect the tableau at this point tells us that we have not made any of either product X_1 or X_2 and that our unused labor, X_3, and unused raw material, X_4, are 24 and 10 units, respectively.

Step 3. Determine whether a better feasible solution is possible.
To proceed with step 3 requires that the tableau of Figure 3.5 be completed. The tableau has been designed to facilitate the mathematics connected with this task. To complete the Z_j row we multiply each of the a_{ij} values by the C_j associated with the variable in the solution of the ith row and add the products thus formed in each column. For example we find the value of Z_j under X_1 from

$$Z_j(X_1) = (\text{Var. } C_j \text{ for first row}) (a_{11})$$
$$+ (\text{Var. } C_j \text{ for second row}) (a_{21})$$
$$= 0(3) + 0(2) = 0$$

and the value of Z_j under X_2 would be found from

$$Z_j(X_2) = (\text{Var. } C_j \text{ for first row}) (a_{12})$$
$$+ (\text{Var. } C_j \text{ for second row}) (a_{22})$$
$$= 0(6) + 0(1) = 0$$

$Z_j(X_3)$ and $Z_j(X_4)$ would be found in a similar fashion as would be $Z_j(b)$. In this instance they would all be equal to zero. Remember the values of X_3 and X_4 appeared in the appropriate row under the b column. Where in the tableau would you look to find the value of Z, the objective function? It, too, will appear in the b column in the Z_j row, of course. In this instance the objective function value is zero but that is not surprising since having produced nothing we would not expect to have a profit. Figure 3.6 shows the results of these computations.

Variables in Solution	Var. C_j	C_j	2	3	0	0	
			X_1	X_2	X_3	X_4	b
X_3	0		3	6	1	0	24
X_4	0		2	1	0	1	10
Z_j			0	0	0	0	0
$C_j - Z_j$							

Figure 3.6 Continuing with the initial tableau.

The last row of the tableau is completed by subtracting the computed Z_j from the corresponding C_j at the top of the tableau. Thus under X_1 we would have

$$C_j(X_1) - Z_j(X_1) = 2 - 0 = 2$$

and under X_2

$$C_j(X_2) - Z_j(X_2) = 3 - 0 = 3$$

The process would be continued for each column and the completed row is shown in Figure 3.7.

	C_j	2	3	0	0	
Variables in Solution	Var. C_j	X_1	X_2	X_3	X_4	b
X_3	0	3	6	1	0	24
X_4	0	2	1	0	1	10
Z_j		0	0	0	0	0
$C_j - Z_j$		2	3	0	0	0

Figure 3.7   Computing the $C_j - Z_j$ values.

Remember that this row indicates the incremental increase to the objective function if a unit of the variable heading the column is added to the basic feasible solution. We can now answer the question posed at the beginning of this step: "Is there a better feasible solution?"

If any value in the Z_j row *under a variable* is greater than zero, there is a better feasible solution.* Our algorithm tells us that if there isn't a better feasible solution we have found the optimal solution but this will rarely occur in the initial tableau. In our case we can see two $C_j - Z_j$ values greater than zero and so we know we must go to the next step.

Step 4. Identify the variable whose incremental contribution to the objective function is greatest.

This step can be done by inspection since the variable heading the column containing the maximum positive $C_j - Z_j$ is the variable we are

---

* Actually if, for one column, $C_j - Z_j$ is positive but all the a_{ij} in that column are nonpositive, the objective function is not bounded and can be increased without limit.

looking for. Thus in our problem the variable X_2 whose corresponding $C_j - Z_j = 3$ is designated as the variable to enter into the basic feasible solution. This can be shown on the tableau by placement of a small arrow at the bottom of the tableau as shown in Figure 3.7.

Step 5. Identify the variable to be removed from the basic feasible solution.

This step involves a simple computation for each row where the b_i values are divided by the appropriate a_{ij} values in the column of the entering variable. As a computational aid these values can be entered in the last column of the tableau as they are calculated and in our example the first row b_i / a_{ij} would be 4 (dividing 24 by 6) and the second row would be 10.

Identification of the variable to be removed from the basic feasible solution then follows from its row association with the minimum *positive* value shown in the last column.* (Ties may be broken arbitrarily.) This row can be identified by a small arrow at the end of the tableau. Finally, for later use in the preparation of the next tableau, the intersection of the entering (column) and departing (row) variables is identified by circling the element of the tableau at the intersection. This element is called the pivot element and the completed tableau is shown in Figure 3.8.

Before turning to the next step it may be well to reflect on what we have just done. In essence, having decided that X_2 was to enter the

Variables in Solution	Var. C_j	C_j	2	3	0	0		
		X_1	X_2	X_3	X_4	b	
X_3	0	3	⑥	1	0	24	4	←
X_4	0	2	1	0	1	10	10	
Z_j		0	0	0	0	0		
$C_j - Z_j$		2	3	0	0	0		

↑

Figure 3.8 Determining entering and departing variables.

* Division by zero is meaningless and division by a negative a_{ij} is not allowed since introduction of a variable in a row as a result of a negative b_i / a_{ij} would be an infeasible solution (i.e., it would constitute violation of a constraint).

solution because its incremental contribution to profit was greatest, we proceeded to determine how much of X_2 we could make without violating our constraints. The tableau indicated that we could only make 4 units of X_2 and at the same time indicated that X_3, unused labor, would be removed from our solution when we did so.

Step 6. Perform the necessary computations to introduce the entering variable and remove the departing variable.

What we are about to do involves transforming our initial set of equations with a basic feasible solution into an equivalent set of equations with a different basic feasible solution. We will do this by going directly from our initial tableau to a second tableau one row at a time. We start construction of the tableau exactly as we did before and everything shown in Figure 3.9 can be copied directly from the previous tableau. Note however, that in the first two columns we have entered X_2 and its associated C_j, thus replacing X_3 in the solution.

	C_j	2	3	0	0	
Variables in Solution	Var. C_j	X_1	X_2	X_3	X_4	b
X_2	3					
X_4	0					
Z_j						
$C_j - Z_j$						

Figure 3.9 Starting an improved solution.

The row transformations always start with the row of the entering variable, the pivot row. To transform the pivot row requires that the a_{ij} values in that row be divided by the pivot element value. We circled the pivot element in Figure 3.8 for this use and dividing the pivot row by it permits us to fill in the equivalent row of our new matrix as shown in Figure 3.10.

The transformation of the remaining rows of the tableau is a two-step operation for each row. In order to obtain the particular set of equivalent equations we are after in the remaining rows, it is necessary that the a_{ij} to be entered under the entering X_j column be zero in each of the remaining rows. To do this requires that we first take the transformed pivot row values and multiply them by the a_{ij} value in the pivot column of

Variables in Solution	C_j Var. C_j	2 X_1	3 X_2	0 X_3	0 X_4	b
X_2	3	$^3/_6$	1	$^1/_6$	0	4
X_4	0					
Z_j						
$C_j - Z_j$						

Figure 3.10 Development of an improved solution.

the row we are transforming and second, to subtract those computed values from each of the a_{ij} values of the row we are transforming. The results of this two-step operation are then written directly into the appropriate row of the new tableau we are forming. For our example problem we will have to transform row 2 of Figure 3.8 whose values are 2, 1, 0, 1, 10. We multiply the transformed pivot row values, which are 3/6, 1, 1/6, 0, and 4, by 1, which is the a_{ij} value in the pivotal column of the row to be transformed and subtract those results from the values to be transformed.

$$
\begin{array}{ccccc}
2 & 1 & 0 & 1 & 10 \\
-3/6 & -1 & -1/6 & -0 & -4 \\
\hline
9/6 & 0 & -1/6 & 1 & 6
\end{array}
$$

The results are entered directly into the tableau as shown in Figure 3.11. Our example only has two rows so we have now finished the transformation. If we had had more rows the process for each one would have been identical to that illustrated for the second row. At this point our algorithm tells us to return to step 3 to determine whether a better feasible solution is possible.

Rather than continue by referring to the steps of the algorithm, let us now proceed to complete the solution of the problem by merely working through the tableaus as necessary.

The Z_j-row values are computed under the columns headed:

$$
\begin{aligned}
&X_1 \text{ from } 3(3/6)+0(9/6)=9/6 \\
&X_2 \text{ from } 3(1)+0(0)=3 \\
&X_3 \text{ from } 3(1/6)+0(-1/6)=3/6 \\
&X_4 \text{ from } 3(0)+0(1)=0 \\
&b \text{ from } 3(4)+0(6)=12
\end{aligned}
$$

C_j		2	3	0	0	
Variables in Solution	Var. C_j	X_1	X_2	X_3	X_4	b
X_2	3	$3/6$	1	$1/6$	0	4
X_4	0	$9/6$	0	$-1/6$	1	6
Z_j						
$C_j - Z_j$						

Figure 3.11   Row transformation.

These values can be written into the tableau as they are obtained. The $C_j - Z_j$ row values are merely a subtraction of the foregoing from the C_j values indicated at the top of the tableau and can also be written into the tableau. Figure 3.12 illustrates how the second tableau would appear after having selected X_1 as the next variable to enter the solution since its incremental contribution to profit $(C_j - Z_j)$ is the maximum positive increment shown.

C_j		2	3	0	0	
Variables in Solution	Var. C_j	X_1	X_2	X_3	X_4	b
X_2	3	$3/6$	1	$1/6$	0	4
X_4	0	$9/6$	0	$-1/6$	1	6
Z_j		$9/6$	3	$3/6$	0	12
$C_j - Z_j$		$3/6$	0	$-3/6$	0	-12

Figure 3.12   Computing $C_j - Z_j$ values.

The tableau is then completed by determining which variable will be removed from the solution. You will recall that this is a matter of dividing the b value in a row by the a_{ij} of that row under the column of the variable to enter the solution and selecting that variable heading of the row with the minimum positive value. After circling the pivot element we will have completed the second tableau as shown in Figure 3.13. We now know that by introducing X_1 into the solution in place of X_4 we can improve our profit. Using the tableau in Figure 3.13, can you predict how much improvement will occur in the next iteration of the simplex algorithm?

Variables in Solution	Var. c_j	C_j	2	3	0	0		
			X_1	X_2	X_3	X_4	b	
X_2	3		$3/6$	1	$1/6$	0	4	8
X_4	0		$9/6$	0	$-1/6$	1	6	4
	z_j		$9/6$	3	$3/6$	0	12	
	$c_j - z_j$		$3/6$	0	$-3/6$	0	-12	

Figure 3.13 Determining entering and departing variables.

The last element of the pivot row indicates that 4 units of X_1 will be introduced in the next iteration and the last element of the pivot column indicates the incremental increase to the objective function will be 3/6 of a unit of profit per unit of X_1. We can, therefore, predict the increase in profit to be 2 units. We cannot predict from the tableau in Figure 3.13, however, whether or not that will be the optimum solution.

Repeating the process described above for the next iteration will produce the tableau shown in Figure 3.14. You should reinforce your knowledge of the process by working out the next tableau and comparing your results with those shown. After completing the tableau, you should be able to answer the question of whether or not further iterations are necessary to obtain an optimum solution. Are further iterations necessary?

Inspection of the tableau in Figure 3.14 reveals that there is no positive incremental increase possible for any variable and thus we have found the optimum solution. We can read that solution directly from the b column, which indicates that we should produce

$$2 \text{ units of } X_2$$
$$4 \text{ units of } X_1$$

and that our profit will be 14 units.

	c_j	2	3	0	0	
Variables in Solution	Var. c_j	X_1	X_2	X_3	X_4	b
X_2	3	0	1	$^2/_9$	$^{-3}/_9$	2
X_4	2	1	0	$^{-1}/_9$	$^6/_9$	4
Z_j		2	3	$^4/_9$	$^3/_9$	14
$c_j - z_j$		0	0	$^{-4}/_9$	$^{-3}/_9$	-14

Figure 3.14 The third tableau.

If you feel confident that you have a firm grasp of the mechanics involved in using the simplex algorithm, you may skip the remainder of this section. If, however, you would like to reinforce your grasp on the mechanics, you should solve the following problem:

EXAMPLE

$$\text{Maximize } Z = 2X_1 + 3X_2$$
$$\text{subject to } 4X_1 + 3X_2 + X_3 = 12$$
$$5X_1 + 2X_2 + X_4 = 10$$
$$X_2 + X_5 = 3$$
$$\text{and } X_j \geq 0 \text{ for } j = 1, 2, \ldots 5$$

You may check your work as you proceed by comparing each of your tableaus to the appropriate tableau shown in Figures 3.15 through 3.17. The optimal solution provides

$$X_1 = \frac{3}{4}, \qquad X_2 = 3, \qquad X_3 = 0, \qquad X_4 = \frac{1}{4}, \qquad X_5 = 0, \qquad Z = 10\tfrac{1}{2}$$

(Hint: let $X_1 = X_2 = 0$ and let X_3, X_4, and X_5 be the variables in your basic solution to the initial tableau.)

**3.5
CONVERSION
TO
STANDARD
FORM**

In formulating linear programming problems, we will rarely find the original formulation in standard form. There are various techniques available to convert a problem into standard form, however, and we must become familiar with them in order to be able to employ the simplex algorithm across a broad range of problems.

Starting with the objective function, of course we recognize that we may not always want to maximize it. For example, we may have an objective function that describes the costs associated with a particular activity and we may wish to minimize them. To change a minimization objective function to a maximization objective function merely requires that you multiply the objective function by -1. Thus

Minimize $2X_1 + 3X_2$ is the equivalent of maximize $-2X_1 - 3X_2$

Variables in Solution	Var. C_j	C_j	2	3	0	0	0		
			X_1	X_2	X_3	X_4	X_5	b	
X_3	0		4	3	1	0	0	12	4
X_4	0		5	2	0	1	0	10	5
X_5	0		0	①	0	0	1	3	3 ←
Z_j			0	0	0	0	0	0	
$C_j - Z_j$			2	3	0	0	0	0	

↑

Figure 3.15 The initial tableau.

Variables in Solution	Var. C_j	C_j	2	3	0	0	0		
			X_1	X_2	X_3	X_4	X_5	b	
X_3	0		④	0	1	0	-3	3	$^3/_4$ ←
X_4	0		5	0	0	1	-2	4	$^4/_5$
X_2	3		0	1	0	0	1	3	—
Z_j			0	3	0	0	3	9	
$C_j - Z_j$			2	0	0	0	-3	-9	

↑

Figure 3.16 An improved solution.

	C_j	2	3	0	0	0	
Variables in Solution	Var. C_j	X_1	X_2	X_3	X_4	X_5	b
X_1	2	1	0	$^1/_4$	0	$-^3/_4$	$^3/_4$
X_4	0	0	0	$-^5/_4$	1	$^7/_4$	$^1/_4$
X_2	3	0	1	0	0	1	3
Z_j		2	3	$^2/_4$	0	$^6/_4$	10½
$C_j - Z_j$		0	0	$-^2/_4$	0	$-^6/_4$	$-10½$

Figure 3.17 The optimal solution.

Next we must consider the constraints since they rarely will be expressed as equalities as required by the standard form. We have already dealt briefly with ≤ inequalities but a few more words on that type of constraint is necessary. Clearly each ≤ inequality can be converted to an equality by the addition of a variable that represents the unused portion of the resource being dealt with in the constraint. Thus this variable can take on any value between zero, the instance when all of the resource is used, up to and including the upper value representing the maximum amount of the resource available, the instance where none of the resource is used. Because this variable represents the unused portion of a resource, it is referred to as a slack variable. When a slack variable is added to the objective function, as it must be to comply with the requirement set by the standard form, it contributes nothing to the value of the objective function. Hence the coefficient in the objective function of each slack variable is zero. Thus if our problem contained constraints of the form

$$\sum_{j=1}^{n} a_{ij}X_j \le b_i \qquad i = 1, 2, \ldots m$$

they would be converted to equalities of the form

$$\sum_{j=1}^{n} a_{ij}X_j + S_i = b_i \qquad i = 1, 2, \ldots m$$

and the objective function would become

$$Z = \sum_{j=1}^{n} C_jX_j + \sum_{i=1}^{m} 0S_i$$

where S_i is used to denote the slack variable in the ith constraint.

A somewhat different problem arises when the constraint is a $\geq$ inequality. We can proceed as before with a slack variable but in this case we must subtract it in order to convert the inequality to an equality. However this in itself is not sufficient for we cannot come up with an initial basic solution that is feasible and without doing so we cannot start the algorithm. For example, take the constraint

$$X_1 + 3X_2 \geq 4$$

which converts, through subtraction of a slack variable S_1, to

$$X_1 + 3X_2 - S_1 = 4$$

We would, by letting $X_1 = X_2 = 0$, be able to solve for S_1, which turns out to be equal to -4. Since all variables, including S_1, ≥ 0, this would not be a feasible solution. We can get around this problem by introducing yet another variable that is called an artificial variable. Although we can think of a slack variable as representing unused resources, no real meaning can be attached to the artificial variable; hence its name. Now observe that our constraint becomes

$$X_1 + 3X_2 - S_1 + R_1 = 4 \text{ and by letting}$$
$$X_1 = X_2 = S_1 = 0 \text{ we obtain}$$
$$R_1 = 4, \text{ which is feasible}$$

Since artificial variables have no meaning, we do not want them to appear in our solution. We must insure that they are driven out by attaching a very high penalty to them when they are included in our objective function. Rather than writing large numbers over and over again in our tableaus, we can use the letter M to denote a large coefficient and understanding it is very large, whenever it appears, will insure that the artificial variable is driven out by the simplex algorithm. Thus if our problem contained constraints of the form

$$\sum_{j=1}^{n} a_{ij}X_j \geq b_i \qquad i = 1, 2, \ldots m$$

they would be converted to equalities of the form

$$\sum_{j=1}^{n} a_{ij}X_j - S_i + R_i = b_i \qquad i = 1, 2, \ldots m$$

and the objective function would become

$$Z = \sum_{j=1}^{n} C_jX_j + \sum_{i=1}^{m} 0S_i - \sum_{i=1}^{m} MR_i$$

Note that the introduction of the artificial variables into the objective function requires a penalty and thus rather than adding their contribution, as was done with slack variables, we must subtract their contribution.

While we are discussing constraints, it would be well to look at a constraint that is initially in equality form. You might think that since it meets the requirements prescribed by the standard form nothing need be done to that type of constraint. Unfortunately, that is not the case. Let's suppose our constraint is of the form

$$X_1 + 3X_2 = 4$$

What happens when you let $X_1 = X_2 = 0$? There would be no variable in our initial basic feasible solution from this constraint and our algorithm will not work. We can get around this by introducing an artificial variable and proceeding with that variable as prescribed above. Why can't we use a slack variable to overcome this problem with an equality constraint?

Finally we must look at the b_i values in the constraints before leaving that portion of the standard form. It is possible that a constraint for one reason or another takes the form where the b_i value is negative. The simplex algorithm is specifically designed to prevent infeasible solutions from entering the tableau. We cannot, therefore, permit a negative b_i value to enter our initial tableau since it would be tantamount to permitting an infeasible solution as our point of departure. Division of a constraint by -1 will eliminate a negative b_i. There is no nonnegativity restriction on the a_{ij}, therefore such division is perfectly permissible.

We need to explore one more facet of the standard format before we can leave that subject. Recall that

$$X_j \geq 0 \quad \text{for all } j$$

While this is certainly true in the formulation of a very large number of problems, there are cases where it is not. Take, for example, a machining process where one of the variables is a tolerance that allows $\pm$ variations from a true dimension. We cannot apply the simplex algorithm without converting the tolerance limitations to the standard form. Recall that any variable may be expressed as the difference of two positive variables. Thus an X_j that does not, in fact, have a nonnegativity restriction can be accommodated by a simple substitution of the form

$$X_j = X_k - X_l \quad \text{where } X_k, X_l \geq 0$$

In using such a substitution you must be careful to use it throughout the problem wherever X_j occurs whether it be in the objective function or in a constraint.

There is now no linear programming problem that you cannot put into standard form prior to attempting its solution by the simplex algorithm.

Let us look at an illustrative problem that requires treatment in order to put it in standard form. The problem is to

$$\text{Minimize } Z = -2X_1 - 3X_2$$
$$\text{subject to } X_1 + X_2 \le 3$$
$$2X_1 - X_2 \ge 2$$
$$X_1 = 2$$

where negative values for X_2 are permissible.

We first note that since X_2 may have negative values we must substitute the difference of two other nonnegative variables wherever X_2 appears. Let the substitution be

$$X_2 = X_3 - X_4 \qquad \text{where } X_3, X_4 \ge 0$$

Then, rewriting the objective function as a maximization problem, we have

$$\text{Maximize } Z = 2X_1 + 3X_3 - 3X_4$$

By adding a slack variable, S_1, to the first constraint we have

$$X_1 + X_3 - X_4 + S_1 = 3$$

By subtracting a slack variable, S_2, and adding an artificial variable, R_2, to the second constraint we have

$$2X_1 - X_3 + X_4 - S_2 + R_2 = 2$$

By adding an artificial variable, R_3, to the third constraint we have

$$X_1 + R_3 = 2$$

Finally, providing for all the variables in the objective function and the constraints, we would have

$$\text{Maximize } Z = 2X_1 + 3X_3 - 3X_4 + 0S_1 + 0S_2 - MR_2 - MR_3$$
$$\text{subject to } \quad X_1 + X_3 - X_4 + S_1 + 0S_2 + 0R_2 + 0R_3 = 3$$
$$2X_1 - X_3 + X_4 + 0S_1 - S_2 + R_2 + 0R_3 = 2$$
$$X_1 + 0X_3 + 0X_4 + 0S_1 + 0S_2 + 0R_2 + R_3 = 2$$
$$\text{where all} \qquad X_j, S_i, R_i \ge 0.$$

We see that we can obtain our initial basic feasible solution by letting $X_1 = X_3 = X_4 = S_2 = 0$ and the variables in our solution would then be S_1, R_2, and R_3. You should now be able to construct the initial tableau and should do so. Compare your initial tableau with that shown in Figure 3.18. Completion of the problem is left as an exercise that yields $X_1 = 2$, $X_2 = 1$, $Z = -7$. (Hint: don't forget that you let $X_2 = X_3 - X_4$.)

	C_j	2	3	-3	0	0	-M	-M		
Variables in Solution	Var. C_j	X_1	X_3	X_4	S_1	S_2	R_2	R_3	b	
S_1	0	1	1	-1	1	0	0	0	3	3
R_2	-M	2	-1	1	0	-1	1	0	2	1
R_3	-M	1	0	0	0	0	0	1	2	2
Z_j		-3M	M	-M	0	M	-M	-M	-4M	
$C_j - Z_j$		2+ 3M	3- M	-3+ M	0	-M	0	0	4M	

Figure 3.18 The initial tableau.

<table>
</table>

3.6 DUALITY AND SHADOW PRICES

Consider our original product-mix problem of (3.1), (3.2), and (3.3), which was

$$\text{Maximize } Z = 2X_1 + 3X_2$$
$$\text{subject to} \quad 3X_1 + 6X_2 \leq 24$$
$$2X_1 + X_2 \leq 10$$
$$X_1, X_2 \geq 0$$

EXAMPLE

and another linear programming problem:

$$\text{Minimize } Z = 24Y_1 + 10Y_2$$
$$\text{subject to} \quad 3Y_1 + 2Y_2 \geq 2$$
$$6Y_1 + Y_2 \geq 3$$
$$Y_1, Y_2 \geq 0$$

The final tableau yielding the solution to our original problem was found to be

	C_j	2	3	0	0	
Variable in solution	Var. C_j	X_1	X_2	S_1	S_2	b
X_2	3	0	1	2/9	-1/3	2
X_1	2	1	0	-1/9	2/3	4
Z_j		2	3	4/9	1/3	14
$C_j - Z_j$		0	0	-4/9	-1/3	-14

with a solution of $X_1 = 4$, $X_2 = 2$, and $Z = 14$. The final tableau yielding the solution to the second linear programming problem is

Variable in Solution	Var. C_j	C_j → -24 Y_1	-10 Y_2	0 S_1	0 S_2	$-M$ R_1	$-M$ R_2	b
Y_2	-10	0	1	$-2/3$	$1/3$	$2/3$	$-1/3$	$1/3$
Y_1	-24	1	0	$1/9$	$-2/9$	$-1/9$	$2/9$	$4/9$
Z_j		-24	-10	4	2	-4	-2	14
$C_j - Z_j$		0	0	-4	-2	$-M$ $+4$	$-M$ $+2$	-14

with a solution of $Y_1 = 4/9$, $Y_2 = 1/3$, and $Z = 14$. (You can develop the solution to this problem as another exercise to gain experience with the simplex algorithm if you so desire.)

Note that the optimal solution, $Z = 14$ units, is the same for both product-mix problems. This is no coincidence for the two problems are essentially one and the same, the second one being merely another way of stating the original problem. In linear programming terminology the second problem is called the dual while the original is called the primal. Let's take a look at how the dual is constructed from the primal to get an understanding of why they are essentially the same problem.

First observe that the coefficients in the objective function of the dual (24, 10) are the limits of the constraints in the primal, the coefficients of the first constraint in the dual (3, 2) are the coefficients of the first variable in the primal constraints, and the coefficients of the second constraint in the dual (6, 1) are the coefficients of the second variable in the constraints in the primal. Secondly observe that, in a sense, what we have done is rotate the primal 90° to produce the dual while relabeling the variables from X_1 and X_2 to Y_1 and Y_2. In general, it can be shown that given the primal problem

$$\text{Maximize } Z = \sum_{j=1}^{n} C_j X_j$$

$$\text{subject to } \sum_{j=1}^{n} a_{ij} X_j \leq b_i \qquad i = 1, 2, \ldots m$$

$$X_j \geq 0 \qquad j = 1, 2, \ldots n \qquad\qquad (3.7)$$

it can be expressed in dual form as

$$\text{Minimize } Z = \sum_{i=1}^{m} b_i Y_i$$

$$\text{subject to } \sum_{i=1}^{m} a_{ij} Y_i \geq C_j \quad j = 1, 2, \ldots n$$

$$Y_i \geq 0 \quad i = 1, 2, \ldots m \tag{3.8}$$

and that

$$Z^* = \sum_{j=1}^{n} C_j X_j^*$$

$$= \sum_{i=1}^{m} b_i Y_i^* \quad \text{where } * \text{ denotes optimal values} \tag{3.9}$$

Any primal problem can be put into the form of (3.7) and can be then immediately rewritten in dual form through the use of the following rules:

Primal Relationship	Equivalent Dual Relationship
Maximization	Minimization
Coefficients in objective function	Right-hand side of constraints
Right-hand side of constraints	Coefficients in objective function
Coefficients of the jth variable	Coefficients of the jth constraint
Coefficients of the ith constraint	Coefficients of the ith variable
jth variable ≥ 0	jth constraint $\geq$ inequality
jth variable unrestricted in sign	jth constraint an equality
ith constraint an equality	ith variable unrestricted in sign
ith constraint $\leq$ inequality	ith variable ≥ 0

Now let us return for a moment to (3.9). We note that the optimal value of the objective function can be determined by summing the products formed from multiplying the right hand side of the primal constraints by the optimal value of the corresponding dual variable. In terms of our product-mix problem, (3.9) states that the maximum profit can be determined from summing the products formed by multiplying:

1. The number of man-hours available (24) by the optimal value of a man-hour.

2. The number of raw material units available (10) by the optimal value of a unit of raw material.

In other words, the optimal value of a dual variable must indicate how much the objective function changes for each unit of the corresponding resource. In our problem $Y_1^* = 4/9$ and $Y_2^* = 1/3$ so that one additional man-hour would increase our profit by 4/9 of a unit, whereas one additional unit of raw material would only increase our profit by 1/3 of a unit. Because of what the optimal values of the dual variables mean, they are often referred to as shadow prices.

Do we have to solve the dual problem to obtain the optimal values of the dual variables? Remember earlier we said in effect we had turned the primal on its side to form the dual. If this is so might not the dual variables already be in our simplex tableau? Recall also that the dual variables resulted from the resource constraints in the primal. In putting the primal into standard form we introduced slack variables to represent unused portions of the resources available, and you will recall the row in the tableau labeled Z_j contained the unit contribution for each variable. Look at the final tableau yielding the solution to our original problem and you will see that

$$Z_j(S_1) = \frac{4}{9}$$

$$Z_j(S_2) = \frac{1}{3}$$

That is to say that S_1, which is unused manpower, is contributing 4/9 of a unit of profit per unit of manpower at the optimal solution to our problem. A similar statement can be made for S_2 with respect to raw material. Finally these values are in effect the optimal values of the dual variables. In general the optimal values of the dual variables, and hence the shadow prices of the resources, will be displayed in the final tableau in the Z_j row under the columns provided for the slack variables if there are any and under the columns provided for the artificial variables if there is no slack variable in a constraint.

There is much more to be gained from analyses of the data displayed by the final tableau than has been thus far discussed. Frequently the information obtained from such an analysis will be of as much or even more value than the optimal solution itself. For example, going back to our product-mix problem, the profitability coefficients in our objective function were given as 2 and 3 units of profit per unit of X_1 and X_2 produced, respectively. But what if we were not certain about exactly what the profitability coefficients were. It would then be of some value to us to know the range of the profit coefficients over which our optimal production solution would remain an optimal solution. Postoptimality analysis provides us with a tool for obtaining the answers to questions such as the one posed.

**3.7
POST-
OPTIMALITY
ANALYSIS**

In order to obtain the illustrative variety desired in the discussion that follows, we now introduce a new problem. Let us assume we are confronted with a linear programming problem whose formulation is

EXAMPLE

$$\text{Maximize } Z = X_1 + X_2 + 3X_3$$
$$\text{subject to} \quad X_1 + X_2 \leq 4$$
$$X_2 + X_3 \leq 6$$
$$X_1 + X_3 \leq 8$$
$$X_j \geq 0 \quad j = 1, 2, 3$$

After placing the problem in standard form, the initial and final tableaus would appear as shown in Figures 3.19 and 3.20, respectively.

We already know about shadow prices from our previous discussion, so that would be a good place to start our postoptimality analysis of the illustrative problem. Recall that the values on the Z_j row under the slack variables are the optimal values of the dual variables and hence are the shadow prices. Thus we know in the problem being considered from Figure 3.20 that the shadow price for

$$S_1 \text{ is } 0$$
$$S_2 \text{ is } 2$$
$$S_3 \text{ is } 1$$

Since S_1 is the slack variable for the first resource constraint, adding an additional unit of that resource would be of no value to us. Why? Notice that in our optimal solution $S_1 = 2$, that is, the slack variable in our first resource has a positive value indicating that we did not use all of that resource. Adding more of that resource would do us no good; it would

	c_j	1	1	3	0	0	0		
Variables in Solution	Var. c_j	X_1	X_2	X_3	S_1	S_2	S_3	b	
S_1	0	1	1	0	1	0	0	4	—
S_2	0	0	1	1	0	1	0	6	6
S_3	0	1	0	1	0	0	1	8	8
Z_j		0	0	0	0	0	0	0	
$c_j - z_j$		1	1	3	0	0	0	0	

Figure 3.19   The initial tableau.

Variables in Solution	Var. C_j	X_1	X_2	X_3	S_1	S_2	S_3	b
C_j		1	1	3	0	0	0	
S_1	0	0	2	0	1	1	−1	2
X_3	3	0	1	1	0	1	0	6
X_1	1	1	−1	0	0	−1	1	2
Z_j		1	2	3	0	2	1	20
$C_j - Z_j$		0	−1	0	0	−2	−1	−20

Figure 3.20 The final tableau.

simply mean that we would have more of that resource left over. On the other hand, adding an additional unit of either the second or third resource would be of value as indicated by the shadow price of S_2 and S_3. Why would an additional unit of the second resource result in an increase of 2 units in our objective function?

The next topic for analysis is the objective function itself. To be more specific, let us turn our attention to the coefficients in the objective function. You will recall that the reason we know when we have found the optimal solution is that the $C_j - Z_j$ row in the tableau containing that solution contains values that are ≤0. The presence of one positive value in that row, on the other hand, indicates that we have not yet found the optimal. Thus any change in the coefficients that cause a positive value to appear in the $C_j - Z_j$ of our final tableau will cause a change to the values of the variables in our optimal solution. Information on the range of those changes to the coefficients in the objective function that affect our optimal solution is precisely what we wish to know.

Recall that

$$Z_j(X_j) = \sum_{i=1}^{m} (\text{Var. } C_j \text{ for the } i\text{th row})(a_{ij}) \qquad j = 1, 2, \ldots n \qquad (3.10)$$

and that, based on what we have said, as long as

$$C_j - Z_j(X_j) \leq 0 \qquad (3.11)$$

our optimal solution will not change. In our illustrative problem we note that X_2 is not in our basis so let us consider its coefficients, C_2, first.

Looking at Figure 3.20 we can write from (3.10) and (3.11)

$$C_2 - \sum_{i=1}^{3} (\text{Var. } C_j \text{ for the } i\text{th row})(a_{i2}) \leq 0$$

$$C_2 - [(0)(2) + (3)(1) + (1)(-1)] \leq 0$$

$$C_2 - 2 \leq 0$$

$$C_2 \leq 2$$

We now know that as long as $C_2 \leq 2$ our optimal solution will not change but that when $C_2 \geq 2$, X_2 will enter into our solution. What about X_1 and X_3, which are currently in our optimal solution at 2 and 6 units, respectively? Because they are in the solution their analysis is more time consuming but the principle remains unchanged. Let's consider X_1 first and again looking at Figure 3.20 and using (3.10) and (3.11) as we did before we can write

$$C_1 - \sum_{i=1}^{3} (\text{Var. } C_j \text{ for the } i\text{th row})(a_{i1}) \leq 0$$

$$C_1 - [(0)(0) + (3)(0) + C_1(1)] \leq 0$$

$$C_1 - C_1 = 0$$

In other words, there is nothing you can do to C_1 to cause $C_1 - Z_j(X_1)$ to be >0 because X_1 is already in our basis. (Recall that this was not the case when we looked at C_2 because X_2 was not in our basis.) In general, the same result would obtain for every $C_j - Z_j(X_j)$ you computed provided that the X_j was already in the basis. Put another way, we can say that varying the coefficient of a variable already in our basis can only effect those variables which are not in our basis. Since we want to analyze C_1, we shall have to look at X_2, S_2, and S_3. Doing so we obtain

$$C_j - \sum_{i=1}^{3} (\text{Var. } C_j \text{ for the } i\text{th row})(a_{ij}) \leq 0 \qquad j = 2, 5, 6$$

$$1 - [(0)(2) + (3)(1) + C_1(-1)] \leq 0 \qquad j = 2$$

$$C_1 \leq 2$$

$$0 - [(0)(1) + (3)(1) + C_1(-1)] \leq 0 \qquad j = 5$$

$$C_1 \leq 3$$

$$0 - [(0)(-1) + (3)(0) + C_1(1)] \leq 0 \qquad j = 6$$

$$C_1 \geq 0$$

From these results we can see that if $C_1 > 2$, X_2 would enter our solution and if $C_1 < 0$, S_3 would enter our solution. Our solution of $X_1 = 2$ and

$X_3 = 6$ remains optimal, therefore, as long as

$$0 \leq C_1 \leq 2$$

Determination of the range of C_3, over which our optimal solution remains, is left as an exercise for you. (If you determined that the current optimal solution remains optimal as long as $C_3 \geq 2$ you are correct.)

One final item about the objective function before turning to another aspect of postoptimality analysis is in order. By now you should have a feel that variations in the coefficients of the objective function do not cause changes to the a_{ij} values in the tableau and can only affect the question of optimality. This being the case, questions on any variation or combination of variations to the coefficients in the objective function can be quickly investigated by appropriately changing the C_j and Var. C_j in the final tableau, recomputing the Z_j and $C_j - Z_j$ values, and noting whether or not any $C_j - Z_j$ values become positive. If not, the tableau continues to present the optimal solution; if any $C_j - Z_j$ value does become positive it only remains to continue applying the simplex algorithm until a tableau does present an optimal solution.

There may be cases where we would want to know more about the sensitivity of our problem with respect to changes in the right hand side of our restraint relationships. Of course, we already know some things as a result of our knowledge of shadow prices but this may not be enough. Recall that in our initial tableau we placed the right-hand side constants in the b column but in our final tableau the values in that column contained the solutions to the variables in our basis (any not appearing in the basis are equal to zero). Recall also that the values in our b column must always stay positive if our basis is to be feasible; indeed, the simplex algorithm will not permit a negative value to appear in the b column for any variable in our basis.

Suppose then that we think of adding some increment, say Δ, to the standard form of the ith constraint so that the original constraint

$$\sum_{j=1}^{n} a_{ij}X_j + S_i = b_i$$

becomes

$$\sum_{j=1}^{n} a_{ij}X_j + S_i + \Delta_i = b_i + \Delta_i$$

Note that the coefficients of S_i and Δ_i are both 1 and that whatever we have done during the tableau iterations to the coefficients of S_i will also get done to the coefficient of Δ_i. That is, we have in our final tableau an exact portrayal of what would have happened to the coefficient of Δ_i if we had started out with Δ_i in our initial tableau, in the form of the a_{ij} shown in the final tableau under the S_i column. This fact, plus our knowledge that the values under the b column must remain nonnegative, permits us to say that for a Δ_i

$$b_1{}^* + a_{1i}{}^* \Delta_i \geq 0$$
$$b_2{}^* + a_{2i}{}^* \Delta_i \geq 0$$
$$\vdots \quad \vdots \quad \vdots \quad \vdots$$
$$b_m{}^* + a_{mi}{}^* \Delta_i \geq 0$$

if the optimal solution is to remain feasible. Using this on the first row in our illustrative problem we see that the values under b of our final tableau would become

$$2 + (1)\Delta_1 \geq 0$$
$$6 + (0)\Delta_1 \geq 0$$
$$2 + (0)\Delta_1 \geq 0$$

Solving we find that $\Delta_1 \geq -2$ and hence our final tableau remains feasible as long as the right-hand constant of the first constraint, b_1, is greater than or equal to $b_1 + \Delta_1 = 2$.

Following the same reasoning for our second constraint reveals that

$$2 + (1)\Delta_2 \geq 0, \qquad \Delta_2 \geq -2$$
$$6 + (1)\Delta_2 \geq 0, \qquad \Delta_2 \geq -6$$
$$2 + (-1)\Delta_2 \geq 0, \qquad \Delta_2 \leq 2$$

Hence we know that the limits of feasibility for b_2 are $4 \leq b_2 \leq 8$. Computing the limits of feasibility for b_3 are left to you (the answer is $6 \leq b_3 \leq 10$).

The final topic we should consider in our analysis are the technological coefficients, the a_{ij} in our statement of the original problem. Let us begin by considering the coefficients of nonbasic variables. Using our incremental change approach, suppose we wished to consider the coefficient of a nonbasic variable in the ith constraint, then

$$a_{i1}X_1 + a_{i2}X_2 + \ldots + a_{ij}X_j + \ldots + a_{in}X_n \leq b_i$$

would become

$$a_{i1}X_1 + a_{i2}X_2 + \ldots + (a_{ij} + \Delta_{ij})X_j + \ldots + a_{in}X_n \leq b_i$$

where X_j is the nonbasic variable we are considering. The corresponding dual relationship becomes

$$a_{1j}Y_1 + a_{2j}Y_2 + \ldots + (a_{ij} + \Delta_{ij})Y_i + \ldots + a_{mn}Y_m \geq C_j$$

By substituting the optimal values of the dual variables in this equation we can solve for Δ_{ij}. For example, in our problem X_2 is a nonbasic variable and we want to analyze its coefficient in the second constraint. The dual relationship is

$$Y_1 + (1 + \Delta_{22})Y_2 \geq 1$$

and by substituting the optimal values, Y_1^* and Y_2^*, from our final tableau in Figure 3.20 we have

$$0+(1+\Delta_{22})2 \geq 1$$

from which we find

$$\Delta_{22} \geq -\frac{1}{2}$$

We can conclude, therefore, that if the technological coefficient of X_2 in the second constraint becomes smaller than $1/2$, the dual relationship at the optimal solution will no longer hold and X_2 will enter the solution. What conclusion do you draw from an analysis of the technological coefficient of X_2 in the first constraint? (The problem is insensitive with respect to the value of a_{12}.)

Unfortunately, there is no similar simple way to analyze the technological coefficients of basic variables. However, in the event you wish to investigate the effect of a specific change to those technological coefficients, you can always do so by substituting the changes in the original problem and resolving the problem via the simplex method.

3.8 APPLICATION STUDIES

3.8.1 Fertilizer Blending*

Application Study

Blending operations such as those for gasolines, metal alloys, and commercial fertilizers are areas where applications of linear programming are particularly prevalent. As most people who grow gardens and lawns know, commercial fertilizer is generally rated or graded on its contents and ratios of three basic compounds, nitrogen (N), phosphoric acid (P_2O_5), and potash (K_2O). The common procedure of labeling a bag of commercial fertilizer would be by indicating the percentage analysis of each of these three compounds. For example, a 4-8-4 analysis is 4 parts nitrogen, 8 parts phosphoric acid and 4 parts potash. The remaining 84 percent will normally be inert ingredients in one form or another. Other combinations of the ingredients might be in the forms of 0-12-12, 15-0-10 or 20-20-6 mixtures.

These fertilizers do not normally occur in the ratios specified but are obtained by blending several manufactured or natural fertilizers that contain one or more of the required elements in varying quantities. The required combinations of the three compounds would be determined by crop and soil requirements.

Table 3.1 shows a list of natural and manufactured fertilizers and their analysis that could be used in combination to produce a fertilizer of a

---

* This problem has been adapted from a student project and is used with the permission of W. M. Howe.

Table 3.1 Fertilizer Components

Material	Percent Nitrogen N_j	Percent Phosphoric Acid Ph_j	Percent Potash P_j
M_1 Blood meal	10	1.3	—
M_2 Fish scrap	8	2.9	0.9
M_3 Cotton seed meal	7	1.1	1.8
M_4 Meat meal	12	5.8	—
M_5 Nitrate of soda	16	—	—
M_6 Sulphate of ammonia	20	—	—
M_7 Calcium nitrate	15.5	—	—
M_8 Ammonium chloride	26	—	—
M_9 Ammonium nitrate	35	—	—
M_{10} Leunasaltpeter	26	—	—
M_{11} Cyanamid	22	—	—
M_{12} Urea	46	—	—
M_{13} Calurea	34	—	—
M_{14} Super phosphate	—	35	—
M_{15} Steamed bone meal	2	27	—
M_{16} Dissolved bones	2	15	—
M_{17} Basic or Thomas slag	—	17	—
M_{18} Muriate of potash	—	—	57
M_{19} Sulphate of potash	—	—	50
M_{20} Kainito	—	—	17
M_{21} Potash salts (1)	—	—	21
M_{22} Potash salts (2)	—	—	31
M_{23} Filler (peat, etc.)	—	—	—

desired analysis, say a 10-6-10 mix. A farmer or a fertilizer manufacturer naturally would want to produce this mix at the lowest possible cost. You undoubtedly already sense the ready application of the simplex method of linear programming to this problem.

The variables in this simplex problem would be the quantity of each item from Table 3.1 that could be blended to attain the desired mix. The constraints would be the desired final analysis of the mix and due to labeling laws, these quantities cannot be less than specified. The constraint relationships are established from the analysis requirements of a unit quantity of fertilizer, in this case 10 percent nitrogen, 6 percent phosphoric acid, and 10 percent potash. Finally a constraint is required so that the amounts blended add up to a unit measure of fertilizer. The constraints in this example would be as follows:

1. $X_1N_1 + X_2N_2 + X_3N_3 + \ldots X_{23}N_{23} \geq 10$

2. $X_1Ph_1 + X_2Ph_2 + X_3Ph_3 + \ldots X_{23}Ph_{23} \geq 6$

3. $X_1P_1 + X_2P_2 + X_3P_3 + \ldots X_{23}P_{23} \geq 10$

4. $X_1 + X_2 + X_3 + \ldots X_{23} = 1$

where

X_j = quantity of material M_j from Table 3.1 to be blended
N_j = percent nitrogen in material M_j
Ph_j = percent phosphoric acid in material M_j
P_j = percent potash in material M_j

and where

$$j = 1, 2, \ldots, 23$$

The objective function is to minimize costs and can be expressed as

$$\text{Minimize } Z = \sum_{j=1}^{23} C_j X_j$$

where

C_j = cost per unit of material M_j

X_j = the number of units of material M_j

Note that the first three constraints are $\geq$ inequalities and will, therefore, require subtraction of a slack variable and the addition of an artificial variable to put them into standard form. The fourth constraint will contain only an artificial variable. We assign a very high cost (M) to the artificial variables to insure that they are not in our final solution. Of course, all our X_j in this problem are nonnegative and after changing the problem to a maximization problem by multiplying the objective function by -1, we would be ready to construct the initial tableau in preparation for using the simplex algorithm to obtain the solution. The initial tableau is shown in Figure 3.21 where S_1, S_2, S_3 are the slack variables and R_1, R_2, R_3, R_4 are the artificial variables.

Sharp [14] gives us a company with a number of production channels, which utilize a great deal of common labor, through which various products are manufactured simultaneously. In such a situation an operator might be required at a station to produce either product A or product B, although he is quite capable of producing both products simultaneously. At another station, one operator might be needed to

**3.8.2
The Optimal Use
of Common
Labor***

Application Study

* Reprinted with permission from *Industrial Engineering*, Vol. 3, January 1971. Copyright American Institute of Industrial Engineers, Inc., 25 Technology Park/Atlanta, Norcross, Ga. 30071.

Variables in Solution	C_j	$-C_1$	$-C_2$	—	$-C_{22}$	$-C_{23}$	0	0	0	$-M$	$-M$	$-M$	$-M$	
	Var. C_j	X_1	X_2	—	X_{22}	X_{23}	S_1	S_2	S_3	R_1	R_2	R_3	R_4	b
R_1	$-M$	N_1	N_2	—	N_{22}	N_{23}	-1	0	0	1	0	0	0	10
R_2	$-M$	Ph_1	Ph_2	—	Ph_{22}	Ph_{23}	0	-1	0	0	1	0	0	6
R_3	$-M$	P_1	P_2	—	P_{22}	P_{23}	0	0	-1	0	0	1	0	10
R_4	$-M$	1	1	—	1	1	0	0	0	0	0	0	1	1
Z_j														
$C_j - Z_j$														

Figure 3.21 Fertilizer Blending Initial Tableau.

produce one product, but an additional operator is needed when both products are moving through the process. The variable production costs are mainly labor, so the total variable cost for simultaneously producing two products might be considerably less than the sum of the variable production costs for producing each product at separate times.

Let us assume the company has two plants, each of them capable of producing products A, B, and D. In order not to complicate the problem, we have elected to consider that transportation costs are identical from both plants and thus will not be considered in this problem.

The forecasted demands for the company's products are shown in Table 3.2, the plant capacities are shown in Table 3.3, and raw material availability as well as production needs are shown in Table 3.4.

Table 3.2 Demand Forecast

Product	Forecasted Demand (Units)
A	900
B	1100
D	800

Table 3.3 Plant Capacities

Plant	Packing Capacity (Units)
1	1500
2	1400

Table   3.4   Production   Requirements   and   Materials Availability

Plant	Raw Material Availability (Lb)	Product	Production Requirements (Lb/Units)
1	3200	A	1.6
		B	2.2
		D	2.4
2	3000	A	1.8
		B	2.0
		D	2.4

Table 3.5 Production Components

Plant 1	Plant 2	Symbol $(p = 1, 2)$	Description
$7.00	$8.00	CC_{A_p}	VPC/unit unique to product A
6.50	9.50	CC_{S_p}	VPC/unit unique to product B
6.00	8.50	CC_{D_p}	VPC/unit unique to product D
2.20	3.40	CC_{AUB_p}	VPC/unit common to products A and B
2.30	3.90	CC_{AUD_p}	VPC/unit common to products A and D
2.10	0	CC_{BUD_p}	VPC/unit common to products B and D
3.10	0	CC_{AUBUD_p}	VPC/unit common to products A, B, and D

The variable production cost (VPC) components at the two plants are given in Table 3.5. From those costs, the VPC for various production combinations are calculated as in the following two examples:

$$CA_1 = CC_{A1} + CC_{AUB1} + CC_{AUD1}$$
$$+ CC_{AUBUD1}$$
$$= \$7.00 + 2.20 + 2.30$$
$$+ 3.10$$
$$= \$14.60$$
$$CAB_1 = CC_{A1} + CC_{B1} + CC_{AUB1}$$
$$+ CC_{AUD1} + CC_{BUD1}$$
$$+ CC_{AUBUD1}$$
$$= \$7.00 + 6.50 + 2.20$$
$$+ 2.30 + 2.10$$
$$+ 3.10$$
$$= \$23.20$$

Costs for all possible combinations are listed in Table 3.6.

Table 3.6 Production Costs

Plant 1	Plant 2	Symbol $(p = 1, 2)$	Description
$14.60	$15.30	CA_p	VPC/unit of A produced alone
13.90	12.90	CB_p	VPC/unit of B produced alone
13.50	12.40	CD_p	VPC/unit of D produced alone
23.20	24.80	CAB_p	VPC/unit of A and B produced simultaneously
22.70	23.80	CAD_p	VPC/unit of A and D produced simultaneously
22.20	25.30	CBD_p	VPC/unit of B and D produced simultaneously
29.20	33.30	$CABD_p$	VPC/unit of A, B, and D produced simultaneously

If the common labor situation is ignored and the production costs for A, B, and D produced alone are used, the LP model would be as shown in Figure 3.22. L_{A1}, L_{B1}, L_{D1}, L_{A2}, L_{B2}, L_{D2} represents the levels of production of products A, B, and D at plants 1 and 2, respectively.

$$\min \text{VPC} = \$14.60\, L_{A1} + 13.90\, L_{B1} + 13.50\, L_{D1} + 15.30\, L_{A2} + 12.90\, L_{B2} + 12.40\, L_{D2}$$

$$\begin{array}{llllll}
\text{s.t.} & L_{A1} & & & + L_{A2} & & = 900 \\
& & L_{B1} & & & + L_{B2} & = 1100 \\
& & & L_{D1} & & + L_{D2} & = 800 \\
& L_{A1} & + L_{B1} & + L_{D1} & & & \leq 1500 \\
& & & & L_{A2} & + L_{B2} + L_{D2} & \leq 1400 \\
& 1.6\, L_{A1} + 2.2\, L_{B1} + 2.4\, L_{D1} & & & & & \leq 3200 \\
& & & & 1.8\, L_{A2} + 2.0\, L_{B2} + 2.4\, L_{D2} & & \leq 3000 \\
& \multicolumn{6}{l}{L_{A1}, L_{B1}, L_{D1}, L_{A2}, L_{B2}, L_{D2} \geq 0}
\end{array}$$

Figure 3.22   Production LP Model.

The objective function gives the variable production cost. The first three constraints require that the forecasted demand for each of the products be satisfied. The next two constraints require that packing capacities not be exceeded. The last two constraints require that raw material availabilities not be exceeded. The optimal solution for this model is given in Table 3.7 showing a total variable production of $37,780.

Table 3.7 Optimal Production Solution

$L_{A1}{}^* = 900$	900 ($14.60) = $13,140
$L_{B1}{}^* = 200$	200 (13.90) = 2,780
$L_{D1}{}^* = 300$	300 (13.50) = 4,050
$L_{A2}{}^* = 0$	
$L_{B2}{}^* = 900$	900 (12.90) = 11,610
$L_{D2}{}^* = 500$	500 (12.40) = 6,200
	————
$\text{VPC}^* = \$37,780$	$37,780

However, the actual VPC for that production schedule would be less because of the common labor situation. The actual VPC is calculated in Table 3.8 taking common labor into count, and found to be $34,680.

Table 3.8 Actual Production Costs

200 units of A, B, and D produced simultaneously at plant 1
200 ($29.29) = $5,840
100 units of A and D produced simultaneously at plant 1
100 ($22.70) = 2,270
600 units of A produced alone at plant 1
600 ($14.60) = 8,760
500 units of B and D produced simultaneously at plant 2
500 ($25.20) = 12,650
400 units of B produced alone at plant 2
400 ($12.90) = 5,160
————
$34,680

If the common labor situation is taken into account in advance, it would be possible to obtain a lower cost-production schedule. Various production combinations corresponding to the VPC combinations in Table 3.6 must first be defined:

A_p, B_p, D_p: The level of production of products A, B, and D respectively at plant p involving no common production with the other products ($p = 1, 2$).

AB_p, AD_p, BD_p: the level of simultaneous production of products A and B, A and D, and B and D respectively at plant p involving no common production with the other product ($p = 1, 2$).

ABD_p: the level of simultaneous production of products A, B, and D at plant ($p = 1, 2$).

The model can now be redrawn as shown in Figure 3.23. The objective function and constraints serve exactly the same purposes as in the previous model. The only difference is that there are now more activities, taking into account the common labor situation. It is not necessary to include activity BD_2 since there is no common labor involved in the simultaneous production of these products at plant 2.

The optimal solution for this model is listed in Table 3.9 giving a total VPC of $29,650. Thus by specifically taking into account the common labor situation, VPC can be lowered by almost 15% from $34,680 to $29,650.

$$\min VPC = \$14.60A_1 + 13.90B_1 + 13.50D_1 + 23.20AB_1 + 22.70AD_1 + 22.20BD_1 + 29.20ABD_1 + 15.30A_2 + 12.90B_2 + 12.40D_2 + 24.80AB_2 + 23.80AD_2 + 33.30ABD_2$$

S.T.

$$
\begin{aligned}
A_1 \quad\quad\quad + AB_1 + AD_1 \quad\quad\quad + ABD_1 + A_2 \quad\quad\quad + AB_2 + AD_2 + ABD_2 &= 900 \\
B_1 \quad + AB_1 \quad + BD_1 + ABD_1 \quad + B_2 \quad + AB_2 \quad\quad + ABD_2 &= 1100 \\
D_1 \quad + AD_1 + BD_1 + ABD_1 \quad\quad + D_2 \quad\quad + AD_2 + ABD_2 &= 800 \\
A_1 + B_1 + D_1 + 2AB_1 + 2AD_1 + 2BD_1 + 3ABD_1 &\le 1500 \\
A_2 + B_2 + D_2 + 2AB_2 + 2AD_2 + 3ABD_2 &\le 1400 \\
1.6A_1 + 2.2B_1 + 2.4D_1 + 3.8AB_1 + 4.0AD_1 + 4.6BD_1 + 6.2ABD_1 &\le 3200 \\
1.8A_2 + 2.0B_2 + 2.4D_2 + 3.8AB_2 + 4.2AD_2 + 6.2ABD_2 &\le 3000
\end{aligned}
$$

$$A_1, B_1, D_1, AB_1, AD_1, BD_1, ABD_1, A_2, B_2, D_2, AB_2, AD_2, BD_2, ABD_2 \ge 0$$

Figure 3.23 Revised Production LP Model.

Table 3.9 Revised Optimal Solution

$ABD_1{}^* = 500$	$500\ (\$29.20) = \$14,600$
$ABD_2{}^* = 300$	$300\ (\$33.30) = 9,990$
$AB_2{}^* = 100$	$100\ (\$24.80) = 2,480$
$B_2{}^* = 200$	$200\ (\$12.90) = 2,580$
$VPC^* = \$29,650$	$\$29,650$

In the notation of the previous model:

$$L_{A_1}{}^* = 500$$
$$L_{B_1}{}^* = 500$$
$$L_{D_1}{}^* = 500$$
$$L_{A_2}{}^* = 400$$
$$L_{B_2}{}^* = 600$$
$$L_{D_1}{}^* = 300$$
$$VPC^* = \$29,650$$

3.8.3 Optimizing a Parts-Purchasing Decision*

Application Study

The continued use of the linear programming model described in this application permitted the Diesel Engine Products Department of the General Electric Company to minimize monthly costs of purchased parts from multiple suppliers, each with limited capacity, while the demand for parts fluctuated as reported by Simpson and Pellei [16].

The Diesel Engine Products Department produces diesel engines from 1500 to 4000 horsepower. In order to maintain a proper balance of inventories, parts and stock for components are ordered on a periodic basis. This problem is not concerned with how much stock to order, but who to order it from when each supplier can furnish only a portion of the total requirements. For example, since no one foundry is geared to supply all the monthly requirements for a specific part, the Department has several suppliers, each with limited capacity. The size of order each foundry gets depends on the quantities of each part required each month, and the relationship of its costs to the total costs of a group of parts furnished by that particular foundry and several others. Obviously, the prices of the foundries vary for each of the parts they are able to supply.

Although there is virtually no limitation on the number of suppliers that can be accommodated in the model, we shall limit the number of suppliers and engine sizes in this illustration to three in each case. Denoting the suppliers A, B, C and the monthly quantities of parts by

* Reprinted with permission from *Industrial Engineering*, Vol. 5, April 1973. Copyright © American Institute of Industrial Engineers, Inc., 25 Technology Park/Atlanta, Norcross, Ga. 30071.

engine size by X_j, $j = 1, 2 \ldots 9$, the parts costs and variable relationship is shown in Table 3.10.

Table 3.10 Parts Costs

Supplier	Monthly Costs of Parts by Engine Size		
	8 Cylinder	12 Cylinder	16 Cylinder
A	\$647 (X_1)	\$785 (X_2)	\$842 (X_3)
B	652 (X_4)	762 (X_5)	878 (X_6)
C	683 (X_7)	728 (X_8)	893 (X_9)

Constraints are developed on the basis of facts as they exist for the month. In our particular illustration supplier limitations and the constraints developed therefrom are as follows:

Supplier Limitations	Constraint
A has a capacity limitation of 24 units per month.	$X_1 + X_2 + X_3 \le 24$
B has a capacity limitation of 4 16-cylinder parts per month.	$X_6 \le 4$
B has a capacity limitation of 30 units per month.	$X_4 + X_5 + X_6 \le 30$
B has a contract which insures that he will receive an order for at least 26 units per month.	$X_4 + X_5 + X_6 \ge 26$
C is having problems with tooling this month on his 12-cylinder units and cannot produce this size.	$X_8 = 0$
C measures his capacity in equivalent 8-cylinder units, can make 25 equivalent 8-cylinder units per month. He ratios the equivalent as follows: one 16-cylinder unit = 1.8 equivalent 8-cylinder units; one 12-cylinder unit = 1.4 equivalent 8-cylinder units.	$1.0X_7 + 1.4X_8 + 1.8X_9 \le 25$

Parts requirements for the month being considered are as illustrated below:

$$8\text{-cylinder sizes} = X_1 + X_4 + X_7 = 21$$
$$12\text{-cylinder sizes} = X_2 + X_5 + X_8 = 27$$
$$16\text{-cylinder sizes} = X_3 + X_6 + X_9 = 20$$

Although you can now formulate this problem in standard form, the application of this model at General Electric utilizes a computer for its solution. In doing so, it is necessary that the data be arranged for computer computation by arranging the constraints somewhat differently than we would in our initial tableau, but you will recognize the format as essentially what we have béen doing. It is displayed as follows:

X_1	X_2	X_3	X_4	X_5	X_6	X_7	X_8	X_9	
1	1	1	0	0	0	0	0	0	≤ 24
0	0	0	0	0	1	0	0	0	≤ 4
0	0	0	1	1	1	0	0	0	≤ 30
0	0	0	0	0	0	1	1.4	1.8	≤ 25
1	0	0	1	0	0	1	0	0	$= 21$
0	1	0	0	1	0	0	1	0	$= 27$
0	0	1	0	0	1	0	0	1	$= 20$
0	0	0	0	0	0	0	1	0	$= 0$
0	0	0	1	1	1	0	0	0	≥ 26

The resulting printout is shown in Figure 3.24 and shows the routines followed to determine the optimum costs of purchased parts for the given month. Printout section A lists the entry of the coefficients of each of the variables from the preceding arrangement of "variables." B (line 19) enters the values in the righthand column of the same table. C (line 20) shows the entry of the coefficients of the objective function, or the costs for each size (from "cost per part for engine size" table). Values are entered with negative signs to effect minimization.

A
    10 DATA 1,1,1,0,0,0,0,0,0
    11 DATA 0,0,0,0,0,1,0,0,0
    12 DATA 0,0,0,1,1,1,0,0,0
    13 DATA 0,0,0,0,0,0,1,1.4,1.8
    14 DATA 1,0,0,1,0,0,1,0,0
    15 DATA 0,1,0,0,1,0,0,1,0
    16 DATA 0,0.1,0,0,1,0,0,1
    17 DATA 0,0,0,0,0,0,0,1,0
    18 DATA 0,0,0,1,1,1,0,0,0

B
    19 data 24,4,30,25,21,27,20,0,26

C
    20 DATA −647,−785,−842,−652,−762,−878,−683,−728,−893

D LINPRO

TYPE '2' FOR OUTPUT OF TABLEAUS AND BASIS AT EACH
  ITERATION
  '1' FOR THE BASIS ONLY, OR
  '0' FOR JUST THE SOLUTION.

WHICH ? 0

WHAT ARE M AND N OF THE DATA MATRIX ? 9.9

HOW MANY 'LESS THANS', 'EQUALS',
              'GREATER THANS' ? 4.4.1

        YOUR VARIABLES 1 THROUGH 9
     SURPLUS VARIABLES 10 THROUGH 10
       SLACK VARIABLES 11 THROUGH 14
  ARTIFICIAL VARIABLES 15 THROUGH 19

E ANSWERS:

VARIABLE	VALUE	Supplier
1	4	←── A
4	3	←── B
10	4	
14	11	
7	14	←── C
12	4	
3	20	←── A
8	0	
5	27	←── B

OBJECTIVE FUNCTION VALUE   51520

DUAL
VARIABLES:

COLUMN	VALUE
10	0
11	36
12	0
13	31
14	0
15	−683
16	−793
17	−878
18	65.00001

---

* In our terminology, the surplus variable would be the slack variable in the ninth constraint.

Figure 3.24   Resulting Printout.

After signaling the computer to run, the program asks for additional information, section D. The responding answers are underscored. The first response (0) schedules the amount of detail we would like to see concerning the solution of the problem. The second response (9.9) tells the program the size of the data matrix included (in this case) in lines 10 through 18. The third response (4.4.1) tells the program the equalities or inequalities of the data on line 19. For example, after this response, the program interprets line 19 to read ≤ 24, ≤ 4, ≤ 30, ≤ 25, $= 21$, $= 27$, $= 20$, $= 0$, ≥ 26, and places each of these at the ends of lines 10 through 18.

Under "answers," section E, the values corresponding to variables 1 through 9 are taken from the printout. Identification of the suppliers has been written on the printout. As explained earlier, the variables X_j are assigned to the monthly quantities of a part for a specified supplier. The variable 1 in the printout corresponds to X_1 and its value is the number of 8-cylinder parts to be provided by supplier A. The "objective function value," 51520, is the optimum total cost of purchased parts for the month.

Other information in this printout concerning surplus, slack, artificial, and dual variables concern intermediates set up by the program in arriving at a solution. This information may be disregarded in this case.

Table 3.11 shows the results of combining the values generated by the computer program with the earlier matrices.

We now have the order quantities for each part to be placed with each supplier to give us the minimum total cost for the order period. The program run cost approximately $1.00 of General Electric Time Sharing computer services.

When the technique was used for the first time in the Diesel Engine Products Department, the buyers were able to identify considerable savings over their previous best-choice combinations.

The event that triggered this undertaking was anticipated price increases by several suppliers simultaneously. The Materials organization resorted to linear programming to solve the problem. Once it was

Table 3.11 Combined Values

| Supplier | Monthly Costs of Parts by Engine Sizes | | | |
	8 Cylinder	12 Cylinder	16 Cylinder	Totals
A	$647 × 4 = $2,588		$842 × 20 = $16,840	$19,428
B	$652 × 3 = $1,956	$762 × 27 = $20,574		$22,530
C	$683 × 14 = $9,562			$ 9,562
Totals	$14,106	$20,574	$16,840	$51,520

successfully solved, they realized they had a golden opportunity to use the tool for other components that were not originally considered problems, but were worth looking at to find improvements.

The major difficulty encountered was that of identifying and quantifying all of the constraints. This required input from several people, each knowledgeable in his own area. Their input was documented on flip charts during brainstorming sessions, and the charts were studied later for developing the constraints.

In this illustrative application, you will be introduced to an expanded symbology that is useful in formulating linear programming problems where variables are described by combinations of characteristics. The linear programming principles that have been learned thus far remain completely applicable although the notation may seem a little strange at first.

3.8.4
Effective Use of
School Busing to
Achieve
Desegregation

Application Study

Our problem is to use available transportation routes most effectively in achieving a required ethnic mix in each school of a community. As is usually the case, we shall assume that our community is divided into a number, m, of residential areas or tracts and is served by a number, n, of schools. Furthermore, to keep the illustration perfectly general, let us assume the community contains a number, K, of ethnic groups.

Then we could say:

X_{ijk} = the number of students from the ith tract assigned to the jth school of the kth ethnic group.

S_{ik} = the number of students of the kth ethnic group living in the ith tract.

U_{jk} = the upper limit on the number of students of the kth ethnic group assigned to the jth school.

L_{jk} = the lower limit on the number of students of the kth ethnic group assigned to the jth school.

T_{ij} = daily one-way transportation time over the best route from the ith tract to the jth school.

C_j = the total student capacity of the jth school.

In order to solve this problem, the values of S_{ik}, U_{jk}, T_{ij}, and C_j would have to be known. Obtaining these values should not present any significant problem, however, and sources such as census data, boards of education, courts, and police departments will often have, or can obtain, the necessary information.

Let us assume that transportation time is our measure of how effectively we are busing students to the school. Then our objective function would be

$$\text{Minimize } Z = \sum_{i=1}^{m} \sum_{j=1}^{n} \sum_{k=1}^{K} T_{ij} X_{ijk}$$

Our constraints would be
(for school capacity)

$$\sum_{i=1}^{m} \sum_{k=1}^{K} X_{ijk} \leq C_j \qquad j = 1, 2, \ldots n$$

(availability of students)

$$\sum_{j=1}^{n} X_{ijk} = S_{ik} \qquad i = 1, 2, \ldots m$$

$$k = 1, 2, \ldots K$$

(lower limits on assignment of students)

$$\sum_{i=1}^{m} X_{ijk} \geq L_{jk} \qquad j = 1, 2, \ldots n$$

$$k = 1, 2, \ldots K$$

(upper limits on assignment of students)

$$\sum_{i=1}^{m} X_{ijk} \leq U_{jk} \qquad j = 1, 2, \ldots n$$

$$k = 1, 2, \ldots K$$

and, of course, all

$$X_{ijk} \geq 0$$

You can readily see that even for relatively small numbers for m, n, and K this problem would get quite large very quickly and manual solution would become extremely costly. Of course, a computer solution would be the answer in such a case. There actually are a number of communities that have used linear programming in conjunction with their desegregation efforts.

3.8.5
Use of Linear
Programming in
Air-Cleaner
Design*

Application Study

The method of air-cleaner design presented by Avani [1] in this illustration departs from conventional methods. The mechanical engineering approach to air-cleaner design is to use fluid-mechanics equations. However, the design technique presented here considers in an integrated way basic air-cleaner requirements such as dust-collection efficiency, allowable pressure loss, and real-life constraints such as material shortage and minimum demand requirements. Put another way, there

---

* This problem has been adapted from S. Avani, "A Linear Programming Approach to Air-Cleaner Design," *Operations Research*, Vol. 22, No. 2, March–April 1974. Used with the permission of the Operations Research Society of America.

are many conflicting factors involved in achieving the final design—the linear programming approach helps find the optimal solution that strikes an acceptable compromise among all the conflicting factors. This problem was encountered in tractor manufacturing in Bombay, India, where a small-scale manufacturing unit received orders from the subcontracting department of a tractor manufacturer to produce air-cleaners for a 60 horsepower tractor.

The limiting specifications for the air cleaners provided that the diameters of the main body and exit duct should not exceed $6\frac{1}{4}$ inches and $2\frac{1}{2}$ inches, respectively, in order to keep the dust-collection efficiency within permissible limits. In addition, these diameters could not go below $3\frac{3}{4}$ inches and $1\frac{1}{2}$ inches, respectively, in order to keep the pressure drop across the air cleaner (and, hence, the consequent horsepower loss) within permissible limits. The length of the main body and exit duct were to be maintained at a constant 10 inches and $2\frac{3}{4}$ inches, respectively (see Figure 3.25). Finally, a minimum of 50 air cleaners were to be produced each month.

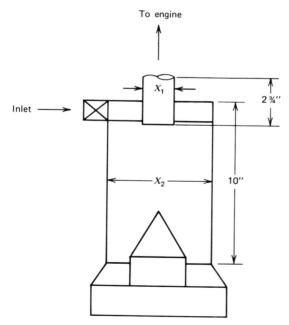

Figure 3.25   Air cleaner.

There was a national shortage of sheet metal, and the government would only sanction 15,000 square inches of the material per month out of its limited imported stock. (This situation is common in developing countries.)

It was assumed that scrap and other minor parts of the air cleaner used, respectively, 20 percent and 40 percent of the amount of sheet metal needed to make both the main body and exit duct. Thus, all areas had to be multiplied by 1.6 to obtain metal requirements. Although the manufacturing design should use as little sheet metal as possible, other considerations, such as minimum air cleaner weight requirements, dictated that the amount of metal to be used per air cleaner should be no less than 250 square inches.

The linear programming problem then was to determine the maximum number of air cleaners that would be produced per month and the resulting dimensions in the face of the restrictions enumerated. In order to maximize the number of air cleaners that could be produced, it would be necessary to minimize the amount of material used per air cleaner. The objective function then becomes

$$\text{Minimize } Z = (1.6)(2.75\pi X_1) + (1.6)(10\pi X_2)$$

subject to the constraints
(dimensional restrictions)

$$X_1 \geq 1.5$$
$$X_1 \leq 2.5$$
$$X_2 \geq 3.75$$
$$X_2 \leq 6.25$$

(area restriction)

$$(1.6)(2.75\pi X_1) + (1.6)(10\pi X_2) \geq 250$$

(material restriction)

$$50(1.6)(2.75\pi X_1 + 10\pi X_2) \leq 15{,}000$$

$$X_1, X_2 \geq 0$$

The solution, manually or by computer, is straightforward and yields the following:

$$Z_{min} = 250.24 \text{ square inches}$$
$$X_1 = 1.5 \text{ inches}$$
$$X_2 = 4.57 \text{ inches}$$

which provided for $15{,}000/250.24 = 59.9$ (59) air cleaners per month.

A number of approaches to capital budgeting exist. The utilization of a theoretically optimal investment criterion—such as accepting any investment proposal that has a net present value greater than zero or accepting those projects with the highest rate of return until the cutoff rate is reached—does not directly consider many practical constraints that exist in real life. Furthermore, a pragmatic approach such as "accept those projects that appear desirable" is equally unpalatable. One possible method of treating both theoretical and practical considerations is to examine all possible combinations of investment alternatives to determine the effect of each combination on all of the corporate objectives. Although this method will certainly work, the computational task becomes huge when a large number of projects is considered.

A possible approach to this problem is to use linear programming to determine the optimal set of investment proposals. The objective of the approach would be to maximize the IRR (internal rate of return) or the NPV (net present value) of those investment alternatives subject to a set of constraints. The constraints, in addition to the supply of capital available, would be those factors, such as earnings per share, return on investments, dividends per share, R & D expenditures, and the like, that management feels should be considered as operational or practical objectives of the firm.

The relevant information for an assumed company is shown in Table 3.12. The company is relatively small, with after-tax earnings of $500,000 for the year just ended. Since there are 100,000 shares outstanding the earnings per share were $5.00. Management estimates earnings for the current year before any new investments to be $470,000 or $4.70 per share. Total cash currently available is $1.2 million and estimated cash flow for the current year from existing projects without any new investment is $1.13 million.

The table also summarizes the factors that the management feels reflect the company's operational goals. Desirous of a 6 percent growth in earnings per share (EPS), next year's goal is earnings of at least $5.30 per share, or $530,000 total. Management feels that a 40 percent dividend payout ratio is appropriate. Therefore a dividend of $2 per share ($200,000) is expected to be paid soon based on last year's earnings. Management estimates that $300,000 should be expended for R & D projects, and $60,000 is required for certain other necessary projects. Since the total capital available is $1.2 million, the amount available for new projects is $640,000. A minimum cash flow of $1.3 million is considered desirable for the current year.

3.8.6
A Capital
Budgeting
Decision*

Application Study

---

* This problem has been adapted from A. A. Robichek, D. G. Ogilvie and J. C. Roach, "Capital Budgeting: A Pragmatic Approach," *Financial Executive*, April 1969. Used with the permission of the Financial Executive Institute.

Table 3.12 Company Information

A.	Current Data	
	Actual earnings after taxes last year	$ 500,000
	Number of shares outstanding	100,000
	Earnings per share	5.00
	Cash Available for investments and dividends	1,200,000
	Estimated earnings for current year without new investment	470,000
	Estimated cash flow for current year without new investment	1,130,000
B.	Goals and Requirements for Current Year	
	Earnings per share—minimum (6 percent increase)	5.30
	Total earnings required	530,000
	Less: estimated earnings without new investment	470,000
	Incremental earnings required from new investment	60,000
	Cash flow required—minimum	1,300,000
	Less estimated cash flow without new investment	1,130,000
	Incremental cash flow required from new investments	170,000
	Minimum R & D expenditures	300,000
	Minimum "necessary" expenditures	60,000
	Minimum dividends on last year's earnings (40 percent of earnings)	200,000
	Cash available for new investments	1,200,000
	Less: R & D expenditures $300,000	
	Necessary expenditures 60,000	
	Dividends 200,000	560,000
	Net cash available for new investments	$ 640,000

With this company background information in mind, we can now analyze the investment opportunities open for consideration. Table 3.13 summarizes five possible investment alternatives. The data for these projects are presented so that both the accounting income and the cash flow for each year are evident. The calculations in the table assume that the revenues and expenses estimated for determining the marginal accounting income are identical to the marginal revenues and marginal expenses necessary for calculating the cash flows. Under traditional accounting practices, this equality is not always maintained. Also for the sake of simplicity, straight-line depreciation is assumed for all projects for both tax and reporting purposes.

Table 3.14 shows the initial investment required, the first year's accounting income, the first year's cash flow, and the computed internal rate of return for each of the five projects. In calculating the rate of return,

Table 3.13 Investment Opportunities (all figures in $1000s)

Period (1)	Investment (2)	Revenues (3)	Expenses (4)	Depreciation (5)	Operating Income (6)=(3)−(4+5)	Taxes (50 percent) (7)=.5(6)	Accounting Income (8)=(6)−(7)	Cash Flow (9)=(3)− (4)−(7)
				Project A				
1	100	140	85	25	30	15	15	40
2		175	100	25	50	25	25	50
3		175	100	25	50	25	25	50
4		175	100	25	50	25	25	50
				Project B				
1	300	100	80	60	(40)	(20)	(20)	40
2		400	200	60	140	70	70	130
3		1100	600	60	440	220	220	280
4		900	400	60	440	220	220	280
5		1500	800	60	640	320	320	380
				Project C				
1	200	300	140	100	60	30	30	130
2		200	80	100	20	10	10	110
				Project D				
1	300	230	105	75	50	25	25	100
2		300	125	75	100	50	50	125
3		350	145	75	130	65	65	140
4		400	165	75	160	80	80	155
				Project E				
1	200	200	110	40	50	25	25	65
2		200	110	40	50	25	25	65
3		220	120	40	60	30	30	70
4		240	130	40	70	35	35	75
5		270	140	40	90	45	45	85

Table 3.14 Investment Summary

	Project				
	A	B	C	D	E
Initial Investment ($1000s)	100	300	200	300	200
First Year's Accounting Income ($1000s)	15	−20	30	25	25
First Year's Cash Flow ($1000s)	40	40	130	100	65
Internal Rate of Return (percent)	30.4	45.6	13.5	24.2	22.2

the investment cost was assumed to have been incurred on the first day of the first year, and all of the revenues and expenses were assumed to occur at the end of the respective periods.

For this particular problem, the assumption will be made that management wishes to maximize the average IRR subject to the various constraints noted above. The formulation of the problem is as follows:

$$\text{Maximize } Z = 0.304X_1 + 0.456X_2 + 0.135X_3 + 0.242X_4 + 0.222X_5$$

where the X_j's represent the amount of funds (in thousand of dollars) committed to project j and the coefficients preceding each X_j stand for the project IRR's shown in Table 3.14. Average IRR is obtained by dividing Z by 640, the total funds available (assuming the total funds are utilized).

Subject to

(budget constraint)

$$X_1 + X_2 + X_3 + X_4 + X_5 \leq 640$$

The amount allocated to all projects cannot exceed $640,000, the total amount available.

(project constraints)

$$0 \leq X_1 \leq 100$$
$$0 \leq X_2 \leq 300$$
$$0 \leq X_3 \leq 200$$
$$0 \leq X_4 \leq 300$$
$$0 \leq X_5 \leq 200$$

The commitments of funds to any one project cannot exceed the project's maximum required funds or be negative.

(earnings constraint)

$$\frac{15}{100}X_1 - \frac{20}{300}X_2 + \frac{30}{200}X_3 + \frac{25}{300}X_4 + \frac{25}{200}X_5 \geq 60$$

The first year's earnings contributions from the accepted new project must be at least $60,000.

(cash flow constraint)

$$\frac{40}{100}X_1 + \frac{40}{300}X_2 + \frac{130}{200}X_3 + \frac{100}{300}X_4 + \frac{65}{200}X_5 \geq 170$$

The first year's cash flow from the new projects must be at least $170,000.

The solution to this problem shows that

$$X_1 = \text{project A} = 100.0$$
$$X_2 = \text{project B} = 55.5$$
$$X_3 = \text{project C} = 0$$
$$X_4 = \text{project D} = 284.5$$
$$X_5 = \text{project E} = 200.0$$
$$Z = \text{objective} = 168.97$$

$$\text{Average IRR} = \frac{Z}{640} = \frac{168.97}{640} = 26.4 \text{ percent}$$

Even though the optimal allocation has been determined, postoptimality analysis will reveal several items which could be quite significant to management. For example, knowledge of the optimal values of the dual variables would reveal that the addition of $1000 to cash available for new projects would increase Z by .36; that is, the IRR on the marginal $1000 would be 36 percent. With this type of evidence, management may well decide to either raise additional capital from outside sources or to reduce the originally planned level of expenditures for R & D, necessary projects, or dividends.

Even more striking is the value of the dual variable for the earnings constraint: 1.42. This means that if management were to reduce their earnings requirement by $1000 (from $60,000 to $59,000) the value of Z would increase by 1.42 and the average IRR would rise from 26.40 percent to 26.73 percent. This increase is accomplished by switching $6,667 from project D to project B. In other words, the reduction in earnings requirements permits a shift of funds from a project with a relatively low IRR but attractive first-year earnings to a project that offers a very high rate of return, but reports an accounting loss in the first year. Although ours is not the job to judge the validity or reasonableness of this earnings requirement, the LP solution points out the dramatic and severe opportunity cost associated with this policy.

On the other hand, analysis of the LP solution indicates that the minimum cash requirement presents no problems and that for practical purposes the minimum cash constraint has no effect on the allocation procedure.

3.8.7
Solution of a
Two-Person
Game

Application Study

Recall the problem of selecting optimum strategies for two players in a zero-sum game discussed in Chapter 2. We will now examine a linear programming solution to any such $m \times n$ game.

Given such a game, you will remember it can be portrayed in matrix form as

Player B

		Y_1	Y_2	$\ldots$	Y_n
	X_1	a_{11}	a_{12}	$\ldots$	a_{1n}
Player A	X_2	a_{21}	a_{22}	$\ldots$	a_{2n}
	$\vdots$	$\vdots$	$\vdots$	$\vdots$	$\vdots$
	X_m	a_{m1}	a_{m2}	$\ldots$	a_{mn}

where X_i is the probability with which A selects his ith strategy, Y_j is the probability with which B selects his jth strategy, and the a_{ij} are A's payoffs.

Then, as you will recall from Section 2.6, the optimum strategy for A is to maximize his minimum expected payoffs so that

$$\max_{X_i} \left\{ \min \left(\sum_{i=1}^{m} a_{i1}X_i, \sum_{i=1}^{m} a_{i2}X_i, \ldots, \sum_{i=1}^{m} a_{in}X_i \right) \right\}$$

where

$$\sum_{i=1}^{m} X_i = 1$$

If we let $V =$ the value of the game then we wish to

Maximize $Z = V$

subject to

$$\sum_{i=1}^{m} a_{ij}X_i \geq V \qquad j = 1, 2, \ldots, n$$

$$\sum_{i=1}^{m} X_i = 1$$

$$X_i \geq 0 \qquad i = 1, 2, \ldots, m$$

Now note that max $V \equiv \min (1/V)$ and that if we divide* the second constraint by V we have

$$\sum_{i=1}^{m} \frac{X_i}{V} = \frac{1}{V}$$

so that

$$\max V \equiv \min \frac{1}{V} = \sum_{i=1}^{m} \frac{X_i}{V}$$

Letting $S_i = X_i/V$ and dividing all constraints by V we can write

$$\min Z = \sum S_i$$

subject to

$$\sum_{i=1}^{m} a_{ij}S_i \geq 1 \qquad j = 1, 2, \ldots n$$

$$S_i \geq 0 \qquad i = 1, 2, \ldots m$$

You will recognize the foregoing as a linear programming problem which, after it is placed in standard form, can be solved via the simplex algorithm. Having done so you will obtain the optimal values of S_i and Z from which you can obtain the X_i^* since

$$S_i^* = \frac{X_i^*}{V^*}$$

$$Z^* = \frac{1}{V^*}$$

Would it be necessary to reformulate the problem to find B's optimal Y_j using the minimax strategy? A moment's reflection will reveal that such a formulation is the dual of the problem we already solved and thus the Y_j^* are in our final tableau in the form

$$R_j^* = \frac{Y_j^*}{V^*}$$

1. (a) Max $Z = 12X_1 + 5X_2$
   subject to $5X_1 + 3X_2 \leq 15$
   $7X_1 + 2X_2 \leq 14$
   $X_1, \quad X_2 \geq 0$

---

* This division is only proper as long as $V > 0$. This presents no problem since a sufficiently large constant, K, can be added to each of the a_{ij} making the value of the game $V + K$. Once the optimum X_i are obtained, the true value of the game can be found by subtracting K.

(b) Max $Z = 10X_1 + 2X_2$
    subject to same constraints as 1(a)
(c) Max $Z = X_1 + X_2$
    subject to same constraints as 1(a)

2. Min $Z = 12X_1 + 5X_2$
   subject to $5X_1 + 3X_2 \geq 15$
   $7X_1 + 2X_2 \geq 14$
   $X_1, \quad X_2 \geq 0$

3. Max $Z = 22X_1 + 5X_2$
   subject to $7X_1 + 3X_2 \leq 21$
   $3X_1 + 2X_2 \geq 6$
   $X_1 \leq 2$
   $X_1, \quad X_2 \geq 0$

4. Max $Z = 3X_1 + 5X_2$
   subject to $X_1 - X_2 \leq 4$
   $3X_1 - 2X_2 \geq 3$
   $6X_1 + 7X_2 \geq 42$
   X_1, X_2 unrestricted in sign

Put problems 5 and 6 in standard form:

5. Min $Z = 12X_1 + 5X_2$
   subject to $5X_1 + 3X_2 \geq 15$
   $7X_1 + 2X_2 \leq 14$
   $X_1, \quad X_2 \geq 0$

6. Min $Z = 3X_1 + 5X_2$
   subject to $X_1 - X_2 \leq 4$
   $3X_1 - 2X_2 = 3$
   $6X_1 + 7X_2 \leq 42$
   $X_1 \geq 0, X_2$ unrestricted in sign

Solve problems 7 through 9 via the simplex algorithm:

7. Max $Z = 3X_1 + 2X_2$
   subject to $X_1 + X_2 \geq 5$
   $X_1 + X_2 \leq 11$
   $X_1 - X_2 \leq 1$
   $X_2 - X_1 \geq 5$
   $X_1, \quad X_2 \geq 0$

8. Min $Z = 3X_1 + 2X_2 + X_3$
   subject to $3X_1 + X_2 + 3X_3 \geq 2$
   $$3X_1 + 2X_2 \qquad = 6$$
   $$X_1 - X_2 \qquad \leq 1$$
   $$X_1, X_2, X_3 \qquad \geq 0$$

9. Max $Z = 6X + 10X_2$
   subject to $2X_1 - 2X_2 \leq 8$
   $$3X_1 - 2X_2 \geq 3$$
   $$X_1 \qquad \geq 0, X_2 \text{ unrestricted in sign}$$

10. Write the dual of problem 7.
11. Write the dual of problem 8.
12. Show that the dual of the dual is the primal.
13. A manufacturing company makes three products, each of which requires three operations as part of the manufacturing process. The company can sell all of the products it can manufacture but its production capability is limited by the capacity of its operations centers. Additional data concerning the company is as follows:

Product	Manufacturing Requirement, Hours/Unit			Cost ($)	Selling Price ($)
	Center 1	Center 2	Center 3		
A	1	3	2	11	15
B	3	4	1	12	20
C	2	2	2	10	16
Hours avail.	160	120	80		

What should the product mix be?

14. A wood-screw manufacturer plans on putting up a package of assorted screw sizes for household use in response to requests from wholesalers. Each package is to contain at least 8 ounces of screws in three sizes. Manufacturing costs are $5, $3, and $2 per 50 pounds for sizes 1, 2, and 3, respectively. In discussing the package makeup with his wholesalers, the manufacturer has decided that:

   (a) the weight of size 3 cannot exceed 4 ounces.
   (b) the combined weight of sizes 2 and 3 cannot exceed 6 ounces.

What should the package composition be if the package can be sold to wholesalers for 4¢? For 3¢?

15. A company can produce four products, each of which requires four operations as part of the manufacturing process. The company has no warehousing facilities for finished product inventory and its products

are shipped directly to customers. Additional data concerning the company are as follows:

(a) From the sales department:

Product	Maximum Sales Units	Sales Price ($/Unit)
1	100	3
2	50	4
3	70	2
4	30	12

(b) From the production department:

Product	Center 1	Center 2	Center 3	Center 4	Cost ($/Unit)
	Production Requirements Hours/Unit				
1	3	8	2	6	1.5
2	4	3	1	0	2
3	2	1	3	4	1
4	10	8	8	6	6
Total production capability	1400	1000	800	2000	

(c) From the bill of materials and raw-material inventory records:

Product	1/16"	1/8"	1/4"
	Stock Requirements ft.^{2}/Unit		
1	4	2	0
2	7	4	4
3	1	1	6
4	6	0	4
Total stock availability	1500	1200	600

What should the company produce?

16. An advertising agency has been approached by one of its clients who is contemplating the introduction of an additional product to its product line. The client proposes to spend $1,000,000 the first year on

advertising but feels that unless it can obtain a 10 percent share of the market, the introduction of the new product will not be a financial success. Four advertising media are being considered: newspapers, periodicals, TV, and home mailings. The client wishes to know what its best advertising strategy would be and the least share of the market that strategy would be apt to produce. The advertising agency has put together a payoff matrix containing its best estimates that has been reviewed and agreed to by the marketing division of its client.

(a) The matrix, showing percent of market captured, is shown below; what are the client's minimum prospects if he adopts the best strategy?

(b) Competition is currently following a strategy that allocates the following resources to each of the media: (1) 50 percent to TV, (2) 25 percent to newspapers, (3) 25 percent to periodicals, and (4) nothing to home mailing. What are the client's prospects if he follows his best strategy and the competition persists in its strategy?

	Media	1	2	3	4	Media
						1 TV
	1	8	16	12	7	2 Newspapers
Client	2	9	10	15	11	3 Home mailing
	3	2	5	14	4	4 Periodicals
	4	14	11	5	2	

Competition spans columns 1–4. *Media* right column lists TV, Newspapers, Home mailing, Periodicals.

17. The owner of a poultry farm has been mixing equal parts of three types of feed for his chicken feed. He has recently read a report that indicated that poultry should be fed three essential ingredients in those feeds in certain minimum proportions. Shown below is the data concerning the feed and ingredients. How should he blend the feeds?

Ingredient	Percent Ingredient by Weight			Minimum Requirement (percent)
	Feed 1	Feed 2	Feed 3	
1	30	40	0	30
2	20	10	30	15
3	30	20	60	Not prescribed
4	20	30	10	10
cost $/lb	.40	.50	.30	

18. You have the option of investing your savings in two plans. The first plan guarantees that each dollar invested will earn a rate of return of 12 percent per annum while the second plan guarantees a rate of return of 30 percent biannually. In the second plan only investments for a two-year period are allowed. You wish to liquidate your investments at the end of three years. What should your investment strategy be?

19. You are operating a McDonald's drive-in franchise and are contemplating trying an experimental 24-hour operation. History of previous operations and best estimates indicate that the following number of counter clerks will be needed.

Counter Clerks Required	Time of Day
8	6–10
11	10–14
7	14–18
14	18–22
5	22–2
4	2–6

Each clerk works an eight consecutive-hour shift. How would you schedule the clerks to satisfy these requirements while minimizing your daily clerk force?

20. A manufacturing company produces two products, each of which requires stamping, assembly, and painting operations. Total productive capacity by operation if it were devoted solely to one product or the other is:

Productive Capacity (Units per Week)		
Operation	Product A	Product B
Stamping	500	700
Assembly	650	330
Painting	450	700

Pro-rata allocation of productive capacity is permissible so that combinations of production of the two products are permissible. Demand for the two products is unlimited and the profits on A and B are $15 and $12, respectively.

The company wishes to expand its product line subject to equaling or increasing the total profit it can realize. Its marketing manager has determined that there is an unlimited market for a third product and the production manager states that the third product could be manufactured with a slight change in facilities. If that change is made the new production capacities would be:

	Productive Capacity (Units per Week)		
Operation	Product A	Product B	Product C
Stamping	450	600	240
Assembly	600	200	200
Painting	400	650	160

The pro-rata allocation of productive capacity capability continues to exist but the profits on A and B would change to $15 and $9.50, respectively. Profit for the third item is estimated to be $16.

Should the company extend its product line by including product C? (Hint: treat each operation capability as 100 percent and allocate the percentage of capability by product line on a pro-rata percent basis.)

21. A floor-covering wholesaler receives a solicitation to bid on an order for carpeting from a building contractor for a high-rise apartment under construction. Carpeting comes in standard rolls of either 12 or 15 feet width with 200 and 250 square yards to the roll, respectively. Data on the solicitation is:

Color	Width in Feet	Square Yards Required
Green	4	400
	9	2000
	14	900
Blue	4	600
	9	3000
	14	1200
Gold	4	800
	9	4000
	14	1800

The grade of carpeting specified in the solicitation is a commercial grade that bears a standard cost regardless of manufacturer and the only cost edge the wholesaler can obtain on his competition is to minimize waste. Remnants (leftover pieces once a roll has been cut into) have a reduced value to the wholesaler on the retail market. These reduced values are as shown below:

Remnant Width	Value as a Percent of Standard Value
Under 27″	None
27″–48″	25
49″–59″	30
60″–108″	40
108″–143″	50

(a) Formulate this problem to solve for the cutting pattern of the carpeting rolls so that losses due to the creation of remnants are minimized.

(b) Solve the problem using a computer.

22. A large manufacturing corporation makes one of its products in eight different factories and has 12 distribution centers to which it ships the product. There are two other small companies who make the same product from whom the large corporation could buy the product for its distribution centers. It costs the corporation 50¢ per unit to produce it; it costs 55¢ to buy the product from the smaller companies.

The distribution center's requirements for the products and manufacturing capabilities are:

Distribution Center	Requirement	Factory	Production Capability
1	2,000	1, 2, 3	1000 each
2	3,000	4, 8	2000 each
3	4,000	5, 6, 7	2500 each
4	2,500	9, 10, 11, 12	3000 each
5	6,000		
6	3,000		
7	1,000		
8	5,000		
Total	26,500		

Transportation costs in cents per unit from each factory or small company to each distribution center are:

Distribution Center	Factory											Company	
	1	2	3	4	5	6	7	8	9	10	11	12 A	B
1	5	6	7	8	9	10	11	12	13	14	15	16 3	4
2	2	3	4	5	6	7	7	6	5	4	3	2 2	1
3	7	6	5	4	3	2	7	6	5	4	3	2 9	1
4	16	15	14	13	12	11	10	9	8	7	6	5 18	5
5	3	8	13	4	9	14	5	10	15	6	11	16 3	8
6	16	11	6	3	8	13	15	10	5	14	9	4 19	7
7	4	9	14	5	10	15	13	8	3	6	11	16 3	9
8	1	7	3	2	8	4	5	9	6	11	14	8 1	1

Each of the two small companies can produce 1000 of the product.
    Formulate this problem to obtain the manufacturing and purchasing plan to stock the distribution centers while minimizing costs.
    23. Consider the linear programming problem:

$$\text{Max } Z = 2X_2 - 5X_3$$
$$\text{subject to } X_1 + X_3 \geq 2$$
$$2X_1 + X_2 + 6X_3 \leq 6$$
$$X_1 - X_2 + 3X_3 = 0$$
$$\text{all } X\text{'s} \geq 0$$

The final tableau yielding the optimal solution is:

	C_j	0	2	-5	0	0	$-M$	$-M$	
Variable in Solution	Var. C_j	X_1	X_2	X_3	S_1	S_2	R_1	R_3	b
X_2	2	0	1	0	0	1/3	0	-2/3	2
S_1	0	0	0	2	1	1/3	-1	1/3	0
X_1	0	1	0	3	0	1/3	0	1/3	2
Z_j		0	2	0	0	2/3	0	-4/3	4
$C_j - Z_j$		0	0	-5	0	-2/3	$-M$	$-M$ +4/3	

(a) What are the shadow prices (optimal value of the dual variables) of each of the constraints in the primal?

(b) Over what range of coefficients for each variable in the objective function will the optimal solution remain optimal?

(c) Over what range of constraint constants will the optimal solution remain feasible?

(d) Over what range of technical coefficients of X_3 in the second constraint will X_3 remain nonbasic? In the first constraint? In the third constraint?

24. Consider the linear programming problem:

$$\text{Max } Z = 12X_1 + 5X_2$$
$$\text{subject to } 5X_1 + 3X_2 \leq 15$$
$$7X_1 + 2X_2 \leq 14$$
$$X_1, \quad X_2 \geq 0$$

The final tableau yielding the optimal solution is:

Variable in Solution	Var. C_j	C_j 12 X_1	5 X_2	0 S_1	0 S_2	b
X_2	5	0	1	7/11	−5/11	35/11
X_1	12	1	0	−2/11	21/77	12/11
Z_j		12	5	1	1	29
$C_j - Z_j$		0	0	−1	−1	

(a) How much would the objective function increase if one additional unit of the first constraint were available? For one additional unit of the second constraint?

(b) Would the optimal solution remain optimal if the coefficient in the objective function for X_1 were changed by a positive increment? If the coefficient for X_2 were changed by a positive increment? Explain your answers.

(c) How would you determine the effect on the optimal solution when the technical coefficient of X_1 in the first constraint is changed to read 6?

(d) What would be the effect on the feasibility of the optimal solution if the constant in the first constraint were reduced to 11? To 9? How would the first change effect the values of the optimal solution?

25. You have solved the problem for the wood-screw manufacturer of problem 14. In discussing your solution with the president of the company, he poses the following questions to you.

(a) What would be the effect on profit per package if it were permissible to increase the weight of the size 3 screw by 25 percent? To limit the weight of the size 1 screw to not more than 1 ounce?

(b) A 10-ounce package can be sold for 5¢. Would it be to the company's advantage to put up such a package given the original constraints?

(c) Given the original constraints, how much would a 9-ounce package have to sell for in order to increase the package profit?

(d) What is the minimum the 9-ounce package would have to sell for in order to realize a 2¢ profit assuming the original constraints?

26. Consider the problem confronting the manufacturer of problem 20.

(a) It would cost $25 and $50 per percentage increase in assembly and painting capability, respectively. How much would it cost to increase the stamping capability in order to bring product C into the optimal solution?

(b) How much of an increase in the paint capacity would be required so that the total profit after introducing product C would equal the total profit before its introduction? Given that the increase was funded, would the company be in a position to realize its objective?

(c) It would cost $75 per percentage increase in stamping capability. What would the least cost be to provide the necessary capabilities to permit at least 50 of each product line?

(d) How much would it cost to obtain a 10-percent increase over current profits, expand the product line, and manufacture at least 50 of each product line?

(e) The company operates on a policy of requiring a 15-percent return on capital investments. Would you recommend the expenditure of the funds required in (d) or the use of those funds to increase the capacities in the current situation?

REFERENCES

1. Avani, S., "A Linear Programming Approach to Air-Cleaner Design," *Operations Research*, Vol. 22, No. 2, March–April 1974.
2. Bierman, H., Jr., C. P. Bonini, and W. H. Hausman, *Quantitative Analysis for Business Decisions*, fourth edition, Richard D. Irwin, Inc., Homewood, Ill., 1973.
3. Cooper, L. and D. Steinberg, *Methods and Applications of Linear Programming*, W. B. Saunders Co., Philadelphia, 1974.
4. Dantzig, G. B., *Linear Programming and Extensions*, Princeton University Press, Princeton, N.J., 1963.

5. Frazer, R. J., *Applied Linear Programming*, Prentice-Hall, Englewood Cliffs, N.J., 1968.

6. Garvin, W. W., *Introduction to Linear Programming*, McGraw-Hill, New York, 1960.

7. Levin, R. I. and C. A. Kirkpatrick, *Quantitative Approaches to Management*, McGraw-Hill, New York, third edition, 1975.

8. Llewellyn, R. W., *Linear Programming*, Holt, Rinehart and Winston, New York, 1964.

9. Loomba, N. P. and E. Turban, *Applied Programming for Management*, Holt, Rinehart and Winston, New York, 1974.

10. McMillan, C., Jr., *Mathematical Programming*, Wiley, New York, second edition, 1975.

11. Plane, D. R. and G. A. Kochenberger, *Operations Research for Managerial Decisions*, Richard D. Irwin, Inc., Homewood, Ill., 1972.

12. Robichek, A. A., D. G. Ogilvie and J. C. Roach, "Capital Budgeting: A Pragmatic Approach," *Financial Executive*, April 1969.

13. Shamblin, J. E. and G. T. Stevens, *Operations Research, A Fundamental Approach*, McGraw-Hill, New York, 1974.

14. Sharp, J. F., "Linear Programming Optimizes Use of Common Labor," *Industrial Engineering*, Vol. 3, No. 1, January 1971.

15. Simmons, D. M., *Linear Programming for Operations Research*, Holden-Day, Inc., San Francisco, Cal., 1972.

16. Simpson, J. L. and D. J. Pellei, "Linear Programming Guides Part Buyers," *Industrial Engineering*, Vol. 5, No. 4, April 1973.

17. Smythe, W. R., Jr. and L. A. Johnson, *Introduction to Linear Programming, with Applications*, Prentice-Hall, Englewood Cliffs, N.J., 1966.

18. Taha, H. A., *Operations Research, An Introduction*, Macmillan, New York, second edition, 1976.

specialized mathematical programming topics 4

Mathematical programming, as a body of knowledge, embraces the techniques used in finding optimal solutions to real-world problems via mathematical representations of those problems. The reader will at once recognize that he has already been introduced to, and hopefully has become proficient in, one of those techniques—linear programming. It would not be possible, within the scope of this text, to treat mathematical programming in its entirety but a student interested in operations research deserves more than proficiency in the simplex method of solving linear programming problems. Accordingly in this chapter we look at a number of additional selected topics in mathematical programming; the references at the end of the chapter can be used by those wishing to delve further into this fascinating and useful topic.

A particular type of linear programming problem that is often encountered involves the distribution of a product or resource from various sources to various destinations or users. Although problems of this type do not necessarily involve the movement of goods in the generally accepted sense associated with the word transportation, they can all be solved using the so called transportation model.

A transportation problem can be completely defined by the matrix:

Sources	Destinations				Supply
	1	2	$\ldots$	n	
1	C_{11}	C_{12}	$\ldots$	C_{1n}	S_1
2	C_{21}	C_{22}	$\ldots$	C_{2n}	S_2
$\vdots$	$\vdots$	$\vdots$	$\vdots$	$\vdots$	$\vdots$
m	C_{m1}	C_{m2}	$\ldots$	C_{mn}	S_m
Demand	D_1	D_2	$\ldots$	D_n	

where C_{ij} is the cost of getting one unit of the product or resource from the ith source to the jth destination. It should be noted that this cost may be a variable production cost, purchasing cost, shipping cost, combination thereof or for that matter any relative value indexing that we may wish to assign to a unit of the product or resource X_{ij}. A linear program representation of the problem would be

$$\text{Minimize} \sum_{i=1}^{m} \sum_{j=1}^{n} C_{ij}X_{ij}$$

subject to

$$\sum_{i=1}^{m} X_{ij} \geq D_j \qquad j = 1, 2, \ldots n$$

$$\sum_{j=1}^{n} X_{ij} \leq S_i \qquad i = 1, 2, \ldots m$$

$$X_{ij} \geq 0 \qquad \text{for all } i \text{ and } j$$

When $\sum_{j=1}^{n} D_j = \sum_{i=1}^{m} S_i$, that is, when total supply and demand are equal, this type of problem can be solved by a simplified algorithm. This is not a severe restriction limiting the use of the transportation model algorithm that we are about to look at. For example, in those cases where the supply exceeds the demand, the problem can be reformulated with the addition of a dummy destination whose demand would equal the excess supply. In the final solution each of the X_{ij} to the dummy destination would simply be interpreted as remaining or not being produced at the ith source. Since we intend to neither move nor produce the product for the dummy destination, what values would you assign to the C_{ij} in the dummy destination column?

All that remains to be done before tackling an example problem using the transportation algorithm is a definition of the transportation tableau, shown in Figure 4.1. The C_{ij} are entered in the small boxes in the upper left-hand corner of each of the ij matrix positions and the X_{ij} are entered in the matrix positions. The available product quantity from each source is entered in the S_i (supply) column and the required product quantity to each destination is entered in the D_j (demand) row. Note that any dummy used to create the condition $\sum_{j=1}^{n} D_j = \sum_{i=1}^{m} S_i$ must be included in the tableau. Finally the v_i column and w_j row are provided for computational aids in connection with the algorithm and their use is explained in the example discussed below.

The transportation algorithm itself may be described as follows:

STEP 1.   Set up the problem in the standard transportation tableau.

STEP 2.   Find an initial basic feasible solution.

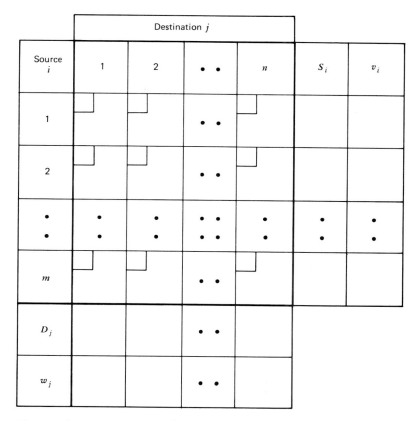

Figure 4.1 A transportation tableau format.

STEP 3. Determine whether a better feasible solution is possible. If not the optimal solution has been found. If a better feasible solution is possible proceed to step 4.

STEP 4. Determine the improved basic feasible solution.

STEP 5. Return to step 3.

EXAMPLE Now let us proceed with an illustrative problem. A company has three plants from which it must supply two distributors. The first distributor requires 2100 units of the product, the second requires 2500. The data on the three plants are as shown in Table 4.1.

How should we meet the distributor requirements so as to minimize costs?

Step 1. Set up the problem in the standard transportation tableau.

We see immediately that total supply is 6200 units but that the total requirement is only 4600 units. In order to make demand equal supply we

Table 4.1 Plant Data

Plant	Cap. Unit	Unit Cost, $	Unit Shipping Cost, $, to Distr.	
			1	2
1	2000	5000	1000	1000
2	2200	4000	2000	3000
3	2000	7000	2000	2000

introduce a dummy distributor, $j = 3$, with a requirement for 1600 units. Produce on a sheet of paper the initial transportation tableau with quantity and cost data in thousands of dollars and hundreds of units, respectively. Your tableau should look like Figure 4.2.

Step 2. Find an initial basic feasible solution.
    There are several ways to accomplish this step; among the simplest is the so-called northwest corner solution. Look at your tableau; the 1,1

Figure 4.2 Filling in the initial tableau.

matrix position is referred to as the northwest corner and the solution was so named because we will start with that matrix position. Obviously X_{11} cannot be more than either the available supply, S_1, or the distributor demand, D_1. In our case X_{11} is 20. Note that this fails to satisfy D_1 but exhausts S_1 and we know therefore that $X_{12} = X_{13} = 0$. From the remaining matrix positions defined by $i = 2, 3$ and $j = 2, 3$, we can continue developing the northwest corner solution with position 2, 1. We see that X_{21} cannot exceed 1 despite the availability of 22 from S_2. Thus we let $X_{21} = 1$. Now $X_{22} = 21$, which is all that remains in S_2, and, although this exhausts S_2, it leaves D_2 with a further requirement of 4 units. At this point your tableau should look like Figure 4.3. Note that the system used

| | Distributor | | | | |
Plant	1	2	3	S_i	v_i
1	6 / 20	6 / 0	0 / 0	2̶0̶ / 20	
2	6 / 1	7 / 21	0	2̶2̶ / 21	
3	9	9	0	20	
D_j	2̶1̶ / 1̶	2̶5̶ / 4	16		
w_j					

Figure 4.3 Developing the initial basic feasible solution.

in posting the D_j and S_i quantities in order to keep track of what is being done as the northwest solution is being developed. You can now determine X_{23}; what is it? Of course, since S_2 has been exhausted, it must be zero. What is the value of X_{31}? Finally, although 20 units are available from S_3, we see that only 4 units are yet required in D_2. Therefore, X_{32} must be 4 thus leaving 16 units for distribution elsewhere. Finish the northwest solution in your tableau and compare it to Figure 4.4. We now have an initial basic feasible solution.

	Distributor				
Plant	1	2	3	S_i	v_i
1	6 / 20	6 / 0	0 / 0	20	
2	6 / 1	7 / 21	0 / 0	22 / 21	
3	9 / 0	9 / 4	0 / 16	20 / 16	
D_j	21 /	25 /	16 /		
w_j					

Figure 4.4 The initial basic feasible solution.

Step 3. Determine whether a better feasible solution is possible.

In our basic feasible solution shown in Figure 4.4 it is obvious that the C_{ij} entering into the determination of the cost of that solution are $C_{11} = 6$, $C_{21} = 6$, $C_{22} = 7$, $C_{32} = 9$, and $C_{33} = 0$. Now suppose we altered our solution by one unit so that $X_{11} = 19$. Then $X_{12} = 1$, $X_{22} = 20$, and $X_{21} = 2$. We have not violated any of our row or column constraints but we have introduced C_{21} into our solution cost. Verify that in the original solution that

$$\sum_{i=1}^{m} \sum_{j=1}^{n} C_{ij}X_{ij} = 309$$

(in tens of thousands) whereas in the second solution it equals 308. Clearly this is a reduction in cost and it would be an improvement. Obviously we would not desire to continue improving our solution by this hit-and-miss trial method; fortunately it is not necessary to do so. In effect what happened in our changed solution is that we found a path where a unit shift provided us with an incremental cost reduction and we have a method whereby such incremental costs can be quickly found. Let us define w_j and v_i such that for a basic feasible solution for the X_{ij} in our basis

$$C_{ij} = v_i + w_j \qquad \text{for each } X_{ij} \text{ in the basis} \qquad (4.1)$$

To keep track of what we are doing let us employ the device of circling the C_{ij} of our basis; do that to your tableau so it looks like Figure 4.5.

Figure 4.5 Identifying the variables in the basis.

From our tableau and (4.1) we can produce the set of equations

$$C_{11} = 6 = v_1 + w_1$$
$$C_{21} = 6 = v_2 + w_1$$
$$C_{22} = 7 = v_2 + w_2 \qquad (4.2)$$
$$C_{32} = 9 = v_3 + w_2$$
$$C_{33} = 0 = v_3 + w_3$$

and we see that we have five equations and six unknowns. In general we will always have $m+n$ unknowns and can structure our problem so it will always contain $m+n-1$ equations. Although there are an infinite number of solutions that will satisfy (4.2), for our purposes any one of those solutions would suffice. We therefore could assign any value to any one of the unknowns and proceed from there. A common practice is to let $v_1 = 0$ and that is what we will do in our example. Thus

$$C_{11} = 6 = 0 + w_1 \qquad w_1 = 6$$
$$C_{21} = 6 = v_2 + 6 \qquad v_2 = 0, \text{ etc.}$$

Complete the solution of (4.2) and enter the v_i and w_j values in your tableau; it should now look like Figure 4.6.

Plant	Distributor 1	Distributor 2	Distributor 3	S_i	v_i
1	⑥ 20	6 — 0	0 — 0	~~20~~	[0]
2	⑥ 1	⑦ 21	0 — 0	~~22~~ 21	[0]
3	9 — 0	⑨ 4	⓪ 16	~~20~~ 18	[2]
D_j	~~21~~ 1	~~28~~ 4	18		
w_j	[6]	[7]	[-2]		

Figure 4.6 Developing the $C_{ij} - Z_{ij}$ values.

Now let us define the cost contributions to the objective function total by Z_{ij} (similar to the way we did with the simplex tableau) such that for each X_{ij}

$$Z_{ij} = v_i + w_j \qquad i = 1, 2, \ldots m$$
$$j = 1, 2, \ldots n \qquad (4.3)$$

Then

$$Z_{11} = v_1 + w_1 = 0 + 6 = 6$$

$$Z_{12} = v_1 + w_2 = 0 + 7 = 7, \text{ etc.}$$

Do not bother to complete (4.3) just yet because we want to combine another step in our calculations. Recall that in our simplex tableau what we really were looking for, in order to determine whether or not our feasible solution could be improved, was the incremental cost of adding one unit of an X_{ij} to the basis; that is, the $C_{ij} - Z_{ij}$. Since all C_{ij} are displayed in our tableau and the Z_{ij} can be determined by (4.3) it is simple enough to push the computations one step further so that

$$C_{ij} - Z_{ij} = C_{ij} - v_i - w_j \qquad \begin{array}{l} i = 1, 2, \ldots m \\[4pt] j = 1, 2, \ldots n \end{array} \qquad (4.4)$$

Now

$$C_{11} - Z_{11} = 6 - 0 - 6 = 0$$

$$C_{12} - Z_{12} = 6 - 0 - 7 = -1, \text{ etc.}$$

You should now complete (4.4) entering the incremental costs for each X_{ij} in your tableau just to the right of the corresponding C_{ij} block of each ij matrix position. Your tableau should look like Figure 4.7 when you are done.

The presence of a negative $C_{ij} - Z_{ij}$ value indicates that the value of the objective function can be reduced; that is, our current basic feasible solution can be improved and we are ready to proceed to the next step of our algorithm.

Step 4. Determine the improved basic feasible solution.
In general any negative $C_{ij} - Z_{ij}$ can be used to produce an improved solution but if there were more than one such value as a result of completing (4.4), which one would you use to construct your next solution? Intuitively we would think that the most negative one should be used and our general procedure does just that. In our illustrative example only one such value exists, $C_{12} - Z_{12} = -1$, and we will use it. If one unit in X_{12} gives us a reduction then the greater X_{12}, the greater the gross reduction; accordingly we shall try to make X_{12} *as large as possible*.

To determine how large we can make the entering variable we must construct a so called $+-$ path in the matrix. We know that the matrix position holding the most negative $C_{ij} - Z_{ij}$ contains the entering variable; that is, we are going to add increments to the matrix position's X_{ij}. In our example position 1, 2 is therefore a $+$ position and we can note this in

Plant	Distributor, 1		Distributor, 2		Distributor, 3		S_i	v_i
1	⑥	0	6	−1	0	2	2̶0̶	0
	20		0		0			
2	⑥	0	⑦	0	0	2	2̶2̶ 2̶1̶	0
	1		21		0			
3	9	1	⑨	0	⓪	0	2̶0̶ 1̶8̶	2
	0		4		16			
D_j	2̶1̶ 1̶		2̶5̶ 4̶		1̶6̶			
w_j	6		7		−2			

Figure 4.7 Posting the $C_{ij} - Z_{ij}$ values.

our tableau by placing a + in the lower left-hand corner of that cell; do so in your tableau. We note immediately, in order to maintain our S_i and D_j conditions, that whatever increments are added to cell 1, 2 will have to be subtracted someplace from row 1 and column 2. There are two matters that must be kept in mind as the + − path is constructed. First, we cannot have a − cell wherever $X_{ij} = 0$ since subtraction of positive nonzero increments from such a cell would result in a negative X_{ij}. Second, since we selected the X_{ij} cell with the greatest contribution to the objective function as the entering variable, no other $X_{ij} = 0$ may have an increment added to it. In short, once we have selected the X_{ij} to enter the solution the remainder of the + − path must pass through cells in the current basis.

In our current example we can make either cell 2, 2 or 3, 2 a minus cell on our path. If we select 3, 2 then 3, 3 would have to be a plus cell but there is no other cell in column 3 that can be made a minus cell; this would therefore be an improper choice. On the other hand if we were to select 2, 2 as a minus cell, cell 1, 1 could be minus and we would have a closed path leading back to cell 1, 2. In general this process is used to generate a

	Distributor				
Plant	1	2	3	S_i	v_i
1	(6) 0 20 −	6 −1 0 +	0 2 0	~~20~~	0
2	(6) 0 1 +	(7) 0 21 −	0 2 0	~~22~~ ~~21~~	0
3	9 1 0	(9) 0 4	(0) 0 16	~~20~~ ~~16~~	2
D_j	~~21~~ ~~1~~	~~25~~ ~~4~~	~~16~~		
w_j	6	7	−2		

Figure 4.8 Establishing the +− path.

closed +− path and in our example it led to the path shown in Figure 4.8. Now we know that the increment to be added and subtracted along our +− path can only be as large as the smallest X_{ij} in the − cells along our path (otherwise we will wind up with a negative X_{ij}). In our example the X_{ij} in the − cells are $X_{11}=20$ and $X_{22}=21$ and our increment is therefore 20, the lesser of the two.

Now we can set up another transportation tableau (Figure 4.2) for the next improved feasible solution. The improved X_{12} will be the old $X_{12}+$(because it is a + cell) our increment of 20. Hence we can enter $X_{12}=20$ in our improved solution. Similarly our improved X_{22} will be the old $X_{22}-20$ and we can enter $X_{22}=1$ in our new tableau. You should complete the calculations around the +− path entering the new X_{ij} in your tableau as you do so. When the path is complete, all the remaining new X_{ij} can be filled in by direct transcription from the old tableau. After doing so your tableau should look like Figure 4.9, which is an improved solution over that shown in Figure 4.7. Verify that our improved solution has reduced our cost to 289 now before we proceed to the next step of our algorithm.

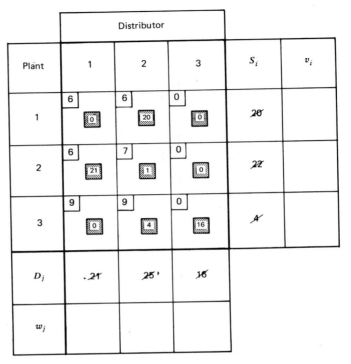

Figure 4.9   Improving the basic feasible solution.

Step 5.   Determine whether a better feasible solution is possible.

Since this step is exactly like step 3, its completion is left to the reader as a practice exercise. The completed tableau is shown in Figure 4.10. Note now that all $C_{ij} - Z_{ij}$ are nonnegative and, therefore, the current basic solution cannot be improved. It must then be the optimal solution and our problem is completed. With the experience you have gained you should be well on your way to gaining the ability to look at an initial basic feasible solution (Figure 4.7), pick the +− path (Figure 4.8) and move directly to the next improved solution (Figure 4.9) with a minimal effort.

EXAMPLE   Although we now know how to solve the transportation model we are not quite through with the subject. Let us make one change in the requirements of our illustrative problem so that the first distributor requires 2000 units (rather than 2100 as was originally stated) and then solve the new problem. Performance of the first and second steps of the transportation algorithm is left to the reader as an exercise to gain experience with the transportation model. Your tableau with the initial basic feasible solution should look like Figure 4.11.

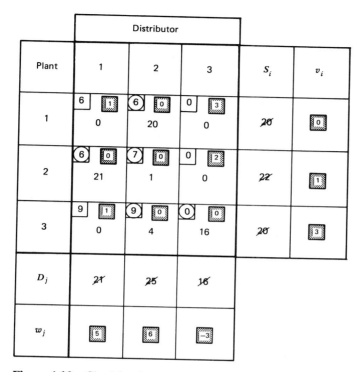

Figure 4.10 Checking for further solution improvements.

Now let us proceed to the third step and attempt to determine whether a better feasible solution is possible. We would discover that

$$C_{11} = 6 = v_1 + w_1$$
$$C_{22} = 7 = v_2 + w_2$$
$$C_{32} = 9 = v_3 + w_2$$
$$C_{33} = 0 = v_3 + w_3$$

and that even after assuming $v_1 = 0$, we would be left with five unknowns and only four equations. In short we cannot solve for the v_i and w_j values. What has happened is that, in utilizing our northwest corner technique, we have developed a degenerate basic feasible solution. This will occur every time that a sum of some subset of the available supplies (S_i) equals the sum of some subset of the required distributions (D_j). In the instant problem such a condition existed since $S_1 = 20 = D_1$.

Whenever such a condition exists it can be overcome by perturbating the S_i or D_j. That is to say we can add a small increment, say ε, to either

Distributor					
Plant	1	2	3	S_i	v_i
1	6 20	6	0	~~20~~	
2	6	7 22	0	~~22~~	
3	9	9 3	0 17	~~20~~ ~~17~~	
D_j	~~20~~	~~25~~ ~~3~~	~~17~~		
w_j					

Figure 4.11 A degenerate solution.

the S_i or D_j and either $m\varepsilon$ or $n\varepsilon$ to D_n or S_m. In our case let

$$\varepsilon = .01$$

$$S_i' = S_i + \varepsilon \qquad i = 1, 2, 3$$

Then

$$D_j' = D_j \qquad j = 1, 2$$

$$D_3' = D_3 + 3\varepsilon = D_3 + .03$$

and the initial basic feasible solution would appear in the tableau as shown in Figure 4.12.

The completion of the problem is now left as an exercise. The optimal solution you should obtain is

$$X_{12} = 20.01 \qquad X_{21} = 20 \qquad X_{22} = 2.01 \qquad X_{32} = 2.98 \qquad X_{33} = 17.03$$

But hold on, these answers contain our perturbations and it is necessary to remove them. Remember our $\varepsilon = .01$ and our answers could be written as

$$X_{12} = 20 + \varepsilon \qquad X_{21} = 20 \qquad X_{22} = 2 + \varepsilon \qquad X_{32} = 3 - 2\varepsilon \qquad X_{33} = 17 + 3\varepsilon$$

Plant	Distributor				
	1	2	3	S_i	v_i
1	6 20	6 .01	0	~~20.01~~ .01	
2	6	7 22.01	0	~~22.01~~	
3	9	9 2.98	0 17.03	~~20.01~~ ~~17.03~~	
D_j	~~20~~	~~20~~ ~~2.98~~	~~17.03~~		
w_j					

Figure 4.12 Perturbating a degenerate solution.

Now suppose we make ε smaller and smaller so that it has less and less effect on the solution. In fact, let's make $\varepsilon = 0$ so that it has no effect on our answer; then the answer to our perturbated problem becomes

$$X_{12} = 20 \qquad X_{21} = 20 \qquad X_{22} = 2 \qquad X_{32} = 3 \qquad X_{33} = 17$$

which is also the answer to the unperturbated problem. The perturbation method will always permit us to get around degeneracy in using our transportation model and we can now move on to our next topic in mathematical programming.

The assignment model is a particular type of transportation model where $m = n$ and each S_i can be used once and only once to satisfy one D_j. As such it is, of course, also a type of linear programming problem. There are, as you will see, a number of problems where this situation arises. In such cases we can adopt the convention

$$X_{ij} = \begin{cases} 1 \text{ if } S_i \text{ is used to satisfy } D_j \\ 0 \text{ otherwise} \end{cases}$$

**4.3
THE
ASSIGNMENT
MODEL**

Then our mathematical description of the problem would be

$$\text{Minimize} \quad \sum_{i=1}^{m} \sum_{j=1}^{n} C_{ij} X_{ij}$$

subject to

$$\sum_{i=1}^{m} X_{ij} = 1 \qquad j = 1, 2, \ldots n$$

$$\sum_{j=1}^{n} X_{ij} = 1 \qquad i = 1, 2, \ldots m$$

$$X_{ij} = 0 \text{ or } 1$$

If, in a given problem, $n \neq m$, no difficulty is presented in using the assignment model since we can always use dummy S_i or D_j to make $n = m$. As you will recall $C_{ij} = 0$ where a dummy is involved. Suppose you have a situation where a particular S_i cannot be used to satisfy a D_j; what would the C_{ij} be in that event? Of course since we would want to be sure that X_{ij} would not be in our solution we could make its C_{ij} prohibitively large. You should also have noticed that $S_i = D_j = 1$.

As in the transportation model we can construct a cost matrix for our assignment problem, which would be

$$
\begin{array}{cccc}
C_{11} & C_{12} & \cdots & C_{1n} \\
C_{21} & C_{22} & \cdots & C_{2n} \\
\vdots & \vdots & \cdots & \vdots \\
C_{n1} & C_{n2} & \cdots & C_{nn}
\end{array}
$$

What effect would adding a constant, r_i, to the ith row have on our optimal solution X_0^*? We know that

$$X_0^* = \sum_{i=1}^{n} \sum_{j=1}^{n} C_{ij} X_{ij}^* \tag{4.5}$$

and

$$X_0^{*\prime} = \sum_{i=1}^{n} \sum_{j=1}^{n} (C_{ij} + r_i) X_{ij}^* \tag{4.6}$$

Expanding (4.6) we get

$$X_0^{*\prime} = \sum_{i=1}^{n} \sum_{j=1}^{n} C_{ij} X_{ij}^* + \sum_{i=1}^{n} r_i \sum_{j=1}^{n} X_{ij}^* \tag{4.7}$$

But $\sum_{j=1}^{n} X_{ij}^* = 1$ and by substituting (4.5) in (4.7)

$$X_0^{*\prime} = X_0^* + \sum_{i=1}^{n} r_i = X_0^* + \text{constant}$$

In other words, the addition of constants to the rows of our cost matrix would not change our optimal solution of X_{ij}. The reader can prove that a similar condition exists with respect to the addition of a constant to the columns of the cost matrix. This suggests that if a second cost matrix can be developed from the original matrix by the introduction of constants to the rows and columns of the original such that an X_{ij} path can be found where its C_{ij} all equal zero, we will have found the $X_{ij}*$.

Let us see how this works in an illustrative problem. Suppose we **EXAMPLE** have three workers and three jobs. The three workers have different levels of expertise necessary to do the three jobs that in themselves require different amounts of the various levels of expertise possessed by the three workers. Consequently, labor costs will vary depending on which worker is assigned to each job. The cost matrix for this situation is shown in Table 4.2. We wish to know which job to assign to each worker so as to minimize our costs.

Table 4.2 Worker/Job Costs (in dollars)

Job Worker	1	2	3
1	7	9	11
2	15	11	13
3	15	13	13

We can create a zero in rows 1, 2, and 3 by the subtraction from each row of a 7, 11 and 13, respectively. These constants were selected because they represented the least cost in each row. Our new matrix is shown in Figure 4.13. X_{11}, X_{22}, X_{23} is not an acceptable solution since that assigns job 2 to both worker 2 and 3 and does not provide for job 3. However, X_{11}, X_{22}, and X_{33} is an acceptable solution. From our original matrix we see that the optimal solution yields a cost of $C_{11} + C_{22} + C_{33} = 7 + 11 + 13 = 31$, which is also the sum of the r_i. This is a perfectly general condition and we can always say that the sum of the constants removed from the rows will provide us with the cost of the optimal solution.

Suppose, in our original matrix, $C_{33} = 16$ rather than the 13 it was. **EXAMPLE** Then our reduced cost matrix would be as shown in Figure 4.14.

Job / Worker	1	2	3	r_i
1	0	2	4	7
2	4	0	2	11
3	2	0	0	13

Figure 4.13 The reduced cost matrix.

Job / Worker	1	2	3	r_i
1	0	2	4	7
2	4	0	2	11
3	2	0	3	13

Figure 4.14 An incompletely reduced cost matrix.

Now we cannot find an acceptable zero path but remember we can operate on the columns just as we did on the rows. Doing so our next matrix could be reduced as shown in Figure 4.15.

Job / Worker	1	2	3	r_i
1	0	2	2	7
2	4	0	0	11
3	2	0	1	13
k_j	0	0	2	

Figure 4.15 Row and column reduction.

The solution X_{11}, X_{23}, and X_{32} is an acceptable solution and must therefore be optimal. The cost associated with it is $\sum k_j + \sum r_i = 33$. Verify this cost from the original matrix.

Sometimes not even the combination of row and column manipulations will yield an acceptable zero path. For example suppose our original cost matrix read as shown in Table 4.3. Operate on this matrix as we have

Table 4.3 Worker/Jobs Costs (in dollars)

Worker \ Job	1	2	3
1	7	9	8
2	15	11	13
3	15	13	16

before; what is the result? As you see you still cannot find a suitable zero path. But there is a way to continue operating on the matrix by eliminating the zero matrix positions from further consideration. Let us continue to see how this works.

We want to delete from consideration the minimum number of rows and columns such that their elimination will remove the matrix positions containing a zero. Examination of the reduced matrix clearly shows that elimination of the first row and the second column will accomplish this and we draw lines through the selected row(s) and column(s). Our reduced matrix now should look like the one shown in Figure 4.16.

We now examine the remaining matrix positions to determine the minimum cell. We subtract the value of the minimum cell from each of the remaining cells and add that value to each matrix position at an intersection of a row and column elimination. Thus, in our case, the minimum remaining matrix position is $X_{23} = 1$; we subtract that value from X_{21}, X_{23}, X_{32}, and X_{33}; finally we add that value to X_{12}. This operation produces the matrix shown in Figure 4.17. It is now possible to select a zero path that proves to be X_{32}, X_{23}, X_{11} for which the total cost is

$$C_{32} + C_{23} + C_{11} = 13 + 13 + 7 = 33$$

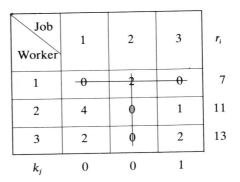

Job \ Worker	1	2	3	r_i
1	0	2	0	7
2	4	0	1	11
3	2	0	2	13
k_j	0	0	1	

Figure 4.16 Manipulating a reduced matrix.

Job \ Worker	1	2	3	r_i
1	0	3	0	7
2	3	0	0	11
3	1	0	1	13
k_j	0	0	1	

Figure 4.17 The reduced matrix.

The procedure of eliminating rows and columns is, in general, reiterative. Should its first application fail to provide a feasible zero path, it can be used as many times as may be necessary on successive matrices until a feasible zero path is found.

4.4
THE
TRANSSHIPMENT
MODEL

We are going to look at another type of problem that you may encounter by using a very simple example to illustrate its features. Suppose we have two tons of a product to ship from a source to two destinations, each destination requiring one ton of product. The relative position of the source and destination are as shown in Figure 4.18. We have three possible alternative shipping schemes. We could ship one ton to each destination directly, we could ship two tons to D_1 and then one ton to D_2, or we could ship two tons to D_2 and then one ton to D_1. Now suppose the capacity of the shippers carriers is two tons and he charges $1 per ton mile for less than carload lots and $2 per ton mile for carload lots. It is simple

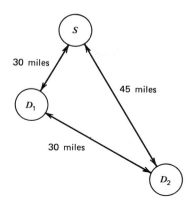

Figure 4.18 Source/destination distances.

enough to calculate the costs of each alternative and if we were to do so we would find that the second one is the cheapest, costing $120. What we have done in effect is transshipped one ton to D_2 via D_1; in effect D_1 became the supplier for D_2. Problems where suppliers may serve as destinations and/or destinations may serve as suppliers are called transshipment problems and they do not fit the transportation model directly. The technique to employ then is to structure a transshipment problem to make it fit the transportation model.

Let us use a three-source, two-destination example to illustrate the **EXAMPLE** technique. We know from the previous discussion that sources can act as destinations and vice-versa and, therefore, rather than a 2×3 matrix to define our cost matrix we need a 5×5 matrix to do so. In general the transshipment cost matrix would be

	Destinations					
Source	1	... n	$n+1$	... $n+m$	Supply
1	C_{11}	... C_{1n}	$C_{1,n+1}$	... $C_{1,n+m}$	S_1
	.	... .	.	... .	.
	.	... .	.	... .	.
	.	... .	.	... .	.
m	C_{m1}	... C_{mn}	$C_{m,n+1}$	... $C_{m,n+m}$	S_m
$m+1$	$C_{m+1,1}$	... $C_{m+1,n}$	$C_{m+1,n+1}$	... $C_{m+1,n+m}$	
.	.	... .	.	...	
.	.	... .	.	...	
$m+n$	$C_{m+n,1}$	... $C_{m+n,n}$	$C_{m+n,n+1}$	... $C_{m+n,n+m}$	
Demand	D_1	... D_n			

Notice that the matrix is incomplete in that there are no supply values after the mth row nor demands after the nth column. This is because the matrix provides for destinations to act as sources and vice-versa and neither supplies nor demands exist for those provisions. For our three-source, two-destination problem the cost matrix appears in Table 4.4. We have adopted the convention in this matrix display where true sources are listed first in both the rows and columns so that X_{11} indicates shipping from source 1 to source 1; C_{11} is shown as zero as are all the C_{ii}. Note also that this leaves us without a value for D_1, D_2, D_3, S_4, and S_5.

Table 4.4 Shipping Cost Matrix (in dollars)

		Destination				
Source	1	2	3	4	5	Supply
1	0	5	8	6	6	20
2	6	0	9	6	7	22
3	7	8	0	9	9	4
4	9	10	11	0	10	S_4
5	4	8	9	9	0	S_5
Demand	D_1	D_2	D_3	21	25	

Recall now each source or destination represents a potential supply or demand at any point in the transshipment process. It must follow, therefore, that all of the available supply could be present at any transshipment point. Remember also to utilize the transportation model that

$$\sum_{i=1}^{m+n} S_i = \sum_{j=1}^{n+m} D_j$$

All these conditions can be met by the simple expedient of adding a quantity of dummy supply (often referred to as a buffer stock), say B, to each row and column such that

$$B \ge \sum_{i=1}^{m} S_i$$

In our case $\sum_{i=1}^{m} S_i = 46$ and we shall let $B = 46$. Doing so permits us to place the problem into a standard transportation tableau, which is shown in Figure 4.19, and we can then proceed to solve the problem via our transportation algorithm. If you feel that working this problem would provide a beneficial transportation model drill, you should do so. Your final tableau should appear as shown in Figure 4.20.

		Destination j						
		$S(1)$	$S(2)$	$S(3)$	$D(1)$	$D(2)$		
Source i		1	2	3	4	5	S_i	v_i
$S(1)$	1	0	5	8	6	6	66	
$S(2)$	2	6	0	9	6	7	68	
$S(3)$	3	1	8	0	9	9	50	
$D(1)$	4	9	10	11	0	10	46	
$D(2)$	5	4	8	9	9	0	46	
D_j		46	46	46	67	71		
w_j								

Figure 4.19   Transshipment transportation tableau.

Interpretation of the solution shown in Figure 4.20 reveals that X_{11}, X_{22}, X_{33}, X_{44}, and X_{55} are shipments from a location to itself and have no physical meaning. In general the diagonal in a transshipment model may be ignored. Since $X_{31} = 4$ we see that the third source ships 4 units to the first source (raising its supplies to 24 units) and that since $X_{15} = 24$, the first source ships its 20 units and transships the 4 units from the third source all to the second destination. Furthermore, we see that the demand of 25 units at the second destination is finally satisfied by the shipment of 1 unit from the second source ($X_{25} = 1$) and that the first destination is fully satisfied with the remaining 21 units at the second source ($X_{24} = 21$). The network of shipments is shown in Figure 4.21.

There are a number of combinatorial problems that present vast numbers of possible solutions. The enumeration of those solutions is an unappealing prospect. The so-called traveling salesman problem can be used to illustrate the point.

Source i		$S(1)$ 1	$S(2)$ 2	$S(3)$ 3	$D(1)$ 4	$D(2)$ 5	S_i	v_i
$S(1)$	1	[0] 42	[5]	[8]	[6]	[6] 24	66	
$S(2)$	2	[6]	[0] 46	[9]	[6] 21	[7] 1	68	
$S(3)$	3	[1] 4	[8]	[0] 46	[9]	[9]	50	
$D(1)$	4	[9]	[10]	[11]	[0] 46	[10]	46	
$D(2)$	5	[4]	[8]	[9]	[9]	[0] 46	46	
D_j		46	46	46	67	71		
w_j								

Destination j heading spans columns $S(1), S(2), S(3), D(1), D(2)$.

Figure 4.20 Transshipment solution.

EXAMPLE Consider the traveling saleman who has 10 cities to visit in his assigned territory. On each circuit of his territory he wishes to visit each city once and only once arriving back at the city from which he started. After spending the necessary time to clean up his paperwork he intends to embark on the same tour with the cycle being repetitive. His transportation represents a significant part of the costs associated with his business and he wishes to determine the tour sequence that will represent the least cost. Let us also assume that the cost of going from A to B may not equal the cost of going from B to A, a condition which could arise for a number of reasons. How many possible tour arrangements exist? He must start at one of the 10 cities and for anyone he picks he can then go to anyone of the 9 cities remaining; for each of the 9 he picks to visit he can then go to any one of the 8 cities remaining, and so on. In short, he can traverse the territory 9! different ways and in general he will have $(n-1)!$ different circuits to evaluate. In our case this represents 362,880 different sequences. Just adding one city to this problem increases the different

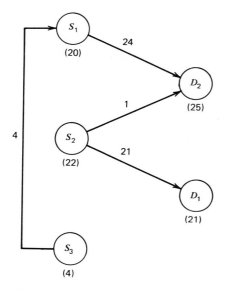

Figure 4.21   Shipment network.

possibilities to 3,628,800 and, as you can see, the problem rapidly gets out of hand.

The branch-and-bound algorithm is another technique that permits us to search the solution space selectively in a fashion that arrives at an optimal solution much more quickly than would complete enumeration. According to this algorithm the following steps must be followed:

STEP 1.   Select the first leg of the trip (or the first assignment) to be considered.

STEP 2.   Compute the lower bound of the costs of all solutions that include the first leg.

STEP 3.   Compute the lower bound of the costs of all solutions that do not include the first leg.

STEP 4.   Select the next leg of the trip for that branch that has the lowest lower bound.

STEP 5.   Compute the lower bound of the costs of all trips that include the next leg.

STEP 6.   Compute the lower bound of the costs of all trips that do not include the next leg.

STEP 7.   Return to step 4 and continue the process until the optimal solution has been determined.

EXAMPLE   Let us do a simple four-city problem to illustrate the details connected with the branch-and-bound algorithm. Noting that a leg of the trip
cannot be from a city to the same city, the trip cost matrix for our problem
is shown in Table 4.5.

Table 4.5 Trip Cost Matrix (in dollars)

		To City			
	j	1	2	3	4
i					
	1	∞	3	8	7
From	2	4	∞	14	3
City	3	4	5	∞	2
	4	7	8	13	∞

Step 1. Select the first leg of the trip to be considered.

We arbitrarily select the first leg and, if it were not a correct choice,
the algorithm would eventually move us to the correct branch. Rather
than do that, however, we begin the solution using the technique we will
use throughout in successively selecting legs. If the thought has occurred
to you that this problem is not unlike the assignment model, you would be
correct, and, like the solution to that model, we will start by reducing the
matrix by row and column operations. By doing so the reduced matrix will
appear as shown in Figure 4.22. Any leg with a zero value in the reduced

i \ j	1	2	3	4	r_i
1	∞	0	0	2	3
2	1	∞	6	0	3
3	2	3	∞	0	2
4	0	1	1	∞	7
k_j	0	0	5	0	

Figure 4.22   Reduced trip cost matrix.

matrix is a candidate for our first selection but which one should we pick? A moment's reflection should lead us intuitively to the conclusion that we would prefer to pick the one that if it were excluded would increase the cost of the round trip the most. Let us see what that means in connection with our reduced matrix.

Taking cell 1, 2 first we see that if we exclude it from our solution we will have to include either 1, 3 or 1, 4. The best we could hope for from these choices is that we would include 1, 3 since its reduced cost is the lesser of the two. Notice also that we would be compelled to include either 3, 2 or 4, 2 since the exclusion of 1, 2 means that we will have to get to city 2 from some city other than 1. The best we could hope for from these two choices is 4, 2. Thus the best we could hope for if we exclude cell 1, 2 from our initial solution is an added cost to our solution resulting from the inclusion of 1, 3 and 4, 2. That added cost, which we call the cost of exclusion, is 1. We can partition the upper right-hand corner of cell 1, 2 and place its cost of exclusion there.

This process can be repeated for each of the cells that contains a zero in Figure 4.22 by simply searching the row and column in which the cell is located. The sum of least values of exclusion in the cell's row and column will be the cost of exclusion for the cell in question. Thus the cost of excluding cell 1, 3 would be 0 (from 1, 2) + 1 (from 4, 3) and the cost of exclusion would be entered in the upper-right corner of cell 1, 3. Continuing for cells 2, 4; 3, 4; and 4, 1 would result in the matrix shown in Figure 4.23. The cell containing the greatest cost of exclusion is a logical

i \\ j	1	2	3	4	r_i
1	∞	0 [1]	0 [1]	2	3
2	1	∞	6	0 [1]	3
3	2	3	∞	0 [2]	2
4	0 [2]	1	1	∞	7
k_j	0	0	5	0	

Figure 4.23 Cost of exclusion computations.

candidate for inclusion; we adopt the rule of breaking ties by arbitrary selection. In our illustrative problem we pick cell 3, 4 as the starting point. We shall also adopt the technique of using an inverted tree network to keep track of work as we proceed through the algorithm. Thus far our network looks like the one shown in Figure 4.24. The top node represents all possible solutions; the lower-right node represents all solutions that contain leg 3, 4; the lower-left node represents all solutions that do not contain leg 3, 4, for example, $\overline{3, 4}$.

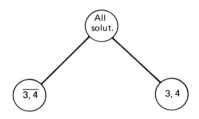

Figure 4.24 Developing the branch-and-bound network.

Step 2. Compute the lower bound of the cost of all solutions that include the first leg.

We know from our previous work with reduced matrices that the best we can hope for as the lowest cost to the reduced matrix is $\sum_{i=1}^{m} r_i + \sum_{j=1}^{n} k_j$. In our case then the lower bound for all solutions would be $LB_{AS} = 3+3+2+7+5 = 20$. What would be the lower bound of all solutions containing cell 3, 4? If we were to examine Figure 4.22 we would note that since our solutions will contain cell 3, 4 we can eliminate row 3 (we cannot go from city 3 to any other city) and column 4 from further consideration. Furthermore, we know that we shall not be able to go to city 3 from city 4 (making $C_{43} = \infty$) thus leaving us with a new matrix shown in Figure 4.25. We note in Figure 4.25 that we no longer have a reduced matrix by virtue of the fact that row 2 does not contain a zero cost cell. Of course by reducing row 2 with an $r_2 = 1$ we can restore the situation and by doing so we also note that the lower bound of solutions containing cell 3, 4 must therefore be the lower bound of all solutions $(LB_{AS} = 20)$ plus the reductions necessary to reduce the matrix of Figure 4.21 $(r_2 = 1)$. Thus $LB_{3,4} = 21$. (We note here that if Figure 4.25 had contained a zero in each row and column thereby eliminating the requirement for any additional reduction that $LB_{3,4} = LB_{AS}$.)

Step 3. Compute the lower bound of the costs of all solutions that do not include the first leg.

 i \ j	1	2	3
1	∞	0	0
2	1	∞	6
4	0	1	∞

Figure 4.25   Remaining matrix.

What, then is the lower bound of solutions not containing 3, 4; for example, $LB_{\overline{3,4}}$? We know that the cost of exclusion of 3, 4 is 2 from Figure 4.23 and it is obvious that if that cost were added to LB_{AS} we would have $LB_{\overline{3,4}}$. With our knowledge of the lower bounds our tree network can be updated to look like Figure 4.26.

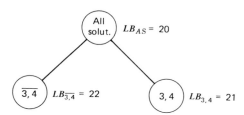

Figure 4.26   Lower bounds.

Step 4.   Select the next leg of the trip for that branch that has the lowest bound.

The branch of solutions containing cell 3, 4 has the lowest bound and therefore our task is to select the next leg for that branch. Returning to Figure 4.25 and remembering that it must be reduced by $r_2 = 1$, we again compute the cost of exclusions for the cells containing a zero cost. You should do so for the practice and can check your work against Figure 4.27. We see that we can select either 1, 3 or 2, 1 and arbitrarily select 1, 3.

Step 5.   Compute the lower bound of the costs of all trips that include the next leg.

The technique used in step 2 is perfectly general and can be used in carrying out the computations for step 5; the actual work is left to you. We find that $LB_{1,3} = 22$.

i \ j	1	2	3
1	∞	[1] 0	[5] 0
2	[5] 0	∞	5
4	[1] 0	1	∞

Figure 4.27 Continuing matrix manipulation.

Step 6. Compute the lower bound of the costs of all trips that do not include the next leg.

Again the technique used in step 3 was perfectly general and can be applied here to yield $LB_{\overline{1,3}} = 26$. Our tree network has developed as shown in Figure 4.28.

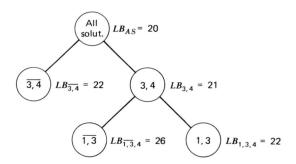

Figure 4.28 The developing network.

Step 7. Return to step 4, until the optimal round trip has been determined.

Observe now that we have three nodes from which we can proceed, for example, $3, 4$; $1, 3$; and $1, 3$. We are to select the node which has the lowest lower bound and therefore could proceed from either $\overline{3,4}$ or $1, 3$ since they are equal. We elect $1, 3$ for which the reduced matrix and costs of exclusions appear as shown in Figure 4.29. From this we select $2, 1$ as our next node, the lower bound of which is computed to be $LB_{2,1} = 22$.

j i	1	2
2	0	∞
4	0	0

Figure 4.29 Continuing matrix manipulation.

We also determine that $LB_{\overline{2,1}} = \infty$ and by updating our tree we arrive at Figure 4.30. We continue our process from 2, 1 and after eliminating row 2 and column 1 of Figure 4.29 there is only one choice, to wit, 4, 2. Our tree network row is complete as shown in Figure 4.31.

We should note that although the algorithm has yielded an optimal solution of cost = 22, the legs of the circuit are not, and will not necessarily be, in logical sequence. However it is not a serious problem to rearrange them. For example the round-trip circuit is, from Figure 4.31, from city 3 to 4 to 2 to 1 to 3. Go back to our original cost matrix in Table 4.1 and verify that the cost of the round trip selected is 22.

Our work with the branch-and-bound technique is not over because we have not looked at the methodology to be used if we proceed down any of the branches that do not include a selected node. We shall now do so using the same illustrative problem. Return to step 1 of the algorithm

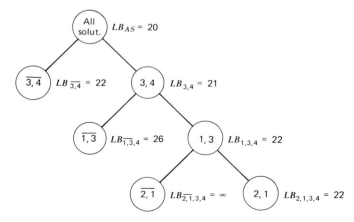

Figure 4.30 Continued network development.

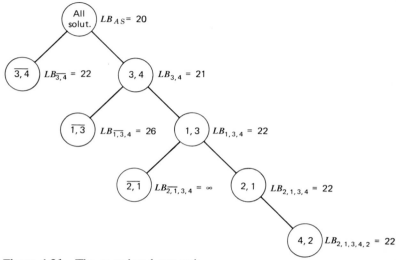

Figure 4.31 The completed network.

and specifically to Figure 4.23. Recall that we had two candidates from which we could select our first leg: 3, 4 or 4, 1. Originally we selected 3, 4—which turned out to be a fortuitous choice since it led us to an optimal solution. What would have happened had we selected 4, 1? Using 4, 1 as the first leg selected, you should complete steps 2 and 3 of the algorithm for practice and should be able to arrive at the tree network shown in Figure 4.32 at the conclusion of step 3. Proceeding to step 4, we

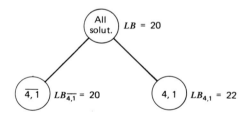

Figure 4.32 Developing an alternative node.

see that we will be picking the next leg after cell 4, 1; again, two possibilities exist: 1, 3 or 2, 4, both of which have a cost of exclusion of 6. Selecting 2, 4 (step 4) complete steps 5 and 6 and you should arrive at the tree network shown in Figure 4.33. Step 7 requires us to return to step 4 to continue the process but now note that the lowest lower bound is $LB_{\overline{4,1}} = 22$. The methodology for proceeding with our algorithm differs

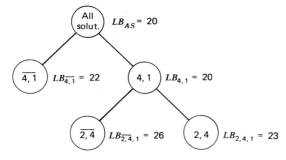

Figure 4.33   Continuing the alternative network.

somewhat now since we must return to the cost matrix associated with the node with which we are going to be working. In our case this means returning to the reduced cost matrix, shown in Figure 4.22. Now since we are going to exclude 4, 1 from all our solutions we must insure that the cost of cell 4, 1 is prohibitive to keep it from entering our solution; the easy way to do that is to substitute ∞ for the cost shown in cell 4, 1. This presents us with a matrix that does not include a zero in either row 4 or column 1 but we can continue reduction as we have been doing all along. By doing so and computing the cost of exclusions as we did before we arrive at the cost matrix for node $\overline{4, 1}$, shown in Figure 4.34. As before, the sum of the r_i and k_j should provide us with the cost of all solutions excluding 4, 1 and a quick check shows us that it does. The next leg is

i \ j	1	2	3	4	r_i
1	∞	0 $\boxed{0}$	0 $\boxed{0}$	2	3
2	0 $\boxed{1}$	∞	6	0 $\boxed{0}$	3
3	1	3	∞	0 $\boxed{1}$	2
4	∞	0 $\boxed{0}$	0 $\boxed{0}$	∞	8
k_j	1	0	5	0	

Figure 4.34   The new reduced cost matrix.

determined by the cell containing the largest cost of exclusion and we see we have two candidates 2, 1 and 3, 4. Let us select 2, 1. The techniques for computing the lower bounds for the new nodes remain and by their application you should arrive at the network shown in Figure 4.35. We now have examined the complete methodology necessary in the branch-and-bound algorithm and the completion of the network after Figure 4.35 is left to the reader. You should arrive at the same answer we obtained before.

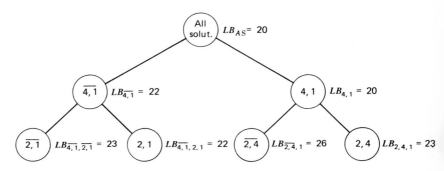

Figure 4.35 Continued network development.

**4.6
SEPARABLE
PROGRAMMING**

There are a number of problems that are encountered that do not permit the use of any of the foregoing techniques for reasons of non-linearity. Although an exhaustive treatment of all the techniques available for dealing with such problems is beyond the scope of this text, we cannot move on without a treatment of at least one such technique. Take for example the problem:

EXAMPLE

$$\text{Maximize } -X^2 + 8X + 4$$

subject to

$$1 \le X \le 7$$

We have thus far discussed no technique that would permit us to solve this problem. It should be clear, however, that if we could express the objective function as a linear function, we could handle its solution easily. While the latter is not precisely possible, examination of the graphical presentation of the objective function does show that it can be approximated by a series of straight lines as shown in Figure 4.36. That is in the range of values of x of interest to us we now can express an approximation of $f(x)$ in terms of x linearly. Recalling that the equation for a straight line can be expressed as

$$f(x) = y = mx + c = \frac{y_j - y_i}{x_j - x_i} x + y_i - \left(\frac{y_j - y_i}{x_j - x_i} \right) x_i$$

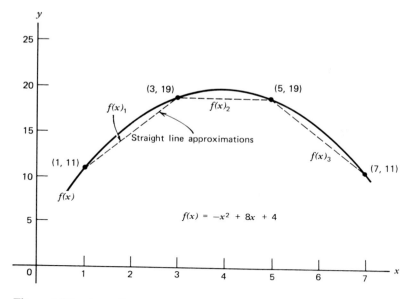

Figure 4.36 A nonlinear function.

and using subscripts to denote each of linear segments, we can for the first segment, $f(x)_1$, say

$$m_1 = \frac{y_2 - y_1}{x_2 - x_1} = \frac{19 - 11}{3 - 1} = 4$$

and

$$c_1 = y_1 - m_1 x_1 = 11 - 4(1) = 7$$

Thus

$$f(x)_1 = 4x + 7 \qquad 1 \le x \le 3$$

and, similarly, we can determine that

$$f(x)_2 = 19 \qquad 3 \le x \le 5$$

and

$$f(x)_3 = -4x + 39 \qquad 5 \le x \le 7$$

What we have done is used pairs of successive points along $f(x)$ to obtain our approximations $f(x)_i$. If we denote the first point of a successive pair as x_k, y_k and the second point of the pair as x_{k+1}, y_{k+1}, then, in general, we could say that

$$f(x)_i = \left(\frac{y_{k+1}-y_k}{x_{k+1}-x_k}\right)x + y_k - \left(\frac{y_{k+1}-y_k}{x_{k+1}-x_k}\right)x_k$$

$$= \left(\frac{y_{k+1}-y_k}{x_{k+1}-x_k}\right)(x - x_k) + y_k \qquad x_k \leq x \leq x_{k+1} \qquad (4.8)$$

Furthermore, we can say that any x in a particular interval can be expressed as the sum of some fractional part, for example, λ_{k+1} of x_{k+1} and some fractional part, $1-\lambda_{k+1}$, of x_k. Thus

$$x = \lambda_{k+1}x_{k+1} + (1-\lambda_{k+1})x_k$$

which, after expansion and rearrangement of terms, gives us

$$x - x_k = \lambda_{k+1}(x_{k+1}-x_k) \qquad (4.9)$$

Substituting (4.9) in (4.8) we obtain

$$f(x)_i = \left(\frac{y_{k+1}-y_k}{x_{k+1}-x_k}\right)\lambda_{k+1}(x_{k+1}-x_k) + y_k$$

$$= \lambda_{k+1}(y_{k+1}-y_k) + y_k$$

$$= (1-\lambda_{k+1})y_k + \lambda_{k+1}y_{k+1} \qquad x_k \leq x \leq x_{k+1} \qquad (4.10)$$

Letting $1-\lambda_{k+1} = \lambda_k$ we have, from (4.10),

$$f(x)_i = \lambda_k y_k + \lambda_{k+1}y_{k+1} \qquad x_k \leq x \leq x_{k+1} \qquad (4.11)$$

where

$$\lambda_k + \lambda_{k+1} = 1$$

and

$$\lambda_k, \lambda_{k+1} \geq 0$$

Now if we let $k = 0$ denote the first point in our range of interest, and $k = s$ denote the last point in that range, then $s =$ the number of linear piecewise segments we are using to approximate our original function. Using this notation we can use (4.11) to write a single expression that approximates the original function we are trying to evaluate as follows:

$$f(x) \simeq \lambda_0 y_0 + \lambda_1 y_1 + \lambda_2 y_2 + \ldots + \lambda_s y_s$$

$$\simeq \sum_{k=0}^{s} \lambda_k y_k \qquad (4.12)$$

where

$$\sum_{k=0}^{s} \lambda_k = 1 \qquad \lambda_k \geq 0$$

Note that when any two adjacent points of one linear segment of the approximation are being evaluated as in (4.11) that the sum of the lambdas associated with those adjacent points must equal one and, therefore, all other lambdas must equal zero.

This technique of piecewise linear approximation is perfectly general **EXAMPLE** and can be applied to a continuous nonlinear function of more than one variable provided that the function is separable. For example, suppose we had the function

$$f = 4X_1 + 3X_1^2 - X_2$$

Inspection reveals that the function can easily be separated into two separate functions such that

$$f_1(X_1) = 4X_1 + 3X_1^2$$
$$f_2(X_2) = X_2$$

and, hence,

$$f(X_1, X_2) = f_1(X_1) - f_2(X_2) \qquad (4.13)$$

Then by utilizing (4.12) we could write

$$f \approx \sum_{k=0}^{s_1} \lambda_{1k} y_{1k} - \sum_{k=0}^{s_2} \lambda_{2k} y_{2k}$$

Since the process is perfectly general (provided that the function we are dealing with is separable*) we could say, for any continuous nonlinear separable function,

$$f(X_1, X_2 \ldots X_n)$$

that a piecewise linear approximation can be developed so that

$$f(X_1, X_2 \ldots X_n) \approx \sum_{k=0}^{s_1} \lambda_{1k} y_{1k} + \sum_{k=0}^{s_2} \lambda_{2k} y_{2k} + \ldots + \sum_{k=0}^{s_n} \lambda_{nk} y_{nk} \qquad (4.14)$$

provided that

$$\sum_{k=0}^{s_j} \lambda_{jk} = 1 \qquad j = 1, 2, \ldots n$$

$$\lambda_{jk} \geq 0 \qquad \begin{cases} j = 1, 2, \ldots n \\ k = 0, 1, \ldots s_j \end{cases}$$

---

* There are techniques available whereby many functions that do not appear to be separable can, in fact, be separated; however, such treatment is beyond the scope of this text. The interested reader should consult C. McMillan Jr., *Mathematical Programming*, Wiley, New York, 2nd ed., 1975.

Now let us utilize separable programming in an optimization problem. Of course, by now you probably have deduced that we are going to take a continuous nonlinear separable function, approximate it by a piecewise linear function, and then operate on the approximation by the simplex algorithm. And that is essentially what we do via the following algorithm.

STEP 1. Express the functions involved in the problem as separate functions.

STEP 2. Partition the domain of each variable into a number of segments.

STEP 3. Evaluate the separate functions at the endpoints of each segment.

STEP 4. Generate a linear programming problem in the λ_{jk} with suitable constraints on the λ_{jk}.

STEP 5. Solve for the λ_{jk}.

STEP 6. Solve for the original variables.

EXAMPLE

For illustrative purposes let us solve the problem

$$\text{Maximize} \quad X_1^2 - X_1 + X_2$$
$$\text{subject to} \quad X_1 + X_2^2 \leq 4$$
$$X_1, X_2 \geq 0$$

Step 1. Express the functions as separate functions.

This can be done very easily by utilizing (4.13) once you have determined that the functions are indeed separable. In our illustrative example this is the case, and so we can say that

$$f(X_1, X_2) = f_1(X_1) + f_2(X_2)$$
where
$$f_1(X_1) = X_1^2 - X_1, f_2(X_2) = X_2$$

Note, however, that the first constraint is also a separable function and we must also operate on it. Since Equation 4.13 is general we can say, for all constraints, that

$$g_i = g_{i1}(X_1) + g_{i2}(X_2) + \ldots + g_{in}(X_n) \qquad i = 1, 2, \ldots m$$

In this case we have only the one constraint to concern ourselves with and we have

$$g_1(X_1, X_2) = g_{11}(X_1) + g_{12}(X_2)$$
where
$$g_{11}(X_1) = X_1, g_{12}(X_2) = X_2^2$$

Step 2. Partition the domain of each variable into segments.

From our original problem we see that both X_1 and X_2 must be ≥ 0 but the first constraint indicates that $X_1 \leq 4$ and $X_2 \leq 2$. (The variables do not necessarily have to have the same domain.) The number of segments to be used is purely arbitrary and, although the more segments the more accurate the linear approximation, it does not always follow that more segments will lead to a more accurate final answer. (Refer to Figure 4.36 and decide for yourself why this is so.) In our case let us partition the domain of each variable into four segments; thus we will have five points.

Step 3. Evaluate the separate functions at the end points of each segment.

Utilizing a tabular format as shown in Figure 4.37 permits efficient completion of this step. Using that format, you should construct a table outline for the illustrative problem. After you have completed it, com-pare your table outline with Figure 4.38. You can now begin to fill in your table. We know that at $k = 0$, $X_{1k} = X_{1,0}$, and, this being the lower range of our domain of interest, we know that $X_{1,0} = 0$. Furthermore, at $k = 1$, $X_{1,1} = 1$ (from step 2 above) and $X_{1,2} = 2$. You can complete the columns X_{1k} and X_{2k} yourself now and after doing so we can start on the column headed $f_1(X_{1k})$. From step 1 above we know that

$$f_1(X_{1k}) = X_{1k}{}^2 - X_{1k}$$

and at

$$k = 0 \qquad X_{1,0} = 0$$

Thus

$$f_1(X_{1k}) = 0 \qquad k = 0$$

Similarly,

$$f_1(X_{1k}) = 0 \qquad k = 1$$

You should now be able to complete the evaluation of the separate functions as required by this step of the algorithm and should do so. Compare your evaluation with that shown in Figure 4.39.

Step 4. Generate a linear programming problem in the λ_{jk}.

We are now ready to utilize (4.14) and it, in combination with our evaluation in Figure 4.39, permits us to write the following problem:

$$\text{Maximize} \quad f(X_1, X_2) \simeq \sum_{k=0}^{4} \lambda_{1k} f_{1k} + \sum_{k=0}^{4} \lambda_{2k} f_{2k} =$$

$$2\lambda_{12} + 6\lambda_{13} + 12\lambda_{14} + .5\lambda_{21} + \lambda_{22} + 1.5\lambda_{23} + 2\lambda_{24}$$

k	X_{1k}	X_{2k}	$\cdots$	X_{nk}	$f_2(X_{1k})$	$f_2(X_{2k})$	$\cdots$	$f_n(X_{nk})$	$g_{11}(X_{1k})$	$g_{12}(X_{2k})$	$\cdots$	$g_{1n}(X_{nk})$	$g_{21}(X_{1k})$	$g_{22}(X_{2k})$	$\cdots$	$g_{2n}(X_{nk})$	$g_{m1}(X_{1k})$	$g_{m2}(X_{2k})$	$\cdots$	$g_{mn}(X_{nk})$
0																				
1																				
2																				
$\cdot$																				
$\cdot$																				
s																				

Figure 4.37 Tabular Format for Evaluating Functions.

k	X_{1k}	X_{2k}	$f_1(X_{1k})$	$f_2(X_{2k})$	$g_{11}(X_{1k})$	$g_{12}(X_{2k})$
0						
1						
2						
3						
4						

Figure 4.38   Table Outline for Illustrative Problem.

k	X_{1k}	X_{2k}	$f_1(X_{1k})$	$f_2(X_{2k})$	$g_{11}(X_{1k})$	$g_{12}(X_{2k})$
0	0	0	0	0	0	0
1	1	.5	0	.5	1	.25
2	2	1	2	1	2	1
3	3	1.5	6	1.5	3	2.25
4	4	2	12	2	4	4

Figure 4.39   The Completed Evaluation Table.

subject to

$$g_1(X_1, X_2) \simeq \sum_{k=0}^{4} \lambda_{1k}g_{1k} + \sum_{k=0}^{4} \lambda_{2k}g_{2k} =$$

$$\lambda_{11} + 2\lambda_{12} + 3\lambda_{13} + 4\lambda_{14} + .25\lambda_{21}$$

$$+ \lambda_{22} + 2.25\lambda_{23} + 4\lambda_{24} \le 4$$

$$\sum_{k=0}^{4} \lambda_{1k} = \lambda_{10} + \lambda_{11} + \lambda_{12} + \lambda_{13} + \lambda_{14} = 1$$

$$\sum_{k=0}^{4} \lambda_{2k} = \lambda_{20} + \lambda_{21} + \lambda_{22} + \lambda_{23} + \lambda_{24} = 1$$

$$\lambda_{jk} \ge 0 \quad \begin{cases} j = 1, 2 \\ k = 0, 1, 2, 3, 4 \end{cases}$$

For ease in utilizing the complex algorithm in subsequent steps, the condition exists that no more than two of the lambdas associated with X_1 and X_2 are greater than zero, and if two lambdas associated with a variable are greater than zero, then the fact that those two lambdas must be adjacent points has not been stated mathematically as a constraint. However, we must remember to keep this constraint in mind as we move from tableau to tableau.

Step 5. Solve for the λ_{jk}.

We are now on familiar ground and by introducing a slack variable, S_1, we can write the first constraint as an equality. We must also introduce artificial variables R_2 and R_3 to the second and third constraints and proceed to use the simplex algorithm to solve our piecewise linear approximation. The first tableau that results is shown in Figure 4.40. After driving out the two artificial variables the resulting tableau is shown in Figure 4.41 and yields the solution

$$\lambda_{10} = 1 \qquad \lambda_{20} = 1 \qquad S_1 = 4 \qquad \text{all other variables} = 0$$

and indicates improvement is possible by letting λ_{14} enter the solution.

However, what will happen if we introduce λ_{14} into the basis? It appears that λ_{14} will replace S_1 while λ_{10} and λ_{20} remain in the basis. Clearly λ_{10} and λ_{14} are not adjacent points and this is a situation we cannot tolerate. There is, of course, another alternative in this case in that we could permit λ_{14} to replace λ_{10}. In that case we would have S_1, λ_{14} and λ_{20} in our basis, a perfectly acceptable condition. Doing so would result in the tableau shown in Figure 4.42 which yields the solution $\lambda_{14} = 1$, $\lambda_{20} = 1$, all other variables $= 0$ and indicates improvement is possible by letting λ_{24} enter the solution. Is there any reason why λ_{24} cannot be permitted to enter the solution? Examination of the tableau shows it may replace λ_{20} and there does not appear to be any reason why it should not. However, if you try to do so, and you should, you will discover, in the process of row transformations, that $S_1 = b_1 = -4$. This is a violation of a constraint since no b_i may ever be negative. Next note that there are other $C_j - Z_j$ values in Figure 4.42, which are positive, indicating the possibility that improvement in the objective function may be realized from the insertion of either λ_{21}, λ_{22}, or λ_{23}. In each case this could be done by removing λ_{20} from the basis. Of course we should try λ_{23} first since, of the three, it offers the largest positive increment. This is a perfectly general procedure in separable programming and as long as positive $C_j - Z_j$ increments remain in the tableau we must attempt to bring the corresponding variables into our solution. Two constraints must be kept in mind in doing so, however, and we have encountered both in our illustrative problem. We must remember that if two lambdas associated with one variable enter our solution, they must be an adjacent pair, and second, we

	C_j	0	0	2	6	12	0	.5	1	1.5	2	0	$-M$	$-M$		
Variables In Solution	Var. C_i	λ_{10}	λ_{11}	λ_{12}	λ_{13}	λ_{14}	λ_{20}	λ_{21}	λ_{22}	λ_{23}	λ_{24}	S_1	R_2	R_3	b	
S_1	0	0	1	2	3	4	0	1/4	1	9/4	4	1	0	0	4	—
R_2	$-M$	①	1	1	1	1	0	0	0	0	0	0	1	0	1	1
R_3	$-M$	0	0	0	0	0	1	1	1	1	1	0	0	1	1	—
Z_j		$-M$	$-M$	$-M$	$-M$	$-M$	$-M$	$-M$	$-M$	$-M$	$-M$	0	$-M$	$-M$	$-2M$	
$C_j - Z_j$		M	M	M	M	M	M	M	M	M	M	0	M	M	$2M$	

Figure 4.40 The initial tableau.

C_j	0	0	2	6	12	0	.5	1	1.5	2	0	$-M$	$-M$		
Variables In Solution	Var. C_j	λ_{10}	λ_{11}	λ_{12}	λ_{13}	λ_{14}	λ_{20}	λ_{21}	λ_{22}	λ_{23}	λ_{24}	S_1	R_2	R_3	b	
S_1	0	0	1	2	3	④	0	1/4	1	9/4	4	1	0	0	4	1
λ_{10}	0	1	1	1	1	1	0	0	0	0	0	0	1	0	1	1
λ_{20}	0	0	0	0	0	0	1	1	1	1	1	0	0	1	1	—
Z_j		0	0	0	0	0	0	0	0	0	0	0	0	0	0	
$C_j - Z_j$		0	2	6	12	0	.5	1	1.5	2	0	$-M$	$-M$	0		

Figure 4.41 Improving the initial solution.

Variables In Solution	Var C_j	C_j 0 λ_{10}	0 λ_{11}	2 λ_{12}	6 λ_{13}	12 λ_{14}	0 λ_{20}	.5 λ_{21}	1 λ_{22}	1.5 λ_{23}	2 λ_{24}	0 S_1	$-M$ R_2	$-M$ R_3	b
S_1	0	-4	-3	-2	-1	0	0	$1/4$	1	$9/4$	④	1	-4	0	0
λ_{14}	12	1	1	1	1	1	0	0	0	0	0	0	1	0	1
λ_{20}	0	0	0	0	0	0	1	1	1	1	1	0	0	1	1
Z_j		12	12	12	12	12	0	0	0	0	0	0	0	0	12
$C_j - Z_j$		-12	-12	-10	-6	0	0	.5	1	1.5	2	0	$-M$	$-M$	-12

Figure 4.42 Continuing to improve the solution.

may not bring in any lambda that would cause a b_i value to become negative. In our illustrative problem neither λ_{21}, λ_{22}, or λ_{23} can be brought into the basis by replacing λ_{20}. Substitution of λ_{20} for S_1, which is left as an exercise for the reader, while feasible, will not alter our optimal solution in this case and we must have therefore found the optimal solution to our linear piecewise approximation. It now only remains to translate our solution into terms of the original variables X_1 and X_2.

Step 6. Solve for the original variables.

Recalling the earlier discussion leading to (4.14) we can similarly expand (4.9) to show that

$$X_j = \lambda_{j0}X_{j0} + \lambda_{j1}X_{js_j} + \ldots + \lambda_{js_j}X_{js_j}$$

$$= \sum_{k=0}^{s_j} \lambda_{jk}X_{jk} \qquad j = 1, 2, \ldots n$$

Thus in our illustrative problem we have

$$X_1 = \sum_{k=0}^{4} \lambda_{1k}X_{1k} = (0)(0) + (0)(1) + (0)(2) + (0)(3) + (1)(4) = 4$$

and

$$X_2 = \sum_{k=0}^{4} \lambda_{2k}X_{2k} = (1)(0) + (0)(.5) + (0)(1) + (0)(1.5) + (0)(2) = 0$$

and the evaluation of the objective function yields

$$X_1^2 - X_1 + X_2 = 12$$

4.7 DYNAMIC PROGRAMMING

EXAMPLE

Many times we may find ourselves confronted with a problem containing dynamic elements, such as time considerations, where the system state as it progresses from one stage to another has a profound effect on the final output from the system. Because of this, a decision in the first stage that may not be optimal for that stage may, in fact, be correct since it leads to an optimal outcome after the final stage has been completed. This simple example will illustrate the point; suppose you were based in city A and had to visit city F and wished to minimize travel costs. Suppose also you could make the trip either over route A, B, D, F or route A, C, E, F. Your initial decision would be a matter of deciding whether to visit B or C first but having decided that you would have to visit either D or E depending on your initial decision. Let's also suppose that while the trip to B is cheaper than the trip to C, the trip from B to F is more expensive than the trip from C to F. Now, even though it may be less expensive to travel from A to B than from A to C, we might not elect to travel to B but rather to C if that would be the cheapest overall trip. In problems of this nature the optimizing technique frequently used is called dynamic programming, and fundamental to this technique are the notions of recursion and Bellman's principle of optimality [1].

Recursion in mathematics involves the determination of a successive element by operations on a preceding element according to a formula. Let us look at a simple problem and solve it recursively. We wish to divide 27 kilograms of a raw material into three parts so that the product of the weight of the parts is maximized.

Let $f_n(w)$ = the maximum product of the weights of the parts given a total available weight of w when w is divided into n parts. If we were to "divide" w into one part we would have

$$f_1(w) = w \qquad (4.15)$$

Now suppose we were to divide w into two parts with one of the parts containing y kilograms. Then

$$f_2(w) = \text{maximum of all possible products of } (y)f_1(w-y)$$
$$\text{as } y \text{ varied from 0 to } w$$

$$= \max\{yf_1(w-y)\} \qquad 0 \le y \le w$$

But from (4.15) we know that

$$f_1(w-y) = w - y \text{ and that therefore}$$

$$f_2(w) = \max\{y(w-y)\} \qquad 0 \le y \le w \qquad (4.16)$$

Now by calculus we find the derivative of $f_2(w)$ with respect to y,

$$\frac{d}{dy}f_2(w) = w - 2y$$

and by setting the derivative equal to zero we find that $f_2(w)$ occurs when $y = w/2$. Then, by substituting the value of y in (4.16), we have

$$f_2(w) = (w/2)^2 \qquad (4.17)$$

Having solved for $f_2(w)$ let us solve for $f_3(w)$. We designate z as one of the three parts into which we will divide w. That being the case, then the remainder, $w - z$, will have to be divided into two parts, and we can say

$$f_3(w) = \max_{0 \le z \le w} [zf_2(w-z)] \qquad (4.18)$$

But from (4.17) we know that

$$f_2(w-z) = \left(\frac{w-z}{2}\right)^2$$

and that, therefore,

$$f_3(w) = \max_{0 \le z \le w} \left[z \left(\frac{w-z}{2} \right)^2 \right] \tag{4.19}$$

Utilizing calculus again,

$$\frac{d}{dz} f_3(w) = \frac{w^2 - 4wz + 3z^2}{4}$$

and that $f_3(w)$ occurs when $z = w/3 = 9$

We have now solved our problem recursively and can state from (4.19), (4.17), and (4.15), respectively, that

$$f_3(w) = 9 \left(\frac{27-9}{2} \right)^2 = 729 \qquad z = 9$$

$$f_2(w-z) = (18/2)^2 \quad = 81 \qquad y = 9$$

$$f_1(w - z - y) = 27 - 9 - 9 \ = 9$$

The second concept around which dynamic programming is based, Bellman's principle of optimality, states that an optimal policy has the property that, whatever the initial state and initial decision are, the remaining decisions must constitute an optimal policy with respect to the state resulting from the first decision. Although not explicitly mentioned in the recursive example we just looked at, we were applying Bellman's principle. Look at (4.18), for example, in conjunction with the principle and let us see how it works. Whatever the initial state (e.g., w) and the initial decision (e.g., z) are, the remaining decisions (e.g., y and $w - z - y$) must constitute an optimal policy (e.g., f_2 by definition) with respect to the state resulting from the first decision (the resulting state is $w - z$).

EXAMPLE   Now in order to tie these concepts together in the language of dynamic programming let's redo our illustrative problem. The first thing we want to do is establish our recursive relationship in the framework of Bellman's principle.

Let: $f_N(w)$ be the maximum product of the weights of the parts, given that w is the initial weight to be divided into N parts.

Let: z be the weight of one of the parts as a result of the initial decision.

Then the principle says

$$f_{n+1}(w) = \max_{0 \le z \le w} [zf_n(w-z)] \qquad n = 1, 2, \ldots, N$$

This is a very general recursive relationship for the process we have described since the system could have any number of stages, N, and w could be any weight of raw material. Now knowing that

$$f_1(w) = w$$

we could solve for $f_2(w)$, then $f_3(w)$ and, for that matter, up to $f_N(w)$ where $N =$ whatever the number of stages in our system.

Now that we understand the two concepts fairly well, let's use them in solving another rather simple problem in order to get a better feel for the techniques.

You have been contacted by a distributor who would like to know **EXAMPLE** what his ordering and selling policy should be for a new item he intends to stock. He has an agreement with his supplier that permits him to order on the fifteenth of each month for delivery on the first of the following month at $100 per unit. His initial shipment from the supplier will be 250 units and the supplier will not permit distributors to stock more than 500 units at any given time. The distributor has contacted several of his customers and feels he can sell as many units as he can get at the unit prices shown but is not sure he can sell any beyond the projections shown. The distributor has estimated a schedule of his unit distribution costs for the item which is as indicated.

Month	Distribution Unit Cost($)	Unit Selling Price($)	
0	0	0	(order first shipment)
1	30	145	
2	50	145	
3	45	155	
4	25	155	
5	20	155	
6	20	155	
and thereafter		No sales predictions	

The distributor does not want to take any risk on the new item beyond month 6 at this time but wishes to maximize his profit through that month.

Our problem is to determine how much to order and sell each month. Let us use the following notation:

s_i = sales quantity

p_i = selling price

q_i = quantity ordered, fifteenth   of month$_i$

c_i = distribution unit cost

b_i = inventory levels at beginning

M = maximum beginning inventory

$f_n(b)$ = maximum profit achievable during the *remaining n* months if the stock level is b. Thus f_7 would be the maximum profit achievable for the seven-month period (initial-order month and six months of sales).

We begin by setting up our general recursive relationship. Since our total profit through a month will be the dollars in sales that month ($p_i s_i$) less costs for that month ($c_i s_i + 100 q_i$) plus the profit made in previous months we can say in order to maximize profits that

$$f_{n+1}(b_i) = \max_{\substack{0 \le s_i \le b_i \\ 0 \le q_i \le M - b_i + s_i}} [(p_i - c_i)s_i - 100q_i + f_n(b_{i+1})] \qquad i = 6 - n$$

but

$$b_{i+1} = b_i + q_i - s_i$$

thus

$$f_{n+1}(b_i) = \max_{\substack{0 \le s_i \le b_i \\ 0 \le q_i \le M - b_i + s_i}} [(p_i - c_i)s_i - 100q_i + f_n(b_i + q_i - s_i)] \qquad (4.20)$$

$$i = 6 - n$$

Before we can start applying this recursive relationship in solving the problem we must take a look at the seventh month to determine $f_0(b_7)$. Since we are not sure of any sales in the seventh month, we would not want to order any stock for that month on the fifteenth of the sixth month so that $q_6 = 0$. Furthermore, we would not want to have any stock on hand at the end of the sixth month so that $s_6 = b_6$. Thus

$$f_0(b_7) = f_0(b_6 + q_6 - s_6) = f_0(0) = 0$$

Then, from (4.20),

$$f_1(b_6) = \max_{\substack{0 \le s_6 \le b_6 \\ 0 \le q_6 \le M - b_6 + s_6}} [135s_6 - 100q_6 + f_0(b_7)]$$

$$= 135b_6 = 135(b_5 + q_5 - s_5)$$

from a policy of $s_6 = b_6 = M$ and $q_6 = 0$.

$$f_2(b_5) = \max_{\substack{0 \le s_5 \le b_5 \\ 0 \le q_5 \le M - b_5 + s_5}} [135s_5 - 100q_5 + f_1(b_6)]$$

$$= 135b_5 + 35M$$

from a policy of $s_5 = b_5$ and $q_5 = M$.

$$f_3(b_4) = \max_{\substack{0 \le s_4 \le b_4 \\ 0 \le q_4 \le M - b_4 + s_4}} [130s_4 - 100q_4 + f_2(b_5)]$$

$$= 130b_4 + 70M$$

from a policy of $s_4 = b_4$ and $q_4 = M$.

You should solve for f_4, f_5, f_6, on your own. If your work is correct you should obtain the following:

$f_4(b_3) = 110b_3 + 100M$ from a policy of $s_3 = b_3 = q_3 = M$
$f_5(b_2) = 85b_2 + 110M$ from a policy of $s_2 = b_2$ and $q_2 = M$
$f_6(b_1) = 115b_1 + 110M$ from a policy of $s_1 = b_1$ and $q_1 = 0$
$f_7(b_0) = \$58750$ from a policy of placing initial order for 250

A recapitulation of the order-sell policy is shown in Table 4.6; note that the selling schedule generated is not the maximum sales that would have been possible. What would happen to the profits if maximum possible sales were scheduled?

Table 4.6 Order–Sell Recapitulation

Month i	Inventory Level b_i	Sales s_i	Unit Price p_i	Unit Distr. Costs c_i	Quantity to Order q_i
0	0	0	—	—	250
1	250	250	145	30	0
2	0	0	145	50	500
3	500	500	155	45	500
4	500	500	155	25	500
5	500	500	155	20	500
6	500	500	155	20	0

The general type of problem to be illustrated is first discussed in terms of a simplified example as suggested by Dwyer [6]. A business concern must fill three jobs that demand different abilities and training. Three applicants who can be hired for identical salaries are available. Because of the different abilities, training, and experiences, however, the value of each applicant to the company depends on the job in which he is placed. The estimate of the value of each applicant to the company each year if he were to be assigned to any one of the three jobs is given in Table 4.7.

We want to assign the applicants to the jobs in such a way that the total value to the company is as great as possible. In this problem there are $3! = 6$ possible alternative assignments of the three men and the greatest estimated value to the company, \$24,000 per year, is obtained by assigning applicant 1 to job 3, applicant 2 to job 1, and applicant 3 to job 2.

**4.8
APPLICATION
STUDIES**

4.8.1
*Personnel
Assignment*
(A transportation model
illustration)

Application Study

* This problem has been adapted from P. S. Dwyer, "Solution of the Personnel Classification Problem with the Method of Optimal Regions," *Psychometrika*, Vol. 18, No. 1, March 1954. Used with the permission of *Psychometrika*.

A more general problem is arrived at by denoting by C_{ij} the contribution of individual i to the common effort if he is assigned to job j, in units of the measure of the common effort. Thus in Table 4.7, $C_{11} = 5$, $C_{12} = 4$, $C_{13} = 7$, $C_{21} = 6$, and so on. Sometimes dimensionless C_{ij} may be used to express the relative contributions to the common effort.

Table 4.7 Estimated Value Per Year (in units of $1000)

		Job	
Applicant	1	2	3
1	5	4	7
2	6	7	3
3	8	11	2

A more general problem features M individuals and N jobs in which, as above, the contribution of individual i to the common effort is C_{ij} units if he is assigned to job j. The assignments are then made so that the sum of the corresponding C_{ij} values is a maximum. We set $x_{ij} = 1$ when individual i is assigned to job j and $X_{ij} = 0$ otherwise. Then

$$\sum_i X_{ij} = 1 \qquad \sum_j X_{ij} = 1 \qquad \sum_{i,j} X_{ij} = N$$

and the problem is to maximize

$$T = \sum_{i,j} X_{ij} C_{ij}$$

There are $N!$ values of T, although some of them may be equal, and for N large it becomes impractical to examine them all to determine the maximum.

Frequently there are many identical jobs or jobs that, though not identical, demand the same basic qualifications indicated by the C_{ij}. Such jobs can be combined into a job category. If there are m categories and if the number of jobs grouped in the jth job category is q_j, we have

$$X_{ij} = 1 \text{ if } i \text{ is assigned to } j$$

$$X_{ij} = 0 \text{ otherwise}$$

and

$$\left.\begin{array}{c} \sum_{i=1}^{N} X_{ij} = q_j \\[2em] \sum_{j=1}^{m} X_{ij} = 1 \end{array}\right\} \text{with } \sum_{i,j} X_{ij} = \sum_j q_j = \sum_i 1 = N$$

We wish to maximize the total contribution to the common effort

$$T = \sum_{i,j} X_{ij} C_{ij}$$

The q_j values are called quotas. This formulation of the problem is illustrated in Table 4.8.

Table 4.8 Use of Job Categories

i \ j	1	2	3	$\cdots$	j	$\cdots$	m	
1	c_{11}	c_{12}	c_{13}	$\cdots$	c_{1j}	$\cdots$	c_{1m}	1
2	c_{21}	c_{22}	c_{23}	$\cdots$	c_{2j}	$\cdots$	c_{2m}	1
3	c_{31}	c_{32}	c_{33}	$\cdots$	c_{3j}	$\cdots$	c_{3m}	1
$\cdots$	$\cdots$	$\cdots$	$\cdots$	$\cdots$	$\cdots$	$\cdots$	$\cdots$	1
i	c_{i1}	c_{i2}	c_{i3}	$\cdots$	c_{ij}	$\cdots$	c_{im}	1
$\cdots$	$\cdots$	$\cdots$	$\cdots$	$\cdots$	$\cdots$	$\cdots$	$\cdots$	1
N	c_{N1}	c_{N2}	c_{N3}	$\cdots$	c_{Nj}	$\cdots$	c_{Nm}	1
q_j	q_1	q_2	q_3	$\cdots$	q_j	$\cdots$	q_m	N

Sometimes there are different individuals having identical C_{ij} values or at least the values are close enough so that the individuals may be grouped without serious error. In this case we group these individuals into personnel categories. If there are n personnel categories and the number of individuals grouped in the ith personnel category is f_i, we have

$$X_{ij} = 1 \text{ if some individual in } i \text{ is assigned to } j$$
$$X_{ij} = 0 \text{ otherwise}$$

and

$$\left.\begin{array}{c} \sum_{i=1}^{n} X_{ij} = 1 \\[2em] \sum_{j=1}^{N} X_{ij} = f_i \end{array}\right\} \text{with } \sum_{i,j} X_{ij} = \sum_i f_i = \sum_j 1 = N$$

The values of f_i are called frequencies. This formulation of the problem is illustrated in Table 4.9.

Table 4.9 Use of Personnel Categories

i \ j	1	2	3	$\cdots$	j	$\cdots$	N	f_i
1	c_{11}	c_{12}	c_{13}	$\cdots$	c_{1j}	$\cdots$	c_{1N}	f_1
2	c_{21}	c_{22}	c_{23}	$\cdots$	c_{2j}	$\cdots$	c_{2N}	f_2
3	c_{31}	c_{32}	c_{33}	$\cdots$	c_{3j}	$\cdots$	c_{3N}	f_3
$\cdots$	$\cdots$	$\cdots$	$\cdots$	$\cdots$	$\cdots$	$\cdots$	$\cdots$	$\cdots$
i	c_{i1}	c_{i2}	c_{i3}	$\cdots$	c_{ij}	$\cdots$	c_{iN}	f_i
$\cdots$	$\cdots$	$\cdots$	$\cdots$	$\cdots$	$\cdots$	$\cdots$	$\cdots$	$\cdots$
n	c_{n1}	c_{n2}	c_{n3}	$\cdots$	c_{nj}	$\cdots$	c_{nN}	f_n
q_j	1	1	1	$\cdots$	1	$\cdots$	1	N

A common form of the problem uses both personnel categories and job categories. If, as before, f_i is the number of persons in personnel category i and q_j is the number to be placed in job category j, then

X_{ij} = zero or a positive integer indicating the number of persons in personnel category i assigned to job category j

Then,

$$\sum_{j=1}^{m} X_{ij} = f_i$$

with

$$\sum_{i,j} X_{ij} = \sum_i f_i = \sum_j q_j = N$$

$$\sum_{i=1}^{n} X_{ij} = q_j$$

This formulation of the probem is illustrated in Table 4.10.
Table 4.9 is a special case of Table 4.10 when $q_j = 1$; Table 4.8 is a special case of Table 4.10 when $f_i = 1$, and the square $N \times N$ matrix results when $f_i = 1$ and $q_i = 1$, all of which can be solved with the transportation model algorithm.

Table 4.10 Use of Personnel Categories and Job Categories

i \ j	1	2	3	$\cdots$	j	$\cdots$	m	f_i
1	c_{11}	c_{12}	c_{13}	$\cdots$	c_{1j}	$\cdots$	c_{1m}	f_1
2	c_{21}	c_{22}	c_{23}	$\cdots$	c_{2j}	$\cdots$	c_{2m}	f_2
3	c_{31}	c_{32}	c_{33}	$\cdots$	c_{3j}	$\cdots$	c_{3m}	f_3
$\cdots$	$\cdots$	$\cdots$	$\cdots$	$\cdots$	$\cdots$	$\cdots$	$\cdots$	$\cdots$
i	c_{i1}	c_{i2}	c_{i3}	$\cdots$	c_{ij}	$\cdots$	c_{im}	f_i
$\cdots$	$\cdots$	$\cdots$	$\cdots$	$\cdots$	$\cdots$	$\cdots$	$\cdots$	$\cdots$
n	c_{n1}	c_{n2}	c_{n3}	$\cdots$	c_{nj}	$\cdots$	c_{nm}	f_n
q_j	q_1	q_2	q_3	$\cdots$	q_j	$\cdots$	q_m	N

Consider a multiproduct line that is capable of producing a family of several different product models. Each product part is a discrete item with physical shape, size, weight, and composition. A finished product may consist of only one part, or it may be an assembly of two or more parts. The operation routing for the several products are similar, but there are some differences. The operations, themselves, may vary considerably from one product to another. It will be assumed that the operation routings and the content of each operation on each product has been previously established by a process design department as illustrated by Young [21].

Consider further that demand schedules for the several products are established on a daily, weekly, or monthly basis by a production control department, and that the production line has been physically arranged with a certain number of production stages and a set number of machines or work stations at each stage. The general arrangement of the stages has also been established as part of the plant layout function.

For a given demand period (day, week, month, and so forth) a selected group of products is to be scheduled into the production line. This group may be only a part of the family of products that can be scheduled through the line. Products are to be scheduled through the production line in economic lots, limited by the total demands for the period. That is, one or more batch runs of each product may be made during the demand period, but no batch run may exceed the demand for the given period.

4.8.2
Production
Line
Scheduling*
(An Assignment
Model
Illustration)

Application Study

* Reprinted with permission from *The Journal of Industrial Engineering,* Vol. xviii, January 1967. Copyright © American Institute of Industrial Engineers, Inc., 25 Technology Park/Atlanta, Norcross, Ga. 30071.

First it is desired to establish an optimum order for scheduling the products into the production line, considering the costs of converting the production line setup from one product to another. We will assume that these conversion costs can be estimated or computed from historical data.

In computing the conversion costs from one product to another, considering the time for tool changeover and machine resetting, it also is desirable to include machine and operator delay time costs.

It is desired to find an optimum ordering of the product batch runs that will minimize the total setup costs for the entire schedule of products within a given demand period. In order to examine the use of the assignment model for optimizing this sequence, consider a schedule of five products with the conversion (or setup) costs shown in Table 4.11. The numbers represent the line conversion costs from (source) product to (designation) product (the 1000's on the diagonal are artificial and preclude a product from following itself).

Table 4.11 A Setup Cost Matrix for Solution by the Assignment Model of Linear Programming

		Product to Follow (Destination)					
		1	2	3	4	5	Supply
Product to	1	1000	60	100	70	50	1
Precede	2	90	1000	110	80	30	1
(Source)	3	100	65	1000	80	40	1
	4	80	70	120	1000	50	1
	5	20	75	90	90	1000	1
Demand		1	1	1	1	1	

Table 4.12 Solution Matrix

	Follower				
Predecessor	1	2	3	4	5
1	950	$\cancel{0}$	$\boxed{0}$	$\cancel{0}$	$\cancel{0}$
2	60	950	30	10	$\boxed{0}$
3	60	5	910	$\boxed{0}$	$\cancel{0}$
4	30	$\boxed{0}$	20	910	$\cancel{0}$
5	$\boxed{0}$	35	30	30	980

The solution matrix is shown in Table 4.12 and reveals the least-cost solution, arbitrarily starting with product 1, would be $1 \rightarrow 3 \rightarrow 4 \rightarrow 2 \rightarrow 5$ at a cost of $300.

However, the assignment model by itself may not define an optimum product sequence. In addition, it seems desirable to include a dummy variable in the matrix to allow for the initial condition of the line. Consider the setup cost matrix of Table 4.13 including an initialization variable where:

> I = dummy variable, and where Row I is the initialization costs to set up product i from scratch.
> Column I is the departure costs for the last product scheduled, equal to zero except for C_{II}.
> N = a large number.

Table 4.13 Setup Cost Matrix with Initialization Cost Included

Predecessor	Follower					
	1	2	3	4	5	I
I	4	5	3	7	6	N
1	N	2	5	7	1	0
2	6	N	3	8	2	0
3	8	7	N	4	7	0
4	12	4	6	N	5	0
5	1	3	2	8	N	0

The solution matrix to this problem is shown in Table 4.14 and reveals the least cost solution starting with product 3 to be $I \rightarrow 3 \rightarrow 4 \rightarrow 2 \rightarrow 5 \rightarrow 1 \rightarrow I$ at a cost of $14.

It should be noted that the solution provides one setup and one batch run on each product before any product is scheduled for a second batch run. The running of all products to be sequenced may be considered a run cycle. If additional run cycles are required, new cost values would be introduced into the matrix for the initialization variable I. It may be noted that one value would be zero, the case where the last product scheduled during the first-run cycle becomes the first product scheduled during the second-run cycle.

These optimal sequence models may easily be solved by hand computation for a small number of products. Where a larger number of products is to be sequenced into the line or where on-line computer control is desired, computerized procedures are available.

Table 4.14 Solution Matrix

			Follower			
Predecessor	1	2	3	4	5	I
I	⊠	⊠	[0]	3	2	N
1	N	⊠	5	3	⊠	[0]
2	5	N	3	4	[0]	⊠
3	7	5	N	[0]	6	⊠
4	9	[0]	4	N	2	⊠
5	[0]	1	2	4	N	⊠

Table 4.15 Shipping Cost Data

	S_1	S_2	S_3	D_1	D_2	D_3	D_4	D_5	S_i	
	0	2	1	3	2	3	4	1	100	S_1
	2	0	3	4	1	2	4	2	125	S_2
	1	3	0	1	0	5	3	2	75	S_3
	3	4	1	0	4	1	3	2		D_1
	2	1	0	4	0	2	1	5		D_2
	3	2	5	1	2	0	2	1		D_3
	4	4	3	3	1	2	0	3		D_4
	1	2	2	2	5	1	3	0		D_5
D_j				100	60	40	75	25		

Consider the cost array shown in Table 4.15, which depicts the unit costs of shipping goods from three factories and five warehouses to each other, the factories' capacities to produce the goods, and the warehouses' demands for the goods as suggested by Garvin [8].

The dummy supply, B, is established at 300 units the total of the three factories' capacities. An initial feasible solution was developed and is shown in Table 4.16. After four iterations we reach the optimal solution shown in Table 4.17. The difference between $B = 300$ and the X_{ii} (shown along the main diagonal) represents the amount that each point

4.8.3
Factory–Warehouse Distribution*
(A transshipment model illustration)

Application Study

Table 4.16 An Initial Solution

Each cell below shows the unit cost, followed by the allocation (in parentheses) where one exists.

	S_1	S_2	S_3	D_1	D_2	D_3	D_4	D_5	S_i
S_1	0 (300)	2	1	3 (25)	2	3	4 (50)	1 (25)	400
S_2	2	0 (300)	3	4	1 (60)	2 (40)	4 (25)	2	425
S_3	1	3	0 (300)	1 (75)	0	5	3	2	375
D_1	3	4	1	0 (300)	4	1	3	2	300
D_2	2	1	0	4	0 (300)	2	1	5	300
D_3	3	2	5	1	2	0 (300)	2	1	300
D_4	4	4	3	3	1	2	0 (300)	3	300
D_5	1	2	2	2	5	1	3	0 (300)	300
D_j	300	300	300	400	360	340	375	325	

Table 4.17 The Optimal Solution

	S_1	S_2	S_3	D_1	D_2	D_3	D_4	D_5	S_i	
cost	0	2	1	3	2	3	4	1	400	S_1
alloc	300		35					65		
cost	2	0	3	4	1	2	4	2	425	S_2
alloc		300			125					
cost	1	3	0	1	0	5	3	2	375	S_3
alloc			265	100	10					
cost	3	4	1	0	4	1	3	2		D_1
alloc				300					300	
cost	2	1	0	4	0	2	1	5		D_2
alloc					225		75		300	
cost	3	2	5	1	2	0	2	1		D_3
alloc						300			300	
cost	4	4	3	3	1	2	0	3		D_4
alloc							300		300	
cost	1	2	2	2	5	1	3	0		D_5
alloc						40		260	300	
D_j	300	300	300	400	360	340	375	325		
	S_1	S_2	S_3	D_1	D_2	D_3	D_4	D_5		

transships. We see that factory 3 transships 35 units, warehouse 2 transships 75 units, and warehouse 5 transships 40 units, and all other points transship nothing. Interpreting the off-diagonal boxes, we see that factory 1 ships 35 units to factory 3 and 65 units to warehouse 5. Factory 2 ships 125 units to warehouse 2. Factory 3 ships 100 units to warehouse 1 and 10 units to warehouse 2. Warehouses 1, 3, and 4 ship nothing, but warehouse 2 ships 75 units to warehouse 4, and warehouse 5 ships 40 units to warehouse 3. This shipping pattern is shown in Figure 4.43. We can readily verify that this pattern of shipments satisfies the factory productions and the warehouse demands.

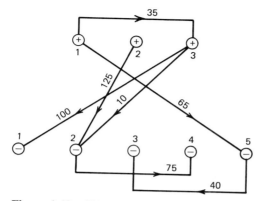

Figure 4.43   Shipping pattern.

4.8.4
Shipment
Loading*
(a branch-and-
bound
illustration)

Application Study

Consider the problem of loading a number of shipments on a cargo carrier where each shipment may not be broken into parts and the total weight of all shipments to be loaded exceeds the weight capacity of the cargo carrier suggested by Kolesar [9]. We wish to maximize the total value of the shipments loaded on the carrier where load capacity is $W = 100$; pertinent data on the shipments are given in the following table:

Shipment No.	Weight (w_i)	Value (v_i)
1	40	40
2	50	60
3	30	10
4	10	10
5	10	3
6	40	20
7	30	60

A preliminary test reveals that the problem possesses a nonempty feasible solution and is not trivial, because $\sum w_i > 100$. We compute the ratios v_i/w_i and reorder the items. They are given overleaf with the new indexing.

* This problem has been adapted from P. J. Kolesar, "A Branch and Bound Algorithm for the Knapsack Problem," *Management Science*, Vol. 13, No. 9, May 1967. Used with permission of *Management Science*.

New Index	Shipment	w_i	v_i	v_i/w_i
1	7	30	60	2
2	2	50	60	6/5
3	1	40	40	1
4	4	10	10	1
5	6	40	20	1/2
6	3	30	10	1/3
7	5	10	3	3/10

The first node shown in Figure 4.44 is that including all possible solutions. The first branching uses index 1 as the first pivot and at node 2 where this index is excluded (noted by an asterisk) from the solution the upper bound is computed by

$$B(2) = v_2 + v_3 + v_4 = 110$$

Note that since we are seeking to maximize the total value of the loading we are concerned with working with upper bounds rather than lower bounds and that we cannot proceed beyond v_4 in determining that bound since $w_2 + w_3 + w_4 = 100 = W$.

At node 3, where index 1 is included, we obtain

$$B(3) = v_1 + v_2 + 1/2 v_3 = 140$$

Note that $w_1 + w_2 + 1/2 w_3 = 100 = W$ and we could not proceed down this branch beyond $1/2 w_3$. Since what we are concerned with here are upper bounds, it is perfectly permissible to divide a shipment for that purpose as long as we do not include a divided shipment in our loadings; infeasible loading is noted by a bound of -999.

Since $B(3)$ is the maximum upper bound, the next branching is made at node 3 and index 2 is selected as the pivot. The results of the repeated application of the process are given in Figure 4.44. The optimum is reached at node 15. The total value is 133 and is attained by loading items 7, 2, 4, and 5.

4.8.5
Capital
Budgeting*
(a dynamic
programming
illustration)

The problem of selecting projects for investment given a limited budget is generally called the capital budgeting problem and is treated by Nemhauser [14]. One procedure for choosing the "best" projects is to rank them according to decreasing interest rate of return and then to select projects from the "top of the list" up to and including project k, where k is defined such that if project $k+1$ were chosen the budget

* Reprinted with permission from *The Journal of Industrial Engineering*, Vol. xviii, June 1967. Copyright © American Institute of Industrial Engineers, Inc., 25 Technology Park/Atlanta, Norcross, Ga. 30071.

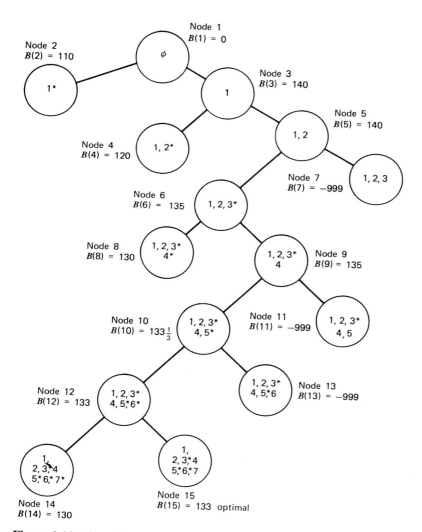

Figure 4.44   Complete tree.

constraint would be violated. However, this procedure may not maximize the present worth* of the projects chosen. Weingartner [20] stated:

Application Study

> ... it is possible that a single large project may have a high ratio of present value to cost, but its size may preclude the execution of a higher net present value through fuller exploitation of the budget constraint.

When there are not more than three budget constraints, cleverly organized dynamic programming calculations are probably most efficient in this type of problem.†

The dynamic programming procedure with one budget constraint will be illustrated. Let a_n be the present worth of project n, c_n be the investment required for project n, K be the total capital available for investment, and N the number of projects. Applying the dynamic programming principle of optimality yields the recursion equations

$$f_n(x) = f_{n-1}(x) \qquad x - c_n < 0$$
$$f_n(x) = \max\left[f_{n-1}(x),\ a_n + f_{n-1}(x - c_n)\right] \qquad x - c_n \geq 0$$
$$\text{for } n = 1, \ldots, N \qquad \text{and} \qquad 0 \leq x \leq K$$

where x is the budget available to allocate among projects 1 through n and $f_n(x) = $ maximum present worth attainable from projects 1 through n with budget x. The procedure is initiated with $f_0(x) = 0$.

These equations simply state that, for budget x, project n should be selected if and only if its present worth plus the maximum present worth attainable from projects 1 through $n-1$ with budget $x - c_n$ exceeds the maximum present worth attainable from projects 1 through $n-1$ with budget x.

With an effective program, these equations can be solved for large values of N very rapidly on a digital computer. It is important to note that $f_n(x)$ is a monotonic nondecreasing step function and that only f_n values where there is a change in the step function have to be calculated.

To illustrate the calculations, consider a problem with the data given in Table 4.18 where $K = 100$.

For $n = 1$

$$f_1(x) = \max(0, 63) \qquad x - 51 \geq 0$$
$$f_1(x) = 0 \qquad x - 51 < 0$$

---

* The present worth or value of a project is

$$PW = \sum_{n=0}^{N} S_n/(1+r)^n$$

where r is the firm's internal rate of return. Maximizing the present worth of all the projects is, under reasonable assumptions, equivalent to maximizing the firm's net worth.
† More than one budget constraint can arise when investments are required in more than one period or when more than one type of resource is restricted.

Table 4.18 Capital Budget Data

n	1	2	3	4	5
a_n	63	52	40	28	20
c_n	51	42	32	23	15

Thus

$$f_1(x) = 63 \qquad 51 \leq x \leq 100 \quad \text{(project 1 accepted)}$$
$$= 0 \qquad 0 \leq x \leq 50 \qquad \text{(project 1 rejected)}$$

For $n = 2$

$$f_2(x) = \max\,[f_1(x),\, 52 + f_1(x - 42)]$$

A series of simple comparisons yields the results given in Table 4.19. The results for $n = 3$ and 4 are summarized in Tables 4.20 and 4.21, respectively.

Table 4.19 Calculations for $n = 2$

$a \leq x \leq b$			
a	b	$f_2(x)$	Projects Accepted
0	41	0	None
42	50	52	2
51	92	63	1
93	100	115	1, 2

Table 4.20 Calculations for $n = 3$

$a \leq x \leq b$			
a	b	$f_3(x)$	Projects Accepted
62	73	63	1
74	82	92	2, 3
83	92	103	1, 3
93	100	115	1, 2

For $n = 3$, values of x below 62 do not need to be considered since the maximum investment in projects 4 and 5 is 38.

Table 4.21 Calculations for $n = 4$

$a \le x \le b$		$f_4(x)$	Projects Accepted
a	b		
85	92	103	1, 3
93	96	115	1, 2
97	100	120	2, 3, 4

For $n = 4$, values of x below 85 need not be considered since the investment in project 5 is 15.

At $n = 5$, with $x = 100$

$$f_5(100) = \max \left[f_4(100), 20 + f_4(85) \right]$$
$$= \max (120, 123) = 123$$

Hence projects 1, 3, and 5 are accepted and the optimal present worth is 123.

**4.9
PROBLEMS**

Set up the standard transportation tableau for problems 1 through 3 and develop an initial basic feasible solution.

1. Minimize $\sum_{i=1}^{m} \sum_{j=1}^{n} C_{ij} X_{ij}$ subject to

$$\sum_{i=1}^{3} X_{ij} \ge D_j \qquad j = 1, 2, 3, 4$$

$$\sum_{j=1}^{4} X_{ij} \ge S_i \qquad i = 1, 2, 3$$

$$X_{ij} \ge 0 \qquad \text{for all } i \text{ and } j$$

	1	2	3	4
A	4	5	6	7
$C_{ij} = $ B	8	7	4	3
C	2	1	6	2

$j =$	1	2	3	4
$D_j =$	10	15	17	13

$i =$	A	B	C
$S_i =$	17	18	20

2. Minimize $\quad 4X_{11}+5X_{12}+6X_{13}+8X_{21}+7X_{22}+4X_{23}+2X_{31}+$ $X_{32}+6X_{33}$ subject to

$$X_{11}+X_{21}+X_{31}=10$$
$$X_{12}+X_{22}+X_{32}=15$$
$$X_{13}+X_{23}+X_{33}=17$$
$$X_{11}+X_{12}+X_{13}\leq17$$
$$X_{21}+X_{22}+X_{23}\leq18$$
$$X_{31}+X_{32}+X_{33}\leq20$$

$$X_{ij}\geq0 \text{ for all } i \text{ and } j$$

3. Maximize $5X_{11} + 6X_{12} + 7X_{13} + 7X_{21} + 4X_{22} + 3X_{23} + X_{31} +$ $6X_{32}+2X_{33}$ subject to

$$X_{11}+X_{21}+X_{31}\leq25$$
$$X_{12}+X_{22}+X_{32}\leq18$$
$$X_{13}+X_{23}+X_{33}\leq12$$

$$\sum_{j=1}^{3} X_{ij} = 14 \qquad i = 1, 2, 3$$

$$X_{ij}\geq0 \qquad \text{for all } i \text{ and } j$$

4. Solve problem 1.
5. Solve problem 2.
6. Solve problem 3.
7. A manufacturer has three plants from which he supplies five warehouses by truck transport. Road distances from the plants to the warehouses are shown in Table 4.22. The manufacturer has a contract

Table 4.22 Road Distance (Miles)

Plant \ W'hse	1	2	3	4	5
A	62.5	93.75	125	187.5	250
B	250	125	62.5	93.75	125
C	125	62.5	250	187.5	312.5

with a freight hauling firm that charges him $.05 per metric ton kilometer for transporting his products to the warehouses. The plants' monthly capacities and the warehouses' monthly requirements are shown in Table 4.23. The manufacturer wishes to minimize his transportation costs.

Table 4.23 Capacities and Requirements (short tons)

Plant Capacity			Warehouse Requirements				
A	B	C	1	2	3	4	5
220.51	165.38	137.82	110.25	82.69	137.82	165.38	55.13

What should the shipping pattern be and how much will it cost per month?

8. The personnel manager of a manufacturing company is in the process of filling 175 jobs in six different entry level skills due to the establishment of a third shift by the company. Union wage scales and requirements for the skills are shown in Table 4.24. Two-hundred and

Table 4.24 Pay Scales and Skill Requirements

Entry Level Skill	A	B	C	D	E	F
Wage scale, $/week	100	110	120	130	140	150
Number required	25	29	31	40	33	17

thirty applicants for the jobs have been tested and their aptitudes and skills for the jobs in question have been matched against company standards and evaluated. The applicants have been grouped into four categories by their abilities; the grouping and values of each category to the company are shown in Table 4.25. How many applicants of each category should the personnel manager hire and for which jobs?

Table 4.25 Category Value ($/week)

Applicant Category	A	B	C	D	E	F	Number of Applicants
I	100	110	150	140	140	145	54
II	120	125	120	135	140	140	57
III	100	110	120	140	150	160	45
IV	150	150	160	140	140	150	74

9. A large trucking firm servicing five metropolitan areas has its trucks and trailers located as shown in Table 4.26. For the past six months the firm has been experiencing a shift in its customer demands and management has decided to relocate its vehicles in order to reduce costs.

Table 4.26 Truck Locations and Requirements

City	Number Trucks	
	Current	Required
Alphaville	31	25
Bravoburg	43	29
Charlesville	66	68
Deltadown	29	36
Easyton	86	78

Based on statistics available, management has approved the forecasted requirements shown also in Table 4.26. You have been requested to recommend a movement plan for the trucks while minimizing the cost of relocating them. The road distances between the cities is shown in Table 4.27. You also know that the cheapest route between Charlesville and

Table 4.27 Road Distances (miles)

City	A	B	C	D	E
A	0	39	163	132	105
B	39	0	34	176	49
C	163	34	0	76	92
D	132	176	76	0	63
E	105	49	92	63	0

Deltadown involves tolls and barging that triples the normal mileage cost of movement between those cities. Finally because of flood damage to roads and bridges, truck movement between Charlesville and Alphaville should not be attempted at this time. What disposition do you recommend for the truck fleet?

10. Solve the following problems:

Minimize $\sum_{i=1}^{4} \sum_{j=1}^{4} C_{ij} X_{ij}$ subject to

$$\sum_{i=1}^{4} X_{ij} = 1 \qquad j = 1, 2, 3, 4$$

$$\sum_{j=1}^{4} X_{ij} = 1 \qquad i = 1, 2, 3, 4$$

$$X_{ij} = 0 \qquad \text{or} \qquad 1$$

(a)

	1	2	3	4
1	12	6	8	5
2	14	13	13	12
3	16	10	8	9
4	6	7	12	8

$C_{ij} =$ (rows 1–4)

(b)

	1	2	3	4
1	12	6	8	5
2	14	13	12	13
3	16	10	8	9
4	6	6	12	8

$C_{ij} =$ (rows 1–4)

11. A large conglomerate with several divisions located across the country, conducts campus interviews each year for new personnel recruitment. It feels that personnel from any division can conduct these initial interviews for any other division. In order to reduce costs the corporation has decided that all interviews on each campus will be conducted during a single visit. Additionally, knowing the type of personnel desired in a particular year, the conglomerate can narrow down the universities/colleges to be visited. Utilizing suitable personnel from each division, up to four recruiting teams per division can be formed but salary costs and travel costs vary from team to team. In the year in question the cost of a team visit in hundreds of dollars is as shown in Table 4.28. Management has decided that one team cannot make more than one visit. Which teams should visit which campuses?

12. Solve problem 1 with the proviso that transshipments are permitted where the following additional cost data pertain:

$$C_{ij} = C_{ji} \qquad C_{13} = 2$$
$$C_{AB} = 1 \qquad C_{14} = 1$$
$$C_{AC} = 3 \qquad C_{23} = 4$$
$$C_{CB} = 9 \qquad C_{24} = 5$$
$$C_{12} = 3 \qquad C_{34} = 3$$

13. Solve problem 2 with the proviso that transshipments are permitted wherein the following additional cost data pertain:

$$C_{ij} = C_{ji} \qquad D_1 \text{ to } D_3 = 3$$
$$S_1 \text{ to } S_2 = 2 \qquad D_2 \text{ to } D_3 = 2$$
$$S_1 \text{ to } S_3 = 1 \qquad \text{(Hint: handling the}$$
$$S_2 \text{ to } S_3 = 2 \qquad \text{dummy will require}$$
$$D_1 \text{ to } D_2 = 4 \qquad \text{special consideration)}$$

Table 4.28 Team Visit Costs ($100)

Division	Team	Campus													
		1	2	3	4	5	6	7	8	9	10	11	12	13	14
1	1	6.6	7.2	7.8	8.4	9.2	10.4	11.2	12	12.8	6	6.66	6.72	6.78	6.84
	2	7.92	8.64	9.36	10.08	10.8	11.52	12.24	12.96	13.68	7.2	8	8.06	8.12	8.18
	3	8.58	9.36	10.14	10.92	11.64	12.42	13.2	13.98	14.76	7.8	8.66	8.74	8.81	8.9
	4	9.24	10.68	10.92	11.76	12.88	14.56	15.68	16.8	17.92	8.4	9.32	9.4	9.49	9.58
2	1	8.6	9.4	10.1	10.9	11.6	12.4	13.2	14	14.8	7.8	8.7	8.7	8.8	8.9
	2	10	11.4	11.6	12.5	13.6	15.3	16.4	17.6	18.6	9.1	10	10.1	10.2	10.3
	3	11	12.54	12.76	13.75	14.96	16.83	18.04	19.36	20.46	10	11	11.11	11.22	11.33
	4	8.6	9.4	10.1	10.9	11.6	12.4	13.2	14	14.8	7.8	8.7	8.7	8.8	8.9
3	1	11.33	11.22	11.11	11	10	20.46	19.36	18.04	16.83	14.96	13.75	12.76	12.54	11
	2	8.9	8.8	8.7	8.7	7.8	14.8	14	13.2	12.4	11.6	10.9	10.1	9.4	8.6
	3	10.3	10.2	10.1	10	9.1	18.6	17.6	16.4	15.3	13.6	12.5	11.6	11.4	10
	4	8.9	8.8	8.7	8.7	7.8	14.8	14	13.2	12.4	11.6	10.9	10.1	9.4	8.6
4	1	6.8	6.8	6.7	6.7	6	12.9	12	11.2	10.4	9.2	8.4	7.8	7.2	6.6
	2	9.58	9.49	9.4	9.32	8.4	17.9	16.8	15.7	14.6	12.9	11.8	10.9	10.7	9.24
	3	8.18	8.12	8.06	8	7.2	13.68	12.96	12.24	11.52	10.8	10.08	9.36	8.64	7.92
	4	8.9	8.81	8.74	8.66	7.8	14.76	13.98	13.2	12.42	11.64	10.92	10.14	9.36	8.58

14. A wholesale distributor has three distribution centers from which he services five sales districts. The Adams center receives and fills orders from the first and second districts, the Baker center works with the third district, and the Cranston center works with the fourth and fifth districts. Demand is fairly consistent, although variations do occur and each center maintains a buffer stock of 5 percent of its monthly shipments to handle these variations in demand. The average monthly distribution is shown in Table 4.29 and average shipping costs between centers and districts is shown in Table 4.30. Centers are supplied from manufacturers that are located in the proximity of the centers and unit shipping costs to the centers are essentially equal. The manufacturers have the capability of providing each center with up to 35 percent more in goods per month. What recommendations would you make to the wholesale distributor with regard to the basic operations of its centers?

Table 4.29 Average Units Distributed

District	Avg. Mo. Distribution
1st	2600
2nd	650
3rd	1950
4th	1040
5th	1560

Table 4.30 Average Unit Shipping Cost ($)

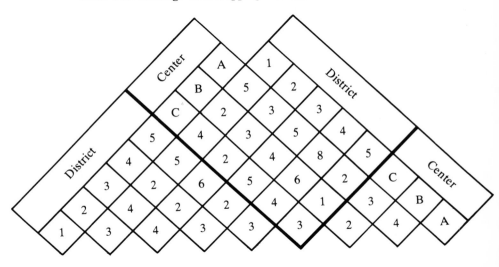

15. With the added stipulation that $i \neq j$ for any X_{ij}, solve problems 10(a) and (b) as traveling salesman problems by the branch-and-bound algorithm.

16. Solve problem 10(b) without computing cost of exclusions, selecting the lowest valued cell as the first cell to be utilized in a branch-and-bound solution.

17. Solve the production line scheduling problem illustrated in Section 4.8.2 using the branch-and-bound technique. Do not use cost of exclusions and use cell 1, 5 of Table 4.13 as the first cell of the network.

18. Solve the following problem by separable programming and verify your answer graphically.

$$\text{Maximize } X_1 - X_2 - X_1^2$$
$$\text{subject to } X_1 + X_2 \geq 4$$
$$X_1, X_2 \geq 0$$

If your answer is $X_1 = 1$, $X_2 = 3$, $f(X_1, X_2) = -3$, how do you account for the fact that you obtained an exact answer by an approximation method? If your answer was close to -3 what could you have done to obtain a more accurate answer?

19. Solve the following problem:

$$\text{Minimize } 4X_1 + 2X_2 - X_1 X_2$$
$$\text{subject to } \quad X_1 + X_2^2 \geq 5$$
$$X_1 X_2 \leq 4$$
$$X_1, X_2 \geq 0$$

(Hint: let $X_3 = \frac{1}{2}(X_1 + X_2)$ and $X_4 = \frac{1}{2}(X_1 - X_2)$ Solve for $X_3^2 - X_4^2$).

20. A frozen-food distributor is installing an additional walk-in freezer. After conducting a survey among his customers he has developed the following profit functions for each of three products that he plans to add to his inventory:

Product	Profit Function
A	$3X^{1/2}$
B	$X^2/128$
C	$5X - X^2/8$

where X is the quantity of the product included in inventory.

The characteristics of each product are given in Table 4.31, the walk-in box is rated at 28 cubic meters of useable storage space and/or 40 metric tons of net storage load. The distributor does not want to tie up

Table 4.31 Product Characteristics

		Per Case		
Product	Weight	Volume	Distr. Cost	No. Units
A	22 kg	.02 cu m	$27	48
B	22 kg	.03 cu m	$32	48
C	14 kg	.02 cu m	$40	24

more than $32,000 in product inventory in stocking the new box. How should he stock the new walk-in box?

21. Solve the order-selling policy for the distributor problem of Section 4.7 with the additional condition that:

(a) Once the initial order of 250 units is placed, each monthly subsequent order on the supplier must be for at least 100 units.

(b) As a promotional incentive, the supplier is quoting a unit price of $90 for the initial and the first month's orders.

22. A manufacturer has several subcontractors providing components for him that must be picked up at the subcontractor's plants. In addition to the cost of the components, it costs the manufacturer C dollars per hundred weight per working day when subcontractors must hold components pending pickup by the manufacturer. The subcontractors' total daily production for components, P_t, for the next 30 working days are known to the manufacturer and it costs him S dollars for a truck that can make the pickup circuit of his subcontractors. Daily pickups can result in less than truckload pickups but the manufacturer has agreed that in any event he will make a pickup run not less than every five working days. Formulate the recursive relationships to minimize costs (holding and shipping) and show the optimization function when there is a single period remaining.

23. A plant has five work operations it must perform to produce a finished product and has alternative work stations through which the product could be routed in performing the operations. Because of equipment, operator and location differences for the different work stations, the cost of producing the product is dependent on the routing used through work stations in carrying out the five operations. Figure 4.45 shows a schematic of the plant layout with movement and work station costs, C_{ij} and C_i, respectively, for the product in question. Using dynamic programming, what is the optimum routing through the five operations?

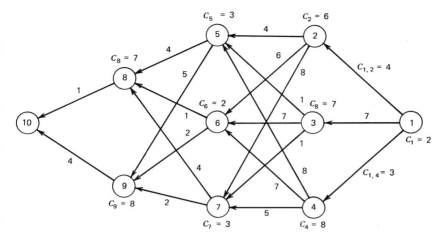

Figure 4.45 Plant schematic.

1. Bellman, R., *Dynamic Programming*, Princeton University Press, Princeton, N.J., 1957.
2. Bellman, R. and S. Dreyfus, *Applied Dynamic Programming*, Princeton University Press, Princeton, N.J., 1962.
3. Bierman, H. Jr., C. P. Bonini, and W. H. Hausman, *Quantitative Analysis for Business Decisions*, fourth edition, Richard D. Irwin, Inc., Homewood, Ill., 1973.
4. Cooper, L. and D. Steinberg, *Methods and Applications of Linear Programming*, W. B. Saunders Co., Philadelphia, 1974.
5. Dantzig, G. B., *Linear Programming and Extensions*, Princeton University Press, Princeton, N.J., 1963.
6. Dwyer, P. S., "Solution of the Personnel Classification Problem with the Method of Optimal Regions," *Psychometrika*, Vol. 18, No. 1, March 1954.
7. Frazer, R. J., *Applied Linear Programming*, Prentice-Hall, Englewood Cliffs, N.J., 1968.
8. Garvin, W. W., *Introduction to Linear Programming*, McGraw-Hill, New York, 1960.
9. Kolesar, P. J., "A Branch and Bound Algorithm for the Knapsack Problem," *Management Science*, Vol. 13, No. 9, May 1967.
10. Levin, R. I. and C. A. Kirkpatrick, *Quantitative Approaches to Management*, McGraw-Hill, New York, third edition, 1975.
11. Llewellyn, R. W., *Linear Programming*, Holt, Rinehart and Winston, New York, 1964.
12. Loomba, N. P. and E. Turban, *Applied Programming for Management*, Holt, Rinehart and Winston, New York, 1974.

REFERENCES

13. McMillan, C. Jr., *Mathematical Programming*, Wiley, New York, second edition, 1975.

14. Nemhauser, G. L., "A Note on Capital Budgeting," *The Journal of Industrial Engineering*, Vol. xviii, No. 6, June 1967.

15. Plane, D. R. and G. A. Kochenberger, *Operations Research for Managerial Decisions*, Richard D. Irwin, Inc., Homewood, Ill., 1972.

16. Shamblin, J. E. and G. T. Stevens, *Operations Research, A Fundamental Approach*, McGraw-Hill, New York, 1974.

17. Simmons, D. M., *Linear Programming for Operations Research*, Holden-Day, Inc., San Francisco, Cal., 1972.

18. Smythe, W. R. Jr. and L. A. Johnson, *Introduction to Linear Programming, with Applications*, Prentice-Hall, Englewood Cliffs, N.J., 1966.

19. Taha, H. A., *Operations Research, An Introduction*, The Macmillan Co., New York, second edition, 1976.

20. Weingartner, H., *Mathematical Programming and the Analysis of Capital Budgeting Problems*, Prentice-Hall, Englewood Cliffs, N.J., 1963.

21. Young, H. H., "Optimization Problems for Production Lines," *The Journal of Industrial Engineering*, Vol. xviii, No. 1, January 1967.

network
techniques 5

Networks and network analyses are playing an increasingly important role in the description and improvement of operational systems. The ease with which systems can be modeled in network form is the fundamental reason for this significant increase in the use of networks. Other reasons for using networks are (1) the need for communication mechanisms to discuss the operational system in terms of its significant features, (2) a means for specifying the data requirements for analysis of the system, and (3) a starting point for analysis and scheduling of the operational systems. The latter of these reasons was the original motive for network construction and use. The advantages that occurred outside of the analysis procedure soon justified the network approach, and further efforts toward improving and extending network analysis procedures have not kept pace with the applications of networks.

In this chapter we discuss activity networks, PERT, CPM, shortest path analysis, and maximal flow analysis.

5.1
INTRODUCTION

The heart of critical path methods is a network portrayal of the plan for carrying out a project. Such a network shows the precedence relationships of the elements of the program leading to the program's completion and is called an *arrow diagram* or *precedence diagram.*. The idea of using the arrow diagram is not new; however, it wasn't until 1958, when PERT and CPM were available, that the technique became popular. The arrow diagram is an outgrowth of the familiar Gantt chart.

The development of the arrow diagram occurs in the planning phase of the project. Costs, resources, and times are neglected at this point. We

5.2
ACTIVITY NETWORKS: CPM AND PERT

5.2.1
Activity
Diagrams*

---

* The analysis in this section assumes that time-consuming activities are represented by arrows of the network. The British often use a system where the time-consuming activities are represented by the nodes of the network.

ask three questions about each element of the project:
1. What immediately precedes this element?
2. What can be done concurrently?
3. What immediately follows this job?

With these questions answered we are prepared to draw an arrow diagram of a project. The diagram has two elements:
1. *Arrow* or *arc* represents the activities of the project under consideration.
2. *Node* or *event* represents the intersection of activities.

The node rule for an arrow diagram is that no activity can start from an event until all activities entering this event are complete.

EXAMPLE   Consider a project for which the analysis has resulted in the definition of five activities: A, B, C, D, and E. Furthermore, assume the following precedence relationships between these activities:
1. A and B can be started simultaneously.
2. Activity C can be started only upon the completion of A.
3. Activity D can be started when B is completed.
4. Both C and D must be complete before E may be started.

In the analysis, estimated durations of these activities have not been specified. Consequently, the lengths of the arrows used in the diagram representing these activities do not correspond to any specific lengths of time. Only the relative positions of the arrows have any significance. The five-activity project for which the precedence relationships have been defined may therefore be shown as an arrow diagram in Figure 5.1a.

EXAMPLE   Suppose the precedence relationships for this example were changed slightly to read:
1. A and B can be started simultaneously.
2. Activity C can be started only upon the completion of A.
3. Activity D can be started *when A and B are completed.*
4. Both C and D must be complete before E may be started.

The arrow diagram as shown in Figure 5.1a is no longer appropriate for the new problem because it violates the restriction that activity D be dependent on activity A. We might consider redrawing the network as shown in Figure 5.1b, but this is also incorrect. This diagram implies that activity C is dependent on activity B, which is not the case. To display this relationship, it will be necessary to introduce another type of activity called a *dummy activity*. A dummy activity, represented by a broken-line arrow, has a duration of zero. If we introduce a dummy as shown in Figure 5.1c, the new precedence relationship can be modeled. The arrow diagram says that activity D cannot start until both the dummy activity and activity B are completed. But the dummy must wait for activity A to be completed, so activity D is dependent on activities A and B.

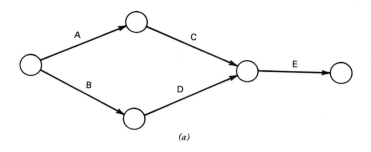

(a)

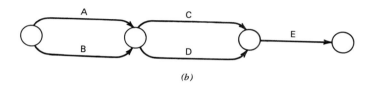

(b)

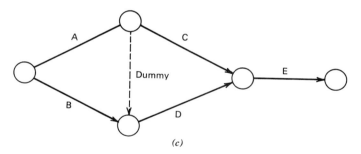

(c)

Figure 5.1 An example of the use of dummies in an activity
network.

In real life we must determine the interrelationships among the
activities in the project we are modeling. The following example illustrates how you proceed to establish your own interrelationships.

Consider an example from everyday life—a grease job and oil **EXAMPLE**
change for your car. Make a list of all the jobs involved, arranging them in
more or less chronological order. Your list might look something like this:
    Hoist car.
    Remove drain plug, drain oil.
    Grease underside fittings.
    Inspect tires and exhaust system.
    Check differential and transmission levels.

Replace drain plug.
Lower car.
Refill crankcase.
Grease upper fittings.
Oil generator and distributor.
Check radiator and battery.

Assume there are two service-station attendants to work on your car. Now prepare a diagram of the work, using arrows to represent the jobs you have listed. It is logical to hoist the car first so that the oil can be drained at the outset. Therefore, start the arrow diagram with a job arrow marked "hoist car."

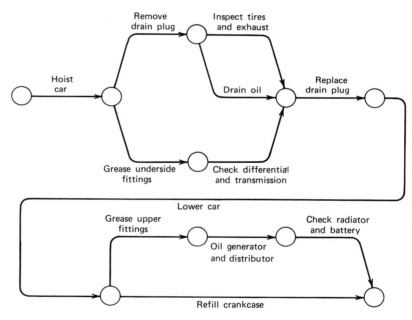

Figure 5.2 Arrow diagram for servicing a car.

The next job on the list is "remove drain plug and drain oil." What other job(s) must be completed before this job can start? Obviously, "hoist car" is the only job that must be done before the oil can be drained.

What job(s) can be done while this is being done? There are three such jobs: "grease underside fittings," "inspect tires and exhaust system," and "check differential and transmission." It is logical to expect that one attendant will drain the oil and inspect tires and exhaust *while* the oil is draining. The other attendant will grease the underside fittings and check differential and transmission while the first is draining the oil and inspecting.

What job(s) cannot start until this job ("remove drain plug and drain oil") is done? All of the remaining jobs must wait until the oil is drained. Obviously, the next job *is* to "replace the drain plug" and then "lower the car." This done, one of the attendants can "refill the crankcase" while the other "greases the upper fittings," "oils the generator and distributor," and "checks the radiator and battery." Add these job arrows in their logical positions. Our arrow diagram will then look like Figure 5.2.

Now that we are *experts* on drawing arrow diagrams, let us add time to the diagram. Adding the time dimension will allow scheduling of the various elements of the project.

Estimating the time required for each task is usually done by one or more people thoroughly familiar with the task. This estimate is the total elapsed time required from the start to the finish of a task and is called the *time duration*. It is the time required to accomplish the task most economically. Later adjustments can be made to lengthen or shorten this time duration as required. Some systems have expensive procedures for arriving at time durations based on several estimates involving statistics and probability. At present we assume one estimate per task. To illustrate the inclusion of time into an arrow diagram, consider Figure 5.3a. The numbers on the arrows represent the time estimates to complete that activity. For example, task F is estimated to take eight time units.

In the arrow diagram, Figure 5.3a, the project starts with tasks A and **EXAMPLE** J. At the completion of task A, both tasks B and D may start. Task C

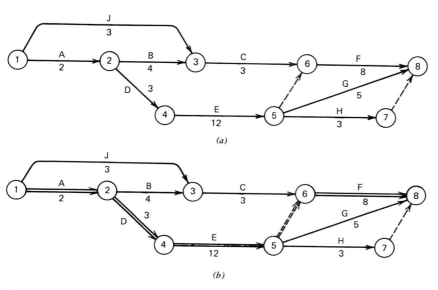

Figure 5.3 An example of a project activity diagram.

follows B and J, and task E follows D. Tasks G and H can start at the completion of task E. Task F can start after the completion of task C and task E. Since it is not necessary for tasks G and H to follow C, they are not connected to task C, and the relationship of tasks E and F is shown by the use of a dummy. The project is finished after completion of tasks F, G, and H. Since tasks G and H would have the same numbers of their start and finish nodes, a dummy was used to connect task H to the finish. This allowed task H to have different node numbers from task G. This unique identification is required by some computer packages developed to analyze activity networks.

By inspecting Figure 5.3a, we can see that route or path A, B, C, F would require 17 days; path J, C, F would require 14 days; path A, D, E, G would require 22 days; path A, D, E, H would require 20 days; and path A, D, E, F would require 25 days. Therefore, path A, D, E, F is the *critical path* as shown in Figure 5.3b. If any shortening of the project is to be accomplished, it must first be along this path A, D, E, F. Shortening of tasks B, C, G, H, or J by using overtime, double shifting, or more men, machines, or materials would not shorten the completion time of the project. Shortening the tasks on the critical path (task A, D, E, and F) would shorten the project time, and it is these tasks that must receive special attention. Shortening of tasks along the critical path can eventually cause other paths to become critical. For example, if task F is shortened to less than five days, task G becomes critical since A, D, E, G would be a critical path.

In the example shown in Figure 5.3b, all of the relationships that have been mentioned are apparent by inspection and mental arithmetic. What happens, however, when the tasks increase in number from 9 to 90 or to 900? Exactly the same procedure is followed up to and through the creation of the arrow diagram and the list of node numbers, durations, and task descriptions. A computer is usually used to do the work of analyzing the project and creating the schedule data.

We now present an algorithm for determining the critical path and other scheduling information in a mechanical fashion. The technique can either be applied by hand or programmed for the computer.

The network is first solved from source to sink by what are often referred to as *forward-pass rules*. These rules are stated as follows:

STEP 1. The earliest event time for the source event is assumed to be zero.

STEP 2. Each activity is assumed to start as soon as the event at which it starts is realized. The earliest finish time for an activity is equal to its earliest start time plus its duration.

STEP 3. The earliest event time is equal to the latest of the earliest finish times of the activities merging on the event. Return to step 2.

Next the network is analyzed in similar manner working backward from the sink. The rules are as follows and are often called *backward-pass rules*:

The earliest event time for the sink is equated to its latest allowable event time.

STEP 1.

The latest allowable finish time for an activity is equated to its successor event's latest allowable time. The latest start time for an activity is its latest finish time minus its duration.

STEP 2.

The latest allowable time for an event is the earliest of the latest start times for the activities emanating from the event. Return to step 2.

STEP 3.

This algorithm can be stated in equation form using the following nomenclature:

t = single estimate of mean activity duration time
T_E = earliest event occurrence time
T_L = latest allowable event occurrence time
ES = earliest (activity) start time
EF = earliest (activity) finish time
LS = latest allowable (activity) start time
LF = latest allowable (activity) finish time

FORWARD-PASS RULES
1. $T_E = 0$ (for the source node)
2. $ES = T_E$ (for the predecessor event)
   $EF = ES + t$
3. $T_E = \max (EF_1, EF_2, \ldots, EF_n)$ for an event with n activities merging on it. Return to step 2.

BACKWARD-PASS RULES
1. $T_L = T_E$ (for the sink node)
2. $LF = T_L$ (for successor event)
   $LS = LF - t$
3. $T_L = \min (LS_1, LS_2, \ldots, LS_n)$ for an event with n activities originating from it.
   Return to step 2.

If you are applying this algorithm, you can either apply it directly on the arrow diagram or solve it in a tabular form. Figure 5.4 shows these rules as applied to the arrow diagram introduced in Figure 5.3. These results are also tabulated in Table 5.1.

EXAMPLE

Figure 5.4 and Table 5.1 are derived as follows. Referring to Figure 5.3, we see that tasks A and J are started immediately at zero time. They have time durations of 2 days and 3 days, respectively; therefore, their earliest starting times are zero and their earliest finish times are 2 days and 3 days, respectively. At the finish of task A, tasks B and D may start.

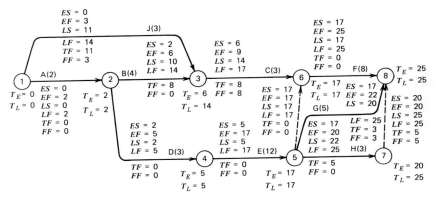

Figure 5.4 An example of a project arrow diagram showing calculations.

Table 5.1 Critical Path Calculation

Nodes		t	Description of Tasks	ES	EF	LS	LF	TF	FF
From	To								
1	2	2	A	0	2	0	2	0*	0
1	3	3	J	0	3	11	14	11	3
2	3	4	B	2	6	10	14	8	0
2	4	3	D	2	5	2	5	0*	0
3	6	3	C	6	9	14	17	8	8
4	5	12	E	5	17	5	17	0*	0
5	6	0	Dummy	17	17	17	17	0*	0
5	7	3	H	17	20	22	25	5	0
5	8	5	G	17	22	20	25	3	3
6	8	8	F	17	25	17	25	0*	0
7	8	0	Dummy	20	20	25	25	5	5

(* = Critical Path)   (Project completion = 25)

Since task A has an earliest finish of 2 days, tasks B and D have an earliest start date of 2 days. Adding their time durations to their earliest start times, we find that they have earliest finish times of 6 days and 5 days, respectively. Task C can start at the finish of both tasks B and J and cannot start until both are finished; therefore, it can start on the sixth day. Its earliest finish would be 9 days. Continuing through the project, we can see that task F has an earliest finish of 25 days. This is the earliest the project can be completed under the conditions set forth in the arrow diagram and the time duration estimates. Reversing the procedure, we can calculate the latest start and latest finish for each of the tasks. The latest finish of the last task in the project is the same as the earliest finish of this task. Subtracting the time duration from this date gives the latest start of that task.

The next two items of the scheduling procedure concern what is called *float* or *slack*. Float is a measure of allowable delay or leeway. There are two types of floats normally considered: *total float* and *free float*. Total float (TF) is the time any given task may be delayed before it will affect the project completion time. We compute it by subtracting the earliest finish from the latest finish. Free float (FF) is the time any task may be delayed before it will affect the earliest starting date of any of the tasks immediately following. We compute it by subtracting the earliest finish time from the earliest start date of the very next task. These quantities are reported in Table 5.1 and Figure 5.4. We notice that those items on the *critical path* can be identified by the fact that their total floats equal zero.

PERT introduces uncertainty into the time estimates for activities and hence in the project duration. It is, therefore, well suited for situations where there is either insufficient data to predict activity durations or where the project activities involve research and development.

The first step in a PERT analysis is to create an arrow diagram as described in Section 5.2.1. PERT uses an activity duration called the *expected mean time* (t_e) together with an associated measure of uncertainty of this activity duration. The uncertainty may be expressed as either the standard deviation (σ_{t_e}) or the variance (V_{t_e}) of the duration. These two quantities are related by the relationship $V_{t_e} = \sigma_{t_e}^2$.

PERT uses three time estimates for each activity:

5.2.2
PERT: Program
Evaluation and
Review
Technique—Introducing
uncertainty into
activity times

a, the optimistic time (which should have only a very low probability of occurring)

m, the most likely time (or the mode of the distribution)

b, the pessimistic time (which also should have only a very low probability of occurring)

PERT then assumes that these three estimates can be used to describe a beta distribution for each activity duration (see Figure 5.5). Then t_e, the expected time for the activity, σ_{t_e}, the standard deviation of t_e, and V_{t_e}, the variance of t_e, can be computed as follows:

$$t_e = \frac{a + 4m + b}{6}$$

$$\sigma_{t_e} = \frac{b - a}{6}$$

$$V_{t_e} = \left(\frac{b - a}{6}\right)^2$$

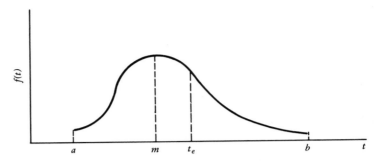

Figure 5.5   PERT beta distribution.

EXAMPLE   For example, for the PERT network shown in Figure 5.6, the activity going from event 3 to event 5 has time estimates of $a = 0$, $m = 6$, and $b = 18$. The parameters for this activity would be calculated as follows:

$$t_e = \frac{0 + 4(6) + 18}{6} = 7$$

$$\sigma_{t_e} = \frac{18 - 0}{6} = 3$$

$$V_{t_e} = \left(\frac{18 - 0}{6}\right)^2 = 9$$

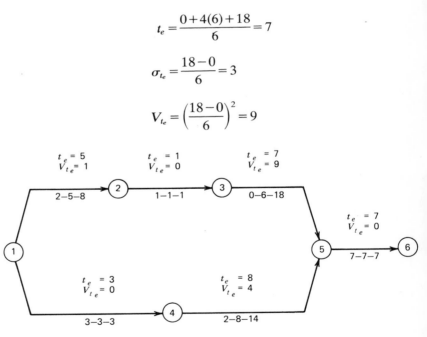

Figure 5.6   Sample PERT network.

The analysis of the arrow diagram proceeds in a fashion similar to that described in Section 5.2.1 with particular emphasis on determining the variance of the T_E and T_L of the events.

To permit the finding of the variance of the earliest $(\sigma_{T_E}{}^2)$ and latest $(\sigma_{T_L}{}^2)$ times, we assume that the elapsed times for individual activities are statistically independent. For only one path to an event, the earliest time equals the elapsed times to the event. Therefore the expected value and the variance of the earliest time equal the sum of the expected values and the sum of the variances, respectively, to the event. For example, there exists only one path to event 3 in Figure 5.6—that being from 1–2–3. The expected value of the earliest time (μ_{T_E}) is $5+1=6$, and the expected value of the variance of the earliest time is $1+0=1$. For the case of one path, the expected latest time (μ_{T_L}) is calculated in a similar manner.

Now consider the case where there exists more than one path to an event. For event 5, two possible paths exist: 1–2–3–5 and 1–4–5. The earliest time of event 5 equals the greater of the total elapsed times along these paths. However, it is difficult to find the exact expected value and variance for the maximum time. Therefore, the largest total elapsed time is said to always occur on the path with the largest expected total elapsed time. The expected total elapsed times to event 5 are 13 and 11. Path 1–2–3–5 has the larger value (13), so it is assumed that the actual total elapsed time is greater on this path. With this assumption, an approximation for the expected value of the total of the elapsed time is 13. The variances of T_E and T_L are calculated under the same assumption, that is, the path with the largest expected time will always dominate other paths. Therefore, for our example, an approximation for the variance for the T_E for node 5 equals $10(1+0+9)$.

Slack for the PERT-type network is defined as the expected latest time for an event (μ_{T_L}) minus the expected earliest time for an event (μ_{T_E}). Slack is similar to the float defined in Section 5.2.1 except that it is defined with respect to events instead of activities.

The calculations for a PERT network are usually summarized as shown in Table 5.2 which describes Figure 5.6.

Table 5.2 PERT Calculations

Event Number	Earliest Time (T_E)		Latest Time (T_L)		Slack
	Expected Value μ_{T_E}	Variance $\sigma_{T_E}^2$	Expected Value μ_{T_L}	Variance $\sigma_{T_L}^2$	
1	0	0	0	10	0
2	5	1	5	9	0
3	6	1	6	9	0
4	3	0	5	4	2
5	13	10	13	0	0
6	20	10	20	0	0

To find the critical path, examine the slack column of Table 5.2. Where there is a zero slack, an event is in a critical path. The critical path for the given example is shown to be 1–2–3–5–6. Once the expected earliest time of an event (μ_{T_E}) and its standard deviation (σ_{T_E}) have been determined, it is possible to use probability theory to calculate the chances of meeting a specific scheduled time (T_s) for a node. Based on the central limit theorem, the earliest completion for an event is assumed to have a normal probability distribution with a mean of μ_{T_E} and a standard deviation of σ_{T_E}.

To calculate the probability of meeting a scheduled time T_s for a particular event, it is necessary to visualize a normal distribution centered at μ_{T_E} as illustrated in Figure 5.7. The probability of meeting the desired scheduled time T_s is obtained by finding the area under the normal curve to the left to T_s.

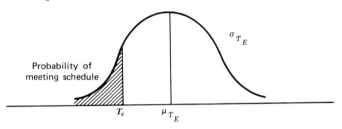

Figure 5.7 Calculation of the probability of meeting schedule.

The familiar Z statistic of the normal distribution can be calculated if we realize that $T_s = \mu_{T_E} + Z\sigma_{T_E}$. Therefore:

$$Z = \frac{T_s - \mu_{T_E}}{\sigma_{T_E}}$$

The Z value can be converted to a probability by means of Appendix B.

EXAMPLE   For the PERT network described in Figure 5.6, let us find the probability of completing the project within 18 time units. This is the same as asking what is the probability of realizing event 6 before time 18? From Table 5.2 we find $\mu_{T_E} = 20$ and $V_{T_E} = 10$. Realizing that $\sigma_{T_E} = \sqrt{V_{T_E}} = \sqrt{10}$, we can calculate Z:

$$Z = \frac{18 - 20}{\sqrt{10}} = -.63$$

Therefore, we can see from Appendix B that there is a probability of about .26 that the project will be finished in 18 time units or less. This approach for finding the probability of meeting a schedule can be applied to any event in the network, not just to the last event.

CPM was developed at about the same time as PERT and has been used extensively within the construction industry where previous experience in similar work can be used to predict time durations and cost within a tight range. It is difficult to give a universally acceptable description of CPM because many companies have developed their own versions of a cost model based on activity networks. The initial step in CPM is the preparation of an arrow diagram. Next is the assignment of estimated durations and costs to each activity on the arrow diagram. Although there are many methods currently used to determine time and cost estimates, a procedure utilizing two time/cost estimates will be illustrated in this book. These two estimates are called the "normal" and "crash" time/cost estimates. Based on the relationship between time and money, these two estimates can be defined as follows:

1. Normal time and cost—the duration to complete the project requiring the least amount of money.
2. Crash time and cost—the minimum possible time to complete the activity and the associated increased cost.

Since each activity is assigned a duration range and related cost, obviously there is a range of durations available for the project depending on the individual time selections for each activity. Each one of these various project durations also presents a different project cost. A CPM computer program is used to develop these various project durations from which the optimum schedule will be selected. In each instance only the lowest possible cost for each different project duration is produced.

5.2.3
CPM:
Critical
Path
Method—
Introducing
Cost Data
into
Activity
Network*

CPM Example. Using the activity network illustrated in Figure 5.8 and assigning time/cost estimates to each activity as shown in Table 5.3, we are ready to begin the scheduling processes of CPM.

From our definition of the critical path, the longest project duration using normal time estimates would be 16 days along path A–D–G. To shorten the project's duration, either activity A, D, or G will have to be expedited. To ensure that this acceleration will be done at the lowest possible cost, we must calculate one further figure for each activity that we will call the *activity cost slope.* Using activity B as an example and assuming a linear relationship, we can present the cost curve for activity B graphically, as shown in Figure 5.9.

EXAMPLE

---

* Some authors refer to the material in this section as PERT/COST.

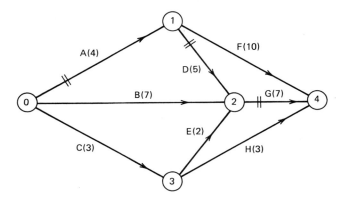

Figure 5.8 All-normal CPM network.

Table 5.3 Cost Table

	Normal		Crash	
Activities	Days	Dollars	Days	Dollars
A	4	$100	3	$200
B	7	280	5	520
C	3	50	2	100
D	5	200	3	360
E	2	160	2	160
F	10	230	8	350
G	7	200	5	480
H	2	100	1	200
	Total	$1320	Total	$2370

The cost slope of this curve is computed by the formula:

$$\frac{\text{crash cost} - \text{normal cost}}{\text{normal time} - \text{crash time}}$$

For activity B, the cost slope is:

$$\frac{\$520 - \$280}{7 \text{ days} - 5 \text{ days}} = \frac{\$240}{2 \text{ days}} = \$120 \text{ per day reduced}$$

If we perform this calculation for each activity, an additional column can be added to our cost table as shown in Table 5.4.

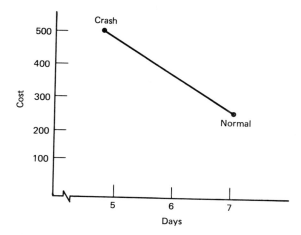

Figure 5.9 Time-cost curve for activity B.

Table 5.4 Cost Table

Activities	Normal		Crash		Cost Slope
	Days	Dollars	Days	Dollars	
A	4	$100	3	$200	$100
B	7	280	5	520	120
C	3	50	2	100	50
D	5	200	3	360	80
E	2	160	2	160	—
F	10	230	8	350	60
G	7	200	5	480	140
H	2	100	1	200	100
	Total	$1320	Total	$2370	

With this information we can now develop various project durations using the logic of CPM:

16-DAY SCHEDULE—normal duration for this project—cost $1320.

15-DAY SCHEDULE—the least expensive way to gain one day would be to reduce activity D for an additional cost of $80, project cost $1400. If the other activities on the critical path were reduced, activity A or G would have been more costly.

14-DAY SCHEDULE—another day can also be gained by expediting D for an additional cost of $80, project cost $1480. In the 14-day schedule, it is apparent that there are three critical paths, activities A–F, A–D–G, and B–G. Further cuts in activity D will not help since the project's duration is also determined by other activities.

13-DAY SCHEDULE—the cheapest way to attain a 13-day duration is to cut A and G each one day for an additional cost of $240. However, in doing this we can extend D by one day (allocation of one day of float), gaining $80. The net result is an additional cost of $160, project cost $1640.

12-DAY SCHEDULE—activities F and G can be accelerated for an additional $200, project cost $1840.

11-DAY SCHEDULE—to cut down to 11 days, an activity on each of our three critical paths must be expedited. The cheapest combination of reductions would be B, D, and F for an additional cost of $260 and a project cost of $2100.

The project cannot be performed in less than 11 days; therefore, we have determined six different project durations and costs from which we must choose a schedule.

Selection of a particular schedule from among the many alternatives depends mainly on your project objectives. If time is the primary concern, a schedule between 11 and 16 days can be selected directly. If the completion date calls for a project duration of less than 11 days, it will be necessary to reconsider your arrow diagram to see if any efficiencies can be gained.

If total project cost is the deciding factor, more information is required than the direct project investment already calculated. Indirect expenses, lost revenue, penalties, and similar costs must be added to the direct costs. Total indirect expenses increase as the project duration increases. The sum of the direct and indirect expenses gives a U-shaped total project cost curve. The optimum schedule for implementing the project is the schedule corresponding to the minimum point on this curve. The relationship among direct, indirect, and total project costs for our example is shown in Table 5.5 and graphically in Figure 5.10. From the table, the optimum schedule is 14 days at a cost of $2880.

A very flat total cost curve is not uncommon in practical applications. This flatness indicates that, for only a nominal additional investment, the

Table 5.5 Total Cost Table

Days	16	15	14	13	12	11
Direct costs	1320	1400	1480	1640	1840	2100
Indirect costs	1600	1500	1400	1300	1200	1100
Total cost	2920	2900	2880	2940	3040	3200

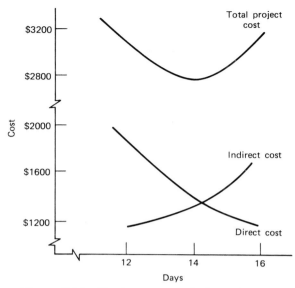

Figure 5.10 Total cost analysis for selecting the "optimum" project duration.

project duration can be reduced. In our case we can reduce the project duration to 13 days at a cost of $60 ($2940 − $2880) or to 12 days at a cost of $160.

The material in this section is really a way of managing the resources connected with a project. There are a number of algorithms [1, 11] available for *resource allocation* that are beyond the scope of this text. It should, however, be noted that network costs can be in terms of time, cost, man hours, pounds of material, and so on, and all can be treated as a limited resource using the same computational techniques presented in this section.

All the methods described so far have been used for planning and scheduling, and they are employed before the project begins. The final phase of project management, the control phase, is needed to provide the project manager with the information for managing his project. This monitoring is achieved by a comparison of the actual status of the project against the CPM or PERT schedule. The outgrowth of this comparison is a revised strategy. The monitoring phase is usually performed using a computer, although limited success can be achieved by using hand calculations. By periodically feeding the computer such data as (1) completed activities, (2) changes in the durations of activities, and (3) changes in the detailed structure of the network, the project manager obtains from the computer a monitor report illustrating the current status

5.2.4
Project Control

of the project. The monitor indicates those activities which are ahead of or behind schedule. Using new and improved data, the computer predicts when the project will be completed. It identifies critical activities and those about to become critical. The manager thus can see how the total project is progressing and can determine where maximum effort should be placed.

**5.3
SHORTEST
PATH
ANALYSIS**

If we consider the parameter on an activity network to be distance, we might be interested in finding the shortest path through the network.

We will now consider solutions to the following three shortest-path problems:

1. Find the shortest path between the origin and the terminal point of a network.
2. Find the shortest paths from the origin to all the nodes in the network.
3. Find the shortest routes through a network.

In this section we will consider a class of networks which are called *acyclic-directed networks*. This means that all the paths are directed and contain no cycles or loops. Because of the special nature of these networks, we can always number the nodes in such a way that all activities lead from a smaller-numbered node to a node of larger number. Consider the network shown in Figure 5.11*a*. We can number the nodes as shown in Figure 5.11*b* so that all activities lead from smaller-numbered nodes to higher-numbered nodes. Because of this feature, the algorithms for finding the shortest paths in acyclic-directed networks are quite simple.

Let us first consider the problem of finding the shortest path from node 1 to node 7 in Figure 5.11*b*. Thus we are seeking the shortest path from the source to the sink in this network. This problem can be solved by the following algorithm:

STEP 1. Label node 1 with the designation $m_1 = 0$.

STEP 2. Continue to label the remaining nodes (chosen in ascending order) according to the following formula:

$$m_j = \min_{i=1,2,\ldots,j-1} (m_i + d_{i,j})$$

where $d_{i,j}$ is the distance between node i and node j. $d_{i,j}$ can be assumed to approach infinity for those combinations of i and j that do not have paths in the network of interest.

STEP 3. When the last node, n, has been labeled, m_n is the shortest path through the network. The path is determined by tracing backward from node n to

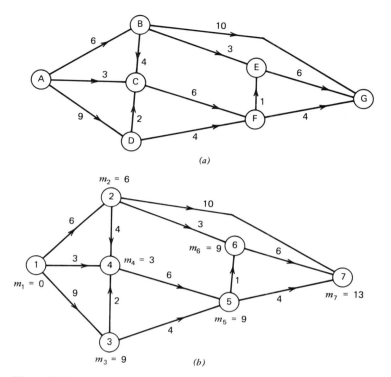

Figure 5.11 Node numbering for a directed acyclic network.

all nodes so that $m_i + d_{i,j} = m_j$ for $j = n, n-1, n-2, \ldots, 1$. That is, any path satisfying the equality $m_i + d_{i,j} = m_j$ is a candidate for being on the shortest path from the origin to the terminal of the network.

Now let us apply this algorithm to the network shown in Figure 5.11b.

$$m_1 = 0$$

STEP 1.

$$m_2 = \min (m_1 + d_{1,2}) = \min (0+6) = 6$$
$$m_3 = \min (m_1 + d_{1,3}) = \min (0+9) = 9$$
$$m_4 = \min (m_1 + d_{1,4}, m_2 + d_{2,4}, m_3 + d_{3,4})$$
$$\quad = (0+3, 6+4, 9+2) = 3$$
$$m_5 = \min (m_3 + d_{3,5}, m_4 + d_{4,5}) = \min (9+4, 3+6) = 9$$
$$m_6 = \min (m_2 + d_{2,6}, m_5 + d_{5,6}) = \min (6+3, 9+1) = 9$$
$$m_7 = \min (m_2 + d_{2,7}, m_5 + d_{5,7}, m_6 + d_{6,7})$$
$$\quad = \min (6+10, 9+4, 9+6) = 13$$

STEP 2.

EXAMPLE

STEP 3.   Since node 7 has been labeled, we conclude that the shortest path through the network is of length 13. Checking for the path, we find that activities $(5, 7)$, $(2, 6)$, $(4, 5)$, $(1, 4)$, and $(1, 3)$ satisfy the equality $m_i + d_{i,j} = m_j$. Thus the shortest path from 1 to 7 will be $(1, 4)$, $(4, 5)$, and $(5, 7)$ because it is the only complete path from node 1 to node 7.

It is interesting to note that the algorithm just presented also solves the problem of finding the shortest path from the origin to any node in the network. The m labels give the lengths of such paths. The actual paths are determined from the set of activities satisfying the equality $m_i + d_{i,j} = m_j$.

EXAMPLE   For the example shown in Figure 5.11b, $m_6 = 9$; therefore, the shortest path from node 1 to node 6 is 9. The path includes activities $(1, 2)$ and $(2, 6)$. Similarly, $m_3 = 9$, so the shortest path from node 1 to node 3 is of length 9 and includes only activity $(1, 3)$.

A simple modification to the algorithm will allow us to determine the shortest path between all pairs of nodes. Due to the special nature of acyclic-directed networks we observe that a node can only have a path to a node of higher number. Therefore, it is possible for us to have a path from node 2 to node 5, but not from node 5 to node 2. To find the shortest path from node h to nodes k, $k > h$, consider the portion of network including all nodes of higher number than h and apply the same procedure outlined above with $m_h = 0$.

EXAMPLE   For example, if we were interested in the shortest paths from node 3 to nodes 4, 5, 6, and 7, we would first modify the network as shown in Figure 5.12 and then apply our algorithm:

STEP 1. $$m_3 = 0$$

STEP 2. $$m_4 = \min (m_3 + d_{3,4}) = \min (0+2) = 2$$
$$m_5 = \min (m_3 + d_{3,5}, m_4 + d_{4,5}) = \min (0+4, 2+6) = 4$$
$$m_6 = \min (m_5 + d_{5,6}) = \min (4+1) = 5$$
$$m_7 = \min (m_5 + d_{5,7}, m_6 + d_{6,7}) = \min (4+4, 5+6) = 8$$

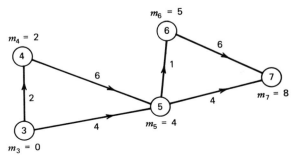

Figure 5.12   Modified acyclic network.

Activities (3, 4), (3, 5), (5, 6), and (5, 7) satisfy the equality $m_i + d_{i,j} =$ STEP 3.
m_j; so the results of our calculations are summarized in Table 5.6.

Table 5.6 Shortest Paths from Node 3

Shortest Path from Node 3 to	Length	Includes Activities
Node 4	2	(3, 4)
Node 5	4	(3, 5)
Node 6	5	(3, 5)(5, 6)
Node 7	8	(3, 5)(5, 7)

The problem of finding the k-shortest paths between nodes is an interesting and important concept. For example, it might not be feasible to use the shortest route. Thus some path such as the second or third shortest might be adopted. Sensitivity analysis is another important use for this approach. For instance, we might be interested in what it will cost us to deviate from the optimum shortest-path solution.

This problem can be handled by a slight modification of procedure just discussed. Let the notation $\min_1$ denote the minimum, $\min_2$ denote the second minimum, and so on. The general step of the procedure is as follows. For each node j, consider the set of nodes i that are connected to j. The kth shortest distance is found using the following equation:

$$m_j^{(k)} = \min_k_{\substack{\text{all } i \\ \text{connected} \\ \text{to } j}} (m_i^{(r)} + d_{i,j}) \qquad \text{for } 1 < r < k \qquad k = 1, 2, \ldots, n$$

where $m_j^{(k)}$ is the kth shortest path to node j.

To illustrate, let us determine the three shortest paths for the **EXAMPLE** network illustrated in Figure 5.11b. For node 1, $m_1^{(1)} = 0$ since we assume node 1 occurs at time 0. $m_1^{(2)}$ and $m_1^{(3)}$ are undefined since there is only one possible time.

We are now ready to apply our procedure:

node 2: $m_2^{(1)} = 6$ $m_2^{(2)}$ and $m_2^{(3)}$ are undefined
node 3: $m_3^{(1)} = 9$ $m_3^{(2)}$ and $m_3^{(3)}$ are undefined
node 4: $m_4^{(1)} = 3$ $m_4^{(2)} = 10$ $m_4^{(3)} = 11$
node 5: $m_5^{(1)} = 9$ $m_5^{(2)} = 13$ $m_5^{(3)} = 16$
node 6: $m_6^{(6)} = 9$ $m_6^{(2)} = 10$ $m_6^{(3)} = 14$
node 7: $m_7^{(1)} = 13$ $m_7^{(2)} = 15$ $m_7^{(3)} = 16$

As an example of the calculations involved, consider node 7 which is connected to nodes 2, 5, and 6.

$$m_7^{(1)} = \min_1 (m_2^{(1)} + d_{2,7}; \, m_5^{(1)} + d_{5,7}; \, m_6^{(1)} = d_{6,7})$$
$$= \min_1 (16, 13, 15) = 13$$
$$m_7^{(2)} = \min_2 (m_2^{(1)} + d_{2,7}; \, m_2^{(2)} + d_{2,7}; \, m_5^{(1)} + d_{5,7}; \, m_5^{(2)} + d_{5,7};$$
$$m_6^{(1)} + d_{6,7}; \, m_6^{(2)} + d_{6,7}) = \min_2 (16, \text{undefined},$$
$$13, 17, 15, 16) = 15$$
$$m_7^{(3)} = \min_3 (m_2^{(1)} + d_{2,7}; \, m_2^{(2)} + d_{2,7}; \, m_2^{(3)} + d_{2,7}; \, \dots ;$$
$$m_6^{(3)} + d_{6,7}) = 16$$

5.4 MAXIMAL FLOW METHODS

If we consider the parameter on our network to be flow capacity, an important question that can be asked about networks is: "What is the maximum possible flow between two points in a network?" There are a number of physical interpretations of this problem, for example, telephone messages in the Bell System's network, fuel oil being shipped by pipe from the Gulf coast to other areas of the country, and traffic flowing on a highway network between two or more cities.

There are a number of labeling techniques for solving this problem but here we consider an intuitive approach for finding the maximum flow in a network. We assume that there is conservation of flow at each node of the network; that is, the flow into each node must equal the flow out of each node. Obviously, the conservation-of-flow restriction does not hold for the source, where commodities only flow out, and the sink, where commodities only flow in. It is interesting to note, however, that the amount flowing out of the source will equal the amount flowing into the sink because of the conservation of flow at all other nodes. The flow problem also has flow constraints implied for each arc of the network. The flow capacities can, however, be assumed to be infinite for certain of the arcs in the network.

Consider a network such as that shown in Figure 5.13a. An intuitive approach to finding the maximum flow is the following:

STEP 1. Start at the source and move along branches of positive capacity until we reach the sink. Consider the capacities of the branches on the path from the source to the sink. Let M denote the minimum of these capacities. Next deduct M from each of the capacities for the branches on the path. The remainder on each branch can be viewed as the excess branch capacity.

STEP 2. Repeat the above processes on the new network capacities until there is no longer a path from the source to the sink that can carry flow. The maximal flow is the sum of all of the flows found at each step.

We will apply our procedure to the network shown in Figure 5.13a. First consider the path 1–2–4–6. The minimum capacity along the path is 3, which occurs on the branch from node 2 to node 4. Thus 3 units of flow can be sent along path 1–2–4–6, and the residual capacities can be calculated by reducing every unit along this path by 3. The revised network is shown in Figure 5.13b. Next the path 1–2–3–4–6 is considered from Figure 5.13b. The maximum quantity that can flow along this path is 3 units, as restricted by the branch from node 2 to node 3. After the

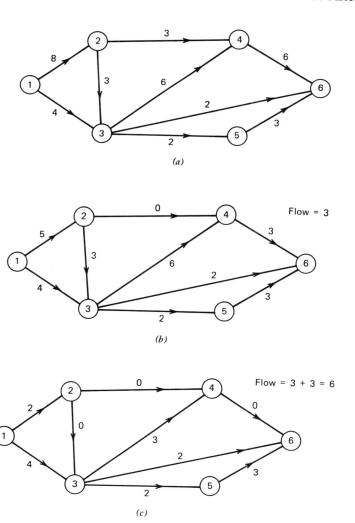

Figure 5.13 An example of the intuitive approach to network flow analysis.

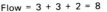

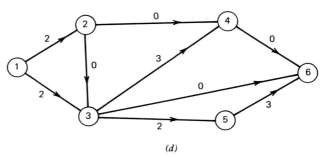

(d)

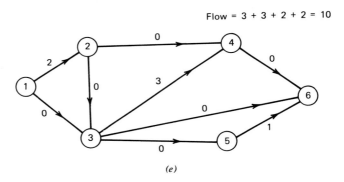

(e)

Figure 5.13 (d) and (e).

capacities are modified the network will appear as shown in Figure 5.13c, and 6 units have flowed through the network. Next it is observed that 2 units can flow along the path 1–3–6, which yields Figure 5.13d. Finally, 2 units can flow through the path 1–3–5–6, which yields the network shown in Figure 5.13e. Examining Figure 5.13e we can find no other path that can accommodate a positive flow; so our procedure terminates with a total flow of 10 units.

The obvious question to ask is whether the maximal flow for this network is 10? The answer is yes, but we must consider ourselves lucky because, had we chosen our flow paths in a slightly different order, we might not have achieved the flow of 10. Figure 5.14 illustrates one such sequence.

EXAMPLE

Examining Figure 5.14e we see no path that will accommodate a positive flow. Therefore, we would assume the maximum flow in the network to be 9 units. The algorithm has failed us. It is not tolerable to have a method that yields different results as a function of the arbitrary

ordering of the paths selected. The algorithm can be modified to allow
fictional flows in the wrong direction. That is, step 2 of our approach can
be modified to allow flow in the wrong direction as long as the net flow
remains nonnegative.

Viewing Figure 5.14e, we see that with the concept of negative flow,
1 unit can flow along the path 1–2–4–3–5–6 which will reduce the flow in
arc (3, 4) to 1, which is still feasible. It is, therefore, possible to obtain the
optimal solution to the network flow problem using this approach. But

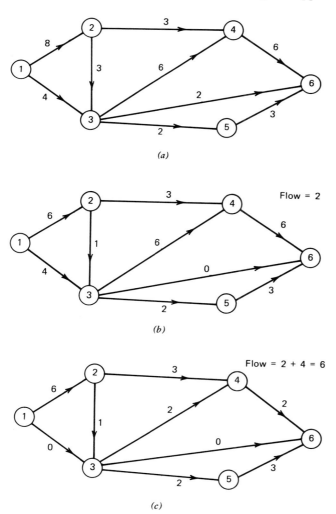

Figure 5.14   An example of where the intuitive network
flow approach fails.

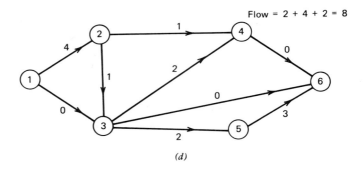

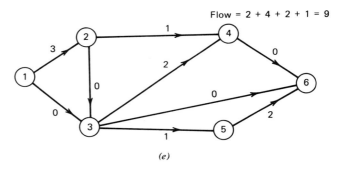

Figure 5.14 (d) and (e).

this technique is inconvenient for complicated networks so computer programs consider a systematic labeling procedure that will do away with some of the objections to this method.

5.5
APPLICATION
STUDIES

5.5.1
Launching a
New Product*

Application Study

Assume that we have been appointed project managers to direct the launching of a new product. We will assume that the product is a consumer item such as an air conditioner or vacuum cleaner. Our company has had no experience with similar products, so detailed market studies will be performed. A list of the steps involved in the launching of this product is developed next. Our analysis might lead to the following activities broken down into departmental responsibility.

---

* Material in this section is an adaption of material appearing in Whitehouse, G. E. *Systems Analysis and Design Using Network Techniques*, Prentice-Hall, Englewood Cliffs, N.J. Used with the permission of Prentice-Hall.

Market Analysis Department Activities

1. *Develop product planning specifications.* This is where the CPM program is begun, where the tasks are defined and assigned, and where the monitorships are established.
2. *Conduct market research.* This activity determines the demand for the product.
3. *Develop price demand schedule.* This activity determines the various grades, models, and prices of the product and relates them to the potential market.
4. *Conduct profit-and-loss analysis.* From the work of the market analysis section, a profit-and-loss estimate is made, and it is determined whether to continue on with product development and what the characteristics of the product will be.
5. *Conduct product appraisal.* This activity determines whether or not the design presented by engineering meets requirements of cost analysis and permits a profitable undertaking. It uses information on costs from engineering with known direct and indirect costs of all types and grades of product under consideration in making its determination.
6. *Determine price.* This activity determines the price from cost data and market research so that it will be profitable and competitive.

Engineering Department Activities

1. *Conduct engineering research.* This is the activity where the preliminary design is made and where necessary information is gathered for making decisions regarding make-or-buy components.
2. *Conduct patent search.* This activity determines whether or not the product is patentable or infringes on the other patents. It also determines if a need to license patent rights for manufacture exists.
3. *Prepare cost estimates.* This engineering function estimates production costs and material costs.
4. *Develop laboratory model.* In conjunction with engineering design, this activity makes a model of the product. The model is used for testing and as an example for production of the final product. The product is made by production people from drawings from the design section, and it is modified as tests and cost figures become available and as improved design drawings become available.
5. *Design final product.* This activity uses information from the laboratory-model testing and from market research activities.
6. *Issue drawings and specifications.* This engineering activity issues necessary drawings and specifications for manufacturing processes.
7. *Determine manufacturing methods.* This activity establishes efficient manufacturing methods and decides what equipment is needed; it

determines job requirements at each station in the manufacturing process.

8. *Prepare service literature.* This activity prepares literature concerning servicing of the product for service people, outlets, and customers.

9. *Train service organization.* This activity trains manufacturing outlets' service people in the proper methods of servicing the product.

10. *Test.* This engineering function is the responsibility of the quality-control section.

Sales and Advertising

1. *Train sales force.* This activity instructs the firm's sales force concerning its new product so that the sales force can obtain new sales outlets and orders for the new product.

2. *Prepare advertising.* This activity prepares an advertising campaign stressing the new product's outstanding features.

3. *Establish distribution outlets.* This activity is accomplished by the sales force and takes initial orders from dealers.

4. *Release advertising.* This activity contracts for advertising display and will be coordinated with dealer and product availability.

5. *Design and procedure packaging.* This activity develops and procures attractive and secure packaging.

Purchasing Department Activities

1. *Procure raw materials.* This activity covers the purchase of raw materials for timely delivery to the production process.

2. *Procure "buy" items.* This activity covers purchases of items such as screws, tools, and product components used in the production process.

Production Department Activities

1. *Train production personnel.* This activity sets up the production line and trains personnel in their assigned jobs.

2. *Manufacture "make" items.* This is the production line.

3. *Assemble.* This activity assembles make items and buy items into finished product.

4. *Box, pack, and ship.* This activity represents the last step before the product is available to the consumer.

We can now consider the interrelationships among these activities and develop an activity network. The activity network is shown in Figure 5.15 and was developed using the following logic.

The market analysis department is responsible for the product planning specifications, market research, and price demand schedule activities. Since they are all interrelated and concerned with consumer preferences and the associated markets, they are placed first. From these

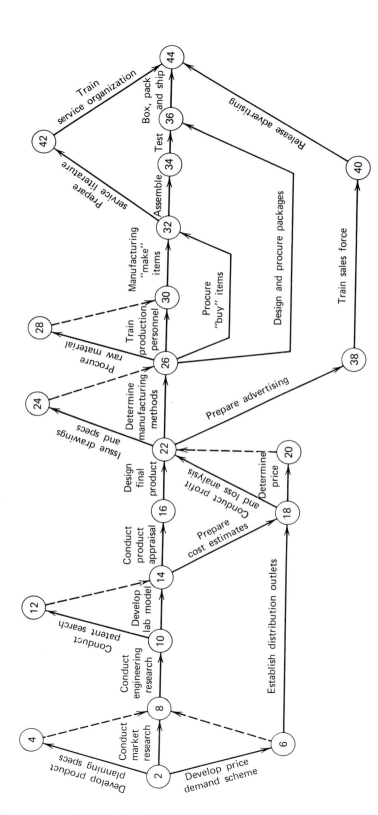

Figure 5.15 Activity network for "launching a new product."

specifications of the market, the creative engineering research and development activities are carried on in sequence. At this time distribution outlets are also established for the product.

Product appraisal consists of a review of the preceding activities, resulting in final product specifications that are transmitted to the final design group. In parallel with this activity, cost estimates are made and combined with the distribution cost data to determine the total cost of producing and selling the product. In the latter portion of the final design phase, a profit-and-loss analysis is accomplished to establish a market price for the product. This price analysis utilizes the cost estimates and distribution information to calculate and "engineer in" a fair profit for the company.

Work on the project can be stopped at any phase of development; however, the most logical point would be at event 22. Beyond this point tooling, material, and machines will be committed to the production of the product. We will consider this as a "point of no return" in committing resources to the production of the product.

If the product meets the profit criteria, it is then committed to the production phase. At this point production personnel determine manufacturing methods including make-or-buy decisions. After the make-or-buy decisions are made, drawings are released for bid or use in the production department. Advertising material for the product is started at this time.

At the same time that the purchased items are procured, the packaging is designed and procured. Production personnel are then trained, raw materials procured, and the manufacturing process begun. The service literature is prepared only after both the make items and buy items are on hand. This will make the preparation of product description and photographic copy much simpler to perform. After this literature has been prepared and made available, the service organization is trained.

While the assembly, testing, and packing phases are under way, the sales force is trained using the actual assembly line-produced items for demonstrations. After sales personnel are trained, but just prior to shipment, the advertising is released. With the shipment of the product, the activity network is complete.

The interrelationships of our activities have been determined and we have developed an activity network describing the project. Our next step is to determine the time and cost data associated with each activity. The normal and crash information is shown in Table 5.8. We now have enough information to use an available computer package. Using the normal time for each activity, the network would yield a project duration of 52 weeks. The results of the analysis are shown in Figure 5.16. The earliest and latest times for each node are shown on the figure along with the critical path.

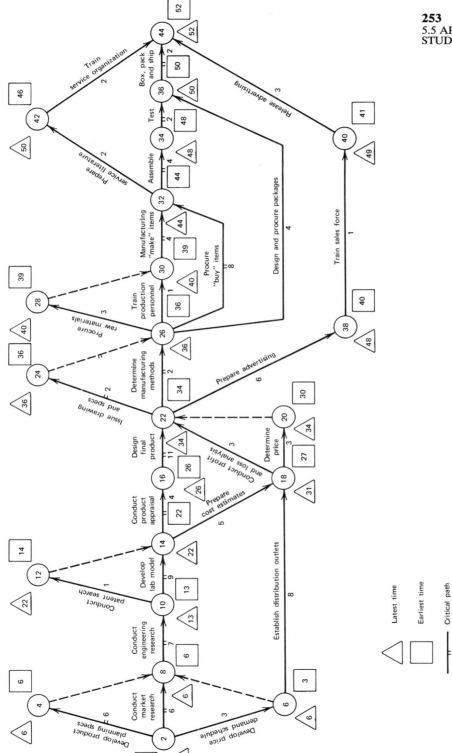

Figure 5.16 All normal schedule for "launching a new product."

Table 5.7 Time and Cost Information for Launching a Product

Activity Description	Normal		Crash	
	Duration	Cost	Duration	Cost
Conduct market research	6	$30,000	2	$125,000
Develop price demand schedules	3	6,250	1	27,400
Develop product planning specifications	6	28,120	4	48,500
Conduct engineering research	7	33,750	4	159,590
Conduct patent search	1	10,000	1	10,000
Prepare cost estimates	5	9,380	2	26,420
Develop laboratory model	9	51,250	5	158,760
Conduct product appraisal	4	15,650	2	51,950
Conduct profit-and-loss analysis	3	5,630	1	24,570
Design final product	8	40,620	5	151,870
Train sales force	1	5,000	1	5,000
Prepare advertising	6	18,750	3	47,500
Issue drawings and specifications	2	3,120	1	7,100
Determine price	3	5,130	1	16,420
Establish distribution outlets	8	56,250	5	132,500
Release advertising	3	4,380	3	4,380
Determine manufacturing methods	2	5,630	1	14,200
Procure raw material	3	3,750	2	9,250
Procure "buy" items	8	11,880	5	28,880
Prepare service literature	2	5,000	1	12,000
Design and procure packaging	4	10,500	1	73,700
Train production personnel	1	9,370	1	9,370
Manufacture "make" items	4	68,750	1	237,380
Assemble	4	49,380	3	95,750
Train service organization	2	11,500	1	27,500
Test	2	12,500	2	12,500
Box, pack and ship	2	5,000	1	11,230
		$516,540		$1,528,900

When consumer products are marketed, timing is extremely important. The longer it takes to get a product on the market, the lower the anticipated profits from the endeavor. We know, however, that it will cost us money (crashing cost) to expedite the project. Thus, there is a cost tradeoff. We can also save on indirect project costs if we decide to expedite the project. Historically, the indirect costs for a project of this nature could be calculated from the following formula:

$$\text{Indirect costs} = \$600,000 + \$10,000 \times (\text{project duration})$$

The marketing department's preliminary estimates of the market potential of this product are shown in Table 5.8.

Table 5.8 Market Potential of the New Product

If Shipped by Week	Total Anticipated Market
30	$2,750,000
31	2,695,000
32	2,650,000
33	2,610,000
34	2,575,000
35	2,540,000
36	2,510,000
37	2,485,000
38	2,460,000
39	2,440,000
40	2,422,000
41	2,406,000
42	2,390,000
43	2,375,000
44	2,360,000
45	2,341,000
46	2,335,000
47	2,325,000
48	2,315,000
49	2,310,000
50	2,305,000
51	2,300,000
52	2,295,000

The procedure for determining the optimum project duration is as follows:

1. Develop the computer input for this project. The computer will determine the direct costs and schedules for various project durations.
2. Determine the total project costs for each feasible schedule calculated by the computer by adding indirect costs (computed initially by the formula, $600,000 + $10,000 \times$ project duration) to the direct cost.
3. Determine the profit for each schedule by subtracting total costs as determined in step 2 from the anticipated market values provided.
4. Select the schedule that will yield the maximum profit.

Table 5.9 Total Profit Analysis for the Product Launching

Duration	Direct Cost	Indirect Cost	Anticipated Market	Profit
52	$516,540	$1,120,000	$2,295,000	$658,460
51	522,200	1,110,000	2,300,000	667,800
50	528,430	1,100,000	2,305,000	676,570
49	539,600	1,090,000	2,310,000	680,400
48	552,150	1,080,000	2,315,000	682,850
47	570,300	1,070,000	2,325,000	684,700
46	588,450	1,060,000	2,335,000	686,550[a]
45	615,327	1,050,000	2,341,000	675,673
44	642,205	1,040,000	2,360,000	677,795
43	669,082	1,030,000	2,375,000	675,918
42	695,960	1,020,000	2,390,000	674,040
41	729,900	1,010,000	2,406,000	666,100
40	763,840	1,000,000	2,422,000	658,160
39	805,920	990,000	2,440,000	654,080
38	838,000	980,000	2,460,000	642,000
37	879,947	970,000	2,485,000	635,053
36	921,893	960,000	2,510,000	628,107
35	963,840	950,000	2,540,000	626,160
34	1,006,610	940,000	2,575,000	628,390
33	1,052,908	930,000	2,610,000	627,020
32	1,114,860	920,000	2,650,000	615,140

[a] Optimum schedule.

Table 5.9 shows the results of applying our procedure to this project. Since our objective is to select the project duration with the maximum profit, we select the 46-week schedule. The optimum schedule is shown in Figure 5.17. The profit curve is fairly flat, so the company might select a somewhat different schedule based on intangible considerations.

5.5.2 Project Management for the Construction of a Warehouse

Application Study

The Walker Portland Company is currently in the process of planning to construct a new warehouse facility to reduce the company's inventory storage problems. Most of the work will be performed by the company's own construction division, but certain portions of the project, such as electrical and plumbing work, will be subcontracted.

Assume you have been retained by the company as a consultant to aid in the planning and administrative control of the project. You have decided to use PERT (program evaluation and review technique) to perform this function. Before beginning the PERT network, you called a meeting with the general foreman, estimator, and chief engineer, all from

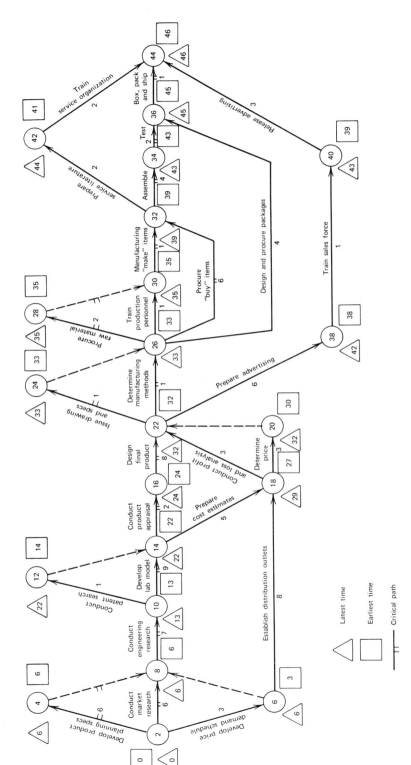

Figure 5.17 Optimum profit schedule for "launching a new product."

the company's construction division. Together, you have prepared a series of time estimates for the various separate portions of the project. These include an optimistic, pessimistic, and most likely time estimate. These separate jobs or activities and the three time estimates for each appear in Table 5.10.

In addition to determining the list of activities, the estimator and foreman discussed in some detail how these activities should be sequenced since the list in Table 5.10 does not necessarily indicate the order in which the work should be performed. During their discussion, you made the following notes:

Corporate management approval must be obtained before any work or procurement of supplies can begin.

Procurement of materials and subcontracting negotiations can begin as soon as approval is obtained.

Grading can begin as soon as subcontracting negotiations are completed.

Foundation can be poured following excavation and after concrete arrives.

Building footings can be poured as soon as excavation work is completed.

Framework must be erected in conjunction with (simultaneously) pouring of building footings.

Floor slab can be poured at completion of foundation pouring. Extra time is allowed in estimates for safety reasons so that floor work does not interfere with framework construction.

Exterior walls can be put up following completion of steel framework and arrival of supplies.

Roof can be installed after steel framework is up. Roof slab pouring must precede roofing installation.

Electrical and plumbing work can commence as soon as steel framework is up.

Insulation and interior walls can be put up after electrical and plumbing work.

Interior painting must await installation of interior walls.

Work for sewer drain, driveway, and parking lot can begin as soon as building site is graded and excavated. Final backfilling and grading must await completion of these activities.

Installation of fuel oil tank and heating system must be started after the foundation has been poured. It must be completed before the interior walls are put in.

Cleanup is the final work before job acceptance.

Company management has requested that your PERT analysis be included with the proposal that comes before them. They also would like to know the probability of finishing the project in 65 days.

Table 5.10 Probabilistic Data for the Walker Portland Company Warehouse

Activity Code	Activity	Opti- mistic Time Days[a]	Most Likely Time Days[a]	Pessi- mistic Time Days[a]
a	Obtain corporate management approval	2	5	8
b	Complete subcontractor negotiations	1	3	7
c	Grade building site and excavate for foundation	5	7	9
d	Procure structural steel for framework	10	15	20
e	Procure concrete for foundation	1	3	5
f	Procure exterior window and door frames	5	7	11
g	Procure supplies for exterior walls and roofing	1	3	5
h	Pour concrete for foundation	9	10	15
i	Pour building footings	4	5	10
j	Erect steel framework	8	11	14
k	Pour floor slab and lay concrete flooring	5	9	13
l	Erect exterior walls	21	24	27
m	Pour roof slab	9	12	15
n	Lay roofing	2	3	8
o	Electrical work—subcontracted	8	10	14
p	Plumbing—subcontracted	7	10	13
q	Install insulation and interior walls	10	15	20
r	Paint interior	3	5	9
s	Install fuel tank and heating system	8	10	16
t	Excavate and lay sewer drain	5	8	11
u	Driveway and parking lot— subcontracted	9	12	15
v	Backfill around building and grade	6	8	10
w	Clean up building and grounds	2	2	2
x	Obtain job acceptance	3	5	9

[a] Working days only, 5 days per week.

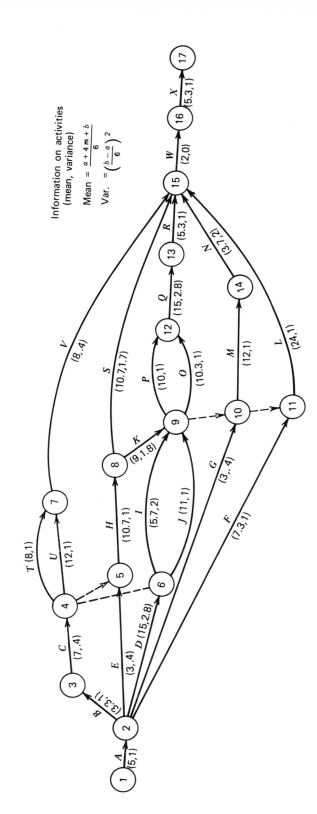

Information on activities
(mean, variance)

Mean $= \dfrac{a + 4m + b}{6}$

Var. $= \left(\dfrac{b - a}{6}\right)^2$

Figure 5.18 PERT network for Walker Portland Company Warehouse.

The PERT activity network for the Walker Portland Company Warehouse is shown in Figure 5.18. The PERT Network is analyzed in Table 5.11. We see that the expected project duration is 72.9 days. To find the probability of meeting a 65-day schedule a Z-value must be calculated.

$$Z = \frac{65 - 72.9}{\sqrt{11}} = -2.4$$

Referring to Appendix B we see that there is a less than 1 percent chance of making the 65-day schedule. However, a review of the critical path shows that time might be saved if electrical work could be completed before the floor slab is laid. The analyst should check the feasibility of this proposal, modify the activity network, and reanalyze the system.

Table 5.11 PERT Analysis for Walker Portland Company Warehouse

Node	T_E Mean	T_E Var.	T_L Mean	T_L Var.	Critical Path
1	0	0	0	11.0	✓
2	5	1	5	10.0	✓
3	8.3	2	8.3	9.0	✓
4	15.3	2.4	15.3	8.6	✓
5	15.3	2.4	15.3	8.6	✓
6	20	3.8	24	6.8	
7	27.3	3.4	57.6	1.4	
8	26	3.4	26	7.6	✓
9	35	5.2	35	5.8	✓
10	35	5.2	49.9	3	
11	35	5.2	41.6	2	
12	45.3	6.2	45.3	4.8	✓
13	60.3	9.0	60.3	3	✓
14	47	6.2	61.9	2	
15	65.6	10.0	65.6	1	✓
16	67.6	10.0	67.6	1	✓
17	72.9	11.0	72.9	0	✓

Ronald Hanson [6] has written an interesting article describing the use of activity networks in planning the move of a hospital to a new location.

5.5.3 Planning to Move a Hospital to New Location*

* Adapted with permission from *Industrial Engineering,* November 1972. Copyright © American Institute of Industrial Engineers, Inc., 25 Technology Park/Atlanta, Norcross, Ga. 30071.

Application Study

There are many factors to be considered when planning to move a hospital. Hanson discusses factors involved in planning a specific move, that of St. Vincent Hospital and Medical Center, Portland, Oregon. St. Vincent moved from a 373-bed hillside facility in the city to a new 403-bed facility five miles away in a suburban area.

Several basic decisions were made early. Due to construction delays, much of the new equipment planned for immediate installation in the new hospital was delivered to, and put into use in, the old hospital. Thus, there was a large volume of equipment to be moved from the old to new hospital. This resulted in a decision to employ a moving firm to perform the moving.

The basic planning tool utilized was critical path scheduling. This technique was invaluable in assuring consideration of the myriad of details involved in planning the move, according to Hanson.

The application of critical path networks provided the move coordinator a detailed, systematized plan and time schedule before the project began. As work progressed, time estimates were refined to provide tighter controls over all required elements of the move. The networks and output reports provided the coordinator with the means to:

1. Define the project tasks and establish the time relationships of the project and the events within the project.
2. Ascertain the interdependence of project activities and the effect of these on project duration.
3. Evaluate progress.
4. Manage the reallocation of resources on an exception basis.
5. Summarize the status of the project for hospital administration.

Since the nature of the move was such that a fixed move date could not be established until the last 60 days (and in our case, was changed 35 days before the planned date), it was decided to do all the planning on the basis of the number of days the event would be prior to or after the patient-move day. This day (M day) was a variable, but all events were fixed in relation to it. For example, an event such as the appointment of a medical staff committee, to advise on necessary premove and postmove admission policies, was to occur at M minus 170 days. A simplified version of the critical path chart is shown in Figure 5.19. After initial revisions, the chart served as the basic coordinating tool for the last eight months prior to the actual move.

Hospital department heads were involved early in planning the move of the individual departments. The move coordinator and the mover's coordinator discussed with each department head the problems of moving his department and its equipment. This early involvement of department heads assured maximum consideration of the particular problems of each department and opened channels of communication.

Early discussions were held with private ambulance companies whose assistance would be necessary even with the use of army ambulance-buses; with local merchants, who would be affected by the moving activities; with local police agencies; city traffic engineers; the other hospitals in the area; and with the outside firms involved in the moving of specialized hospital equipment. In-hospital discussions involved planning of public relations activities, dedication of the new hospital, orientation of employees at the new hospital, cleaning of the new hospital and of the equipment on arrival at the new hospital, and food-service requirements before, during, and after the move. A major decision, that evolved from the discussion with the police, was a plan to move the patients on a Sunday morning, to minimize traffic problems.

A committee of the medical staff and the administration met to formulate admitting and scheduling policies for the premove and immediate postmove periods. As much of the equipment was being moved from the existing operating room suite, it was necessary to plan a reduction in operating room use to allow for equipment transfer. A considerable amount of negotiation was necessary with the contractors as they desired almost all fixed equipment six months in advance of our ability to relinquish it. It was also a paramount consideration that all patients in the hospital at the time of the move be in reasonable condition for moving. This committee, after much consideration, arrived at the policy proposals that formed the basis for the policies followed during the move period. It was necessary, as a part of these policies, to obtain cooperation from other hospitals in the area, for us to divert some emergency ambulance cases during the last week prior to the move and for several days after the move.

The policies formed a logical basis for the hospital to plan the move. The advisory committee also served as a focal point for discussions of M day plans. Discussions with the physicians on the committee served to validate planning of the hospital personnel. The advisory committee also decided on the suitability of the ambulance-bus as a vehicle for the transfer of patients.

Discussions continued with outside individuals and firms on the many factors involved in the move and many plans were finalized as time passed. Concurrent with the previously described events, detailed plans were evolving for the moving of hospital equipment. Estimates of the mover were converted into detailed schedules and were discussed and confirmed with hospital departments. Almost all plans were confirmed and finalized prior to the final month before the actual move.

The final move day was not confirmed until less than two months before the date. There were many modifications to plans as events and passage of time dictated. However, the basic planning document, the critical path network, remained unchanged in the last seven months,

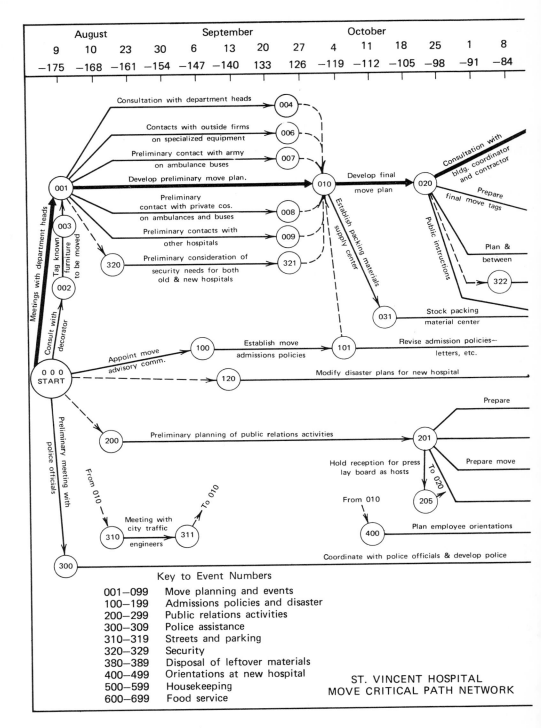

Figure 5.19 St. Vincent Hospital move critical-path network.

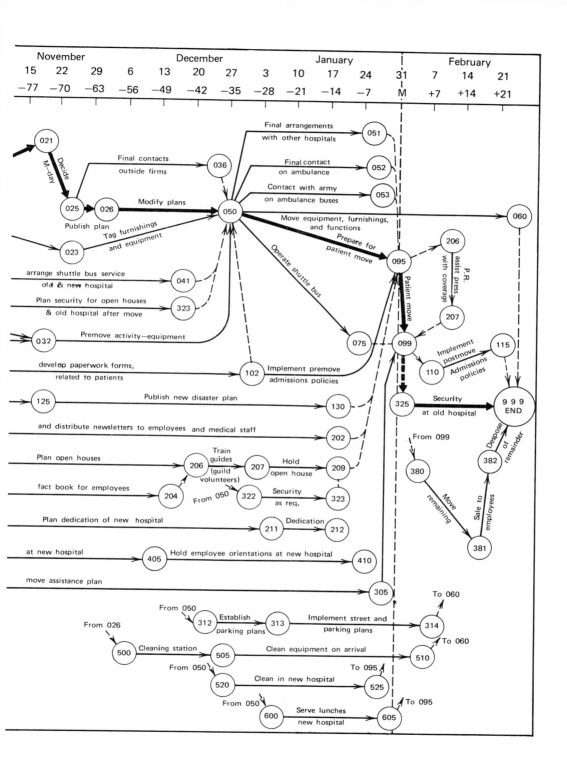

confirming the faith placed in the scheduling method. It remained the constant framework around which all other plans were based and developed.

As Hanson points out, the time spent in the early development of sound plans proved a wise investment.

5.5.4 Equipment Replacement Problem

Application Study

An interesting application of shortest path analysis is in the area of equipment replacement. For example, a company is planning its equipment policy for the next five years. They are able to forecast the cost of buying the equipment at the beginning of year i and selling it at the beginning of year j. We will call this cost, $C_{i,j}$. What is the best replacement policy if:

$$C_{1,2} = 700, \quad C_{1,3} = 1400, \quad C_{1,4} = 1700, \quad C_{2,3} = 900$$
$$C_{2,4} = 1300, \quad C_{2,5} = 1700, \quad C_{3,4} = 1000, \quad C_{3,5} = 1200$$
$$C_{3,6} = 2000, \quad C_{4,5} = 800, \quad C_{4,6} = 1200, \quad C_{5,6} = 700$$

We should note that the five-year span that we are analyzing goes from the beginning of year 1 to the beginning of year 6 (which also is the end of year 5).

The network for this application study is shown in Figure 5.20. The nodes represent the beginning of the year in question and the arcs represent the replacement cost.

For example the $C_{1,3}$ cost is placed on the path joining nodes 1 and 3. To find the minimum cost we observe that this is almost the same type of problem discussed in Section 5.3 except we are minimizing costs instead of distance. Since both costs and distance are additive we can use the algorithm by substituting the $C_{i,j}$'s for the $d_{i,j}$'s in algorithm.

$$m_1 = 0$$
$$m_2 = \min (m_1 + C_{1,2}) = 700$$
$$m_3 = \min (m_1 + C_{1,3}, m_2 + C_{2,3})$$
$$\quad = \min (0 + 1400, 700 + 900) = 1400$$
$$m_4 = \min (0 + 1700, 700 + 1300, 1400 + 1000) = 1700$$
$$m_5 = \min (700 + 1700, 1400 + 1200, 1700 + 800) = 2400$$
$$m_6 = \min (1400 + 2000, 1700 + 1200, 2400 + 700) = 2900$$

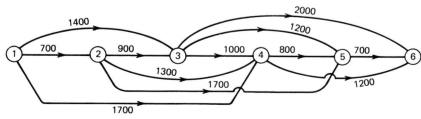

Figure 5.20 Equipment replacement problem.

Therefore the minimum cost path is $2900 and is achieved by buying at the beginning of year 1 and keeping the equipment for three years ($C_{1,4} = 1700$) and then buying at the beginning of year 4 and keeping it two years ($C_{4,6} = 1200$)

The analyst might also be interested in second- and third-best replacement policies, in order to consider some slightly higher cost alternatives. Thus we can apply the m-shortest routes approach discussed in Section 5.3.

$$m_1^{(1)} = 0$$
$$m_2^{(1)} = 700$$
$$m_3^{(1)} = \min_1 (m_1^{(1)} + C_{1,3}, m_2^{(1)} + C_{2,3}) = \min_1 (1400, 1600) = 1400$$
$$m_3^{(2)} = \min_2 (1400, 1600) = 1600$$
$$m_4^{(1)} = \min_1 (m_1^{(1)} + C_{1,4}, m_2^{(1)} + C_{2,4}, m_3^{(1)} + C_{3,4}, m_3^{(2)} + C_{3,4})$$
$$\qquad = \min_1 (1700, 2000, 2400, 2600) = 1700$$
$$m_4^{(2)} = 2000$$
$$m_4^{(3)} = 2400$$
$$m_5^{(1)} = \min_1 (m_2^{(1)} + C_{2,5}, m_3^{(1)} + C_{3,5}, m_3^{(2)} + C_{3,5}, m_4^{(1)} + C_{4,5}, m_4^{(2)}$$
$$\qquad + C_{4,5}, m_4^{(3)} + C_{4,5})$$
$$\qquad = \min_1 (2400, 2600, 2800, 2500, 2800, 3200)$$
$$\qquad = 2400$$
$$m_5^{(2)} = 2500$$
$$m_5^{(3)} = 2600$$
$$m_6^{(1)} = \min_1 (m_3^{(1)} + C_{3,6}, m_3^{(2)} + C_{3,6}, m_4^{(1)} + C_{4,6}, m_4^{(2)} + C_{4,6}, m_4^{(3)}$$
$$\qquad + C_{4,6}, m_5^{(1)} + C_{5,6}, m_5^{(2)} + C_{5,6}, m_5^{(3)} + C_{5,6})$$
$$\qquad = \min_1 (3400, 3600, 2900, 3200, 3600, 3100, 3200, 3300)$$
$$\qquad = 2900$$
$$m_6^{(2)} = 3100$$
$$m_6^{(3)} = 3200$$

So the second-best policy yields a cost of $3100 and is obtained by buying in years 1, 2, and 5. There are two third-best policies yielding a cost of $3200.

Often an interesting result is available from simple modifications of the shortest path analysis. Consider the case where an investor has alternate investment strategies available to him. For example, he can buy one-year bonds that yield 4 percent per annum, three-year bonds yielding 6 percent per annum or five-year bonds yielding 5 percent per annum. Given that the investor has a fixed horizon, his problem is to maximize return on investment. For our example assume that we wish to obtain the maximum return over a five-year horizon. The flow of investment can be modeled in network form as shown in Figure 5.21. The nodes represent the beginning of the investment year in question and the arcs represent the investment opportunities. Thus at the beginning of year 1 we can buy

**5.5.5
Maximizing
the Rate of
Return on
Investments**

Application Study

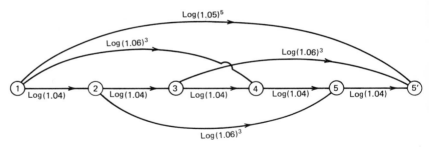

Figure 5.21   Network model for investment flows.

a one-year, three-year, or five-year bond at the beginning of year 2 we can only buy a one-year or three-year bond because a five-year bond will not mature within our five-year planning horizon. We should note that node 5′ represents the end of year 5 and thus the end of our investment plan. The problem is to find the path from node 1 to 5′ which maximizes the rate of return on our money. Since we are dealing with compound interest money invested along path 1–2–5–5′ will yield a return (1.04) $(1.05)^3$ (1.04), thus the coefficients on our activities are multiplicative instead of being additive. But we could take the log of each rate of return and value of the path in question becomes $\log(1.04) + 3\log(1.06) + \log(1.04)$. Since the log increases with the size of a number, this problem can be solved by finding the longest path through the network after the log has been taken of the coefficient of each activity.

We can modify step 2 of the algorithm discussed in Section 5.3 to read

$$m_j = \max\,(m_i + \log R_{i,j}) \qquad i = 1, 2, \ldots j - 1$$

where $R_{i,j}$ is the rate of return realized by buying a bond in year i that matures in year j.

By applying the modified algorithm we could find that the best investment strategy would be to buy series of two one-year bonds and one three-year bond yielding a rate of return of 28.8 percent.

**5.5.6
Maximizing
the Minimum
Level of
Efficiency
in an
Assignment
Problem**

Application Study

In Chapter 4 we discussed the job assignment problem where our goal was to maximize the total efficiency in our system. Now suppose we wish to assign jobs in such a way that the lowest efficiency is as large as possible. We handle this problem as a maximal flow problem. First, an arbitrary assignment is made. The lowest efficiency in the arbitrary assignment is observed and all possible assignments with that efficiency or lower are considered to be illegal. A flow network of the legal assignments is made and another feasible solution is found by network flow methods. Once again, the lowest efficiency is observed and assignments with that efficiency or lower are eliminated from consideration. The process continues until the flow method can no longer find a feasible assignment. The lowest efficiency in the last feasible assignment is then the answer to our problem.

Let's assume the following assignment matrix:

		Person			
Job	1	2	3	4	5
1	10	9	6	5	1
2	2	3	8	4	5
3	7	6	2	1	5
4	4	8	8	4	3
5	4	5	2	4	2

and also that an arbitrary assignment of

$$J_1 \to P_1 \quad (10)$$
$$J_2 \to P_5 \quad (5)$$
$$J_3 \to P_2 \quad (6)$$
$$J_4 \to P_3 \quad (8)$$
$$J_5 \to P_4 \quad (4)$$

has been made. We note that the minimum level of efficiency is $4(J_5 \to P_4)$ for this assignment. We will now remove all assignments with an efficiency of 4 or less and develop a network flow model (Figure 5.22) to test for feasibility. In Figure 5.22 node S is the source and node D is the

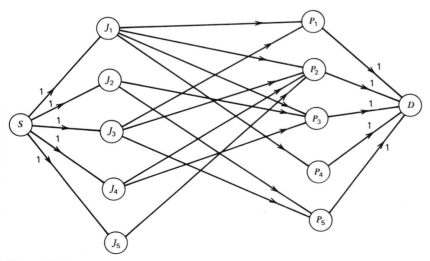

Figure 5.22 Network model of the job assignment problem.

sink. The flow from S to D represents the number of jobs assigned. Thus if this flow is equal to the number of jobs then a feasible assignment has been found. Nodes J_i and P_j represent the jobs and people. The paths joining S to J_i and P_j to D all have capacity of 1 and represent the fact that each job can only be assigned once and each person can only do one job. All feasible assignments are represented by arcs joining appropriate J_i's and P_j's. For example J_5 can only be done by P_5 if our goal is to have a minimum efficiency of 5 or better.

Applying the maximal flow approach described in Section 5.4 we find a maximal flow of 5 associated with

$$
\begin{array}{ll}
J_1 \rightarrow P_4 & (5) \\
J_2 \rightarrow P_5 & (5) \\
J_3 \rightarrow P_1 & (7) \\
J_4 \rightarrow P_3 & (8) \\
J_5 \rightarrow P_2 & (5)
\end{array}
$$

Thus we have a feasible solution and the minimum performance level is 5 and occurs on paths $J_1 \rightarrow P_4$, $J_2 \rightarrow P_5$, and $J_5 \rightarrow P_2$. If all jobs with efficiency 5 are removed, the maximal flow will be less than 5 because J_5 cannot be assigned.

5.5.7
Assignment of
Families to Low-
Income Housing

Application Study

A city must assign n families to $m(n \leq m)$ available low-income houses. Certain assignments are impossible because the houses are too small for the family. Figure 5.23 shows a possible network flow model for this situation. In this model N_i is the number of houses that will hold i people and P_j is the number of families with j people in them. The model has been set up in such a way that the family can live in a house that is bigger than their needs but not in one that is smaller.

We should try to assign families as close as possible to their size needs. The city administration will have to establish a policy for assignments. For example, in Figure 5.23 the policy tested would not assign a house that was too small but would assign a house that had a capacity that exceeded needs by as much as two people. If the network flow equals n then all families can be assigned, otherwise a new policy must be tried.

5.6
PROBLEMS

1. Make an arrow diagram for the following:
   (a) O start of job
       K end of job
       O precedes A, B
       A precedes C, M
       B precedes E, F, G
       C precedes I, H
       E precedes D
       M precedes D

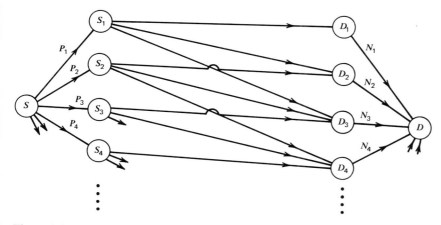

Figure 5.23 Network flow model for assignment of city low-income housing.

   D, F also precede *I, H*
   H, G precede *J*
   I, J precede *K*
  (b) Same as above, except:
   D now only precedes *I*
   F only precedes *H*
   C still precedes both.
2. Make an arrow diagram for the following:
  (a) *A* must precede *B* and *C*
   B must precede *D* and *E*
   C must precede *E*
   D and *E* must precede *F*
  (b) *A* must precede *B, C,* and *D*
   B, C, D must precede *E*
  (c) *A* and *B* must precede *C*
   A must precede *D*
   C and *D* must precede *E*
3. Draw the arrow diagram for the following:
  O is the start of the job
  O precedes *A* and *B*
  A precedes *G* and *H*
  B precedes *E, F,* and *C*
  C, E, and *G* precede *M*
  F precedes *G*
  H precedes *I*
  M and *I* precede *J*
  J is the end of the job

4. Make an arrow diagram for the following problem of servicing a car. Assume that you must remove the air filter before oiling the generator and distributor and consider the following activities:
(a) Hoist car.
(b) Remove drain plug.
(c) Grease underside fittings.
(d) Inspect tires and exhaust system.
(e) Check differential and transmission levels.
(f) Replace drain plug.
(g) Lower car.
(h) Refill crankcase.
(i) Check oil level.
(j) Grease upper fittings.
(k) Open hood.
(l) Oil generator and distributor.
(m) Check radiator and battery.
(n) Drain oil.
(o) Wipe excess off upper fittings.
(p) Remove and clean air filter.
(q) Replace air filter.
(r) Close hood.

5. Considering problem 1(a), construct a table showing the earliest start, latest start, earliest finish, latest finish, total float, and free float for each activity. The time assignments are as follows:

$$O = 2 \quad A = 6 \quad B = 1 \quad E = 4 \quad M = 9$$
$$C = 7 \quad D = 3 \quad F = 12 \quad H = 6 \quad G = 10$$
$$I = 3 \quad J = 5 \quad K = 3$$

6. Consider problem 2(a), analyze the system given the following times:

$$A = 6 \quad B = 10 \quad C = 7$$
$$D = 11 \quad E = 5 \quad F = 3$$

7. Consider problem 3(a), analyze the system given the following times:

$$O = 11 \quad A = 15 \quad B = 6$$
$$G = 3 \quad H = 4 \quad E = 7$$
$$F = 6 \quad C = 3 \quad M = 6$$
$$I = 9 \quad J = 2$$

8. Draw a cost curve considering the following information:
(a) Forty man-hours of work are required.
(b) Miss A is normally assigned.
(c) Misses B and C can be made available if necessary.

(d) First-shift operation costs $2.00/hour.
   Second-shift operation cost $2.20/hour.
   Third-shift operation costs $2.42/hour.

(e) Typists are assigned for eight-hour periods.

(f) One typewriter is available.
   We can rent additional typewriters at $5.00 per 24-hour period, including delivery and pickup.

(g) No girl works overtime (more than 8 hours in any 24-hour period).

(h) There is no additional expense for second- and third-shift super-vision.

9. For the arrow diagram in Figure 5.24, construct a table showing the earliest start, latest start, earliest finish, latest finish, total float, and free float for each activity. Also, indicate the critical path of the diagram.

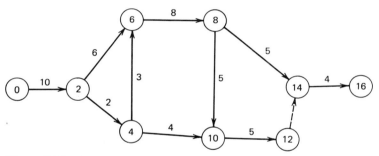

Figure 5.24 Activity network for problem 9.

10. Given the following information and the arrow diagram in Figure 5.25:

Activity	Normal Time	Crash Time	Normal Cost	Crash Cost
A	0	0	0	0
B	15	10	7000	8500
C	6	4	2000	3000
D	2	2	500	500
E	4	4	3500	3500
F	5	3	4000	4400
G	7	5	3000	4000
H	6	6	1000	1000
I	0	0	0	0
J	4	4	3000	3000

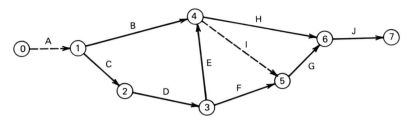

Figure 5.25 Activity network for problem 10.

(a) Construct a table showing earliest start and finish, latest start and finish, cost slope, and the two types of floats.
(b) What is the critical path of this project?
What will the project cost?
(c) What is the shortest possible time in which the project can be completed? What will the critical elements be in this case?
(d) Derive *minimum cost schedules* for all days between the all-normal and the all-crash schedules.
11. Given the activity diagram in Figure 5.26 and the following data:

Activity	Normal Time	Crash Time	Normal Cost	Crash Cost
A	10	7	700	1000
B	12	9	800	1400
C	7	7	1000	1000
D	13	10	1200	1500
E	3	3	500	500
F	7	6	600	900
G	0	0	0	0
H	2	1	1000	5000
I	7	5	1300	1600
J	4	4	2000	2000

(a) Considering normal time, calculate the total and free floats for activities B, D, and E.
(b) If you wish to crash your schedule to 26 days, what would the optimum cost of the project be? Show your work along with the scheduled duration of each activity for the 26-day schedule.
12. Updating problem: the original CPM arrow diagram appeared as shown in Figure 5.27. After 15 days:

    0–2   Complete
    2–6   Complete
    2–10   Complete

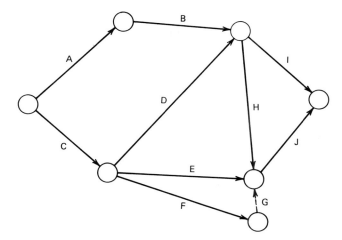

Figure 5.26   Activity network for problem 11.

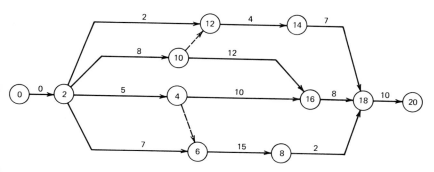

Figure 5.27   Activity network for problem 12.

2–4	Complete
4–16	Five more days left
6–8	Ten days remaining
8–18	Reestimated to four days—not done
	All remaining jobs not started

Draw a new diagram and evaluate the position of the company with respect to its original scheduled completion.

13. (a) Complete the following table for the PERT diagram shown in Figure 5.28.

Event	T_E		T_L			Probability
No.	Mean	Var.	Mean	Var.	Slack	of Slack
1						
2						
3						
4						
5						
6						
7						

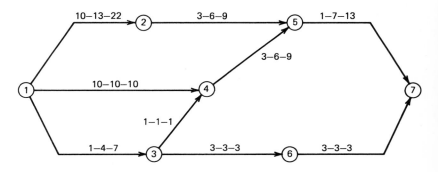

Figure 5.28 Activity network for problem 13.

(b) What is the critical path?

(c) If the scheduled completion time is 28 days, what is the likelihood of meeting the schedule?

(d) If event 3 is scheduled for day 3, what is the probability of meeting the schedule?

14. Write a computer program to evaluate an activity network.

15. Modify the activity network algorithm presented in this chapter so that it gives not only the longest path through a network, but also the second- and third-longest paths.

For each of the following acyclic networks find:

(a) Shortest path between the origin and terminal nodes.

(b) Shortest paths from the origin to all nodes in the network.

(c) Shortest paths between all nodes in the network.

(d) Three shortest paths from the source to the sink.

16.

Arc	Duration
1–2	7
1–3	6
1–4	10
2–3	2
2–4	4
3–4	2
3–5	7
4–5	3

17.

Arc	Duration
1–2	3
1–3	1
2–3	2
2–4	1
3–4	8
3–6	12
3–5	9
4–5	2
4–6	10
5–6	6

18.

Arc	Duration	Arc	Duration
1–2	6	5–7	3
1–3	9	6–7	6
2–3	6	6–8	4
2–4	2	7–8	3
2–5	5	7–9	8
3–4	8	8–9	4
3–6	3		
4–5	1		
4–7	7		

19. Develop a computer program for finding the shortest path between all pairs of nodes in a directed acyclic network. Test your routine on problem 16.

20. Find the maximal flow in the following network:

Arc	$C_{i,j}$
1–2	6
1–3	4
2–3	3
2–4	9
3–4	1
3–5	4
4–5	6

21. Find the maximal flow in the following network:

Arc	$C_{i,j}$
1–2	10
1–3	11
2–3	6
2–4	7
3–4	4
3–5	5
3–6	3
4–5	4
4–6	5
5–6	5

22. Petersen General Contractors is currently preparing a bid for the erection of a 225-foot television antenna tower and the construction of a building adjacent to the tower that will be used to house transmission and electrical equipment. Petersen is bidding only on the tower and its electrical equipment, the building, the connecting cable between tower and building, and site preparation. Transmission equipment and other equipment to be housed in the building are not to be included in the bid and will be obtained separately by the television station. The site for the tower is at the top of a hill to minimize the required height of the tower, with the building to be constructed at a slightly lower elevation than the base of the tower and near a main road. Between the tower and building will be a crushed-gravel service road and an underground cable. Adjacent to the building, a fuel tank will be installed above ground on a concrete slab.

Prior to preparing the detailed cost estimates, Petersen's estimator met with the company's general foreman to go over the plans and blueprints for the job. In addition to preparing a cost estimate, the estimator was also preparing an estimate of the time it would take to complete the job. The television station management was very concerned about the time factor. It requested that bids be prepared on the basis of the most likely time for completing the job and also for the most optimistic and most pessimistic times for completing the job. During the conference between the estimator and general foreman, it was determined that the activities shown in Table 5.12 would be necessary to complete the job. The estimator prepared time estimates for these activities as shown in Table 5.12.

Table 5.12 Television Tower and Building Construction Time and Cost Estimate

Activity Code	Activity	Most Likely Time Days[a]	Opti-mistic Time Days[a]	Pessi-mistic Time Days[a]
a	Sign contract and complete subcontractor negotiations	5	5	5
b	Survey site	6	4	8
c	Grade building site and excavate for basement	8	6	10
d	Grade tower site	30	21	39
e	Procure structural steel for tower	85	85	85
f	Procure electrical equipment for tower and connecting underground cable	120	120	120
g	Pour concrete for tower footings and anchors	42	25	59
h	Erect tower and install electrical equipment	38	25	51
i	Install connecting cable in tower site	8	4	12
j	Install drain tile and storm drain in tower site	35	18	52
k	Backfill and grade tower site	8	4	12
l	Pour building footings	29	21	37
m	Pour basement slab and fuel tank slab	14	11	17
n	Pour outside basement walls	34	30	38
o	Pour walls for basement rooms	9	7	11
p	Pour concrete floor beams	11	10	12
q	Pour main floor slab and lay concrete block walls	12	10	14
r	Pour roof slab	15	13	17

Table 5.12 continued

Activity Code	Activity	Most Likely Time Days[a]	Optimistic Time Days[a]	Pessimistic Time Days[a]
s	Complete interior framing and utilities	42	30	54
t	Lay roofing	3	2	4
u	Paint building interior, install fixtures, and clean up	19	13	25
v	Install main cable between tower site and building	35	25	45
w	Install fuel tank	3	2	4
x	Install building septic tank	12	8	16
y	Install drain tile and storm drain in building site	15	10	20
z	Backfill around building, grade, and surface with crushed rock	9	7	11
aa	Lay base for connecting road between tower and building	15	13	17
bb	Complete grading and surface connecting road	8	5	11
cc	Clean up tower site	5	3	7
dd	Clean up building site	3	2	4
ee	Obtain job acceptance	5	5	5

[a] Days shown are working days only.

In addition to determining the list of activities, the estimator and foreman discussed in detail how these activities could be sequenced since the list of activities in Table 5.12 did not necessarily indicate the order in which the work could be performed. In the course of the discussion, the estimator made the notes as follows:

Survey work and procurement of the structural steel and electrical equipment so that tower can start as soon as contract is signed.

Grading of tower and building sites can begin when survey is completed.

After tower site is graded, footings and anchors can be poured.

After building site is graded and basement excavated, building footings can be poured.

Septic tank can be installed when grading and excavating of building site is done.

Construction of connecting road can start as soon as survey is completed.

Exterior and interior basement walls can be poured as soon as footings are in.

Basement floor and fuel tank slab should go in after basement walls.

Floor beams can go in after the basement walls and basement floor.

Main floor slab and concrete block walls go in after floor beams.

Roof slab can go on after block walls are up.

Interior can be completed as soon as roof slab is on.

Put in fuel tank any time after slab is in.

Drain tile and storm drain for building go in after septic tank.

As soon as tower footings and anchors are in and tower steel and equipment are available, tower can be erected.

Connecting cable in tower site, drain tile, and storm drain can be put in as soon as tower is up.

Main cable between building and tower goes in after connecting cable at tower site is in and basement walls are up.

Tower site can be backfilled and graded as soon as storm drain, connecting cable, and main cable are in.

Clean up tower site after backfilling and grading is done.

Backfill around building and grade after main cable is in and after storm drain is in.

Clean up building site after backfilling and grading is done.

(a) Prepare a PERT network that portrays the plan for the construction project.

(b) Identify the critical path in the network. What is the most likely time estimate for the project?

(c) Under the most optimistic circumstances, would it be possible to complete the project within a 195-day period? If so, what portions of the job must be supervised most closely in order to achieve completion within this time?

23. Suppose you want to write a thesis. Construct an activity diagram of the various activities and events that would constitute such an endeavor from start to finish. Perform an analysis similar to that presented in this chapter for this situation.

24. Suppose that you wish to install a computer center in a company that previously had no computer. Construct an activity diagram that will describe all the activities and events that would constitute such an endeavor. Perform an analysis similar to that presented in this chapter for this situation.

25. Consider the following equipment replacement model. A company is planning its equipment policy for the next six years. $C_{i,j}$ is the cost of buying the equipment at the beginning of the year i and selling it at the beginning of year j. No equipment can be kept more than three years.

Find the best replacement policy if:

$C_{1,2} = 1800$ $C_{1,3} = 2400$ $C_{1,4} = 3700$ $C_{2,3} = 1900$ $C_{2,4} = 3300$
$C_{2,5} = 4700$ $C_{3,4} = 4000$ $C_{3,5} = 3200$ $C_{3,6} = 3000$ $C_{4,5} = 1800$
$C_{4,6} = 2200$ and $C_{5,6} = 1700$

How much better is this policy than the second- and third-best methods?

26. A company is considering an investment plan with a horizon of seven years. How should they invest, if opportunities include

one-year bonds at 5 percent/year
four-year bonds at 8 percent/year
six-year bonds at 7 percent/year

27. How would your answer in problem 26 change if the planning horizon was eight years?

28. Given the following reliability network, find the most reliable route through the network:

Arc	Reliability
1–2	.80
1–3	.80
2–3	.70
2–4	.90
3–4	.90
3–5	.75
3–5	.75
4–5	.80

Note: reliability is the probability a given element functions.

29. In Chapter 4, we discussed the transportation model. A variatioh of this model is the capacitated transportation model that considers the possibility of limiting the flow $(C_{i,j})$ from sources (s_i) to destination (d_j). Develop a network flow model to find if there is a feasible distribution pattern and try your approach on the following data:

$$s_1 = 10 \quad d_1 = 10 \quad C_{1,2} = 5$$
$$s_2 = 10 \quad d_2 = 10 \quad C_{1,3} = 5$$
$$s_3 = 20 \quad d_3 = 5 \quad C_{1,4} = 2$$
$$d_4 = 10 \quad C_{2,1} = 10$$
$$C_{2,2} = 5$$
$$C_{2,4} = 6$$
$$C_{3,1} = 8$$
$$C_{3,2} = 8$$
$$C_{3,3} = 8$$
$$C_{3,4} = 8$$

30. The matrix below shows the jobs that can be handled by machines in a job shop. If each machine can handle only two jobs, what is the maximum number of jobs that can be processed?

Job/Machine	A	B	C	D
a	✓		✓	
b	✓	✓		✓
c	✓			✓
d	✓			✓
e	✓	✓		
f	✓		✓	
g	✓			
h	✓	✓	✓	
i	✓		✓	
j	✓		✓	
k	✓	✓		
l	✓			

31. In Section 5.5.6 a method for maximizing the minimum level of efficiency in an assignment problem was discussed. Apply this approach to the following assignment matrix.

Job/Person	1	2	3	4	5	6
1	4	9	3	6	7	2
2	3	0	5	2	5	8
3	9	6	7	3	9	7
4	10	3	4	6	3	6
5	4	2	2	2	3	7
6	1	8	1	9	2	1

32. Solve the housing problem discussed in Section 5.5.7 given

$$
\begin{aligned}
P_1 &= 14 & N_1 &= 12 \\
P_2 &= 30 & N_2 &= 35 \\
P_3 &= 41 & N_3 &= 35 \\
P_5 &= 30 & N_4 &= 30 \\
P_6 &= 15 & N_6 &= 30 \\
& & N_8 &= 20
\end{aligned}
$$

33. A company wishes to develop an optimum replacement policy for some pollution equipment it needs for the next seven years. Assume that P_i will be the purchase price at the beginning of year i, and $P_1 = 200$, $P_2 = 210$, $P_3 = 225$, $P_4 = 250$, $P_5 = 270$, $P_6 = 290$, and $P_7 = 300$.

The salvage value of a one-year-old piece of equipment is 100, and it is 50 for a two-year-old piece of equipment. Older equipment is worthless. The operating costs for equipment in use for K consecutive periods is $Y_1 = 50$, $Y_2 = 75$, $Y_3 = 100$, $Y_4 = 150$, $Y_5 = 200$, $Y_6 = 300$, and $Y_7 = 450$. Can you help the company solve this problem?

34. Reanalyze the Walker Portland Company Warehouse system discussed in Section 5.5.2, assuming that the electrical work could be completed before the floor slab was laid. What is the probability of meeting the 65-day schedule?

REFERENCES

1. Antill, J. M. and R. W. Woodhead, *Critical Path Methods in Construction Practice*, Wiley, New York, 1966.
2. Battersby, A., *Network Analysis for Planning and Scheduling*, Macmillan and Co., London, 1967.
3. Elmaghraby, S. E., *Network Models in Management Science*, Springer-Verlag Lecture Series on Operations Research, 1970.
4. Elmaghraby, S. E., "Theory of Networks and Management Science I and II," *Management Science*, Vol. 17, Nos. 1 and 2, September and October 1970.
5. Ford, L. R. and D. R. Fulkerson, *Flows in Networks*, Princeton University Press, Princeton, N.J., 1962.
6. Hanson, R. S., "Moving the Hospital to a New Location," *Industrial Engineering*, Vol. 4, No. 11, November 1972.
7. Hu, T. C., *Integer Programming and Network Flows*, Addison-Wesley Publishing Co., Reading, Mass., 1969.
8. Iannone, A. L., *Management Program Planning and Control with PERT, MOST, LOB*, Prentice-Hall, Englewood Cliffs, N.J., 1967.
9. Kelley, J. E., Jr., "Critical Path Planning and Scheduling: Mathematical Basis," *Operations Research*, Vol. 9, No. 3, May–June, 1962.
10. Levin, R. and C. Kirkpatrick, *Planning and Control with PERT/CPM*, McGraw-Hill, New York, 1966.
11. Moder, J. J. and C. R. Phillips, *Project Management with CPM and PERT*, Van Nostrand-Reinhold Publishing Co., New York, 1970.
12. Phillips, C. R., "Fifteen Key Features of Computer Programs for CPM and PERT," *Journal of Industrial Engineering*, January–February, 1964.
13. Whitehouse, G. E., *Systems Analysis and Design Using Network Techniques*, Prentice-Hall, Englewood Cliffs, N.J., 1973.
14. Wiest, J. and F. Levy, *Management Guide to PERT–CPM*, Prentice-Hall, Englewood Cliffs, N.J., 1969.

inventory
models 6

The development of inventory models was one of the first areas of study in operations research. The inventory models that we will study occur when it is necessary to stock physical goods in order to satisfy a demand for these items over a specified time period. Almost every business uses inventory to guarantee smooth and efficient running of its operations. The basic decisions to be made are when and how much to order. The optimum inventory decision is the one that minimizes the following costs:

6.1 STRUCTURE OF THE INVENTORY MODELS

Setup cost: the fixed cost of starting up a production run or of placing an order for items from an outside vendor. This cost will be assumed to be independent of the number of units ordered or produced.

Holding cost: the cost of carrying items in storage. The major components of this cost include the cost of capital invested in the items, storage costs, insurance costs, depreciation costs, and the like. We will assume that this cost varies directly with the level of inventory and the length of time the item is held in stock.

Purchase or production cost: the per unit cost of buying or making a unit of product. The purchase price will become important when "quantity discounts" or "price breaks" can be secured for purchases above a certain quantity or when economies of scale suggest that the per unit production cost can be reduced by a longer production run.

Shortage costs: the penalty costs for running out of stock when there is a demand for an item. This cost includes the loss of potential profit and the loss of goodwill. In some cases the unfilled demand can be satisfied when product becomes available (the backorder case). In other cases the unfilled demand is lost (lost sales case). The shortage cost is usually assumed to vary directly with the shortage quantity and the delay in filling the order for the back-order case, while it is assumed to be proportional to only the shortage quantity in the lost sale case.

Like several topics in this text, entire books [3, 4, 5] have been written on the use of operations research to study inventory and production situations. We will only study the very basic models. Before we begin our study, however, let's consider some basic characteristics of inventory models that will be important from an analysis standpoint.

1. DEMAND. The demand pattern can be assumed to be either *deterministic* or *probabilistic*. The deterministic models operate under assumed certainty. The demand over future periods is assumed to be known with certainty. The demand can be the same from period to period (the *static* case) or it can vary (the *dynamic* case). The probabilistic demand models are decisions under risk. That is, we assume that we know the probability distribution of demand over a given period. The probabilistic distribution is either *stationary* or *nonstationary* over time, which are equivalent to the static and dynamic cases, respectively. The demand can be assumed to be satisfied *instantaneously* at the beginning of the period or *uniformly* over time.

2. ORDERING CYCLE. The ordering cycle is the time period between two successive orders. The orders can be placed as a result of a *continuous review* process where the status of the inventory level is updated continuously until a certain level (the *reorder point*) is reached at which time an order is placed. The alternative is a *periodic review* process where orders are placed at equally spaced intervals (the *reorder cycle*).

3. LEAD TIMES. The lead time is the time between the placing of an order and the receipt of the order. The lead time may be either deterministic or probabilistic. If the lead time is zero, we have the special case of *instantaneous* delivery.

4. STOCK REPLENISHMENT. The rate at which stock is replaced is also an important parameter in inventory models. If product is received from an outside vendor, replenishment is *instantaneous*. Replenishment will, however, occur at a *uniform* rate when the item is manufactured within one's own factory.

5. NUMBER OF ITEMS. Inventory models often assume that different items of inventory behave independently. If, however, the various items in inventory must compete for limited capital or floor space, special inventory models are needed.

6. NUMBER OF SUPPLY ECHELONS. An inventory system may consist of several levels (echelons) of inventories to supply customer needs. For example, a company might have inventory at the factory which supplies inventories to district warehouses, which supply inventories to distributors, which supply the customers. Such sys-

287
6.2
DETERMINISTIC
MODELS
(ECONOMIC-
LOT-SIZE
MODELS)

tems are referred to as *multiechelon* systems and are very difficult to analyze.

In this chapter we will concentrate mainly on single-item, single-echelon systems with deterministic and probabilistic demands.

**6.2 DETER-
MINISTIC
MODELS
(ECONOMIC-
LOT-SIZE
MODELS)**

6.2.1 Introduction

In this section we assume that demand for items is known with certainty. We will be using the following notation in our models:

C = purchase price or manufacture cost per unit of inventory
K = setup or order cost
h = holding cost per unit per unit of time
p = shortage cost per unit per unit of time
a = production rate per unit of time
b = usage rate per unit of time

6.2.2
Single-Item
Production
Model with
No Shortage
Allowed

This model assumes that a company is producing items at a constant rate, a units per unit time. The demand for the item is also assumed to be at a constant rate b units per unit time (where $b < a$). Demand and production will happen simultaneously for a period of time t_1. During this time inventory will be building at a rate of $(a - b)$. After production ceases, inventory will decrease at the rate of b for a period of time t_2. The entire inventory cycle takes t_0 time units where $t_0 = t_1 + t_2$. The inventory profile for this model is shown in Figure 6.1. We now define

Z = Maximum inventory on hand during the order cycle
Q = Number of units produced per order cycle

Observe that

$$Q = bt_0 = at_1 \tag{6.1}$$

and, from Figure 6.1,

$$Z = t_1(a - b) = (Q/a)(a - b) = Q(1 - b/a) \tag{6.2}$$

The average inventory for the cycle is the area under the inventory profile and equals $Z(t_0/2)$.

The total cost of an order cycle is a function of Q, $TC(Q)$, and is made up of three components:

Manufacture cost = (cost/unit)(order quantity) = CQ
Setup cost = (setup cost per cycle) = K
Inventory cost = (holding cost per unit per unit of time)
        × (average inventory level for the
        order cycle) = $h[Z(t_0/2)]$

Thus

$$TC(Q) = [CQ + K + h(Z(t_0/2))] \tag{6.3}$$

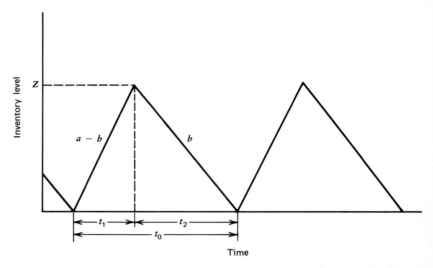

Figure 6.1 Inventory profile for a single-item production model with no shortages allowed.

Substituting (6.2) into (6.3) yields

$$TC(Q) = CQ + K + \frac{hQ(1 - b/a)t_0}{2} \tag{6.4}$$

The objective is to minimize the total cost per unit time $TCU(Q)$, which is given by

$$TCU(Q) = \frac{TC(Q)}{t_0} \tag{6.5}$$

Substituting (6.4) into (6.5) yields

$$TCU(Q) = \frac{CQ}{t_0} + \frac{K}{t_0} + \frac{hQ(1 - b/a)}{2}$$

which reduces to

$$TCU(Q) = Cb + \frac{Kb}{Q} + \frac{hQ(1 - b/a)}{2} \tag{6.6}$$

because

$$t_0 = Q/b$$

To find the optimum order quantity, Q^*, differentiate (6.6) with respect to Q, equate the derivative to zero, and solve for Q.

$$\frac{dTCU(Q)}{dQ} = -\frac{Kb}{Q^2} + \frac{h}{2}\left(1 - \frac{b}{a}\right) = 0$$

289
6.2
DETERMINISTIC
MODELS
(ECONOMIC-
LOT-SIZE
MODELS)

so

$$Q^* = \sqrt{\frac{2Kb}{h(1-b/a)}} \tag{6.7}$$

From (6.1) we observe that $t_0 = Q/b$ so the optimum order cycle, t_0^*, is

$$t_0^* = \sqrt{\frac{2K}{bh(1-b/a)}} \tag{6.8}$$

and substituting (6.7) into (6.6) we find the optimum cost per unit time, $TCU(Q^*)$, is

$$TCU(Q^*) = \sqrt{2bhK(1-b/a)} + Cb \tag{6.9}$$

Note (6.9) will only give the $TCU(Q)$ where $Q = Q^*$. For $Q \neq Q^*$, the $TCU(Q)$ can be found using (6.6).

EXAMPLE

An item costs \$1, it can be produced at the rate of 1000 units per week, and it is used at the rate of 100 units per week. The holding cost is \$.10 per unit per week and the ordering cost is \$300.
  Using (6.7), (6.8), and (6.9) with

$$a = 1000 \text{ units/week}$$
$$b = 100 \text{ units/week}$$
$$K = \$300$$
$$h = \$.10/\text{unit/week}$$
$$C = \$1.00$$

yields

$$Q^* = \sqrt{\frac{2(300)(100)}{.10(1-100/1000)}} = 816 \text{ units}$$

$$t_0^* = \sqrt{\frac{2(300)}{(100)(.10)(1-100/1000)}} = 8.16 \text{ weeks}$$

$$TCU(Q^*) = \sqrt{2(100)(.10)(300)(1-100/1000)} + (1)(100)$$
$$= \$173/\text{week}$$

**6.2.3
Single-Item
Purchase Model
with No
Shortage
allowed**

This model assumes that items are purchased from an outside vendor. The entire lot is delivered at one time. This model is equivalent to the purchase model where a, the production rate, is assumed to be infinite. The inventory profile for this system is shown in Figure 6.2. The optimum results for this model can be obtained by substituting $a = \infty$ into

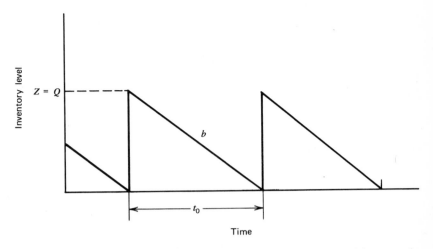

Figure 6.2 Inventory profile for a single-item purchase model with no stock-outs allowed.

(6.7), (6.8), and (6.9), which yields:

$$Q^* = \sqrt{\frac{2Kb}{h}} \tag{6.10}$$

$$t_0^* = \sqrt{\frac{2K}{bh}} \tag{6.11}$$

$$TCU(Q^*) = \sqrt{2bhK} + Cb \tag{6.12}$$

Now consider the example discussed in Section 6.2.2 as a purchase model.

EXAMPLE   Using (6.10), (6.11), and (6.12) with

$b = 100$ units/week

$K = \$300$

$h = \$.10$/unit/week

$C = \$1.00$

$$Q^* = \sqrt{\frac{2(300)(100)}{.10}} = 775 \text{ units}$$

$$t_0^* = \sqrt{\frac{2(300)}{(100)(.10)}} = 7.75 \text{ weeks}$$

$$TCU(Q^*) = \sqrt{2(100)(.10)(300)} + (1)(100) = \$177/\text{week}$$

291
6.2
DETERMINISTIC
MODELS
(ECONOMIC-
LOT-SIZE
MODELS)

6.2.4
Single-Item
Inventory
Models with
Shortages
Allowed

In this section we will consider the models discussed in Sections 6.2.2 and 6.2.3 modified to allow for stockouts. It is assumed that the items stocked out will be back ordered. The inventory profile for the production model is shown in Figure 6.3. During the time interval t_1 the system is producing product and filling back orders. The system is producing product and building inventory during t_2. The plant is not producing product during t_3 and t_4. During t_3 inventory is being drawn down while during t_4 back orders will be built up. In Figure 6.3, Z is the maximum

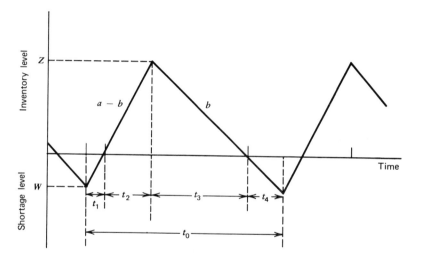

Figure 6.3 Inventory profile for a single-item production model with stockouts allowed.

inventory level and w is the maximum shortage. The geometry of Figure 6.3 suggests the following relationships.

$$t_1 = \frac{w}{a-b}$$

$$t_2 = \frac{Z}{a-b}$$

$$t_3 = \frac{Z}{b}$$

$$t_4 = \frac{w}{b}$$

Total inventory during the order cycle

$$= \frac{Z(t_2 + t_3)}{2} = \frac{Z^2}{2b(1 - b/a)}$$

Total stockout during the order cycle

$$= \frac{w(t_1 + t_4)}{2} = \frac{w^2}{2b(1 - b/a)}$$

As was the case in the model discussed in Section 6.2.2 the order quantity Q is related to t_0 as follows:

$$Q = bt_0 \tag{6.13}$$

also

$$Q = a(t_1 + t_2) \tag{6.14}$$

Another relationship from the geometry of Figure 6.3 is

$$Z + w = (t_1 + t_2)(a - b)$$

Substituting (6.14) into this equation we can solve for Z as a function of Q and w

$$Z = Q(1 - b/a) - w$$

Thus the total inventory during the order cycle can be found as a function of Q and w

Total inventory during the order cycle

$$= \frac{[Q(1 - b/a) - w]^2}{2b(1 - b/a)}$$

The total cost during an order cycle can now be developed as a function of Q and w. $TC(Q, w)$ consists of the sum of four components

Purchase cost $= $ (cost/unit)(order quantity) $= CQ$

Order cost $\quad = $ (order cost per cycle) $= K$

Inventory cost $= $ (holding cost per unit of time)
$\quad\quad\quad\quad\quad\quad \times $ (total inventory for the order cycle)

$$= h\left[\frac{(Q(1 - b/a) - w)^2}{2b(1 - b/a)} \right]$$

Shortage cost $= $ (shortage cost per unit per unit time)
$\quad\quad\quad\quad\quad\quad \times $ (total shortages for the order cycle)

$$= p\left[\frac{w^2}{2b(1 - b/a)} \right]$$

293
6.2
DETERMINISTIC
MODELS
(ECONOMIC-
LOT-SIZE
MODELS)

The total cost per unit time $TCU(Q, w)$ can now be calculated from (6.5) and (6.13)

$$TCU(Q, w) = Cb + \frac{Kb}{Q} + \frac{h[Q(1-b/a) - w]^2 + pw^2}{2(1-b/a)Q} \qquad (6.15)$$

The optimum value of Q and w can be found by solving the following optimization conditions derived from the partial derivatives

$$\frac{\partial TCU(Q, w)}{\partial Q} = 0$$

$$\frac{\partial TCU(Q, w)}{\partial w} = 0$$

which yields

$$Q^* = \sqrt{\frac{2Kb(p+h)}{ph(1-b/a)}} \qquad (6.16)$$

$$w^* = \sqrt{\frac{2Kbh(1-b/a)}{p(p+h)}} \qquad (6.17)$$

and $TCU(Q^*, w^*)$ becomes

$$TCU(Q^*, w^*) = \sqrt{\left(\frac{2Khpb}{p+h}\right)(1-b/a)} + Cb \qquad (6.18)$$

Now consider the example from Section 6.2.2 as a single-item production model with a shortage penalty of \$.90 per unit per unit of time.

Using (6.16), (6.17), and (6.18) with

EXAMPLE

$$a = 1000 \text{ units/week}$$
$$b = 100 \text{ units/week}$$
$$K = \$300$$
$$h = \$.10/\text{unit/week}$$
$$p = \$.90/\text{unit/week}$$
$$C = \$1.00$$

yields

$$Q^* = \sqrt{\frac{2(300)(100)(.90+.10)}{.90(.10)(1-100/1000)}} = 860 \text{ units}$$

$$w^* = \sqrt{\frac{2(300)(100)(.10)(1-100/1000)}{(.90)(.90+.10)}} = 77 \text{ units}$$

$$TCU(Q^*, w^*) = \sqrt{\frac{2(300)(.10)(.90)(100)(1-100/1000)}{(.90+.10)}} + (1)(100)$$

$$= \$170/\text{week}$$

The results for a single-item purchase model with stockouts allowed can be derived from (6.16), (6.17), and (6.18) by setting a equal to ∞, which yields

$$Q^* = \sqrt{\frac{2Kb(p+h)}{ph}} \tag{6.19}$$

$$w^* = \sqrt{\frac{2Kbh}{p(p+h)}} \tag{6.20}$$

$$TCU(Q^*, w^*) = \sqrt{\frac{2Khpb}{p+h}} + Cb \tag{6.21}$$

Formulas (6.19), (6.20), and (6.21) will yield the following results for the example we have been considering.

EXAMPLE

$$Q^* = \sqrt{\frac{2(300)(100)(.90+.10)}{.90(.10)}}$$
$$= 816 \text{ units}$$

$$w^* = \sqrt{\frac{2(300)(100)(.10)}{(.90)(.90+.10)}} = 82 \text{ units}$$

$$TCU(Q^*, w^*) = \sqrt{\frac{2(300)(.10)(.90)(100)}{.90+.10}} + (1)(100) = \$173/\text{week}$$

**6.3
SINGLE-
PERIOD
PROBABILIS-
TIC MODELS**

**6.3.1
Introduction**

The models in this section assume that we know the probability distribution of the demand. Thus the models will be viewed as decisions under risk. Furthermore the assumption is made that we are dealing with a single period model. This says that we have a situation where the product can be bought only once and there can be no orders to replenish inventory. The classic example of this type of model is the "Christmas tree" model where an individual must place an order in August for the number of trees he wishes. No matter how brisk his sales are in December he cannot obtain new trees. The single-period model is also applicable to the case where we can assume that successive periods in the multiperiod model are independent. Thus if we can optimize a single period, we will have in effect optimized the multiperiod model.

We will use the following notation in our models:

D = demand for an item in a period
$f(D)$ or $g(D)$ = continuous or discrete probability distribution of the demand in a period

h = holding cost for items left over at the end of the period
c = purchase cost for an item
p = penalty cost for understocking an item
Q = quantity of items that we stock to meet our demand
I = items on hand before the order was placed
K = setup cost or purchase cost to place an order

We first consider the case where the demand for an item can be approximated by a continuous probability distribution, $f(D)$. This is a reasonable assumption when we are dealing with large demands for relatively inexpensive items. Our optimization criterion will be to minimize expected cost in the inventory period in question. We want to find the best level, Q, with which to start the period. If the initial inventory level is I, this implies that we will order $Q - I$ items to bring our on-hand inventory of the product up to Q. In this section we will assume that it does not cost us anything to place an order for the $Q - I$ items. Now since D is a random variable it can be either greater than Q or less than Q. Now if $Q < D$ we will stock out and there will be a cost of p per unit stocked out. If $Q > D$ we will have an overstock of items and there will be a cost of h per unit of overstocked items. The cost h might include a holding cost, a spoilage cost, or a scrapping cost while cost p must include lost revenue from a sale and the cost for the loss of goodwill.

6.3.2 Single-period Models with no Set-up Cost

Our goal will be to minimize the expression

$$E(C(Q)) = \text{order cost} + E(\text{holding cost } (Q)) + E(\text{shortage cost } (Q))$$

where

$E(C(Q))$ is the expected single-period cost if we start the period with Q items

order cost equals the number of items ordered times the per unit cost or $(Q - I)c$

E (holding cost (Q)) is the expected holding costs if we have Q items on hand at the beginning of the period. It will be equal to the cost per unit of items left over at the end of the period times the expected number of items left over or

$$h \int_{\substack{D=0 \text{ or} \\ \text{minimum demand}}}^{Q} (Q-D)f(D) \, dD \qquad (6.22)$$

noting that we will have items left over only if $D < Q$.

E (shortage cost (Q)) is the expected shortage cost if we have Q items on hand at the beginning of a period. The cost is equal to the cost per unit of items short (demanded but not supplied) at the end of the period times the expected number of items short or

$$p \int_{D=Q}^{\substack{\infty \text{ or} \\ \text{maximum demand}}} (D-Q)f(D)\, dD \tag{6.23}$$

noting that we will be short only if $D > Q$.

Thus the expected single-period cost becomes

$$E(C(Q)) = c(Q-I) + h \int_{\substack{D=0 \text{ or} \\ \text{minimum demand}}}^{Q} (Q-D)f(D)\, dD$$

$$+ p \int_{D=Q}^{\substack{\infty \text{ or} \\ \text{maximum demand}}} (D-Q)f(D)\, dD \tag{6.24}$$

We want to find the value of Q that minimizes $E(C(Q))$ so we differentiate $E(C(Q))$ with respect to Q. Equate the derivative to 0 and solve for the optimum value of Q, which we will call Q^*. It is possible to develop a general condition to determine Q^*. To develop this condition we must differentiate through the integral signs in (6.24). This operation is discussed by Hadley and Whitin [3] but is beyond the scope of this book. The condition for optimality is dependent on an important function from probability theory called the cumulative frequency function, $F(Q)$, which is defined as the probability that a value drawn from the frequency function $f(D)$ is less than or equal to Q or

$$\int_{\substack{D=0 \text{ or} \\ \text{minimum demand}}}^{Q} f(D)\, dD = F(Q) \tag{6.25}$$

The condition for optimality that yields the best value, Q^*, to have on hand at the beginning of the period is

$$F(Q^*) = \frac{p-c}{h+p} \tag{6.26}$$

So we should order $Q^* - I$ units, assuming that $I < Q^*$

EXAMPLE   Assume that the Lehigh chapter of Alpha Pi Mu decided to sell Christmas trees this year. Trees cost $1.50 each and sell for $5. Trees left over are burned at a cost of $.10 each. If a sale is lost there is no additional cost besides the lost revenue. The demand is equally likely to be any value between 500 and 1000 trees.

Thus we can assume that the demand distribution is a uniform distribution between 500 and 1000 trees so

$$f(D) = 1/500 \qquad \text{for } 500 \leq D \leq 1000$$

$$F(Q) = \int_{D=500}^{Q} 1/500 \, dD = D/500 \Big|_{D=500}^{Q}$$

$$= Q/500 - 1 \qquad \text{for } 500 \leq Q \leq 1000$$

Next (6.26) can be applied with

$c = \$1.50$ purchase price for a tree
$h = \$.10$ burning cost
$p = \$5.00$ lost revenue (selling price)

So

$$Q^*/500 - 1 = \frac{5.00 - 1.50}{5.00 + .10} = 0.686$$

$$Q^* = 500(1 + 0.686) = 843 \text{ trees}$$

Since Alpha Pi Mu had no trees on hand they should place an order for 843 Christmas trees.

As was discussed earlier the demand in the inventory problem is not continuous. When dealing with expensive items that have a small range of demands the continuous approximation should not be used. The problem should be formulated as a discrete problem. If $g(D)$ is defined as the discrete probability of having a demand of exactly D, (6.24) becomes

$$E(C(Q)) = c(Q - I) + h \sum_{\substack{D=0 \text{ or} \\ \text{minimum} \\ \text{demand}}}^{Q} (Q - D)g(D) + p \sum_{\substack{D=Q+1}}^{\substack{\infty \text{ or} \\ \text{maximum} \\ \text{demand}}} (D - Q)g(D)$$

$$(6.27)$$

Now consider the Richardson Submarine Works, which makes boats **EXAMPLE** in the winter for spring and summer sales. Boats cost \$3000 each to make and sell for \$6000. If a boat is not sold Captain Richardson estimates that it will cost \$1000 to keep the boat until next year. There are no boats left over from last year. History suggests the following demand distribution:

D	g(D)
0	.1
1	.2
2	.2
3	.2
4	.2
5	.1

Applying (6.27) as shown in Table 6.1 we find that $Q^* = 2$ because $11,800$ is the minimum expected cost. Since Richardson has no boats on hand from last year he should make two boats during the winter.

Tables such as Table 6.1 are cumbersome to evaluate so authors [3, 4, 5] have developed conditions similar to those in (6.26) for the discrete case. These developments are based on the observation that if Q^* is the optimum level of items with which to start the period, then in the discrete case, becomes

$$E[C(Q^*-1)] \geq E(C(Q^*))$$
$$E[C(Q^*+1)] \geq E(C(Q^*))$$

Table 6.1. Expected Cost Analysis for the Richardson Submarine Works using (6.27) with $c = 3000$, $p = 6000$, $h = 1000$, and $I = 0$

D Q \ g(D)	0 .1	1 .2	2 .2	3 .2	4 .2	5 .1	E(C(Q))
0	0	6,000	12,000	18,000	24,000	30,000	15,000
1	4,000	3,000	9,000	15,000	21,000	27,000	12,700
2	8,000	7,000	6,000	12,000	18,000	24,000	11,800
3	12,000	11,000	10,000	9,000	15,000	21,000	12,300
4	16,000	15,000	14,000	13,000	12,000	18,000	14,200
5	20,000	19,000	18,000	17,000	16,000	15,000	17,500

This simply says that expected cost at Q^* will be less than at Q^*-1 or Q^*+1. The development of the conditions for the discrete case is beyond the scope of this text but can be stated as follows:

$$G(Q^*-1) \leq \frac{p-c}{p+h} \leq G(Q^*) \tag{6.28}$$

where $G(Q)$ is the cumulative probability distribution for the discrete probability distribution of demand and is equal to the probability that $D \leq Q$ or

$$G(Q) = \sum_{\substack{D=0 \text{ or} \\ \text{minimum} \\ \text{demand}}}^{Q} g(D)$$

As can be seen the condition for the discrete case is basically the same as for the continuous analysis. Our operating procedure will be to calculate $(p-c)/(p+h)$. Next we find the cumulative probability distribution $G(Q)$ and the values of Q that $(p-c)/(p+h)$ lies between. The two values will be Q^*-1 and Q^* as stated in (6.28) so we should take the higher value as our optimum level to start the period.

For the Richardson Submarine Works   **EXAMPLE**

$$p = 6000 \qquad c = 3000 \qquad \text{and} \qquad h = 1000$$

so the optimality condition is

$$\frac{p-c}{p+h} = \frac{6000-3000}{6000+1000} = .428$$

The calculation of $G(Q)$ is shown in Table 6.2. The table shows that .428 lies between $Q=1$ and $Q=2$. Thus the condition for optimality

Table 6.2 Development of the Cumulative Probability Distribution for Richardson Submarine Works and Optimum Inventory Level Using (6.28)

D	g(D)	Q	G(Q)	
0	.1	0	.1	
1	.2	1	.3	← .428
2	.2	2	.5	← Q^*
3	.2	3	.7	
4	.2	4	.9	
5	.1	5	1.0	

suggests that $Q^* = 2$. This is the same result that we developed previously.

Some analysts have difficulty visualizing expected cost formulations   **EXAMPLE**
similar to that shown in (6.27). They prefer to view the problem from a

maximizing expected profit standpoint. Their formulation of the
Richardson Submarine Works problem would view costs as negative
revenues.

	For $D \leq Q$	$D > Q$
Building cost	$3000Q$	$3000Q$
Holding cost	$(Q-D)1000$	None
Revenue	$6000D$	$6000Q$

The revenues are developed under the assumption that if $D \leq Q$
then we will have items to sell to whoever wants them but if $D > Q$ we can
only sell Q because that is all we have on hand. The expected profit
expression for the Richardson Submarine Works is

$$E(\text{profit } (Q)) = \sum_{D=0}^{Q} [-3000Q - (Q-D)1000 + 6000D]g(D)$$

$$+ \sum_{D=Q+1}^{5} (-3000Q + 6000Q)g(D)$$

The results of this equation are tabulated in Table 6.3, which once again
tells Captain Richardson to build two boats during the winter. It also tells
him that he can expect a profit of \$3200.

Table 6.3 Expected Profit Analysis for the Richardson Boat Works

D	0	1	2	3	4	5	
Q $g(D)$	.1	.2	.2	.2	.2	.1	$E(\text{profit}(Q))$
0	0	0	0	0	0	0	0
1	−4,000	3,000	3,000	3,000	3,000	3,000	2,300
2	−8,000	−1,000	6,000	6,000	6,000	6,000	3,200
3	−12,000	−5,000	2,000	9,000	9,000	9,000	2,700
4	−16,000	−9,000	−2,000	5,000	12,000	12,000	800
5	−20,000	−13,000	−6,000	1,000	8,000	15,000	−2,500

It would be nice if all single-period probabilistic inventory models
with no setup cost could be solved by applying (6.26) or (6.28) but these
conditions are only valid for the conditions stated earlier in this section. If
your situation does not satisfy these conditions then you have to formulate an expected cost or expected profit relationship and solve for Q^*.
Consider the following problem with which you may be able to
identify.

The brothers of a local fraternity are planning an alumni spring weekend. They are trying to decide how many kegs of Mich to stock in. Each keg costs $18. Their cooler holds only two kegs, so that any more than two kegs must be disposed of or it will go bad. The excess kegs can possibly be sold to some of the neighboring frats for $12 each. The probability distribution of the number of kegs consumed is uniform between 3 and 12. The penalty for kicking is estimated to be $100, which would be contributed by the alumni for a new game room. How many kegs should the fraternity have on hand?

This problem does not conform to the standard form that we have been discussing because the stockout penalty is independent of the number of kegs we are short and we can hold two excess kegs at no penalty. If you have more than two excess kegs there is an effective penalty of $6 per keg (your $18 cost less the $12 that your neighboring fraternities will pay). The expected cost equation can be thought of in three parts as follows:

	$D \leq Q-2$	$Q-2 < D \leq Q$	$D > Q$
Purchase cost	$18Q$	$18Q$	$18Q$
Shortage cost	None	None	$100
Sales to neighboring frats	$12(Q-2-D)$	None	None

The expected cost equation appears as follows:

$$E(C(Q)) = \sum_{D=3}^{Q-2} \{18Q - 12[(Q-2) - D]\}g(D) + \sum_{D=Q-1}^{Q} (18Q)g(D)$$

$$+ \sum_{D=Q+1}^{12} (18Q + 100)g(D)$$

where

$$g(D) = 1/10 \qquad \text{for } D = 3, 4, \ldots, 12$$

$$0 \text{ elsewhere}$$

The evaluation of the cost equation is shown in Table 6.4. We observe that the least cost solution is to stock no kegs of Mich. But this is an unstable problem because if the penalty cost was $200 the optimum number of kegs to stock is 12 kegs. The results for the $200 penalty cost are also shown in Table 6.4.

Table 6.4 Expected Cost Analysis for the Fraternity Alumni Party Example

Q	$E(C(Q))$ Assuming a Stockout Penalty of \$100		$E(C(Q))$ Assuming a Stockout Penalty of \$200	
0	100	← Q^*	200	
1	118		218	
2	136		236	
3	144		234	
4	152		232	
5	160		230	
6	167		227	
7	172		222	
8	181		221	
9	180		210	
10	182		202	
11	173		193	
12	182		182	← Q^*
13	191		192	

**6.3.3
Single-period
Models with
Set-up Costs**

The models in this section are identical to the models discussed in Section 6.3.2 except there is a fixed setup cost, K, associated with making or buying items in a single period. That is, if we decide to buy or produce in a period there will be a cost K in addition to other costs but if we decide not to produce there will be no such cost. When is it advantageous to stay with the number of items at the beginning of the period, I, and not produce?

Let's define $E(\bar{C}(Q))$ as the total expected cost including setup cost:

$$E(\bar{C}(Q)) = K + E(C(Q))$$

Remember that the optimum conditions for $E(C(Q))$ are given by (6.26) and (6.28). Since K is a constant then (6.26) and (6.28) must also be the optimum conditions for $E(\bar{C}(Q))$. Thus the optimal order size if we decide to buy or produce is $Q^* - I$.

We will produce if $E(C(I))$, the expected cost if we enter a period with I units of inventory and decide not to produce, is greater than $E(\bar{C}(Q^*))$, the optimum expected cost if we produce $Q^* - I$ units in order to bring our beginning inventory up to Q^*. Thus the conditions for production are:

If $E(C(I)) \geq E(\bar{C}(Q^*))$ produce $Q^* - I$ iems

and if

$$E(C(I)) < E(\bar{C}(Q^*)) \text{ don't produce} \qquad (6.29)$$

Consider the example where   **EXAMPLE**

$$\begin{aligned}
f(D) &= 1/100 \quad &\text{for } 0 \le D \le 100 \\
p &= \$10 \\
c &= \$5 \\
h &= \$1 \\
K &= \$50 \\
I &= 20
\end{aligned}$$

Applying (6.26) we find that

$$\frac{p-c}{p+h} = .4545$$

$$F(Q) = \int_{D=0}^{Q} (1/100) \, dD = Q/100$$

Therefore $Q^* = (.4545)(100) = 45$ units.

Now $E(C(I))$ can be found by evaluating (6.24) with Q set equal to I, where $I = 20$.

$$E(C(I)) = 5(20-20) + 1 \int_{D=0}^{20} (20-D)(1/100) \, dD$$

$$+ 10 \int_{D=20}^{100} (D-20)(1/100) \, dD$$

$$= 0 + 1 \left(\frac{20D - (D^2/2)}{100} \right) \Big|_{D=0}^{20} + 10 \left(\frac{(D^2/2) - 20D}{100} \right) \Big|_{D=20}^{100}$$

$$= \$322$$

And $E(\bar{C}(Q^*))$ can be calculated by observing that

$$E(\bar{C}(Q^*)) = K + E(C(Q^*))$$

so $E(C(Q^*))$ can also be found from (6.24) with Q set equal to Q^* where $Q^* = 45$

$$E(C(Q^*)) = 5(45-20) + 1 \int_{D=0}^{45} (45-D)(1/100) \, dD$$

$$+ 10 \int_{D=45}^{100} (D-45)(1/100) \, dD$$

$$= 5(25) + 1\left(\frac{(45D - (D^2/2))}{100}\right)\Big|_{D=0}^{45}$$

$$+ 10\left(\frac{(D^2/2) - 45D}{100}\right)\Big|_{D=45}^{100}$$

$$= \$286$$

So $E(\bar{C}(Q^*)) = K + E(C(Q^*)) = \$50 + \$286 = \$336$ and since

$$E(C(I)) < E(\bar{C}(Q^*))$$

condition (6.29) tells us not to produce. If K had been equal to $20 then

$$E(\bar{C}(Q^*)) = \$20 + \$286 = \$306$$

since

$$E(C(I)) \geq E(\bar{C}(Q^*))$$

condition (6.29) would have told us to produce $Q^* - I$ or 25 units.

6.4 MULTIPERIOD PROBABILISTIC MODEL

6.4.1 Reorder Point Model

For the models discussed in Section 6.2 we are effectively assuming that both the demand and lead time are known with certainty. Under these conditions we ordered Q^* units whenever inventory reached a level equal to the demand during the lead time. Thus we assumed that the product would arrive at exactly the point at which inventory hit the zero level in the case of the no back-order model.

When we consider the more realistic model with probabilistic demands it is reasonable to assume that the reorder point (the point at which we place an order for a product) will be set at a point above the average lead-time demand. Because if we reorder when there is enough inventory to serve the average demand during the lead time then we will stock out approximately 50 percent of the time. In order to protect ourselves from the undesirable effect of excess stockouts, safety stocks are introduced in the inventory model. Safety stock, S, is just the difference between the reorder point, R, and the average lead time demand L.

$$R = S + \bar{L} \tag{6.30}$$

Thus if the safety stock increases, the reorder point increases, and the probability of stockout on any given cycle decreases. The inventory profile for the probabilistic reorder point model appears as shown in Figure 6.4. An order for Q^* units is placed whenever stock levels fall to R. On the average the product will arrive when there are S units in stock. Figure 6.4 shows three inventory cycles, the second of which stocked out.

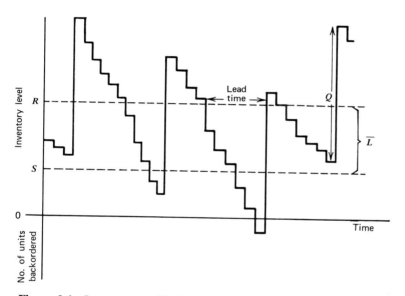

Figure 6.4 Inventory profile for a multiperiod probabilistic inventory model.

Note that if R was slightly higher we could have avoided the stockout. Thus there is tradeoff between reducing the probability and cost of stockouts, and increasing the carrying cost of having a safety stock.

There are two common ways of setting safety stock levels. One is basically an aspiration level approach that chooses the safety stock level guaranteeing that the probability of stockout in a given cycle will not exceed some level that has been set by management. The other approach attempts to minimize the sum of the cost of stockouts and cost of holding safety stock. Both of these methods are, however, dependent on being able to determine the probability distribution of the demand during the lead time.

6.4.2
Calculating
the Safety
Stock Level

Analysts often attempt to build up the demand during the lead time using convolutions of various probability distributions. An alternate approach is to collect historic data on demands during past lead times and fitting a probability distribution to this data. In our opinion the latter approach is preferable if the data are available.

EXAMPLE

Let's assume that a given item has a weekly demand pattern as follows:

D	$g(D)$
0	.1
1	.4
2	.3
3	.2

Furthermore, assume that the lead time is equally likely to be one or two weeks. In order to find the demand during the lead time we will use the following formula:

$$\text{(lead time demand pattern)} = .5 \text{ (one-week demand pattern)}$$
$$+ .5 \text{ (two-week demand pattern)}$$
$$(6.31)$$

We thus need the two-week demand pattern which can be developed by considering all the possible ways of getting particular demands in two weeks and summing their associated probabilities.

For example, consider the finding of the probability of having a demand of 4 in two weeks:

Week 1 Demand	Week 2 Demand	Probability
1	3	$(.4)(.2) = .08$
2	2	$(.3)(.3) = .09$
3	1	$(.2)(.4) = .08$
		$\overline{.25}$

Using similar logic we can find the entire two-week demand schedule as shown in Table 6.5.

Using (6.31) we can finally find the demand during the lead time as shown in Table 6.6.

Table 6.5 Two-week Demand Schedule

Two-Week Demand	Probability
0	.01
1	.08
2	.22
3	.28
4	.25
5	.12
6	.04

Table 6.6 Demand During a Lead Time

Demand During Lead Time D		Probability of D $g(D)$	Probability of a Demand $> D$
0	.5(.1)+.5(.01)	.055	.945
1	.5(.4)+.5(.08)	.240	.705
2	.5(.3)+.5(.22)	.260	.445
3	.5(.2)+.5(.28)	.240	.205
4	.5(.0)+.5(.25)	.125	.080
5	.5(.0)+.5(.12)	.060	.020
6	.5(.0)+.5(.04)	.020	.000

Now, if management wishes to use an aspiration level criterion, they might propose to stockout no more than once in every 20 reorder cycles. This implies that the probability of stocking out in any given cycle is 1/20 or .05. Viewing Table 6.6 we see that the probability of a demand during the lead time greater than 5 is .02 while a demand greater than 4 will happen with probability .08; therefore the reorder point should be set equal to 5. We can find the safety stock level from (6.30) after determining $\bar{L}$ from the information in Table 6.6.

$$\bar{L} = \sum_{D=0}^{6} Dg(D) = 0.(055) + 1(.240) + \ldots + 6(.02) = 2.3$$

therefore

$$S = R - \bar{L} = 5 - 2.3 = 2.7 \text{ units}$$

Management might alternatively wish to set safety stock based on a cost model. The basis of the cost analysis approach for determining the safety stock is a cost formula that includes the cost of carrying safety stock plus the expected cost of stockout. The formula can be stated as follows:

$$E(C(S)) = \begin{pmatrix} \text{safety stock} \\ \text{level} \end{pmatrix} \begin{pmatrix} \text{cost of holding} \\ \text{a unit/period} \end{pmatrix}$$

$$+ \begin{pmatrix} \text{cost of a} \\ \text{stockout} \end{pmatrix} \begin{pmatrix} \text{probability of} \\ \text{stockout in an} \\ \text{inventory cycle} \end{pmatrix} \begin{pmatrix} \text{number of} \\ \text{inventory} \\ \text{cycles/period} \end{pmatrix}$$

$$= Sh + (C_{so})(P_{so}(S))(b/Q^*) \tag{6.32}$$

where

$$P_{so}(S) = \text{prob} \left[\begin{pmatrix} \text{demand during} \\ \text{lead time} \end{pmatrix} > (\bar{L} + S) \right]$$

The procedure for using the cost analysis is to use (6.7) or (6.10) to calculate Q^* and then to use (6.32) to find S.

EXAMPLE   Consider the following purchase model where

$$K = \$400$$
$$h = \$10/\text{unit year}$$
$$c = \$15$$
$$C_{so} = \$100$$
$$b = 1000 \text{ units/year}$$

Assume that the demand during the lead time can be approximated by the following probability distribution

$$g(D) = \left(\frac{D - 15}{100} \right) \quad \text{for } D = 16, \ldots, 25$$

$$= \left(\frac{35 - D}{100} \right) \quad \text{for } D = 26, \ldots, 34$$

$$= 0 \quad \text{elsewhere}$$

First we use (6.10) to find Q^*

$$Q^* = \sqrt{\frac{2Kb}{h}} = \sqrt{\frac{2(400)(1000)}{10}}$$

$$= 283 \text{ units}$$

Next we will need an expression for $P_{so}(S)$, since $\bar{L}=25$ we can sum the probabilities of having a demand in excess of $\bar{L}+S$ or $25+S$. Thus

$$P_{so}(S) = \sum_{D=\bar{L}+S+1}^{34} \frac{35-D}{100}$$

Table 6.7 shows the determination of S^* using (6.32) noting that

$$C_{so}(b/Q^*) = \$100(1000/283) = \$353$$

Table 6.7 shows the cost calculation assuming various levels of S. The

Table 6.7 Calculation of the Optimum Level of Safety Stock

S	Sh	$P_{so}(S)$	$C_{so}(b/Q^*)P_{so}(S)$	$E(C(S))$	
0	0	.45	$158.85	$158.85	
1	10	.36	127.08	137.08	
2	20	.28	98.84	118.84	
3	30	.21	74.13	104.13	
4	40	.15	52.95	92.95	
5	50	.10	35.30	85.30	
6	60	.06	21.18	81.18	
7	70	.03	10.59	80.59	$\leftarrow S^*$
8	80	.01	3.53	83.53	
9	90	.00	0	90.00	

minimum cost occurs at $S=7$, therefore the optimum safety stock level from a cost standpoint is 7 units. The reorder point can be calculated from (6.30)

$$R = S+\bar{L} = 7+25 = 32$$

The optimum inventory policy is to place an order for 283 units every time the inventory level reaches 32 units.

Consider the case where a large investor has monies in the amount of $100,000 per year that become available at a more or less constant rate throughout the year. The investor's brokerage house fee schedule is $50+.02Q$ dollars where Q is the market value of stocks and bonds traded on a given day. The investor estimates that he usually makes 10 percent on the money that is invested.

The inventory in this type of problem is monies accumulating in the hands of the investor before he decides to invest them at the brokerage house. The inventory of money on hand would appear as shown in Figure 6.5. We should note that Figure 6.5 is just the mirror image of Figure 6.2

**6.5
APPLICATION
STUDIES**
6.5.1
Cash
Investments
Through a
Brokerage
House

Application Study

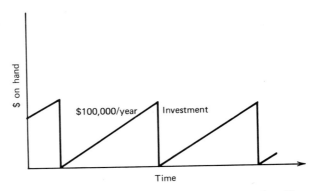

Figure 6.5 Inventory of monies being accumulated by
an investor in anticipation of investment.

so that the average inventory of money in the investment case is identical
to the average inventory of items for the single item purchase model
represented in Figure 6.2. As a matter of fact we can directly apply the
model described in Section 6.2.3 to this problem. The variables will have
the following interpretation for this example:

K is equivalent to the fixed cost charged by the brokerage house for
each investment or $50.

b is equivalent to rate of accumulation of monies available for
investment or $100,000 per year.

h is equivalent to the rate of return lost because money is not
invested. The investor anticipates a return of 10 percent per year,
so h will equal $.10 per dollar per year.

C is equivalent to the variable cost per dollar invested by the broker
or $.02 per dollar invested.

Applying (6.10), (6.11), and (6.12) we draw the following conclusions about this investment example:

(6.10) gives

$$Q^* = \sqrt{\frac{2Kb}{h}} = \sqrt{\frac{2(50)(100,000)}{.10}}$$

$$= \$10,000$$

Thus the investor should invest in lump sums of $10,000.

The optimum time between investments can be found from (6.11)

$$t_0^* = \sqrt{\frac{2K}{bh}} \sqrt{\frac{2(50)}{(100,000)(.10)}}$$

$$= .10 \text{ years or } 5.2 \text{ weeks}$$

The total annual cost of the investment program is given by (6.12)

$$TCU(Q^*) = \sqrt{2bhK} + Cb$$

$$= \sqrt{2(100,000)(.10)(50)} + (.02)(100,000)$$

$$= \$3000 \text{ per year.}$$

Analyses similar to this have also been suggested [3] for the management of borrowed funds for capital expansion and the management of special funds within the company such as petty cash funds.

A very common modification of the economic-lot-size model takes into account the modifications necessary to find the optimum order quantity if financial incentives are given for buying larger quantities of an item. For example, our vendor for the case discussed in Section 6.2.3 might offer the following purchase schedule:

6.5.2·
Quantity
Discount
Model

Application Study

If you order 499 or less items you pay $1.00 each.
If you order 500 to 999 items you pay $.95 each.
If you order 1000 or more items you pay $.90 each.

Thus each price break interval will have its own $TCU_i(Q)$ cost curve that will be a function of the purchase price, C_i, appropriate to that interval. $TCU_i(Q)$ can be derived from (6.6) by substituting C_i for C and observing that we are dealing with a purchase model so a approaches ∞.

$$TCU_i(Q) = C_i b + \frac{Kb}{Q} + \frac{hQ}{2} \tag{6.33}$$

Following arguments similar to those presented in Section 6.2.3 we can show that the minimum for all the $TCU_i(Q)$ curves will be independent of C_i and will occur at

$$Q^* = \sqrt{\frac{2Kb}{h}} \tag{6.34}$$

The $TCU_i(Q)$ curves can be plotted as shown in Figure 6.6. The solid lines show the active cost curve in each price region. Q_1 and Q_2 represent the quantities where the price for a product changes. The candidates for the Q value that gives the minimum for each $TCU_i(Q)$ are
   (i) Q^* if Q^* is in the interval of allowable quantities.
   (ii) *The maximum quantity in the allowable interval* if this value is less than Q^*.
   (iii) *The minimum quantity in the allowable interval* if the value is greater than Q^*.
   In Figure 6.6 the candidates for optimum are marked by ①, ②, and ③. Any candidate that satisfies condition (ii) can be ignored when trying

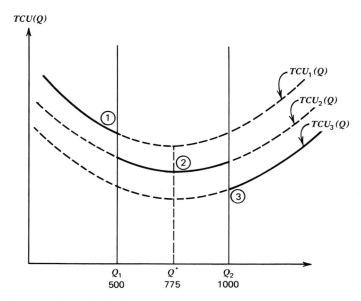

$TCU(Q)$

$TCU_1(Q)$

$TCU_2(Q)$

$TCU_3(Q)$

Q_1
500

Q^{*}
775

Q_2
1000

Figure 6.6 $TCU_i(Q)$ curves for the quantity-discount model.

to find the best quantity Q^{**} for the product. This is because we could always get a better $TCU(Q)$ by moving to the next interval. This is the case for ① on Figure 6.6 because $TCU_1(Q_1) > TCU_2(Q_1)$.

The procedure for finding Q^{**} is to calculate Q^{*} from (6.34).

If $Q^{*} < Q_1$, then Q^{*}, Q_1 and Q_2 are candidates for Q^{**}. Using (6.33) pick the quantity that gives the minimum of $TCU_1(Q^{*})$, $TCU_2(Q_1)$, and $TCU_3(Q_2)$.

If $Q_1 < Q^{*} < Q_2$ then Q^{*} and Q_2 are candidates for Q^{**}. Using (6.33) pick the quantity that gives the minimum of $TCU_2(Q^{*})$, and $TCU_3(Q_2)$.

If $Q^{*} > Q_2$ then Q^{*} equals Q^{**}

Let's consider our example from Section 6.2.3 where

$$b = 100 \text{ units/week}$$
$$K = \$300$$
$$h = \$.10/\text{unit/week}$$
$$C = 1.00 \text{ if } Q < 500$$
$$.95 \text{ if } 500 \leq Q < 1000$$
$$.90 \text{ if } 1000 \leq Q$$

From (6.34)

$$Q^{*} = \sqrt{\frac{2(300)(100)}{.10}} = 775$$

Since $500 \leq Q^* < 1000$ quantities of 775 and 1000 are candidates for Q^{**}. We will, therefore, compare $TCU_2(775)$ and $TCU_3(1000)$ using (6.33)

$$TCU_2(775) = (.95)(100) + \frac{(300)(100)}{(775)} + \frac{(.10)(775)}{2}$$

$$= \$172.46$$

$$TCU_3(1000) = (.90)(100) + \frac{(300)(100)}{(1000)} + \frac{(.10)(1000)}{2}$$

$$= \$170.00$$

Thus $Q^{**} = 1000$ and an order should be placed for 1000 units at a price of $.90 per unit.

Much has been written [1, 2] about various methods for forecasting the demand for a product. In this section we attempt to show the financial value of a forecast. Suppose that demand for an item in a single-period probabilistic model can be predicted in the form of a uniformly distributed random variable such that

6.5.3
The Value
of Forecasting
in Inventory
Management

Application Study

$$g(D) = 1/10 \qquad \text{for } D = 1, 2, \ldots, 10$$

$$= 0 \qquad \text{elsewhere}$$

and assume that

$$c = \$1000$$

$$I = 0$$

$$h = \$100$$

$$p = \$2000$$

Q^* can be found from condition (6.28)

$$\frac{p-c}{p+h} = \frac{2000 - 1000}{2000 + 100} = .48$$

Since $G(4) = .4$ and $G(5) = .5$, (6.28) tells us that $Q^* = 5$.

Now a forecast can be made that will be able to cut the range of uncertainty to a uniform distribution of range 4. That is, if a forecast is d' then

$$g(D) = 1/4 \text{ for } D = d', d'+1, d'+2, d'+3$$

$$= 0 \text{ elsewhere}$$

where $d' = 1, \ldots 7$

Applying (6.28)

$$\frac{p-c}{p+h} = .48$$

Since $G(d') = .25$ and $G(d'+1) = .50$, (6.28) suggests that $Q^* = d'+1$.
The value of the forecast will be a function of d' and can be found by evaluating (6.27) for the no-forecast case (at $Q = 5$) and for the forecast case (at $Q = d'+1$). The value of the forecast will be the difference between these two values of $E(C(Q))$.

For the no-forecast case with $Q = 5$, (6.27) becomes,

if $d' < 5 < d'+3$,

$$E(C(5)) = 1000(5-0) + 100 \sum_{D=d'}^{5} (5-D)1/4 + 2000 \sum_{D=6}^{d'+3} (D-5)1/4$$

if $5 \geq d'+3$

$$E(C(5)) = 1000(5-0) + 100 \sum_{D=d'}^{d'+3} (5-D)1/4$$

and if $5 \leq d'$

$$E(C(5)) = 1000(5-0) + 2000 \sum_{D=d'}^{d'+3} (D-5)1/4$$

When $Q = d'+1$ for the forecast case (6.27) yields

$$E(C(d'+1)) = 1000(d'+1-0) + 100 \sum_{D=d'}^{d'+1} [(d'+1)-D]1/4$$

$$+ 2000 \sum_{D=d'+2}^{d'+3} [D-(d'+1)]1/4$$

$$= 1000d' + 2525$$

These equations are evaluated for various values of d' in Table 6.8. If we assume that each forecast is equally likely then the expected value of the forecast is $975. Therefore we would not be willing to pay more than $975 for the forecast.

6.5.4
A Multistage
Perishable
Fruit
Inventory
Model

Application Study

Consider the following adaption of an inventory model used by a distributor of fresh cranberries in Chicago. The operating procedure that the company is using is to begin to pick berries in New Jersey on Monday and continue to pick until the optimal number of boxes has been picked. The cranberries are stored in New Jersey until Friday night when they are shipped to Chicago by train. They arrive in Chicago in time for Monday demands. The inventory is drawn down throughout the week until Friday.

Table 6.8 Determination of the Value of a Forecast in a Single-Period Probabilistic Inventory Model

d'	No-Forecast Case	Forecast Case	Value of Forecast
1	$5,250	$3,525	$1,725
2	5,150	4,525	625
3	5,575	5,525	50
4	6,525	6,525	0
5	8,000	7,525	475
6	10,000	8,525	1,475
7	12,000	9,525	2,475
		Avg.	$975

If berries are left over they are sold to a discount house at a greatly reduced price. If the company runs out of product there is a cost for loss of goodwill associated with each box that is short. There are also inventory costs in New Jersey and Chicago. Transportation costs are also considered in the model.

This multistage inventory model can be viewed as a single-period probabilistic inventory model. The profit equation can be set up by considering two possible conditions in Chicago: (i) the demand is greater than Q (the quantity picked per week) in which case the inventory profile at Chicago will appear as shown in Figure 6.7a or (ii) the demand is less than Q in which case the inventory profile at Chicago will be as shown in Figure 6.7b. The inventory profile in New Jersey is shown in Figure 6.7c.

Given the following definition of variables, the total profit equation for this problem can be developed:

P = price paid for a case of berries in Chicago
P' = price paid for a case of leftover berries in Chicago
C = cost/box for picking berries in New Jersey
T = cost/box for shipping berries between New Jersey and Chicago
$g(D)$ = demand distribution for weekly needs in Chicago
R = weekly rate of picking berries in New Jersey
I' = weekly inventory cost per box in New Jersey
I'' = weekly inventory cost per box in Chicago
G = goodwill loss per box short in Chicago

The average inventory level in New Jersey is

$$\frac{Q}{2}\left(1+\left(1-\frac{Q}{R}\right)\right) = Q - \frac{Q^2}{2R}$$

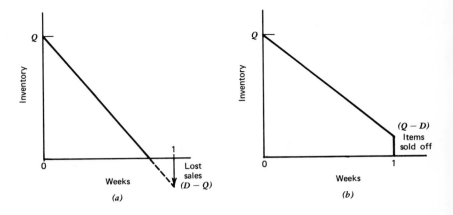

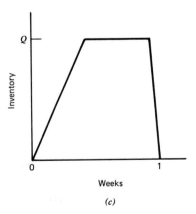

Figure 6.7   Inventory profiles for a perishable-fruit model.

The average inventory level in Chicago given $Q < D$ is

$$\frac{Q^2}{2D}$$

and given $Q > D$ is

$$Q - \frac{D}{2}$$

The elements of the profit equation can now be developed

	$Q \geq D$	$Q < D$
Revenue from selling fresh boxes	PD	PQ
Revenue from selling stale boxes	$P'(Q-D)$	0
Picking cost	CQ	CQ
Transportation cost	TQ	TQ
Loss of goodwill cost	0	$G(D-Q)$
Inventory cost in New Jersey	$I'\left(Q-\dfrac{Q^2}{2R}\right)$	$I'\left(Q-\dfrac{Q^2}{2R}\right)$
Inventory cost in Chicago	$I''(Q-D/2)$	$I''(Q^2/2D)$

The expected total-profit equation can now be formulated.

$$E(TP(Q)) = -CQ - TQ - I'\left(Q - \frac{Q^2}{2R}\right)$$

$$+ \sum_{D=0}^{Q} (PD + P'(Q-D) - I''(Q-D/2))g(D)$$

$$+ \sum_{D=Q+1}^{\infty} (PQ - G(D-Q) - I''(Q^2/2D))g(D)$$

The optimum value of Q^* can be found by using a computer search on various values of Q.

Professors Reed and Stanley [7] reported a study in which the objective was to design a procedure for improved economic control of hospital general inventories. The study was undertaken as a graduate project in the Department of Industrial Engineering with the cooperation of the J. Hillis Miller Health Center, University of Florida. It was desired that the design be practical, efficient, and readily adaptable to existing hospital procedures. Emphasis was placed on determining the order point and order quantity for stores items. Similar analyses and designs were available in the literature for industrial installations where the criteria usually have economic origins. In the hospital it is necessary to consider life and death as well as economic criteria. Practice most often has been to assign an economic cost for all factors. In this presentation, allowance for

**6.5.5
Optimizing
Control of
Hospital
Inventories***

Application Study

* Adapted with permission from January-February 1965 *Journal of Industrial Engineering.* Copyright © American Institute of Industrial Engineers, Inc., 25 Technology Park/Atlanta, Norcross, Ga. 30071.

stockouts is made by means of the model rather than an arbitrarily assigned cost.

It was decided that the A-B-C classification of inventories based on annual dollar usage should be used. The A-B-C classification system states that a small percentage of items (maybe 10 percent) account for a large percentage (maybe 70 percent) of the inventory activity. These items are the A items and should be managed carefully. The B items represent approximately 30 percent of the items and 25 percent of the activity. B items have fairly tight controls but are not watched as closely as A items. The remaining inventory (60 percent of the items that accounts for only 5 percent of the activity) is classified as C inventory and is managed very loosely. Reed and Stanley took a random sample of 200 inventory items that was found satisfactory, producing the A-B-C classification. The resulting distribution is illustrated in Figure 6.8.

It was found that demands could be satisfactorily forecast using Brown's exponential smoothing technique [1]. Demands for the high value class (HVC) and middle value (MVC) items are estimated for the following period using Brown's technique with a smoothing constant $\alpha = .1$. This results in an estimated demand for the next period of $\bar{D}_{n+1}$ and an estimated variance of demand

$$S_D{}^2 = \frac{\sum\limits_{i=1}^{n} (D_i - d_i)^2}{n}$$

where:

D_i = estimated demand for period i
d_i = actual demand for period i
$(D_i - d_i)$ = forecast error for period i
n = number of time periods used in variance determination

The result was that the demand for the next time period could be estimated by a frequency distribution with mean $\bar{D}_{n+1}$ and variance $S_D{}^2$.

To establish an order point for inventory items for which confidence levels could be established, it remained necessary to express lead time as a frequency distribution. It was found that in hospitals in general, the stock item may be purchased from several vendors and the method of purchase for the same vendor may be by either bid or direct purchase order. To overcome these restrictions the following assumptions were made:

1. The time to write and receive approval of the purchase requisition is expected to be the same for all items. This time will generally be small compared to the total lead time.
2. Time required to write bid quotation sheets and purchase orders will be the same for all items and will be constant.

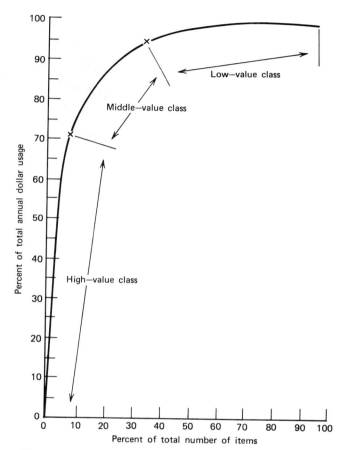

Figure 6.8 Annual dollar usage curve of sample of 200 items stocked at the J. Hillis Miller Health Center, University of Florida.

3. Items that are similar in nature and size are expected to have the same lead time, if generally purchased from the same group of suppliers.

The total lead time for an item, T_T, was then divided into three times, T_1, T_2, and T_3 where:

$T_1 =$ the time required to write and receive approval of the purchase requisition.

$T_2 =$ the time required to write the bid quotation sheets, plus time for vendors to consider this bid, and the time for the hospital to write the purchase order after accepting a bid.

$T_3 =$ the elapsed time from issuance of the purchase order until the units are on the shelf ready for internal distribution. This includes the time for the vendor to make and ship the units, time for transportation, and time for unpacking and inspecting the items.

From assumption 1, a frequency distribution of T_1, compiled from past data of all items, is applicable to all items. Periodic review of T_1 by sampling will prevent significant error due to trends or abrupt changes in procedures. For nonbid items, time T_2 will be equal to the purchase-order writing time, since the bid time will be zero. Time T_2 for bid items was assumed to be equal and constant for all items stocked in the central storeroom. Changes in T_2 can be controlled in the same manner as for T_1.

To overcome sampling restrictions, due to long calendar periods being required to obtain sufficient sample sizes for single items, items of a similar nature and size, having no peculiarities that would significantly affect lead time, were grouped to estimate T_3. The mean and variance for the group T_3 time was then applied to determine the total leadtime estimate for an individual item in the group.

The estimated mean value of the total lead time for an item was then taken as the sum of the sampled mean values of T_1, T_2, and T_3, assuming these three times to be independent. Therefore, the estimated total lead time for the ith item is:

$$\bar{T}_{T_i} = \bar{T}_{1_i} + \bar{T}_{2_i} + \bar{T}_{3_i}$$

An approximation of the variance of the total lead time is found by the theorem of linear combinations applied to sample values. Hence, the estimated total lead-time variance from sample data for the ith item is

$$S_{T_{T_i}}^{\,2} = S_{T_{1_i}}^{\,2} + S_{T_{2_i}}^{\,2} + S_{T_{3_i}}^{\,2}$$

This results in an estimated total lead-time distribution with mean,

$$\bar{T}_{T_i}, \qquad \text{and variance } S_{T_{T_i}}^{\,2}$$

This information, when combined with the demand distribution, permits determination of the order point.

Order-Point Determination for "High Value Class" Items. The demand during lead-time distribution for an item is the product of the demand and lead-time distributions for that item. The order point can be calculated directly from this estimated demand during lead-time distribution for any service level. Let the demand during lead time be denoted by X, the mean of the sample distribution by $\bar{X}$, and the variance by $S_x^{\,2}$. Then, for the ith item,

$$\bar{X}_i = \bar{D}_i \bar{T}_{T_i}$$

and

$$S_{x_i}^{\,2} = S_{D_i}^{\,2} \bar{T}_{T_i} + S_{T_{T_i}}^{\,2} \bar{D}_i^{\,2}$$

The value of X computed for a particular item is the expected number of units of the item needed during the next lead time. If these variables are known and constant, a stock level of X units would be the order point. However, since there is variation expected, an order point of $\bar{X}$ would result in stockouts with about 50 percent of the orders. Safety stock is used to reduce this stockout probability. The size of the safety stock required depends on the variability of the demand during lead-time distribution and the desired service level.

Since both the demand distribution and lead-time distribution are generally unimodal, it was assumed that the product of the two is unimodal. This is a necessary assumption for determining the order point.

To make confidence statements about a unimodal distribution where only the mean and variance are known, use is made of Camp and Meidel's extension of Tchebycheff's inequality. That is,

$$P(X_i > \bar{X} + KS_x) \le \frac{1}{4.5K^2}$$

for sample values.

$P(X_i > \bar{X} + KS_x)$ is the probability of a stockout and is equal to 1 minus the service level, S_L. By assigning a value to the service level, K is readily computed. $(\bar{X} + KS_x)$ = the order point providing a probability of S_L of not having a stockout during order processing and restocking.

The order point computed by this method will provide overprotection. This is desirable since many of the items, such as some medical gases or surgical and medical supplies, may be life-or-death items. This small overprotection, while slightly increasing the inventory cost, adds an extra, although undeterminable, safety factor and is deemed desirable for hospitals.

Order-Point Calculation for "Middle Value Class" Items. The procedure for calculation of the order point for the HVC items is not economical for the MVC items, since the costs of data collection will generally tend to offset savings realized from tighter control.

To reduce cost of data collection, the lead-time estimate is computed in the same manner as for HVC items but for the class rather than for individual items. This value is then applied to each item in the class. The class lead-time value used is the value that, by statistical inference, is large enough to include h percent of the lead times of items in the class. In other words, it is expected that only $(1 - h)$ percent of the orders for items in this class will result in lead-time values greater than the selected value. (Note: it has been stated that the data processing required to establish lead times for individual items is not excessive and should be used rather than class lead time. Such a statement may or may not be true depending on the procedures of the installation. Furthermore, the calendar time over which a sufficient sample must be gathered may make the sample nonrepresentative of present conditions. If applicable and readily available h may be established for each item. It does not change the basic model.)

To find the lead time estimate, the latest 100 orders are selected. It is then assumed that the distribution of these observations is normal, based on the extension of the central limit theorem, which states that when a random variable, X, is the sum of a number of independent variables, $\sum Y$ (where $i = 1, 2, \ldots, n$), the distribution of X approaches the normal form as n gets larger. With the normality assumption, the h percent confidence limit lead time is readily estimated using normal distribution tables.

The demand during lead-time estimate for each item is obtained in the same manner as for HVC items. Again, X refers to the demand during lead time, with X the expected value and S_x^2 the variance. The values are found for the ith term from

$$\bar{X} = \bar{D}_i T_{i(h \text{ percent})}$$

and

$$S_{x_i}^2 = S_{D_i}^2 T_i^2 \text{ } _{(h \text{ percent})}$$

The order point again is found from Camp and Meidel's inequality, using the desired service level.

Order-Point Calculation for the "Low Value Class" Items. LVC items account for very little of the total inventory investment (5 percent in the study). For these low annual value items, larger safety stocks are more economical than detailed, accurate data collection. In order to compensate for greater expected deviations from estimates, larger safety stocks must be kept for each item. The estimate of demand for the next time period is found by dividing the past annual usage (in number of units) by the number of time periods in a year (if the time period is a month, divide by 12, and so forth), and is assumed to remain constant.

Continuous review of the economic order points (EOP) for these items is not economical as a rule. Periodic review and recalculation is sufficient.

Due to the assumption of no variance in the expected demand during lead time, additional safety stock is provided by adding a fixed time factor to the confidence level lead-time value. This is expressed by:

$EOP =$ expected demand during lead time $+$ safety stock where

expected demand during lead time, $\bar{X} = \bar{D}_i \bar{T}_{i(h \text{ percent})}$

and

safety stock $= \bar{D}_i T_s$

where

$T_s =$ fixed time factor. Therefore, $EOP = \bar{D}_i [\bar{T}_{i(h \text{ percent})} + T_s]$

The value of T_s is assigned by qualitative means, being greater if the lead time for the item is relatively long and variable, or if a stockout of the LVC item in question is particularly undesirable.

Application of the Order-Point Calculation Procedure. To illustrate results using the procedure for determining order points, a subsample of 9 items, from the original sample of 200 items, was selected. Using historical data covering a period of two and one-half years, results obtained by application of the method are summarized in Table 6.9.

1. A product can be produced at the rate of 1000 units per week and is demanded at the rate of 400 units per week. Given that

6.6 PROBLEMS

$$\text{Items cost} = \$10$$
$$\text{Setup cost} = \$55$$
$$\text{Holding cost per unit per week} = \$.10$$

find Q^*, $TCU(Q^*)$ and t_0^* for the case where no shortage is allowed.

2. Repeat problem 1 assuming we are dealing with the purchase model, that is, stock is replenished instantaneously.

3. Repeat problem 1 where shortages are allowed at a cost of $1 per unit per week. If the shortage cost was not given and we were told that Q^* is 950, what is the implied shortage cost?

4. Solve problem 3 assuming we are dealing with a purchase model.

5. A machine shop can manufacture 95 gears per day in its manufacturing operations. The production line that uses these gears needs 45 per day. The setup cost is $500 and the holding cost is $.25 per gear per day. The gears are valued at $250. Find Q^*, t_0^*, and $TCU(Q^*)$, assuming that no shortages are allowed.

6. In problem 5 find Q^* and w^*, assuming that shortage costs are $2.00 per gear per day.

7. For the purchase model discussed in Section 6.2.3 find the sensitivity of Q^* and $TCU(Q^*)$ to K, b, and h. Which is the most important variable to have accurate estimates of?

8. An electronics firm requires 100,000 feet of a particular type of wire per day. Shortage cost is estimated to be $0.005 per 1000 feet per day and holding cost is $0.002 per 1000 feet per day. The company has two options: either to manufacture or to purchase the item.

	Purchase	Manufacture
Item cost per 1000 ft	$40	$35
Procurement cost	50	400
Replenishment rate	∞	500,000 feet/day

Should the company make or buy the wire?

Table 6.9 Summary of Procedure Application to Nine Items at the J. Hills Miller Health Center Over a Period of $2\frac{1}{2}$ Years

Item	Class	Assigned Service Level (percent)	Calculated Order Point (units)	Number of Orders Received	Stock Levels at Time Orders Received	Number of Stockouts
Gauze sponge	HVC	95	8	4	1, 6, 4, 7	0
Animal cage paper	HVC	90	40	5	9, 32, 14, 32, 29	0
Cotton balls	HVC	95	22	7	11, 1, 8, 5, 8, 15, 12	0
X-ray film	HVC	95	39	5	14, 16, 8, 12, 23	0
Carbon paper	HVC	95	23	6	8, 14, 15, 12, 17, 9	0
Surgical wadding	MVC	95	10	2	8, 7	0
Pint containers	MVC	95	64	5	17, 27, 3, 21, 42	0
Cotton tip applicators	LVC		11	3	8, 6, 5	0
Nord transfer solution	LVC		21	3	8, 12, 19	0

9. A student once hypothesized that for the purchase model discussed in Section 6.2.3 the average annual cost of holding the product will equal the average annual cost of procuring the product at $Q = Q^*$. Is this a true statement?

10. The demand for an item for a single-period probabilistic model is approximated by the following distribution:

$$f(D) = 1/10 \quad \text{for } 5 \leq D \leq 15$$
$$\qquad\quad 0 \quad \text{elsewhere}$$

Given that $I = 6$, $h = 1$, $c = 5$, $p = 15$, and $K = 0$, find the optimum inventory policy.

11. Repeat the analysis for problem 10, assuming that $K = 50$.

12. The purchase cost per unit is $10, the holding cost is $2 per unit per period, and the shortage cost is $15 per unit per period. What is Q^* if $g(D)$ is defined as follows:

D	0	1	2	3	4	5	6	7
g(D)	.05	.10	.10	.15	.20	.20	.15	.05

There is no setup cost.

13. In problem 12, assume that shortage cost is not known but Q^* is assumed to be 6. What is the implied range on the shortage cost?

14. Solve the single period model discussed in Section 6.3.2, for the case where $c = 1$, $p = 5$, and $h = 1$. $g(D) = 1/5$ for $D = 0, 1, 2, 3, 4$ and $I = 1$.

15. Repeat your analysis for problem 14 but assume that there is a setup cost, K, equal to 10.

16. Resolve the Alpha Pi Mu Christmas-tree problem discussed in Section 6.3.2 under the assumption that the demand for trees can be approximated by a normal distribution with a mean of 750 and a standard deviation of 100.

17. A shipping company has commissioned a large oil tanker. Spare parts such as rudders are usually ordered when the ship is built. The parts are expensive and difficult to obtain if no spare is available. Suppose a part costs $10,000 when the ship is procured but $35,000 if it must be made as a special order. The particular part is needed on the average five times over the life of the ship. The distribution of the demand can be approximated by a Poisson probability distribution. Parts left over when the boat is scrapped are useless. How many spare parts should be ordered?

18. A service station finds that weekly sales of regular gasoline may be considered to be uniformly distributed over the interval from 4000 gallons and 6000 gallons. The station can only replenish its stock once a week and there is no fixed cost of replenishment. Gas costs $.50/gallon and sells for $.65/gallon. It is estimated that there is a loss of goodwill cost

of $.05 per gallon if there is a stockout and the holding cost is $.005 per gallon per week. How many gallons should be ordered?

19. The lead-time demand distribution for a particular product can be approximated by a normal distribution with a mean of 50 and a standard deviation of 10. What is the safety stock and reorder point for an inventory policy that allows no more than one stockout per each 15 order cycles?

20. The probability distribution for lead time demand is approximated by the following probability distribution:

D	10	11	12	13	14	15	16	17
g(D)	.05	.20	.20	.20	.15	.10	.08	.02

We also know that the annual demand rate is 5000 units, the order cost is $50/order, the units cost $10, the inventory cost is $2/unit/year and the cost of a stockout is $10.

What is the optimal order quantity, the reorder point, the safety stock size, and the annual cost of the inventory system?

21. Repeat the analysis in problem 20 when you have the following lead-time information:

Lead Time in Weeks	Probability
1	.1
2	.9

Weekly Demand	Probability
0	.6
1	.2
2	.1
3	.1

22. A company has a petty cash fund that has a more-or-less steady outflow of funds. The fund is replenished from a saving account that pays 5 percent interest. The bank messenger is paid $10 to deliver the money. What is the optimal withdrawal schedule if the annual outlay from the fund is $15,000?

23. Resolve problem 2 considering there is an opportunity for a quantity discount as follows:

Cost/unit	Quantity
$10	$Q < 300$
9.50	$300 \leq Q < 1000$
9.20	$1000 \leq Q < 2000$
8.90	$2000 \leq Q$

24. Resolve problem 4 considering there is an opportunity for a quantity discount as follows:

Cost/unit	Quantity
$10.00	$Q < 200$
9.50	$200 \leq Q < 1000$
9.00	$1000 \leq Q$

25. For the example presented in Section 6.5.3 what would be the value of an exact forecast?

26. Hess Brothers of Allentown must decide what quantity of a high-priced women's leather handbag to procure from France for the winter. They cost $25 each and sell for $60 each. Handbags not sold can be disposed at cost but there is a loss of $3.00 per handbag because of the opportunity cost of the money tied up. The demand is estimated to be uniform on the interval from 50 to 150. How many bags should be bought? Would it be worth $300 for a forecast that would tell the buyer the demand was uniform over the range 75 to 125 handbags?

27. Consider problem 14. What is the value of the forecast d' that would have the following accuracy?

$$g(D) = 1/2 \qquad \text{for } D = d', d' + 1$$

and d' will be equally likely to be 0, 1, 2 or 3.

28. Write a computer program to solve the problem discussed in Section 6.5.4 for the case where

$$C = \$5 \text{ per case}$$
$$T = \$.05 \text{ per case}$$
$$P = \$10 \text{ per case}$$
$$P' = \$4 \text{ per case}$$
$$R = 3000 \text{ cases per week}$$
$$I' = I'' = \$.25 \text{ per case per week}$$
$$G = \$1 \text{ per case}$$
$$g(D) = 1/500 \text{ for } 1000 \leq D \leq 1500$$

REFERENCES

1. Brown, R. G., *Statistical Forecasting for Inventory Control*, McGraw-Hill, New York, 1963.
2. Brown, R. G., *Decision Rules for Inventory Management*, Holt, Rinehart and Winston, New York, 1967.
3. Hadley, G. and T. M. Whitin, *Analysis of Inventory Systems*, Prentice-Hall, Englewood Cliffs, N.J., 1963.
4. Hanssmann, F., *Operations Research in Production and Inventory Control*, Wiley, New York, 1962.
5. Johnson, L. A. and D. C. Montgomery, *Operations Research in Production Planning, Scheduling and Inventory Control*, Wiley, New York, 1974.
6. Miller, D. W. and M. K. Starr, *Inventory Control: Theory and Practice*, Prentice-Hall, Englewood Cliffs, N.J., 1962.
7. Reed, R. and W. E. Stanley, "Optimizing control of hospital inventories," *Journal of Industrial Engineering*, Vol. XVI, No. 1, January–February 1965.

waiting-line
analysis 7

Waiting-line analysis (queueing theory) is one of the earliest problem areas studied in operations research. Waiting-line analysis is of considerable interest to the operations researcher because it is an analytical tool that he can use to make a rational analysis of many problems that he encounters.

Waiting is the condition that exists when a unit that is to be serviced in some way has to wait for the service facility to give service to other units; in other words, the unit joins a *queue* in which it awaits its turn to be serviced by the service facility. Examples of waiting lines are shown in Table 7.1.

Waiting-line analysis (queueing theory) describes the conditions under which waiting lines occur. Most work is concerned with random input to the line or random output or both. In any servicing situation, such as those shown in Table 7.1 the elements of the situation are *arrivals* and servicing *facilities* (often called *channels*) as indicated in Figure 7.1.

There has been little or no standardization of waiting line terminology and classification of models. James Moore [10] has, however, developed a keysort system to catalogue a massive amount of waiting-line literature. Moore suggests that the queueing characteristics be defined in five categories.

1. *Arrival distribution.* How do the customers arrive? If they arrive according to a fixed schedule, it might be possible to schedule the services and a queue would be avoided. This, however, is not usually the case. In most situations the arrivals are controlled by some external factors that produce uncertainties in the arrivals. For this

**7.1
INTRODUCTION
AND
DEFINITION
OF
TERMS***

* Adapted with permission from Industrial Engineering, June, 1974. Copyright © American Institute of Industrial Engineers, Inc., 25 Technology Park/Atlanta, Norcross, Ga. 30071.

Table 7.1 Applications of Waiting-Line Analysis

Arrivals	Servicing Facilities	The Queue
Shoppers	Clerks	Checkout line
Airplanes	Runways	Stack
Machine breakdowns	Repairmen	Idle machines
Telephone calls	Circuits	Uncompleted calls
Patients	Doctor	Waiting room
Fires	Firemen	Burning buildings
Automobiles	Traffic light	Traffic jam
Customers	Inventory	Back orders
Finished goods	Retailers	Inventory
Borrowers	Library books	Waiting list
Quiz questions	Brain	Unanswered questions
Raw materials	Machines	Raw material inventory
Piece parts, subassemblies	Assemblers	In-process inventory
Streams, rain	Water users	Lake behind the dam
Families	Apartments	Waiting list
Apartments	Families	Empty apartments

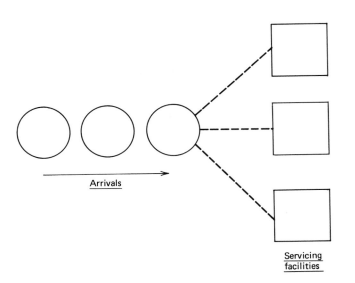

Arrivals

Servicing facilities

Figure 7.1   Structure for a queueing system.

331
7.1
INTRODUCTION
AND
DEFINITION
OF TERMS

reason, the time between successive arrivals is a random variable and its probability distribution is called the arrival distribution.

2. *Service distribution.* Due to factors such as the type of service required and inherent variability among servers, the duration of the time required to provide the service and discharge the customer is also a random variable and its probability distribution is referred to as the service distribution.

3. *Number of service channels.* This refers to the number of servers. There may be one or more servers. If there are multiple servers, it must be specified whether they are in parallel (such as a toll booth where there are three or four toll collectors and the driver of the vehicle has his choice) or in a series where a customer must queue up to go through a second channel that provides another type of service.

4. *Customer population.* There are two distinct classes of queueing situations based on the size of the customer population. If the number of customers is very large and the demand correspondingly small, it is convenient to assume that the customer population is infinite. If the number of customers is small, the finite case must be used. The calculations are far easier for the infinite case. The finite case is more difficult analytically because the number of units in the queueing system affects the number of potential calling units outside the system at any point in time. For a customer population of 250 units or more, the rate at which the input source generates calling units is not significantly affected by the number of units in the queueing system. Thus, this is the number sometimes used to separate the finite and the infinite population cases.

5. *Queue discipline.* This refers to the order in which the customers are accepted into service. The most common discipline is called "first-come-first-served (FCFS)," but there are numerous other disciplines in common use.

Table 7.2 shows Moore's classifications of each of these categories.

Table 7.2 Moore's Waiting Line Classifications

Arrival distributions
Poisson arrival distribution
Erlang arrival distribution
General independent
General arbitrary
Constant arrival time
Uniform arrival distribution

Service distributions
Exponential service time distribution
Erlang service time distribution

Table 7.2 (*Continued*)

General independent
General arbitrary
Constant service time
Uniform service distribution

Number of service channels
One
More than one parallel channel
More than one channel in series
Variable number of channels

Size of population of customers
Infinitely large
Finite population (rule of thumb: less than 250)

Queue discipline
FCFS = first come, first served
Random = customers selected for service in a random order
LCFS = last come, first served
SPT = shortest processing time (customer with shortest servicing time goes first)
SRPT = shortest remaining processing time, i.e., an arriving customer will preempt a customer in service if the processing time of the new customer is less than the remaining processing time of the customer in service. In selecting another customer at the moment of a service completion, the preference is given to the customer with the least remaining processing time.
FP = finite priority, i.e., customers are assigned a unique priority number where the small priority number has preference over the larger priority number.
NP = non-preemptive priority, i.e., if a lower priority customer is being served, it cannot be preempted (ejected out of service facility) to allow a higher priority customer to start service.
SP = semi-preemptive priority, i.e., lower priority customer in service may be preempted by a higher priority customer if its processing time is less than the remaining processing time of customer in service, otherwise he must wait.
PR = preempt resume priority, i.e., preemption causes no loss so that the processing of a preempted job can resume where it left off.
PRW = preempt repeat priority, i.e., preempted customer must repeat its processing from the start.
Balking = customer refuses to join queue if it is too long.
Reneging = customer in queue may leave the system if waiting time is excessive.
Bulk = customers arrive in groups or are served in batches.
Bounded Q = queue size limited to a specific number. When queue size reaches its limit, customers are not allowed to enter.
State dependent arrival rate = arrival rate is expressed as a function of the state of the system, i.e., dependent upon the number of customers in the system.
State dependent service rate = server may be under psychological pressure to increase his service rate if the queue is too long, thus his service rate may be dependent upon the state of the system.

333
7.2 POISSON
ARRIVALS AND
EXPONENTIAL
SERVICE
WAITING-LINE
MODELS

It should be obvious that we cannot develop the results for all the models defined by Moore. We will concentrate on a relatively small subset of the problems described. If the analyst does not find a model appropriate to his situation we suggest that he consult one of the more detailed queueing texts such as Gross and Harris [7], Prabhu [12], Saaty [13], Cox and Smith [3], or Cooper [2]. Another consideration that should always be kept in mind is that many waiting-line systems cannot be handled analytically but must be solved using simulation, as discussed in Chapter 8.

The waiting-line models involving Poisson arrivals and exponential service are the most studied waiting-line systems because they are relatively easy to solve analytically. This is because the time between arrivals for Poisson arrivals is distributed according to an exponential distribution. A very interesting property of the exponential distribution is the "forgetfulness property." The forgetfulness property states that the probability of an event (an arrival or a service) occurring in the next instance of time is independent of when the last event occurred. Suppose customers are arriving at a bank in a Poisson manner; then the forgetfulness property states that the likelihood of a customer arriving in the next element of time (Δt) is the same no matter if the last customer arrived a minute or an hour ago. The same assumption is made about servicing a customer because the service distribution is exponential and also has the forgetfulness property.

7.2 POISSON ARRIVALS AND EXPONENTIAL SERVICE WAITING-LINE MODELS

7.2.1 Formulation

The forgetfulness property allows the operations research analyst to develop equations describing the behavior of the waiting line. Let's define the following terms that will be used in our analysis:

n = number of units in the system. This includes the number in the waiting line as well as those in the service stations.

$P_n(t)$ = probability of n units in the system at time t.

Δt = a small increment of time such that more than one arrival or service during Δt can not occur.

μ_n = mean service rate given that there are n units in the system, units per time period.

λ_n = mean arrival rate given that there are n units in the system, units per time period.

$\mu_n \Delta_t$ = probability that a unit being serviced is completed in the time interval t to $t + \Delta t$ given that there are n units in the system.

$\lambda_n \Delta_t$ = probability that a unit enters the system in the time interval t to $t + \Delta t$ given that there are n units in the system.

We first develop an expression for $P_n(t + \Delta t)$, which is defined as the probability of having n items in the system at time $t + \Delta t$.

$P_n(t+\Delta t) = $ (probability of n items in the system at time t) $\times$ (probability of no arrivals in Δt) $\times$ (probability of no services in Δt) + (probability of $n-1$ items in the system at time t) $\times$ (probability of one arrival in Δt) $\times$ (probability of no services in Δt) + (probability of $n+1$ items in the system at time t) $\times$ (probability of no arrivals in Δt) $\times$ (probability of one service in Δt)

$$P_n(t+\Delta t) = P_n(t)(1-\lambda_n\Delta t)(1-\mu_n\Delta t) + P_{n-1}(t)(\lambda_{n-1}\Delta t)(1-\mu_{n-1}\Delta t)$$

$$+ P_{n+1}(t)(1-\lambda_{n+1}\Delta t)(\mu_{n+1}\Delta t)$$

$$= P_n(t) + (-\lambda_n - \mu_n)\Delta t P_n(t) + \lambda_{n-1}\Delta t P_{n-1}(t)$$

$$+ \mu_{n+1}\Delta t P_{n+1}(t) + \text{terms in } (\Delta t)^2$$

$$\text{for } n = 0, 1, 2 \ldots . \tag{7.1}$$

In (7.1) we note that if $\lambda_n\Delta t$ is the probability of an arrival in time Δt given n items in the system, then $(1-\lambda_n\Delta t)$ is the probability of no arrivals in time Δt given n items in the system. Furthermore, it is assumed that the Δt is sufficiently small so that $(\Delta t)^2$ approaches 0.

Next we realize that the definition of a derivative is

$$\frac{dP_n(t)}{dt} = \lim_{\Delta t \to 0} \left[\frac{P_n(t+\Delta t) - P_n(t)}{\Delta t} \right]$$

so (7.1) becomes

$$\frac{dP_n(t)}{dt} = (-\lambda_n - \mu_n)P_n(t) + \lambda_{n-1}P_{n-1}(t)$$

$$+ \mu_{n+1}P_{n+1}(t) \qquad \text{for } n = 0, 1, 2 \ldots \tag{7.2}$$

So we have a set of differential equations that define the behavior of the waiting line but the solution of sets of equations of this form are difficult and beyond the scope of this text. We will limit our discussion to steady-state results. In steady state, $P_n(t)$ is independent of t and $dP_n(t)/dt$ goes to 0. Therefore (7.2) becomes

$$0 = (-\lambda_n - \mu_n)P_n + \lambda_{n-1}P_{n-1}$$

$$+ \mu_{n+1}P_{n+1} \qquad \text{for } n = 0, 1, 2 \ldots \tag{7.3}$$

where P_n is the steady-state probability of having n items in the system.

335
7.2 POISSON
ARRIVALS AND
EXPONENTIAL
SERVICE
WAITING-LINE
MODELS

Solving (7.3), remembering that λ_n, μ_n, or P_n will equal zero for $n < 0$, we get*

$$P_0 = \frac{1}{1 + \sum\limits_{n=1}^{\infty} \frac{\prod\limits_{i=0}^{n-1} \lambda_i}{\prod\limits_{i=1}^{n} \mu_i}}$$

(7.4)

$$P_n = \frac{\prod\limits_{i=0}^{n-1} \lambda_i}{\prod\limits_{i=1}^{n} \mu_i} P_0 \qquad \text{for } n = 1, 2, \dots$$

In addition to the steady-state probabilities the analyst is often interested in the following measures:

L_s = expected number of items in the system
L_q = expected number of items waiting for service (i.e., in the queue)
W_s = expected waiting time in the system (includes service time)
W_q = expected waiting time in the queue (excludes service time)

If we let c be the number of servers (parallel service channels) in the waiting-line system

$$L_s = \sum_{n=1}^{\infty} n P_n$$

(7.5)

$$L_q = \sum_{n=c+1}^{\infty} (n-c) P_n$$

Now if we assume that λ_n is a constant λ for all n, Little [9] has proved the general result that

$$L_s = \lambda W_s$$

and

(7.6)

$$L_q = \lambda W_q$$

There are several special cases of the Poisson arrival and exponential service waiting-line models that have closed-form solutions for P_n, L_s, L_q, W_s, and W_q and we will look at some of these next. But first let us consider the following example.

---

* $\prod\limits_{i=0}^{n-1} \lambda_i$ is interpreted as $(\lambda_0)(\lambda_1)(\lambda_2) \dots (\lambda_{n-1})$.

EXAMPLE   Consider a barber shop that has two barbers and three chairs for waiting customers. Assume that customers arrive in a Poisson fashion at a rate of 6 per hour and that each barber services customers according to an exponential distribution with a mean time of 15 minutes (i.e., a service rate of 4 per hour). Furthermore, if a customer arrives and there are no empty chairs in the shop he will leave. Let's analyze this using the results we have developed in this section.

From the description of the system we first define λ_n and μ_n as follows:

n	λ_n	μ_n
0	6	0
1	6	4
2	6	8
3	6	8
4	6	8
5	0	8
6 or more	0	0

Customers arrive at the rate of 6 per hour; when the shop is full, they do not enter, therefore $\lambda_5 = 0$. If there are no customers in the shop no one will be serviced (i.e., $\mu_0 = 0$). If there is one customer, one barber will be busy and the shops service will be 4 per hour (i.e., $\mu_1 = 4$). When there are 2 or more customers both barbers will be busy and the shops service rate will be 8 per hour (i.e., $\mu_n = 8$, $n = 2, 3, 4, 5$). Since the maximum number of customers in the shop is 5 (2 having their hair cut and 3 waiting), $\lambda_n = \mu_n = 0$ for $n > 5$.

From (7.4) we can find the steady-state probabilities for the number of customers in the shop.

$$P_0 = \cfrac{1}{1 + \cfrac{6}{4} + \cfrac{(6)^2}{4(8)} + \cfrac{(6)^3}{4(8)^2} + \cfrac{(6)^4}{4(8)^3} + \cfrac{(6)^5}{4(8)^4}} = .1793$$

$$P_1 = \frac{6}{4} P_0 = .2690$$

$$P_2 = \frac{(6)^2}{4(8)} P_0 = .2018$$

$$P_3 = \frac{(6)^3}{4(8)^2} P_0 = .1513$$

337
7.2 POISSON
ARRIVALS AND
EXPONENTIAL
SERVICE
WAITING-LINE
MODELS

$$P_4 = \frac{(6)^4}{4(8)^3} P_0 = .1135$$

$$P_5 = \frac{6^5}{4(8)^4} P_0 = .0851$$

These steady-state probabilities will help us find such information as: What is the probability that the shop is empty?

$$P_0 = .1793$$

What is the probability that a customer will find the shop full and balk?

$$P_5 = .0851$$

What percentage of the time will both barbers be busy?

$$P_2 + P_3 + P_4 + P_5 = .5517$$

What is the expected number of customers in the shop and what is the expected length of the waiting line?
From (7.5) we find

$$L_s = \sum_{n=1}^{\infty} nP_n = 1(.2690) + 2(.2018)$$

$$+ 3(.1513) + 4(.1135)$$

$$+ 5(.0851) = 2.0060 \text{ customers}$$

$$L_q = \sum_{n=c+1}^{\infty} (n-c)P_n = (3-2)(.1513) + (4-2)(.1135)$$

$$+ (5-2)(.0851) = .6336 \text{ customers}$$

Note that (7.6) does not apply to our analysis because $\lambda_n \neq \lambda$ for all n.

This model is a special case of the model presented in Section 7.2.1 where $\lambda_n = \lambda$ for $n = 0, 1, 2, \ldots$ and $\mu_n = \mu$ for $n = 1, 2, 3 \ldots$ From (7.4)

7.2.2 Single Server-Infinite Population of Customers— Infinite Queue

$$P_0 = \frac{1}{1 + \sum\limits_{n=1}^{\infty} \dfrac{\prod\limits_{i=0}^{n-1} \lambda_i}{\prod\limits_{i=1}^{n} \mu_i}}$$

$$= 1 \bigg/ \left(\sum_{n=0}^{\infty} (\lambda/\mu)^n \right)$$

Now if $\lambda/\mu < 1$*

$$P_0 = 1 \Big/ \left(\frac{1}{1-\lambda/\mu}\right) = 1 - \lambda/\mu \tag{7.7}$$

Also, from (7.4),

$$P_n = P_0 \frac{\prod\limits_{i=0}^{n-1} \lambda_i}{\prod\limits_{i=1}^{n} \mu_i} = P_0\left(\frac{\lambda}{\mu}\right)^n \tag{7.8}$$

We should note that if $\lambda/\mu \geq 1$ there will be no steady-state solution for this model. The queue length will approach infinity.

The expected number of units in the system is given by†

$$L_s = \sum_{n=1}^{\infty} nP_n = \sum_{n=1}^{\infty} n\left(\frac{\lambda}{\mu}\right)^n (1-\lambda/\mu)$$

$$= (1-\lambda/\mu)[\lambda/\mu + 2(\lambda/\mu)^2 + 3(\lambda/\mu)^3 + \ldots]$$

$$= (1-\lambda/\mu)(\lambda/\mu)[1 + 2(\lambda/\mu) + 3(\lambda/\mu)^2 + \ldots]$$

$$= (1-\lambda/\mu)(\lambda/\mu)\frac{1}{(1-\lambda/\mu)^2}$$

thus

$$L_s = (\lambda/\mu)\left[\frac{1}{1-(\lambda/\mu)}\right] = \frac{\lambda}{\mu-\lambda} \tag{7.9}$$

---

* If $x < 1$ then $\sum\limits_{n=0}^{\infty} x^n = 1/(1-x)$ so $\sum_{n=0}^{\infty} (\lambda/\mu)^n = 1/[1-(\lambda/\mu)]$ if $\lambda/\mu < 1$.

† Since

$$\text{if } t = 1 + x + x^2 + x^3 + \ldots \qquad x < 1$$

$$\frac{dt}{dx} = 0 + 1 + 2x + 3x^2 + \ldots$$

which is analogous to

$$1 + 2(\lambda/\mu) + 3(\lambda/\mu)^2 + \ldots$$

but

$$t = \frac{1}{1-x}$$

Therefore

$$\frac{dt}{dx} = \frac{-1}{(1-x)^2}(-1) = \frac{1}{(1-x)^2}$$

339
7.2 POISSON
ARRIVALS AND
EXPONENTIAL
SERVICE
WAITING-LINE
MODELS

We can find the expected number in the queue by observing that the average queue length equals the expected number in the system minus the one unit being serviced times the probability a unit is being serviced. Thus

$$L_q = L_s - 1(1 - P_0)$$

$$= \lambda/(\mu - \lambda) - [1 - (1 - \lambda/\mu)]$$

$$= \lambda/(\mu - \lambda) - \lambda/\mu = \frac{\lambda^2}{\mu(\mu - \lambda)} \qquad (7.10)$$

From (7.6) we next find W_s and W_q

$$W_s = \frac{L_s}{\lambda} = \frac{1}{\mu - \lambda} \qquad (7.11)$$

$$W_q = \frac{L_q}{\lambda} = \frac{\lambda}{\mu(\mu - \lambda)} \qquad (7.12)$$

EXAMPLE

In order to see how a waiting-line system behaves as the ratio of the arrival rate to service changes consider Table 7.3.

Obviously the system deteriorates rapidly as the ratio of λ to μ increases. Station idleness decreases as the complement of λ/μ while L_s and W_s increases rapidly as λ/μ approaches 1.

Table 7.3 Comparison of Waiting-Line Behavior as a Function of λ and μ

λ	μ	λ/μ	Station Idleness $P_0 = 1 - (\lambda/\mu)$	Average Number of Units in the System $L_s = \frac{\lambda}{\mu - \lambda}$	Average Waiting Time in the System $W_s = \frac{1}{\mu - \lambda}$	Probability of more than Four units in the System $1 - \sum_{n=0}^{4} P_n = (\lambda/\mu)^5$
1	10	.10	.90	.111	.111	.00001
2	10	.20	.80	.250	.125	.0003
3	10	.30	.70	.429	.143	.002
4	10	.40	.60	.667	.167	.010
5	10	.50	.50	1.000	.200	.031
6	10	.60	.40	1.500	.250	.078
7	10	.70	.30	2.333	.333	.168
8	10	.80	.20	4.000	.500	.328
9	10	.90	.10	9.000	1.000	.590
9.9	10	.99	.01	99.000	10.000	.951

7.2.3
Multiple-Server
Model,
Infinite
Population of
Customers,
Infinite Queue*

In this model the analyst assumes that there are c servers in parallel. Each server has an exponential service distribution with a mean of $1/\mu$ (i.e., each server can handle μ units per time period). There is a further assumption that the customers line up in a single queue and move to the servers as they become available. This assumption eliminates the possibility that there are customers in the queue and idle servers simultaneously. These assumptions allow us to cast this model in the format suggested in Section 7.2.1 where

$$\lambda_n = \lambda \qquad \text{for } n = 0, 1, 2, 3 \dots$$

$$\mu_n = \begin{cases} n\mu & \text{if } 0 \le n < c \\ c\mu & \text{if } n \ge c \end{cases}$$

Following the approaches similar to those used in Section 7.2.2 we get the following steady-state results given that $\lambda \le c\mu$.

$$P_0 = 1 \Big/ \left\langle \left[\sum_{n=0}^{c-1} \frac{(\lambda/\mu)^n}{n!} \right] + \left\{ \frac{(\lambda/\mu)^c}{c![1-(\lambda/c\mu)]} \right\} \right\rangle \qquad (7.13)$$

$$P_n = \begin{cases} \dfrac{(\lambda/\mu)^n}{n!} P_0 & \text{if } 0 < n < c \\[4mm] \dfrac{(\lambda/\mu)^n}{c!c^{n-c}} P_0 & \text{if } n \ge c \end{cases} \qquad (7.14)$$

and

$$L_q = \frac{P_0(\lambda/\mu)^c(\lambda/\mu c)}{c![1-(\lambda/\mu c)]^2} \qquad (7.15)$$

Using the results expressed in (7.6) we get

$$W_q = \frac{L_q}{\lambda} \qquad (7.16)$$

$$W_s = W_q + 1/\mu = L_q/\lambda + 1/\mu \qquad (7.17)$$

and

$$L_s = \lambda W_s = L_q + \lambda/\mu \qquad (7.18)$$

These computations are obviously unattractive to perform so a number of individuals have developed graphs that should ease analysis of multiple-server queueing models. The graphs in this chapter were adapated from the work of John Shelton [14].

341
7.2 POISSON
ARRIVALS AND
EXPONENTIAL
SERVICE
WAITING-LINE
MODELS

Figure 7.2 is a graph that allows the analyst to determine W_q for parallel queueing systems that have as many as 100 servers. This figure requires the use of channel utilization (α), which is defined as the number of arrivals per mean service time divided by the number of channels in the system.

$$\alpha = \frac{\lambda(1/\mu)}{c} = \frac{\lambda}{c\mu} \qquad (7.19)$$

EXAMPLE

Union Bank and Trust Company of Eastern Pennsylvania is considering the use of a new service philosophy in which all customers wait in a single queue and move to the cashiers as they become idle. The bank is interested in the waiting line behavior during peak periods. They plan to have five cashiers, each of which can handle 20 customers per hour. They expect that customers will arrive at the rate of 80 per hour. The assumption of Poisson arrivals and exponential service seems reasonable to the bank.

First we define α from (7.19)

$$\alpha = \frac{80}{5(20)} = .8$$

entering Figure 7.2 with $\alpha = .8$ and $c = 5$, we find that W_q is equal to .55 times the length of the mean service time.

$$W_q = .55(1/20) = .0275 \text{ hours}$$

From (7.16), (7.17), and (7.18) we find that

$$L_q = .0275(80) = 2.2 \text{ customers}$$
$$W_s = .0275 + (1/20) = .0775 \text{ hours}$$

and

$$L_s = 2.2 + 80/20 = 6.2 \text{ customers}$$

Thus the bank agrees that these are very agreeable results from a customer service standpoint.

Shelton [14] also presents some other charts that might be of interest to the operations research analyst. Figure 7.4 provides a vehicle for finding the probability (P) that a customer arriving at the system will move directly into service. The X axis (d) of this figure is defined as the ratio of λ to μ. The analyst enters the figure with d and c, and then reads P from the Y axis. Figure 7.3 allows the analyst to find the probability that the waiting time for an individual customer will be greater than a specified amount. The approach is to define a factor h.

$$h = cT\mu \qquad (7.20)$$

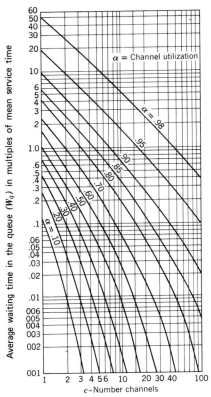

Figure 7.2   Average delay for exponential service time.

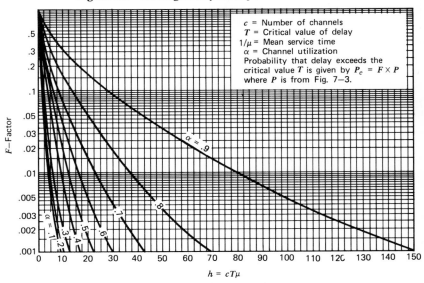

Figure 7.3   Probability that delay exceeds a critical value (exponential service time).

343
7.2 POISSON
ARRIVALS AND
EXPONENTIAL
SERVICE
WAITING-LINE
MODELS

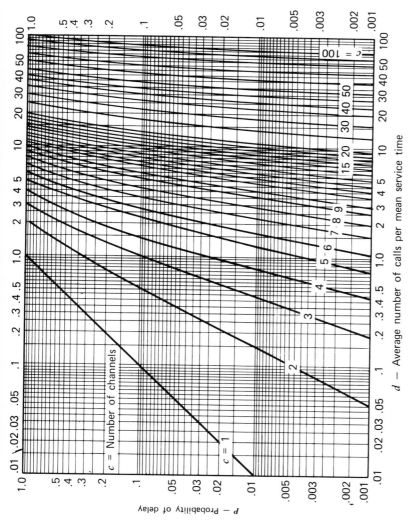

Figure 7.4 Probability of delay for exponential service time.

where
$$c = \text{number of channels}$$
$$T = \text{critical value of delay}$$
$$\mu = \text{service rate per channel}$$

Entering Figure 7.3 with h and α we read a factor F. The factor F multiplied by the P factor derived from the Figure 7.4 gives the desired result (P_c).

EXAMPLE Considering the bank just discussed, what is the probability that a customer will not have to wait for service? Also, what is the probability that a customer will wait in the queue more than five minutes?

For our example $d = 80/20 = 4$, entering Figure 7.4 we find that $P = .55$. Therefore the probability of no delay is .45.

From (7.19) and (7.20) we find $h = (5)(5/60)(20) = 8.33$ and $\alpha = (80)/(5)(20) = .8$. Entering Figure 7.3 we find that $F = .18$. Thus $P_c = F \times P = (.18)(.55) = .099$, which tells us that there is only a 10 percent chance that a customer will wait more than five minutes in the waiting line.

**7.2.4
Finite Queue
Models**

This model is identical to those discussed in Sections 7.2.2 and 7.2.3 except the queue length is limited to a particular size M. Any unit that arrives while the system is "full" leaves the system without being served. The example analyzed in Section 7.2.1 is a finite queueing model with multiple servers. This model is a special case of the system described in Section 7.2.1 where

$$\lambda_n = \begin{cases} \lambda & \text{for } n = 0, 1, 2, \ldots M-1 \\ 0 & \text{for } n \geq M \end{cases}$$

and

$$\mu_n = \begin{cases} n\mu & \text{for } 0 \leq n < c \\ c\mu & \text{for } c \leq n \geq M \\ 0 & \text{for } n > M \end{cases}$$

This model is used when there is only room for M units in the system as in the case of a parking lot or the customers will "balk" if the waiting time is too long as in the case of a barber shop.

Referring to (7.4) and (7.5) we find the following results for the single-server case:

$$P_0 = \frac{1 - (\lambda/\mu)}{1 - (\lambda/\mu)^{M+1}}$$

(7.21)

$$P_n = \left(\frac{1 - (\lambda/\mu)}{1 - (\lambda/\mu)^{M+1}} \right)(\lambda/\mu)^n \quad \text{for } n = 1, 2, \ldots, M$$

345
7.2 POISSON
ARRIVALS AND
EXPONENTIAL
SERVICE
WAITING-LINE
MODELS

$$P_n = 0 \qquad \text{for } n > M$$

$$L_s = \frac{(\lambda/\mu)}{1-(\lambda/\mu)} - \frac{(M+1)(\lambda/\mu)^{M+1}}{1-(\lambda/\mu)^{M+1}} \tag{7.22}$$

and, since $c = 1$,

$$L_q = L_s - (1 - P_0)$$

For the multiple-server case:

$$P_0 = 1 \bigg/ \left[\sum_{n=0}^{c} \frac{(\lambda/\mu)^n}{n!} + \frac{(\lambda/\mu)^c}{c!} \sum_{n=c+1}^{M} \left(\frac{\lambda}{c\mu}\right)^{n-c} \right]$$

$$P_n = \frac{(\lambda/\mu)^n}{n!} P_0 \qquad \text{for } 0 < n < c$$

$$P_n = \frac{(\lambda/\mu)^n}{c!c^{n-c}} P_0 \qquad \text{for } c \le n \le M$$

$$P_n = 0 \qquad \text{for } n > M \tag{7.23}$$

and

$$L_q = \frac{P_0(\lambda/\mu)^c(\lambda/c\mu)}{c!(1-\lambda/c\mu)^2} [1 - (\lambda/c\mu)^{M-c} - (M-c)(\lambda/c\mu)^{M-c}(1-\lambda/c\mu)] \tag{7.24}$$

assuming that $M > c$. It can also be shown that

$$L_s = L_q + \sum_{n=0}^{c-1} nP_n + c\left(1 - \sum_{n=0}^{c-1} P_n\right) \tag{7.25}$$

7.2.5 A Limited-Source Model

A commonly occurring queueing model is the one that has a finite calling population. An example of this model is the machine servicing situation where c servicemen are attending a group of M machines. The machines are in the waiting line when they are down waiting for service. The machines are considered potential arrivals to the queue when they are running. In the model λ is defined as the rate of breakdown *per machine* per time period and μ is the rate of service per serviceman per time period. Using this argument if all the machines are working, the arrival rate to the system is $M\lambda$. If n machines are down the arrival rate is $(M-n)\lambda$. Note that if all the machines are down no arrivals can occur to the system.

Therefore

$$\lambda_n = \begin{cases} (M-n)\lambda & \text{for } n = 0, 1, 2, \ldots, M-1 \\ 0 & \text{for } n \ge M \end{cases}$$

and

$$\mu_n = \begin{cases} n\mu & \text{for } 0 \le n < c \\ c\mu & \text{for } c \ge n \ge M \end{cases}$$

Following approaches similar to that used in Section 7.2.2 we find the following results for single-repairman case (i.e., $c = 1$).

$$P_0 = 1 \Big/ \left[\sum_{n=0}^{M} \frac{M!}{(M-n)!} \left(\frac{\lambda}{\mu}\right)^n \right]$$

$$P_n = \frac{M!}{(M-n)!} \left(\frac{\lambda}{\mu}\right)^n P_0 \qquad (7.26)$$

$$L_q = M - \frac{\lambda + \mu}{\lambda}(1 - P_0)$$

$$(7.27)$$

$$L_s = M - \frac{\mu}{\lambda}(1 - P_0)$$

For the multiple-server case:

$$P_0 = 1 \Big/ \left[\sum_{n=0}^{c-1} \frac{M!}{(M-n)!n!} \left(\frac{\lambda}{\mu}\right)^n + \sum_{n=c}^{M} \frac{M!}{(M-n)!c!c^{(n-c)}} \left(\frac{\lambda}{\mu}\right)^n \right]$$

$$P_n = \begin{cases} P_0 \dfrac{M!}{(M-n)!n!} \left(\dfrac{\lambda}{\mu}\right)^n & \text{if } 0 < n < c \\[3mm] P_0 \dfrac{M!}{(M-n)!c!c^{(n-c)}} \left(\dfrac{\lambda}{\mu}\right)^n & \text{if } c \leq n \leq M \\[3mm] 0 & \text{if } n > M \end{cases} \qquad (7.28)$$

$$L_q = \sum_{n=c}^{M} (n-c)P_n$$

$$L_s = \sum_{n=0}^{c-1} nP_n + L_q + c\left(1 - \sum_{n=0}^{c-1} P_n\right) \qquad (7.29)$$

Extensive tables [4, 11] have been developed to analyze this model. Examples of some tables for this model are given in Section 7.5.3.

EXAMPLE   Assume that one repairman has been assigned to maintain three machines. Assume that the machine running time between each breakdown is exponentially distributed with a mean of 16 hours. Repair time is exponentially distributed with a mean of 4 hours. What is the expected number of machines down?

Using (7.27) we can find L_s

$$L_s = M - \left(\frac{\mu}{\lambda}\right)(1 - P_0)$$

P_0 is defined by (7.26)

$$P_0 = 1 \left/ \left[\sum_{n=0}^{3} \frac{3!}{(3-n)!} \left(\frac{1}{4}\right)^n \right] \right.$$

$$= 1/(1 + 3/4 + 3/8 + 3/32) = .45$$

$$L_s = 3 - (4)(1 - .45)$$

$$= .80 \text{ machines down}$$

On occasion analysts have suggested that we could approximate the **EXAMPLE**
limited-source model with the infinite queue model or finite queue
model. Let's consider the results that these models would suggest.
Using (7.9) with $\lambda = 3/16$ and $\mu = 1/4$ we find

$$L_s = \frac{\lambda}{\mu - \lambda} = \frac{3/16}{1/4 - 3/16} = 3 \text{ machines}$$

Thus in this case, the infinite queue model is a poor choice even though it
is much easier to calculate. This approximation suggests that all the
machines will be down when, in fact, there were only .80 machines down.
Now consider the finite queue model using (7.22) with $\lambda = 3/16$ and
$\mu = 1/4$:

$$L_s = \frac{(\lambda/\mu)}{1 - (\lambda/\mu)} - \frac{(M+1)(\lambda/\mu)^{M+1}}{1 - (\lambda/\mu)^{M+1}}$$

$$= 3 - \frac{4(3/4)^4}{1 - (3/4)^4}$$

$$= 1.15$$

Thus the finite model is a better approximation of the limited-source
model but still we do not suggest this as an approximation.

In models studied in Section 7.2 we assumed that service distribution was **7.3**
exponential; in practice this assumption is often a poor one. Most of the **NON-**
elementary queueing models make the exponential assumption because **EXPONENTIAL**
of ease of derivation with this assumption. In this section we relax this **SERVICE**
assumption. We will consider Erlang service models, constant-service **MODELS**
models, and the Pollaczek–Khintchine formula.

This model is a single-server model with Poisson arrivals and service **7.3.1**
distributed in an Erlang manner. The probability density function for the **Erlang Service**
Erlang distribution is **Model**

$$f(t) = \frac{(\mu k)^k}{(k-1)!} t^{k-1} e^{-k\mu t} \qquad \text{for } t \geq 0 \qquad (7.30)$$

k is assumed to be a positive integer. The Erlang distribution takes many different forms when different values of k are considered. Figure 7.5 shows some of the different forms of the Erlang distributions. We note

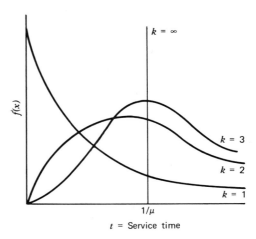

Figure 7.5 Erlang service distributions with mean service time $= 1/\mu$.

that the exponential $(k=1)$ and constant $(k=\infty)$ service models are special cases of the Erlang. The intermediate models have the following characteristics:

$$\begin{aligned}
\text{mean} &= 1/\mu \\
\text{mode} &= (k-1)/\mu k \\
\text{variance} &= 1/k\mu^2
\end{aligned} \tag{7.31}$$

Empirical service-time distributions can usually be reasonably approximated by the Erlang distribution. In practice two of the three characterizations (mean, mode, or variance) of the empirical data are determined. Next k and μ are determined using (7.31). The k value is rounded to closest integer.

The steady-state results for the Erlang model are

$$L_q = \frac{1+k}{2k}\left[\frac{\lambda^2}{\mu(\mu-\lambda)}\right]$$

$$W_q = \frac{1+k}{2k}\left[\frac{\lambda}{\mu(\mu-\lambda)}\right] \tag{7.32}$$

$$W_s = W_q + 1/\mu$$

$$L_s = \lambda W_s$$

349
7.3
NONEXPONENTIAL
SERVICE
MODELS
EXAMPLE

A tool crib has one server and work sampling suggests the following service-time distribution:

Minutes	Number of Services
.5–1.5	5
1.5–2.5	10
2.5–3.5	25
3.5–4.5	15
4.5–5.5	5
5.5–6.5	2

Mechanics arrive in a Poisson manner at the rate of 12 per hour. How long will a mechanic wait in the system on the average?

The mean service time is

$$\frac{5(1)+10(2)+25(3)+15(4)+5(5)+6(2)}{62} = 3.18 \text{ mins} = .053 \text{ hours}$$

The mode is located at 3 minutes or .05 hours. Thus from (7.31)

$$.053 = 1/\mu$$

$$.05 = (k-1)/\mu k$$

so

$$\mu = 18.87$$

and

$$k = 17.7$$

We round k to 18 and using (7.32) we find

$$W_s = W_q + \frac{1}{\mu} = \frac{1+k}{2k} \frac{\lambda}{\mu(\mu-\lambda)} + \frac{1}{\mu}$$

$$= \frac{1+18}{2(18)} \frac{12}{18.87(18.87-12)} + \frac{1}{18.87}$$

$$= 0.102 \text{ hours}$$

**7.3.2
Constant Service
Time***

A special case of the Erlang model is the case where the service time is constant (i.e., $k = \infty$). The resulting equations are

$$L_q = \frac{\lambda^2}{2\mu(\mu - \lambda)}$$

$$W_q = \frac{\lambda}{2\mu(\mu - \lambda)}$$

$$W_s = W_q + \frac{1}{\mu} \tag{7.33}$$

$$L_s = \lambda W_s$$

Note that L_q and W_q are half as large as in the exponential service case discussed in Section 7.2.2.

In addition to the charts presented in Section 7.2.3 Shelton [14] also developed a chart for the multichannel, constant-service-time model similar to that shown in Figure 7.6. The channel-utilization factor (α) is defined by (7.19) and the chart is used in exactly the same manner as the one in Figure 7.2.

**7.3.3
Pollaczek–
Khintchine
Formula**

The Pollaczek–Khintchine formula is derived for the single-server situation with Poisson arrivals with an arrival rate λ and general service time with mean $E(t)$ and var (t).

The resulting formula is

$$L_s = \lambda E(t) + \frac{\lambda^2[(E(t))^2 + \text{var}(t)]}{2[1 - \lambda(E(t))]} \tag{7.34}$$

Thus

$$L_q = L_s - \lambda E(t)$$

$$W_s = L_s/\lambda$$

$$W_q = L_q/\lambda$$

$$P_0 = 1 - \frac{\lambda}{\mu}$$

The operating characteristics for any service time distribution (such as the normal or Beta) can be obtained from (7.34).

---

* The chart in this section is reprinted with permission from *Journal of Industrial Engineering*, July–August 1960. Copyright © American Institute of Industrial Engineers, Inc., 25 Technology Park/Atlanta, Norcross, Ga. 30071.

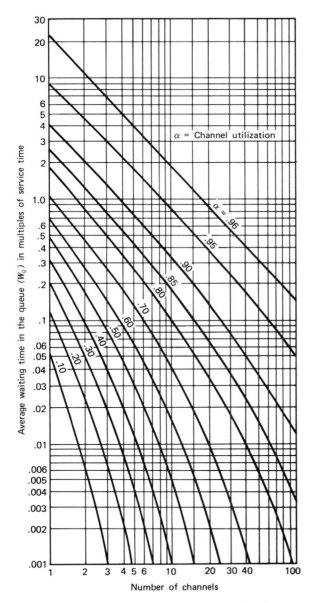

Figure 7.6 Average delay for constant service time.

**7.4
ECONOMIC
MODELS
USING
WAITING-
LINE
ANALYSIS**

Waiting-line problems in operations research generally are concerned with finding answers to the following problems:

1. How many servicing facilities should be established?
2. What will be the effect of increasing the rate of servicing?
3. What accommodations of space, or time will have to be made for arrivals that have to wait?

Hillier [8] has suggested that the conceptual model of waiting-line analysis in operations research is of the form in Figure 7.7. A significant

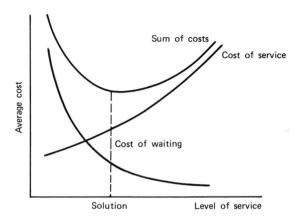

Figure 7.7   Conceptual solution procedure for most industrial waiting-line problems.

part of this model is that which pertains to the cost of waiting and the cost of service. Determination of these costs is an analyst's responsibility and waiting-line theory enables the analyst to find an optimal solution.

Figure 7.8 emphasizes the idea that in a true waiting-line situation, the waiting cannot be eliminated but only transferred from the arrivals to the service facilities, or vice versa. As the level of service is increased, there is more and more idle service facility time and the average delay in the line is decreased as shown in Figure 7.8.

The general approach to solving the economic models of waiting-line analysis is to write an equation describing the cost per unit time as a function of your controllable variable. This equation is ordinarily not continuous, thus enumeration is used rather than differentiation to find the minimum value of the cost equation. A word of caution is in order about setting up the cost equation. There is a great tendency among operations research analysts to develop economic waiting-line equations that are dimensionally incorrect. It is suggested that dimensional analysis be used to check the dimensionality of your equation.

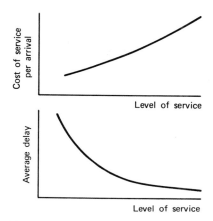

Figure 7.8 Basic information for industrial waiting-line problems.

Consider the case where we are attempting to find the optimum number of parallel servers to place in a system. We are looking for the optimum tradeoff between the cost of service and the cost of delay. We would thus calculate the total cost per hour of the system as a function of number of servers, c.

$$TC(c) = c \cdot C_s + L_s \cdot C_w$$

where

$TC(c) =$ total cost per hour as a function of c
$C_s =$ cost per hour of one server
$L_s =$ expected number of items in the system as a function of c
$C_w =$ cost per hour of an item waiting

Using a similar approach we could analyze the following hypothetical problem of the Bethlehem Steel Company. The company is considering the installation of piers in the Lehigh River to unload "ore." They have room for three piers and have three different types of unloading equipment available.

Type	Fixed Cost $/Day/Pier	Variable Cost $/Day/Pier	Unloading Rate Tons/Day
A	600	600	6000
B	700	900	8000
C	800	1100	9000

EXAMPLE

EXAMPLE

The variable cost is only realized when a pier is busy while the fixed cost is realized whether the pier is busy or not. Ships arrive at the rate of five per week. Ships that cannot move into a pier wait in the river. Ship time is worth $3000 per day. Each ship carries 8000 tons of ore. We wish to determine how many piers and what type of equipment should be used. (Assume that Bethlehem Steel's purchasing department will not allow us to mix equipment.)

The approach to solving this problem is to minimize the cost per day, which is a function of the number of piers and the type of equipment.

$$TC(N, y) = N \cdot FC_y + \bar{N} \cdot VC_y + L_s \cdot \$3000$$
$$= \text{fixed cost} + \text{variable cost} + \text{cost of waiting} \tag{7.35}$$

where

N = number of piers
y = type of equipment
$TC(N, y)$ = total cost per day as a function of N and y
$\bar{N}$ = expected number of piers utilized
FC_y = fixed cost per day per pier using y-type equipment
VC_y = variable cost per day per pier using y-type equipment
L_s = expected number of ships waiting as a function of N and y

We can find $\bar{N}$ by observing

$$\bar{N} = \sum_{i=1}^{3} iP_i + \sum_{i=4}^{\infty} 3P_i = 3 - \sum_{i=0}^{2} (3-i)P_i$$

where P_i = steady-state probability of i ships in the system.

To solve the problem we must find the appropriate model to describe our system. Given this model we can find expressions for L_s and P_i. Next we can solve (7.35) to determine the optimum number of piers and the best type of equipment.

**7.5
APPLICATION
STUDIES**

For plant layout work and material handling planning, waiting-line analysis is extremely useful. In this example, it is used to determine the amount of space necessary for storage of skids.

**7.5.1
In-Process
Storage in a Plant
Layout***

At the finished work end of a production line, each unit is placed on a 3 foot × 3 foot skid and a forklift truck is used to transport the finished unit to the "pack and ship" department, which is located in another part of the plant.

Application Study

---

* The material in this section is adapted from A. F. Gould, "Notes of Waiting Line Theory," Industrial Engineering Department, Lehigh University, 1968. Used with the permission of A. F. Gould.

All units are made to order and all orders are scheduled on a first-in, first-out basis. The manufacturing cycle time varies with the size of a unit and is also increased by a customer's request for extras. As a result of these conditions the units arrive at the skidding area at random intervals when measured in minutes although the number of units produced per week is fairly constant.

The skids are picked up by a forklift truck operator and moved to the packing area in between other material handling jobs assigned to the forklift truck. The other jobs are irregular so that the forklift truck operator cannot schedule his arrival at the skidding area so that he can pick up the work at regular intervals.

The number of finished units that come off the line and are placed on skids averages three per hour and the average interval between trips of the forklift operator is 15 minutes. Management wants space allocated to take care of the skids at least 90 percent of the time.

In other words, what we want is the space required 90 percent of the time for the waiting line.

We can use (7.8) (with $\lambda = 3/\text{hour}$ and $\mu = 4/\text{hour}$), to construct Table 7.4.

At $n = 7$, the cumulative probability is .901, therefore, 63 square feet (7×9) would be required to have space enough to meet management's requirements.

Table 7.4 Cumulative Probability of Needing n Spaces in a Plant Layout

No. in Line (n)	Probability of n	Cumulative Probability
0	.250	.250
1	.187	.437
2	.141	.578
3	.106	.684
4	.079	.763
5	.059	.822
6	.045	.867
7	.034	.901

Vending machines and their use is an example of a service facility with constant servicing time and random arrivals.

7.5.2
Employee Service
Facilities*

* Material in this section is adapted from A. F. Gould, "Notes of Waiting Line Theory," Industrial Engineering Department, Lehigh University, 1968. Used with the permission of A. F. Gould.

Application Study

Consider a vending machine that will give service in 12 seconds and that calls for service occur on the average of one a minute. If we want an employee to begin to receive service within 10 seconds on the average, how many machines should be installed?

For one machine ($c = 1$) and applying (7.19)

$$\alpha = \frac{\lambda}{c\mu} = \frac{1/\text{min}}{(1)(6/\text{min})} = .167$$

We find, from Figure 7.6, that the average delay is given as approximately .08 multiples of the mean service time of 12 seconds, or average delay $= .08 \times 12 = .96$ seconds.

Therefore, one machine is adequate.

7.5.3 Assignment of Operators to Automatic Machines*

Application Study

In Section 7.2.5 we discussed the use of the limited-source model to analyze the machine servicing situation. We observed that the limited-source waiting-line equations are difficult to calculate. A number of tables have been developed to analyze situations involving limited sources. The tables can be used by analysts who are not familiar with waiting-line analysis. An example of such a table was developed by Fetter [5] to determine the optimum number of operators to assign to service automatic machines. An *arrival* is a machine requiring service and the number of operators is the number of service facilities. In this model Fetter assumes the servicing time to be either constant or have an exponential distribution and the calls for service are assumed to be randomly distributed.

The symbols and definitions used are:

s = service time per time unit
m = machine running time per time unit
w = waiting time per time unit
n = number of machines assigned an operator
$K = s/m$ = servicing constant
P_0 = probability of no machines requiring service.

Table 7.5 gives the waiting time and machine availability for values of K from .01 to .4. The degree of worker utilization may be obtained from

$$1 - P_0 = nKm$$

---

* Adapted with permission from the *Journal of Industrial Engineering*, September–October 1965. Copyright © American Institute of Industrial Engineers, Inc., 25 Technology Park/Atlanta, Norcross, Ga. 30071. It was adapted from A. F. Gould, "Notes of Waiting Line Theory," Industrial Engineering Department, Lehigh University, 1968. Used with permission of A. F. Gould.

Table 7.5 Tables of Waiting Time and Machine Availability for Selected Servicing Constants

(Values expressed as percentages of total time where $m + s + w = 100$ percent)

n	(a) w	(a) m	(b) w	(b) m	n	(a) w	(a) m	(b) w	(b) m
		$K = .01$					$K = .01$ (cont.)		
1	.0	99.0	.0	99.0	142			28.9	70.4
10	.1	99.0	.1	98.9	143			29.4	69.9
20	.1	98.9	.2	98.8	144			29.9	69.4
30	.2	98.8	.4	98.6					
40			.6	98.4			$K = .02$		
50			.9	98.1	1	.0	98.0	.0	96.0
60			1.3	97.8	5	.1	98.0	.2	97.9
70			1.8	97.2	10	.2	97.8	.4	97.6
80			2.7	96.3	15	.4	97.7	.7	97.4
85			3.4	95.7	20	.6	97.5	1.1	97.0
90			4.2	94.9	25	.8	97.2	1.6	96.5
95			5.2	93.8	30	1.2	96.9	2.2	95.9
100			6.7	92.4	35			3.1	95.0
105			8.5	90.6	40			4.3	93.8
110			10.7	88.4	45			6.1	92.0
115			13.4	85.8	50			8.7	89.5
120			16.3	82.9	51			9.3	88.9
121			16.9	82.2	52			10.0	88.3
122			17.5	81.7	53			10.7	87.6
123			18.1	81.1	54			11.5	86.8
124			18.8	80.4	55			12.3	86.0
125			19.4	79.8	56			13.1	85.2
126			20.0	79.2	57			14.0	84.3
127			20.6	78.6	58			14.9	83.4
128			21.2	78.1	59			15.9	82.5
129			21.8	77.5	60			16.8	81.5
130			22.4	76.9	61			17.9	80.5
131			22.9	76.3	62			18.9	79.5
132			23.5	75.7	63			19.9	78.5
133			24.1	75.2	64			21.0	77.5
134			24.6	74.6	65			22.0	76.4
135			25.2	74.1	66			23.1	75.4
136			25.7	73.5	67			24.2	74.4
137			26.3	73.0	68			23.2	73.3
138			26.8	72.5	69			26.2	72.3
139			27.3	71.9	70			27.2	71.3
140			27.9	71.4	71			28.2	70.4
141			28.4	70.9	72			29.2	69.4

Table 7.5 (*Continued*)

n	(a) w	(a) m	(b) w	(b) m	n	(a) w	(a) m	(b) w	(b) m
	K = .03					K = .04 (*cont.*)			
1	.0	97.1	.0	97.1	9	.8	95.4	1.5	94.7
5	.2	96.9	.4	96.7	10	1.0	95.2	1.8	94.4
10	.5	96.6	1.0	96.2	11	1.1	95.1	2.1	94.1
15	1.0	95.2	1.8	95.4	12	1.3	94.9	2.4	93.8
20	1.6	95.5	3.0	94.2	13	1.5	94.7	2.8	93.5
25	2.8	94.4	4.7	92.5	14	1.8	94.5	3.2	93.1
26	3.1	94.1	5.2	92.1	15	2.0	94.2	3.6	92.7
27	3.4	93.7	5.7	91.6	16	2.3	94.0	4.0	92.3
28	3.8	93.4	6.2	91.1	17	2.0	93.6	4.5	91.8
29	4.3	92.9	6.8	90.5	18	3.0	93.3	5.1	91.3
30	4.8	92.4	7.4	89.9	19	3.4	92.9	5.7	90.7
31			8.1	89.2	20	3.9	92.4	6.4	90.0
32			8.9	88.5	21	4.5	91.8	7.1	89.3
33			9.7	87.7	22	5.2	91.2	8.0	88.5
34			10.6	86.8	23	6.0	90.4	8.9	87.6
35			11.6	85.9	24	6.8	89.6	9.9	86.7
36			12.6	84.9	25	7.9	88.6	11.0	85.6
37			13.7	83.8	26	9.0	87.5	12.2	84.5
38			14.9	82.8	27	10.4	86.2	13.4	83.2
39			16.1	81.4	28	11.9	84.7	14.8	81.9
40			17.4	80.2	29	13.8	83.0	16.3	80.5
41			18.8	78.9	30	15.5	81.3	17.9	79.0
42			20.1	77.5	31			19.6	77.4
43			21.6	76.2	32			21.3	75.7
44			23.0	74.8	33			23.0	74.0
45			24.4	73.4	34			24.8	72.3
46			25.9	72.0	35			26.6	70.6
47			27.3	70.6	36			28.4	68.9
48			28.7	60.2	37			30.1	67.2
	K = .04					K = .05			
1	.0	96.2	.0	96.2	1	.0	95.2	.0	95.2
2	.1	96.1	.2	96.0	2	.1	95.1	.2	95.0
3	.2	96.0	.3	95.9	3	.2	95.0	.5	94.8
4	.2	95.9	.5	95.7	4	.4	94.9	.7	94.5
5	.3	95.8	.7	95.5	5	.5	94.7	1.0	94.3
6	.5	95.7	.9	95.3	6	.7	94.6	1.4	94.0
7	.6	95.6	1.1	95.1	7	.9	94.4	1.7	93.6
8	.7	95.5	1.3	94.9	8	1.1	94.2	2.1	93.3

Table 7.5 (*Continued*)

n	(a) w	(a) m	(b) w	(b) m	n	(a) w	(a) m	(b) w	(b) m
		K = .05 (*cont.*)					*K* = .06 (*cont.*)		
9	1.4	93.9	2.5	92.9	17	9.3	85.6	12.8	82.3
10	1.6	93.7	3.0	92.4	18	11.1	83.9	14.6	80.6
11	2.0	93.4	3.5	91.9	19	13.2	81.9	16.5	78.8
12	2.3	93.0	4.1	91.4	20	15.6	79.7	18.6	76.8
13	2.7	92.6	4.7	90.8	21			20.8	74.7
14	3.2	92.2	5.4	90.1	22			23.1	72.5
15	3.8	91.7	6.2	89.3	23			25.5	70.3
16	4.4	91.0	7.1	88.5	24			27.9	68.0
17	5.2	90.3	8.1	87.6	25			30.3	65.8
18	6.1	89.5	9.1	86.5					
19	7.1	88.5	10.4	85.4			*K* = .07		
20	8.4	87.3	11.7	84.1					
21	9.8	85.9	13.1	82.7	1	.0	93.5	.0	93.5
22	11.5	84.3	14.7	81.2	2	.2	93.2	.4	93.1
23	13.4	82.5	16.5	79.6	3	.5	93.0	.9	92.6
24	15.5	80.5	18.3	77.8	4	.8	92.7	1.4	92.1
25	17.8	78.2	20.2	76.0	5	1.1	92.4	2.0	91.6
26	20.3	75.9	22.2	74.1	6	1.5	92.1	2.7	91.0
27	22.8	73.6	24.3	72.1	7	1.9	91.7	3.4	90.3
28	25.3	71.2	26.4	70.1	8	2.4	91.2	4.3	89.5
29	27.9	68.8	28.5	68.1	9	3.1	90.6	5.2	88.6
					10	3.8	89.9	6.3	87.6
		K = .06			11	4.7	89.1	7.5	86.4
					12	5.7	88.1	8.9	85.1
1	.0	94.3	.0	94.3	13	7.0	86.9	10.4	83.7
2	.2	94.2	.3	94.0	14	8.6	85.4	12.2	82.1
3	.4	94.0	.7	93.7	15	10.4	83.7	14.1	80.3
4	.6	93.8	1.1	93.3	16	12.6	81.3	16.2	78.3
5	.8	93.6	1.5	92.9	17	15.2	79.3	18.5	76.2
6	1.1	93.3	2.0	92.5	18	18.1	76.6	21.0	73.9
7	1.4	93.1	2.5	92.0	19	21.1	73.7	23.5	71.5
8	1.7	92.7	3.1	91.4	20	24.4	70.7	26.2	69.0
9	2.1	92.4	3.7	90.8	21			28.9	66.5
10	2.6	91.9	4.5	90.1					
11	3.1	91.4	5.3	89.4			*K* = .08		
12	3.8	90.8	6.2	88.5					
13	4.5	90.1	7.3	87.5	1	.0	92.6	.0	92.6
14	5.4	89.2	8.4	86.4	2	.3	92.3	.5	92.1
15	6.5	88.2	9.7	85.2	3	.6	92.0	1.2	91.5
16	7.8	87.0	11.2	83.8	4	1.0	91.7	1.9	90.9

Table 7.5 (Continued)

n	(a)		(b)		n	(a)		(b)	
	w	m	w	m		w	m	w	m
	K = .08 (cont.)					K = .10 (cont.)			
5	1.4	91.2	2.7	90.1	3	1.0	90.0	1.8	89.3
6	2.0	90.8	3.5	89.3	4	1.6	89.5	2.8	88.3
7	2.6	90.2	4.5	88.4	5	2.3	88.8	4.1	87.2
8	3.4	89.5	5.7	87.3	6	3.2	88.0	5.5	85.9
9	4.3	88.6	7.0	86.1	7	4.4	86.9	7.1	84.4
10	5.4	87.6	8.5	84.8	8	5.8	85.7	9.0	82.7
11	6.7	86.4	10.1	83.2	9	7.5	84.1	11.2	80.8
13	8.4	84.8	12.0	81.4	10	9.7	82.1	13.6	78.5
13	10.4	83.0	14.2	79.5	11	12.4	79.8	16.3	76.1
14	12.8	80.8	16.5	77.3	12	15.6	76.8	19.3	73.4
15	15.6	78.2	19.0	75.0	13	19.2	73.4	22.5	70.4
16	18.8	75.2	21.8	72.4	14	23.3	69.8	25.9	67.4
17	22.2	72.0	24.6	69.8	15	27.4	66.0	29.4	64.2
18	25.7	68.8	27.6	67.1	16	31.5	62.0		
19	28.2	66.5	30.5	64.4					
	K = .09					K = .15			
					1	.0	87.0	.0	87.0
1	.0	91.5	.0	91.7	2	.9	86.2	1.7	85.5
2	.4	91.4	.7	91.1	3	2.1	85.1	3.6	83.8
3	.8	91.0	1.4	90.4	4	3.9	83.8	6.0	81.8
4	1.3	90.6	2.3	89.6	5	5.5	82.2	8.7	79.4
5	1.9	90.0	3.3	88.7	6	8.0	80.0	11.8	76.7
6	2.6	89.4	4.5	87.7	7	11.2	72.2	15.4	73.5
7	3.4	88.6	5.8	86.5	8	15.2	73.7	19.5	70.0
8	4.5	87.6	7.3	85.1	9	20.1	70.5	23.8	66.2
9	5.7	86.5	9.0	83.5	10	25.5	64.8	28.4	62.3
10	7.3	83.0	10.9	81.7	11	31.0	60.0		
11	9.3	83.2	13.1	79.7					
12	11.7	81.0	15.6	77.5		K = .20			
13	14.5	78.4	18.3	75.0					
14	17.8	75.4	21.2	72.3	1	.0	83.3	.0	83.3
15	21.5	72.0	24.2	69.5	2	1.3	82.0	2.7	81.1
16	25.3	68.5	27.4	66.6	3	3.6	80.4	6.9	78.1
17	30.2	65.0	30.6	63.7	4	6.3	78.1	9.8	75.2
					5	10.0	75.0	14.2	71.5
	K = .10				6	14.7	71.1	19.2	67.4
					7	20.6	66.2	21.6	62.8
1	.0	90.9	.0	90.9	8	27.3	60.6	30.3	58.1
2	.4	90.5	.8	90.2	9	32.6	56.1		

Table 7.5 (*Continued*)

n	(a)		(b)		n	(a)		(b)	
	w	m	w	m		w	m	w	m
		K = .30					K = .40		
1	.0	76.9	.0	76.9	1	.0	71.4	.0	71.4
2	3.0	74.6	5.1	73.0	2	4.8	68.0	7.5	66.0
3	7.4	71.3	11.1	68.4	3	11.8	63.0	16.3	59.8
4	13.3	66.7	18.0	63.1	4	21.2	56.3	25.6	53.1
5	21.1	60.7	25.4	57.4	5	31.9	48.6	34.9	46.5
6	29.9	53.9	33.0	51.6					

Note: column (a) is for constant servicing times and column (b) is for an exponential distribution of servicing times. *m* is the percentage of running time per time unit and *w* is the percentage of waiting time per time unit.

The machine assignment problem is a problem in optimization in which the cost of idle machines waiting for service is balanced against the cost of assigning a fewer number of machines to an operator.

As an example of the use of Table 7.5, consider a situation where the operator cost is $6 per hour and the cost of idle machine time is $12 per hour per machine. If we have a large number of machines, how many machines should be assigned to an operator?

First, the value of K must be obtained. The value of K is the ratio of s to m for a machine if there was no waiting for service, a situation that exists if an operator is assigned a single machine. Work sampling studies can be used to determine K and for this example, assume that $K = 0.10$. Also, the servicing time is assumed to be distributed exponentially.

As a measure of effectiveness, the total cost per unit of output is used. Actually, the calculation is made on the basis of total cost (idle time and operator cost) per unit machine running time per machine. Table 7.6 shows the total cost per unit of m as a function of n.

We see that the assignment of six machines yields the minimum total cost of machine running time per machine.

Calculations for $n = 3$ are given as follows for the tabular solution in Table 7.6.

STEP 1. Use Table 7.5 to obtain the fraction of waiting time "w" for $n = 3$. The tabular value of w is 1.8 percent under column (b) which is a time fraction of .018 of an hour.

STEP 2. The time fraction of an hour (.018) of waiting time, w, is multiplied by the $12, the cost of idle machine time, to yield a cost of $.216 per hour for idle machine time per machine.

STEP 3. The operator cost per hour per machine is $6/n$. For the case $n = 3$, the cost per machine per hour is $2 (fourth column of Table 7.6).

STEP 4. From Table 7.5 obtain the value of m for $K = .10$ and $n = 3$. The value of m is 89.3 percent or the fraction of an hour that a machine is running is .893 hours.

STEP 5. The last column in Table 7.6 gives the total cost per hour of machine running time and is the total cost per hour divided by the value of m ($2.216 \div .893$).

For $n = 3$, the extent of worker utilization $(1 - P_0)$ is:

$$1 - P_0 = nKm = 3 \times .1 \times .893 = .268 \text{ or } 26.8 \text{ per cent}$$

For the minimum cost assignment of $n = 6$, the operator utilization is:

$$(1 - P_0) = nKm = 6 \times .1 \times .859 = .515 \text{ or } 51.5 \text{ percent}$$

Table 7.6 Determination of the Optimum Number Machines to Assign to an Operator

n	w	$w \times 12$	$6.00/n$	Total Cost	m	Total Cost Per Unit of m
1	0	$ 0	$6.00	$6.000	.909	$6.60
2	.008	.096	3.00	3.096	.902	3.43
3	.018	.216	2.00	2.216	.893	2.48
4	.028	.336	1.50	1.836	.883	2.08
5	.041	.493	1.20	1.693	.872	1.94
6	.055	.660	1.00	1.660	.859	1.93
7	.071	.852	.86	1.712	.844	2.03

7.5.4 Military Car Pool*

Consider a car pool for local use that supplies requests for military cars at an average rate of 16 requests per eight-hour day and the average

Application Study

* Material in this section is adapted from A. F. Gould, "Notes of Waiting Line Theory," Industrial Engineering Department, Lehigh University, 1968. Used with permission of A. F. Gould.

time a car is out is 40 minutes, exponentially distributed. We will assume that the requests are randomly distributed throughout the day although this assumption is one that should be checked.

The general has decided that the pool should have enough cars so that 95 percent of the time a request for a car will be filled within one hour. How few cars can be assigned to the pool?

For this problem use Figure 7.3, which gives an F factor and Figure 7.4, which gives P, the probability of a delay, use in the relationship,

$$P_c = F \times P$$

where P_c is probability of delay exceeding a critical value.

Try $c = 2$, and for Figure 7.3

$$\mu = 3/2$$

$$T = 1 \text{ hour}$$

$$\alpha = \frac{16}{(2)(12)} = 2/3$$

and

$$h = cT\mu = (2)(1)(3/2) = 3$$

and, from Figure 7.3, $F = .3$. From Figure 7.4, $P = .5$ because $d = 1.33$ and

$$P_c = FP = (.3)(.5) = .15$$

This means that 15 percent of the time a request will wait more than an hour and management's criterion is not met.

Try three cars ($c = 3$).

Then

$$\mu = 3/2$$

$$T = 1 \text{ hour}$$

$$\alpha = \frac{16}{(3)(12)} = .44$$

and

$$h = cT\mu = (3)(1)(3/2) = 4.5$$

and, from Figure 7.3, $F = .10$ and, from Figure 7.4, $P = .19$ because $d = 1.33$ and, $P_c = FP = (.10)(.19) = .02$.

Thus, a wait of over one hour will occur only 2 percent of the time and 98 percent of the time the wait for a car will be one hour or less.

Furthermore, $P = .19$ indicates that a request will have to wait only 19 percent of the time and 81 percent of the time a car will be available when the request is made.

Application Study

In 1971 W. Blaker Bolling [1], carried out the following queueing analysis on the emergency room of the Richmond Memorial Hospital. The model was developed to aid the hospital administration in the long-range planning for emergency room operations.

When a patient arrives at the emergency room of a hospital, he wishes to receive the best medical care in as short a time as possible from considerate personnel. The physicians, nurses, and other medical staff in the emergency room are concerned primarily with the quality of care that they can administer to the patient. Many factors, such as available staff, equipment, physical facilities, and ancillary services (radiology, laboratory, and the like) can affect the level of care available at an emergency room and how long it will take to dispense that care.

Since the emergency room is one of the primary contacts of the hospital with the general public, hospital administration is concerned with such things as the level of care offered, legal requirements, costs, and the overall public impression of the receiving areas, processing procedures, patient waiting time, and so on.

In order to assist the administration and emergency room medical staff at Richmond Memorial Hospital in planning for emergency room facilities and staffing, a series of studies and observations were carried out by the hospital's management engineer.

Projecting Demand.   One of the first things noted in the overall review of the problem was the rapid increase in the number of patients using the hospital's emergency room facility. This increase appeared disproportionate to the rise in the Richmond-area population and appeared to follow national trends in emergency room usage. (There has been a growing tendency for persons to go to hospital emergency room facilities rather than a private physician.)

The first step taken to formally evaluate the rise in emergency room visits was to gather data on its operation since its opening in October, 1959. These data were compiled and analyzed in several ways. It was initially decided to plot the average number of visits per day per month as a function of time (Figure 7.9). The independent variable is the month number with number 1 indicating October 1959. Since the number of days per month varies, the average visits per day per month was chosen as the dependent variable. Several things immediately became apparent on review of the plot:

1. There had been a definite increase in emergency room patient visits as a function of time.

---

* Adapted with permission from *Industrial Engineering*, September 1972. Copyright © American Institute of Industrial Engineers, Inc., 25 Technology Park/Atlanta, Norcross, Ga. 30071.

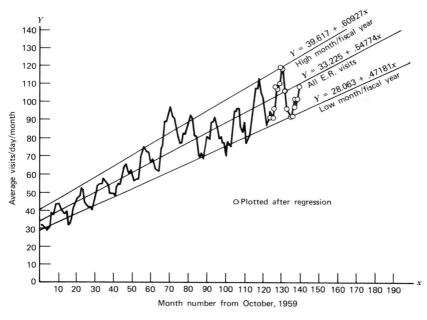

Figure 7.9 Average number of visits per day at hospital's emergency room reveals the upward trend over 12-year period.

2. There had been a seasonal variation with demand—low in winter months, high in summer months.
3. The difference between peaks and valleys (summer and winter) had been increasing with time.

Due to the seasonal trend each month was then plotted separately (Figure 7.10).

Linear regressions were then run on the various plots as follows:
1. All emergency-room patient visits.
2. The month with the highest visits per fiscal year (October 1 to September 30).
3. The month with the lowest visits per fiscal year.
4. Each month—all Octobers, all Novembers, and so on.
5. Admissions through the emergency room.

The data used in the linear regression analysis went through January 1970 (month number 124).

The results as tabulated in Table 7.7 were

$$A = Y \text{ intercept at } x = 0$$
$$B = \text{slope of the line}$$
$$R = \text{correlation coefficients for the data}$$

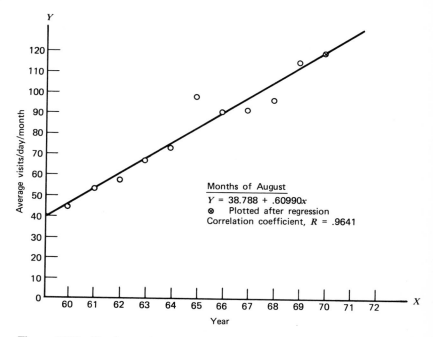

Figure 7.10 To determine seasonal variations in emergency room usage, average visits per day for each of the 12 months were plotted.

The resulting linear regression lines were then plotted (Figures 7.9 and 7.10). Review of the various values of *A* and *B* reinforced the initial observations concerning the plotted data. It should be noted that there was a very high correlation between the dependent and independent variables.

After January 1970, actual data was plotted to check the regression lines. The comparisons appear favorable.

The hospital budgeting for the emergency room and associated services is now based on these projections, with an increase in accuracy over previous methods. For the 1971–1972 fiscal year, these projections were within 2.8 percent of actual.

In addition to the seasonal variation in patient visits to the emergency room, there are variations between the days in a week and the hours in a day. Data were collected from emergency room log books covering 6119 patients at two times of the year—summer and winter—which represented the high- and low-volume periods. These data were broken down into the number of visits by day of the week and by time of day for the two periods. Percentages were computed in order to compare the two periods that had different demand rates.

Table 7.7 Results of Linear Regression Analyses of Emergency Room Visits and Hospital Admissions Through the Emergency Room

	Group		
	A	*B*	*R*
All visits	33.226	.54774	.9203
High months/fiscal year	39.617	.60927	.9627
Low months/fiscal year	28.063	.47181	.9527
October	32.749	.55865	.9584
November	31.744	.51277	.9767
December	31.719	.49004	.9616
January	27.345	.52402	.9764
February	28.167	.47679	.9559
March	29.713	.52433	.9548
April	35.161	.50122	.9548
May	35.524	.55632	.9368
June	35.472	.61900	.9767
July	38.216	.59525	.9653
August	38.788	.60990	.9641
September	36.855	.60990	.9641
All admissions	8.133	.04947	.8000

There were slight differences between the two periods, such as the volume of visits dropping off earlier in the winter months than in the summer months, apparently due to daylight saving time. However, these differences were considered negligible and weighted averages were computed.

The resulting frequency distributions are shown in Figures 7.11 and 7.12. A review of these distributions immediately pointed out a fairly constant daily rate from Monday through Friday, with Saturday and Sunday showing increases. The rate by time of day is very significant, and major changes closely parallel shift changes. These distributions were of some assistance in setting staffing patterns.

Based on these historical data, it is possible to forecast the expected demand at some point in the future. For example, the demand from 8 to 9 P.M. on a Sunday in August 1972, would have been as:

Hours demand = (hours percent)(days percent)(7 days/week)
$$\times (A + Bx \text{ average/day/month})$$
$$= (.0663)(.1633)(7)(38.788 + .60990(155))$$
$$= 10.07 \approx 10 \text{ patients}$$

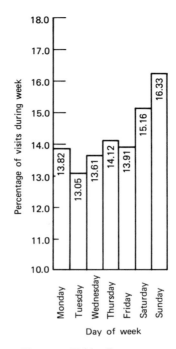

Figure 7.11 Percentage distribution of 6119 visits to the emergency room by the day of the week.

The medical and clerical staff in the emergency room cooperated in collection of other data, including:

1. The number of visitors coming in with each patient.
2. The time from start of treatment to discharge, admission, or death (the service time).

The distribution of the visitors per emergency room patient, Figure 7.13, was checked against the Poisson distribution with unfavorable results, so it was left as an empirical one. However, the distribution of the service time (Figure 7.14) in 10-minute intervals did compare graphically and statistically with the exponential distribution.

A great many things were known at this point about the historical arrival patterns of patients requiring treatment in the Richmond Memorial Hospital emergency room.

However, it was desirable in terms of long-range planning of emergency room facilities and staffing requirements to determine estimates of the system conditions at various points in the future. For example, with the present facilities and staffing and the rising number of

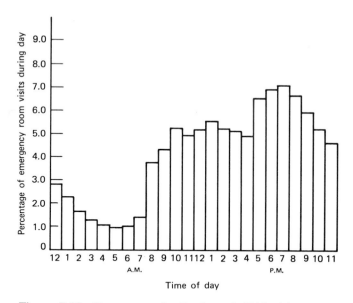

Figure 7.12 Percentage distribution of 6119 visits to the emergency room by time of day.

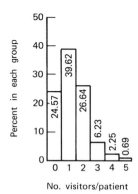

Figure 7.13 Percentage distribution of visitors per patient (average = 1.94).

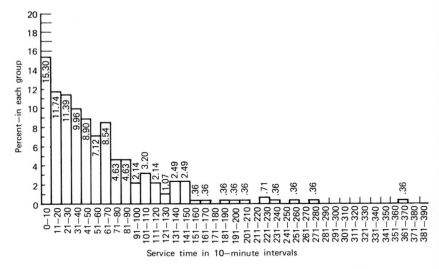

Figure 7.14 Distribution of actual service times: mean = 58.0 minutes.

patients, the waiting time will increase to some point at which it will be considered intolerable, along with the overcrowding of the waiting room. If the waiting-time distributions and distributions of the number of people in the system are known at various points in the future, they can be used as part of the criteria in deciding on expansion of the facilities. Queueing theory could be useful in the evaluation of this emergency room system. By varying the size of the emergency room facilities in a queueing model, it should be possible to evaluate the effect on the system at various points in the future.

In 1971 the emergency facility at the hospital had eight general treatment tables and four beds (primarily for patients awaiting admission). For description of the system only the eight tables should be considered as service channels ($c = 8$). The waiting room has 15 chairs available.

Forecasts of future demand were made, along with the identification of patient arrival distributions, visitors per patient distributions, and treatment (service) time distributions. Therefore, most of the basic requirements for a model of the queueing system in the emergency room are known.

Emergency patient arrivals may be assumed to come from an infinite source (the population and visitors to Richmond). Arrivals at a given time are assumed to follow the Poisson distribution. But the mean arrival rate will be time-dependent and therefore a nonsteady state in terms of long periods. The mean at any given hour may be developed from the various projections if it is assumed that the same patterns will continue.

The mean service rate, μ, was determined to be exponentially distributed with a mean of 58 minutes.

The empirical distribution of visitors per patient has been developed (mean = 1.24) since this adds an extra burden on the waiting room facilities. Space must be provided for both the patient and the visitors while the patient is in the queue, and then for the visitors while the patient is being treated until discharge or admission.

The queueing model would consider various planning horizons and values of C, a procedure could be developed to yield various factors necessary for proper planning of the facility such as:

The probability that a patient would have to wait, and the expected wait time.

The probability of certain numbers of patients waiting.

The expected number of patients (and visitors) in the waiting room.

The expected number of patients in the treatment rooms.

It would then be possible to determine the number of treatment rooms, waiting room facilities, and the staffing needed for the planning horizon.

1. Suggest waiting-line situations that will exhibit the following queue disciplines (refer to Table 7.2).
   (a) Random
   (b) SPT
   (c) Preempt resume priority
   (d) Balking
   (e) Reneging
   (f) State dependent service rate

2. Consider an airport and identify all associated queueing situations. For each situation consider and define (a) the customers, (b) the servers, (c) the arrival distribution, (d) service distribution, (e) number of service channels, (f) size of population of customers, and the (g) queue discipline. Don't forget the queues involving airplane, customers, baggage, and services.

3. Repeat the analysis in problem 2 for the typical short-order restaurant.

4. Consider a barber shop that has two barbers and two chairs for waiting customers. Assume that customers arrive according to a Poisson distribution at a rate of five per hour and that each barber services according to an exponential distribution with a mean service time of 30 minutes. A customer will balk if the shop is full. Define λ_n and μ_n for the system. Find P_n, L_s, and L_q.

5. A service station has one gas pump and the time to service a car is exponential with a mean of four minutes. Cars arrive in a Poisson fashion at the rate of 10 per hour. A customer will balk as follows:

Number in System	Probability of Balking
0	0
1	.25
2	.50
3	1.00

Define λ_n and μ_n. Find P_n, L_s, and L_q.

6. Considering the situation described in problem 5 what is the probability of a customer balking? Should an improved pump that will cut the average service time to three minutes be installed to replace the old pump? The new pump will cost $2 an hour more and each customer adds $1.50 of profit to the service station's operations.

7. Derive an expression for L_q (7.10) for the single server-infinite-population-infinite queue model. Start with the expression

$$L_q = \sum_{n=1}^{\infty} (n-1)P_n$$

8. Consider a one-window drive-in bank. The cars arrive according to a Poisson distribution with a mean of 15 per hour. Cars are serviced according to an exponential distribution with a mean of three minutes.
   (a) What is the probability of not having to wait for service?
   (b) What is the probability that there will be more than three cars in the system?
   (c) Finds L_s, L_q, W_s, and W_q.

9. Consider Table 7.3, add entries for the ratio of λ to μ equal to .92, .95, .97, .999, .9999, and 1.0.

10. Consider the Union Bank example presented in Section 7.2.3:
   (a) How will L_s, L_q, W_s, and W_q change if the arrival rate increases to 85 per hour?
   (b) What will the queueing characteristics be if a sixth teller is added when the arrival rate is 80 per hour?
   (c) What is the probability that the wait in the queue will exceed 15 minutes?

11. An analyst suggested that we could get the same answers as presented in the Union Bank example in Section 7.2.3 by assuming that the model is a one-channel queueing model with an arrival rate of 16 ($80 \div 5$). Compare the results and explain any differences that occur.

12. Determine L_s, L_q, W_s, and W_q for the following multichannel queueing situation. Also determine the probability that the waiting time in the queue will exceed 10 minutes.
   (a) $c = 2$, $\mu = 50$, and $\lambda = 90$

(b) $c = 10$, $\mu = 10$, and $\lambda = 90$
(c) $c = 20$, $\mu = 5$, and $\lambda = 90$
(d) $c = 100$, $\mu = 1$, and $\lambda = 90$

13. A university computing center has five identical terminals for processing student programs. The service time is exponential with a mean of 10 minutes. The arrival rate is Poisson with a mean of 25 per hour. Find L_s, L_q, W_s, W_q, and the probability that the waiting in queue will be less than 5 minutes; 15 minutes; 30 minutes.

14. In a store, customers arrive in a Poisson stream with mean 60 per hour. The service time is exponential with a mean of .005 hours. How many clerks should be available if

(a) The expected waiting time in the system should be less than 10 minutes.
(b) The probability will be greater than .90 that the waiting time in the queue is less than 10 minutes.

15. Consider a queueing system that has a Poisson input, with a mean arrival rate of 10 per hour. The cost per server is $10 an hour while the cost per hour of items being served is $50. Find the number of servers that will minimize the total expected cost of the system given that each server is identical and has an exponential service time with mean of 10 minutes.

16. Using (7.22), (7.23), (7.24), and (7.25) analyze the situations described in problems 4 and 5.

17. Five machines are being attended by an overhead crane. The crane is used to load and unload a machine at the beginning and end of its production cycle. The machine running time is exponential with a mean of 25 minutes. The service time (crane time) is also exponential with mean of 10 minutes.

(a) What percentage of the time is the crane idle?
(b) What is the expected number of machines waiting for service?
(c) What would be the impact of adding a second crane on the number of idle machines? (Assume that the cranes do not interfere with each other.)

18. For a limited source model with $c = 1$, $M = 6$, $\mu = 3$, and $\lambda = 2$, find

(a) P_0, P_3, and P_6
(b) L_s and L_q
(c) Repeat your analysis assuming $c = 2$

19. Assume that one repairman has been assigned the responsibility for servicing four machines. For each machine the running time between breakdowns is distributed exponentially with mean of 10 hours. The repair time is exponential with a mean of 3 hours, find

(a) P_0 and L_q
(b) use the finite queue model to approximate the system
(c) use the infinite queue model to approximate this system

20. Consider a single-server queue with Poisson arrivals, $\lambda = 4$ per hour. Find L_q, L_s, W_q, and W_s for each of the following service distributions:
   (a) exponential with a mean of $\frac{1}{6}$ hour
   (b) Erlang with a mean of $\frac{1}{6}$ hour and $k = 5$
   (c) constant of $\frac{1}{6}$ hour
   (d) normal with mean of $\frac{1}{6}$ hour and variance of $\frac{1}{6}$

21. Consider the situation described in problem 20. An analyst has collected the following data for service times. Use the Erlang model to find L_q, L_s, W_q, and W_s. Also use the Pollaczek–Khintchine formula.

All of the following observations are in minutes 10, 12, 15, 6, 9, 12, 8, 9, 9, 10, 7, 12, 11, 10, 9, 11, 14, 8, 11, 12, 10, 9, 8, 6 and 12.

22. Determine L_s, L_q, W_s, and W_q for the following queueing situations with constant service times.
   (a) $c = 1$, $\mu = 100$, and $\lambda = 90$
   (b) $c = 2$, $\mu = 50$, and $\lambda = 90$
   (c) $c = 10$, $\mu = 10$, and $\lambda = 90$
   (d) $c = 50$, $\mu = 2$, and $\lambda = 90$

23. Repeat the analysis for problem 15 assuming the service time per server is a constant 10 minutes.

24. An airline is considering an alternative plan for overhauling its airplanes. At present only one plane can be handled at a time. History has shown that overhaul takes an average time of 36 hours, and planes arrive on the average of once every 45 hours. The present system costs $7000 per hour. For $8000 per hour we can get a system that will reduce the average overhaul time to 24 hours. Assuming that the cost of waiting planes is $500 per hour and the arrival pattern is Poisson, analyze this problem for each of the following service distributions:
   (a) exponential
   (b) Erlang with $k = 3$
   (c) constant

25. Reanalyze the in-process storage model discussed in Section 7.5.1 with $\mu = 10$ per hour and $\lambda = 9$ per hour.

26. Formulate the in-process storage model as a cost model where space costs $4 per square foot per week and there is a $5 penalty for each item that cannot be accommodated in the plant.

27. Determine the number of machines that should be assigned to each operator for the following situations. Use the method discussed in Section 7.5.3.
   (a) operator cost $6 per hour, cost of waiting $20 per hour and $K = .05$
   (b) operator cost = $4 per hour, cost of waiting $12 per hour and $K = .10$

(c) operator cost = $6 per hour, cost of waiting = $12 per hour and K = .02

28. Formulate the military car pooling model from Section 7.5.4 as a cost model. Consider the cost of cars α ($3/hour) and the cost of officers waiting α ($10/hour).

29. Three knitting machines are being attended by a single operator. Each machine needs attention in a Poisson manner at the rate of three per hour. The operator services the machines at the rate of six per hour. The service distribution is exponential. What percent of the time will the operator be idle? What is the average number of machines down?

30. ABE airport has one runway. Airplanes arrive at the rate of 30 per hour. They can land at the rate of 40 per hour. Assume the Poisson exponential assumption is valid. What will the probability be that a plane will have to circle more than 10 minutes?

31. The Lehigh University police force has requested that the University hire another cop to patrol the "hill" on Saturday night. Capt. Donchez in his eloquent plea to the Forum justified the request by saying that they were not able to get to at least 95 percent of the calls for service within the maximum desired 30 minutes time delay. A student forum representative calculated that on Saturday nights, calls for police service are received at the rate of eight per hour and that it takes on the average 12 minutes to "service" a call. Presently there are two cops patrolling the hill.

(a) What is the average utilization of the two cops presently on Saturday night duty?

(b) What is the average waiting time for a call for police service before a police unit is dispatched to service the call?

(c) Is the captain justified in his statement?

REFERENCES

1. Bolling, W. B., "Queuing Model of a Hospital Emergency Room," *Industrial Engineering*, Vol. 4, No. 9, September 1972.
2. Cooper, R. B., *Introduction to Queuing Theory*, The Macmillan Co., New York, 1972.
3. Cox, D. R. and W. L. Smith, *Queues*, Wiley, New York, 1961.
4. Descloux, A., *Delay Tables*, McGraw-Hill, New York, 1962.
5. Fetter, R. N., "Assignment of Operators Servicing Automatic Machines," *Journal of Industrial Engineering*, Vol. 16, No. 5, September–October 1965.
6. Gould, A. F., "Notes of Waiting Line Theory," Industrial Engineering Department, Lehigh University, 1968.
7. Gross, D. and C. M. Harris, *Fundamentals of Queuing Theory*, Wiley–Interscience, New York, 1974.

8. Hillier, F. S., "Cost Models for the Applications of Priority Waiting Line Theory to Industrial Problems," *Journal of Industrial Engineering*, Vol. 16, No. 3, March 1965.

9. Little, J. D. C., "A Proof for the Queuing Formula: $L = \lambda W$," *Operations Research*, Vol. 9, No. 3, May–June 1961.

10. Moore, J. M., "Queuing Information System," *Industrial Engineering*, Vol. 6, No. 6, June 1974.

11. Peck, L. G. and R. N. Hazelwood, *Finite Queuing Tables*, Wiley, New York, 1958.

12. Prabhu, N. U., *Queues and Inventories: A Study of the Basic Stochastic Processes*, Wiley, New York, 1965.

13. Saaty, T., *Elements of Queuing Theory*, McGraw-Hill, New York, 1961.

14. Shelton, J. R., "Solutions for Waiting-Line Problems," *Journal of Industrial Engineering*, Vol. 11, No. 4, July–August 1960.

simulation 8

Suppose we were going on a vacation to Las Vegas, Nevada, and had set aside $50 to spend for entertainment at the casinos. Upon arriving there we find a number of alternative ways we could spend $50, one of which is playing a game called Chuck-A-Luck. The equipment for the game consists of a cage, containing three dice, on a table that is marked into six sections each bearing a number from 1 to 6. To play the game, a participant places a bet on any number (or numbers) he wishes, the cage is rotated rapidly about its horizontal axis, and when it comes to rest the dice settle on the floor of the cage. The payoff to participants is determined on the basis of the number of dice that show face up the number(s) on which he has bet. For example, if a 1 were showing on all three dice (three 1's) bets on 1 would receive a payment of three times the size of the bets; all other numbers, 2–6, would lose. If a 1, 2, and 3 were showing, one on each die, bets on those three numbers would receive payment equal to the size of the bets; 4, 5, and 6 would lose their bets. Before spending our entertainment money on this game we would like to know how long we could expect the money to last if we were to play. There are several ways we could go about obtaining answers to various questions about systems such as that posed by our illustrative game.

    For one way, we could attempt to obtain answers analytically. That is, we could model the system mathematically and solve the mathematical expressions to obtain the answers. When this method is usable, it generally provides the most effective means for obtaining answers. Unfortunately many real systems defy analytical solutions because they are either too complex or the analyst does not have the analytic capability required by the task. Certainly in the case of our Chuck-A-Luck game, the analytic solution would be the simplest way to obtain an answer to the question posed. For our purposes, however, let us assume that we do not have the necessary analytic capability.

**8.1
INTRODUCTION**

Mankind has been confronted through the ages with systems that defy analytic solutions but has handled many of them through experimentation. Sometimes he has simply experimented with the system itself, sometimes he has constructed a prototype of the system for experimental purposes and sometimes he has built models of the system and experimented on the models. There are, of course, advantages and disadvantages to each of these experimental approaches. For example, using our game as a case in point, we can see that experimentation by actually playing the game entails the risk of exhausting our capital before we obtain our answers. To eliminate that risk, we could obtain a prototype of the game and experiment on it but, with our limited capital, the cost of a prototype would not be very appealing. Finally we could construct a model of the game and experiment on the model. If we could build an inexpensive model that gave us a fairly accurate representation of the game, we could simulate the play of the actual game to get our answer. Of course, in this latter case we must exercise great care that the model is, in fact, an accurate representation of the game. The use of model ships and airplanes used in experiments in water tanks or wind tunnels are good examples of this type of simulation.

Many systems that defy analytic solutions can nevertheless be sufficiently accurately described by a series of relatively simple separate relationships and rules of behavior. The system can then be simulated by progressively and repeatedly evaluating the relationships thereby negating the need for a physical model or prototype. This would be another type of simulation. Until not too long ago this latter type of simulation was frequently unfeasible because of the effort required to evaluate the relationships used to describe the model. Today the availability of high-speed digital computers makes the large number of evaluations necessary in such an experimental situation a very feasible matter. As a matter of fact, the art of computer simulation is generally quite intriguing and one of the dangers confronting the unwary analyst is the indiscriminate use of that technique.

It would be impossible to attempt to describe all the situations where computer simulation would be the preferred technique in handling a problem. The analyst must proceed on a case-by-case basis to make this determination keeping in mind the advantages and disadvantages associated with the technique in light of the circumstances surrounding the case at hand. This then is the initial task that the analyst should address before boldly plunging into a computer simulation. To assist in that task some useful questions for which the analyst should seek the answers would be:

● Can the desired analysis of the system be obtained from observation and experimentation of the actual system itself? Is it safe and economical to do so?

- If it is unwise to use the actual system or it does not exist, can it be described and analyzed analytically?

- Is the cost entailed in developing a computer simulation model (and they are expensive) justified by the use that will be made of it? Don't forget that once it is available, it may be used as often as necessary at relatively little cost.

While these questions are not intended as a comprehensive checklist, their objective evaluation should provide a reasonable starting basis on which to decide whether or not to attempt to construct a computer simulation model. Let us assume that we have done so in the case of our game and that the answers indicate that we should construct such a model from which we can then obtain the answers to our questions.

The first step in developing a computer-aided simulation is the formulation of the model of the system to be simulated. It would probably be more accurate to say the first step consists of starting the formulation of the model. Model formulation is, more often than not, an iterative task and it is not uncommon to find that models undergo continued refinement and sophistication even after they have yielded their first useful results. Nevertheless the task should be undertaken systematically from the outset to insure that the model captures the essence of the system. Equally important during this stage of development is the realization that not everything that one may conjure up should necessarily be included in the model. This differentiation of the important from the trivial, no matter how elegant or intriguing the latter may be, is a key element of good model construction.

8.2 MODEL FORMULATION

A useful and systematic way to start model formulation is to approach it in relatively broad terms with the actual physical system as a basis on which to start visualization of the model. As an example, in developing a model for our game, we say that a single play consists of the following four steps:
1. Determination of the size of the bet.
2. Selection of the number (or numbers) on which we wish to bet.
3. Rotation of the cage.
4. Collection of the payoff, if any, when the cage comes to rest.

The game continues as long as there are any funds available by repeating the four steps of the play; if no funds are available the game is over.

It is frequently quite helpful, particularly when modeling complex systems, to reduce the visualization of the model to a systems flow chart. If you were to do so for any player-Chuck-A-Luck system, you should be able to produce a flowchart much like the one shown in Figure 8.1. We

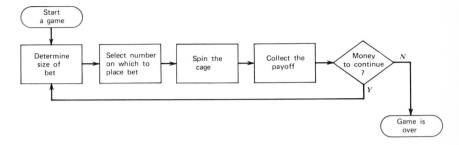

Figure 8.1   The player/game system.

see that the first two steps each involve a myriad of possible choices and if we do not know too much about the system it may be difficult to establish a reasonable set of alternatives to include in the simulation. We could, if that were the case, decide to limit our initial simulation to the third step, that is, the behavior of the cage. We could reason that the analysis of that behavior could lead to the development of reasonable choices that would provide a basis for subsequent experiments.

Another useful technique at this point is the consideration of simplifying valid assumptions that we could make with regard to the system. For example, we could assume that since we know very little about the game it would be risky at this time to bet more than $1 on any number at one time. Going on to the question of which number to bet on we could assume that the game is fair and that each number has an equal probability of appearing. We could also reason that since the cage has no memory, it makes no difference which numbers won what on past plays; each play will produce its winners independently. Thus we could reason that we could pick the number or numbers on which we bet randomly. This being the case, the question is no longer a matter of which number(s) to bet on but rather on how many numbers should we bet on each play. In utilizing this simplifying technique you must be careful to make sure your assumptions are reasonable and you should always state them explicitly as a part of your model. Later on you may even wish to experiment with your model under varying assumptions or conditions to establish the sensitivity of the system to differing conditions. For now let us accept the assumptions and reasoning as described from which we can conceptualize our model with the use of a systems flow chart as shown in Figure 8.2.

After our initial conceptualization of the model, we would normally turn to the task of writing the computer program necessary to exercise the model. Before we can do that for our game, however, there are a number of topics that we must understand and we should explore those topics first.

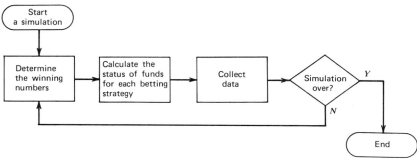

Figure 8.2 The model of the player/game system.
1. $1 will be bet on each number being played each play.
2. Six betting strategies will be examined for each play:
   (a) One number (1).
   (b) Two numbers (1, 2).
   (c) Three numbers (1, 2, 3).
   .
   .
   (f) Six numbers (1, 2, 3, 4, 5, 6).
3. The game is assumed to be fair.

If we are going to conduct our simulation with a physical model of the game we would rotate the cage model and read the winning numbers on the upright faces of the dice. The winning numbers would appear at random. However, the computer with which we are going to conduct our simulation has neither a cage nor dice. What we need in the computer is the ability to generate random numbers of the kind that would appear on the dice in the cage.

The question of whether or not a string of numbers is truly random is somewhat complex. A number of tests have been devised whereby a string can be tested and the reader is referred to Chapter 6, reference [13] where a number of these tests are treated. Tables of random numbers have been published such as those contained in reference [12] which can be used by selecting a starting number at random and then using the numbers in sequence as they appear in the table. Certainly we could make the contents of such a table available to the computer and we could use those numbers during the course of the simulation. A page of random numbers is given in Appendix A.

Another way to obtain random numbers is through computation. For example we could generate a string of numbers from a randomly selected starting number by multiplying the selected number by a constant, say k, dividing the resulting product by another constant that embraces the range of random numbers we want, say m, and use the integer remainder as the next number in the string. The process can be repeated by using the generated number previously obtained as the selected number in the next computation. In our game we could, for example, use $k = 5$, $m = 6$ and arbitrarily start with $x_0 = 2$; let's see what happens.

$$x_0 = 2$$

$$\frac{kx_0}{m} = \frac{(5)(2)}{6} = 1 \text{ with a remainder of } 4.$$

Hence

$$x_1 = 4$$

$$\frac{kx_1}{m} = \frac{(5)(4)}{6} = 3 \text{ with a remainder of } 2.$$

Hence

$$x_2 = 2$$

There is not much point in going on for we can see that we are going to generate a string of alternating 2's and 4's. No sophisticated tests are necessary to determine that such a string is not a random string of numbers representing the face of the dice in our game. The choice of k and m require great care and considerable effort has been expended in devising computational methods that produce anything approaching true random numbers. Fortunately these efforts have not been without some successes and most computer systems contain random number generators that can be called on to produce pseudo random numbers. We describe these numbers by the use of the term "pseudo" because in the purest sense they are reproducible and, hence, not random. However, the numbers so produced pass tests for randomness sufficiently well to be usable in simulations.

The random numbers that are produced by a computer generator are uniformly distributed and have a number of digits in each number. More often than not they are produced as decimal numbers in the range from 0 to 1. For example a string of five such numbers if printed could look like the following :

$$x_0 = .06158 \qquad x_1 = .29022 \qquad x_2 = .69302$$

$$x_3 = .73354 \qquad x_4 = .83784 \tag{8.1}$$

Clearly these numbers do not represent the numbers on the faces of the dice and yet that is what we need. The matter of translating the random numbers from a table or a generator into the random numbers we need in a simulation experiment is the next topic we must discuss.

The transformation of pseudo random numbers into the random number required during a particular simulation experiment is called process generation. There are several ways in which the necessary transformation can be accomplished. We shall first look at a method that uses a probability distribution table in accomplishing the transformation for our Chuck-A-Luck game because it clearly shows the underlying principles of process generation.

We have already assumed that our game is fair and thus the numbers 1–6 should appear randomly with equal probability on each die. To be specific each number on a die has a probability of one out of six chances of appearing, $p = 1/6$. We can construct a probability distribution table by listing the numbers we wish to generate randomly (in our game that would be 1 through 6), show each number's probability of occurrence, $p(x)$, and finally we can show a cumulative total of the probability, $F(x)$, as we proceed through the table. If we did so the table would appear as shown in Table 8.1. Now assuming our random number generator has produced

Table 8.1 Probability Distribution: Chuck-A-Luck Game

x	$p(x)$	$F(x)$
1	.16667	.16667
2	.16667	.33333
3	.16667	.50000
4	.16667	.66667
5	.16667	.83333
6	.16667	1.00000

the string shown in (8.1), we can use Table 8.1 to obtain those values of X needed in our simulation of the game. We note, for example, that $x_0 = .06158$ and that the cumulative distribution for $X = 1$ in our table embraces all x_i where $0 \le x_i \le .1667$; thus the first random number for our game is 1. The process we have just described has generated a random number for our game and can be repeated as many times as necessary. Since in our game we have three dice on each play we can obtain the values for the dice in the first play by using x_0, x_1, and x_2 of (8.1) for the first play. Doing so what would the winning numbers be in our first simulated play? (Your winners should be 1, 2, 5; if they are not, do not go on until you figure them out correctly.)

The process generator we have just described is one that can be used when a simulation requires the generation of discrete random variables that are uniformly distributed over a specified range. The technique, however, is quite general and can be used when the simulation requires discrete or continuous random variables no matter how they are distributed. This last statement is a fairly sweeping one and before we glibly move on, it would be a good idea for us to look at some applications of the technique for varying conditions.

Suppose we wanted to simulate a system that involved, among other things, the number of customers arriving at an existing gas station during successive 10-minute intervals. Let's assume we had no idea how the number of arriving customers are distributed and must resort to observing the gas station over several "typical" days during which we collected the data shown in Table 8.2. We could proceed by constructing either a

Table 8.2 Customer Arrivals Each 10 Minutes

Numbers of Customers Arriving	Frequency of Occurrence
0	31
1	156
2	313
3	313
4	156
5	31
Total occurrences	1000

cumulative frequency table for the random variables similar to the one shown in Table 8.1 or by constructing a cumulative frequency graph as shown in Figure 8.3. Using (8.1) again as the random number string we could generate the number of customers arriving during the first five 10-minute intervals of our simulation. For example, for the first 10 minutes $x_0 = .06158$ and, from Figure 8.3, the number of customers would be 1; while for $x_1 = .29022$ the number of customers arriving the second 10-minute interval would be 2. If you continue processing the string you will see that the random numbers generated under these conditions differ from those generated for our game as well they should.

Let us continue our exploration of process generation by another application of the technique. Returning to our gas station simulation suppose we wanted to generate the time it takes to serve a customer so we

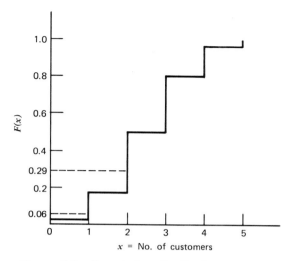

Figure 8.3 Cumulative distribution customer arrivals.

can simulate his departure. Again from our observations of the gas station we are able to plot the cumulative frequencies of serving time and they appear as shown in Figure 8.4. If we were to use our string of random numbers (8.1) we see now that $x_0 = .06158$ translates into a serving time for the first customer of 2.4 minutes. You should and probably did notice that we are no longer dealing with discrete variables. Since we wished to

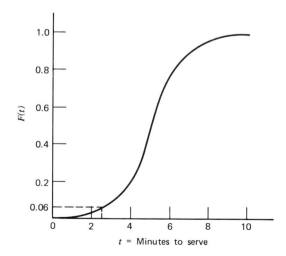

Figure 8.4 Customer serving time.

represent time as a continuous function in this case, we did not restrict the random variables in Figure 8.4 to discrete values as we had done in Figure 8.3. Examine the differences between discrete representation as shown in Figure 8.3 and continuous representation as shown in Figure 8.4.

We have examined a technique for generating random numbers for variables whether they be discrete or continuous and have seen it to be perfectly applicable to any distribution we may encounter. But a moment's reflection will show that it would be a cumbersome technique for computer use. If we could translate that technique into a computational method, the computer could handle it for us very nicely. And this can be done generally as we shall now see.

Recall that the technique we have been using involved the use of the cumulative distribution function for the random variables for which we are seeking to generate random numbers. Suppose that we can define that function and let us denote that definition as $F(x)$. Let $r =$ the uniformly distributed random number generated by a computational technique as discussed in 8.3 such that $0 \le r \le 1$. In effect our technique was using r by setting it equal to $F(x)$ and then solving for x. In other words, since

$$r = F(x)$$

if we can find an expression for x such that

$$x = G(r)$$

it would be a simple matter for the computer to produce x from r.

For an example of how this can be done, recall that the exponential density function with parameter λ is given by

$$f(x) = \lambda e^{-\lambda x} \qquad 0 < x < \infty$$

Its cumulative distribution function by definition is then

$$F(x) = \int_o^x \lambda e^{-\lambda t}\, dt = 1 - e^{-\lambda x} \tag{8.2}$$

Solving (8.2) we obtain

$$e^{-\lambda x} = 1 - F(x)$$

and by taking the logarithms of both sides

$$-\lambda x = \ln\left[1 - F(x)\right]$$

from whence

$$x = -\frac{\ln\left[1 - F(x)\right]}{\lambda} \tag{8.3}$$

Recall our technique set $r = F(x)$ and making that substitution in (8.3) we have

$$x = -\frac{\ln(1-r)}{\lambda} = -\frac{\ln r}{\lambda} \qquad (8.4)$$

which is a perfectly valid exponential process generator since $1-r$ is a random number and can be replaced by r.

Not all process generators are this easily derived and some involve approximation techniques. Nevertheless a number of process generators are available for use with a digital computer and some of the more commonly used ones are shown in Table 8.3. (When empirical data can not be fitted to a known density distribution, the techniques using probability tables or graphs can be used.) For those who wish to explore

Table 8.3 Some Commonly Used Process Generators

Distribution	Parameters Requiring Definition	Process Generator for $X =$	
		Discrete Random Variables	
Uniform	a, b	$= x$ where $\dfrac{x-a}{b-a+1} < r \le \dfrac{x-a+1}{b-a+1}$	
Bernoulli	p	$= \begin{cases} 1 \text{ where } r \le p \\ 0 \text{ where } r > p \end{cases}$	
Binomial	n, p	$= \displaystyle\sum_{i=1}^{n} x_i$ where $x_i = \begin{cases} 1 \text{ where } r_i \le p \\ 0 \text{ where } r_i > p \end{cases}$	
Poisson	λ	$= K-1$ where $\displaystyle\sum_{i=1}^{K-1} -\frac{\ln r_i}{\lambda} \le 1 < \sum_{i=1}^{K} -\frac{\ln r_i}{\lambda}$	
		Continuous Random Variables	
Uniform	a, b	$= a + (b-a)r$	
Exponential	λ	$= -\dfrac{\ln r}{\lambda}$	
Normal (from Ref. [1])	μ, σ, a, b	$= \begin{cases} a \text{ where } v \le a \\ v \text{ where } a < v < b \\ b \text{ where } v \ge b \end{cases}$	where $v =$ $((-2 \ln r_1)^{1/2}$ $(\cos 6.283 r_2)$ $(\sigma) + \mu)$

$a \le X \le b$; $r =$ random number; $p =$ prob. of success; $n =$ no. of Bernoulli trials; $\lambda =$ mean arrival rate per unit of time; $\mu =$ mean; $\sigma =$ standard deviation.

process generation in greater depth, Chapter 7, reference [13] would prove helpful. With an understanding of how we can generate random variables for a simulation in hand, we are ready to discuss the next topic.

**8.5
EVENT-
ORIENTED
SIMULATION**

In general both continuous systems, those which operate continuously over time, and discrete systems, those which operate at discrete intervals in time, are amenable to simulation by digital computer. One way of handling time in a simulation is to break it up into equal intervals. For example if we were interested in simulating the flight of an airplane in order to collect data on its speed from takeoff to landing, we could construct the model so as to obtain an observation on its speed at the end of each minute of simulated flight. While a graph of the plane's actual speed might appear as shown in Figure 8.5, the simulated data might appear as shown in Figure 8.6. If we were interested in obtaining a

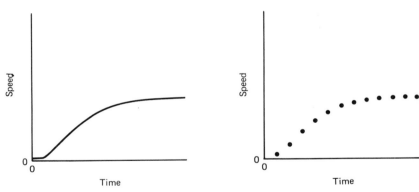

Figure 8.5 Continuous speed over time.

Figure 8.6 Digital simulation of speed.

simulation that more closely approximated the actual performance, we could obtain an observation every second rather than every minute. When digital computers are used to simulate a continuous system this is essentially the manner in which time is treated.

We could deal with time in the same manner even when dealing with a discrete system but there are several reasons why it may not be to our advantage to do so. Our Las Vegas game provides a case in point from which to explore this matter. First, we would not be interested in obtaining observations at equal specific intervals during the game if something of interest were not taking place at those times; essentially our model of the game requires an observation only when the cage comes to rest. Second, it does not follow that the cage will always come to rest after the same time interval. Thus if we used fixed equal intervals for our simulation we might miss some of those instances when the cage does come to rest and if we try to insure against this with very short time intervals we would create a very inefficient simulation model.

The answer in this situation turns out to be quite simple; we simply conduct our simulation by dividing time into unequal increments and tailor the division such that each interval will end precisely as the cage comes to rest. In that way we would not miss any observations and we would not be attempting to take readings when there was nothing of interest to us. This technique for handling time is called event oriented simulation and is quite general in its applicability to discrete systems.

Again we use our game to provide a very simple illustration of how the technique works. We would, in effect, start the game at time equal zero, $t_0 = 0$, and at that instance forecast the time interval, T_1, after which the cage would come to rest. We then advance time to precisely the moment we have forecasted, $t_1 = t_0 + T_1$, and presto, we read the faces of the dice and gather such data as we require. Having completed the first play of the game at t_1, we forecast the time interval after which the cage will come to rest again, T_2, increment our clock so that $t_2 = t_1 + T_2$ and take the next readings from the dice. Assume that playing time is uniformly distributed over the range of from 2 to 5 minutes so that $a = 2$ minutes and $b = 5$ minutes and that our random number generator will produce the string of (8.1). We now manually simulate a portion of the game to illustrate the technique.

1. Initialization: $t_0 = 0$ **EXAMPLE**
   funds $(1) = 50$ (bet on the number 1)
   funds $(2) = 50$ (bets on 1 and 2)
   funds $(3) = 50$ (bets on 1, 2, and 3)
   funds $(4) = 50$ (bets on 1, 2, 3, and 4)
   funds $(5) = 50$ (bets on 1, 2, 3, 4, and 5)
   funds $(6) = 50$ (bets on 1, 2, 3, 4, 5, and 6)
   The six combinations of bets are established so we can keep track of all of them on each play.
2. Forecast when the first play will be over
   $r_1 = .06158$ hence $T_1 = a + (b - a) \, r = 2 + (3).06158 = 2.18$ minutes
3. Read the faces of the dice at $t_1 = t_0 + T_1 = 2.18$ minutes
   $r_2 = .29022$ from Table 8.1 $x_1 = 2$
   $r_3 = .69302$ $x_2 = 5$
   $r_4 = .73354$ $x_3 = 5$
   Hence the bet on 2 pays \$1 and on 5 pays \$2, as well as returning our bets on those numbers if any, from which we can compute the funds remaining for each betting combination at $t_1 = 2.18$ minutes:
   funds $(1) = 49$ (we played only on number 1)

funds (2) = 50 (we played both 1 and 2)
funds (3) = 49 (we played 1, 2, and 3)
funds (4) = 48 (we played 1, 2, 3, and 4)
funds (5) = 50 (we played 1, 2, 3, 4, and 5)
funds (6) = 49 (we played all 6 numbers)

4. Forecast when the second play will be over

$r_5 = .83784$ hence $T_2 = 4.51$ minutes so $t_2 = t_1 + T_2 = 6.69$ minutes
and by continuing to generate random numbers we could translate them
to times and dice faces as done above. When a fund for a particular
betting combination reached zero we would know how many plays that
combination lasted and how long it took before that combination went
broke. Of course simulating one game may not tell us too much since it
depicts only one possible sequence of events; we discuss how long a
simulation run should be later in the chapter.

EXAMPLE   Let us take a look at our gas station again to see how the technique
works in a slightly more complicated system. In that system you will recall
two different kinds of events were possible in that we had customers
arriving and leaving. One way this situation can be treated is to begin by
forecasting the time interval after which the first customer will arrive.
Then

$$t_{A1} = t_0 + T_{A1}$$

and we could place the customer in an "event" file noting both that it is an
arrival and the time of arrival. As you will soon see it is important that we
define the characteristics, or attributes as they are most frequently called,
of each event before the event is placed in the file. Now we know, at $t_0 = 0$,
that the first event to take place is in the event file. We start the simulation
by retrieving the first event from the event file. We know two characteristics about the event, one is the time the event will take place and the other
is that the event is an arrival.

Two events are to follow since another customer is to arrive and
ultimately the first customer will depart after service. The first of these
two events is easily handled; we simply generate the time interval
between arrivals and

$$t_{A2} = t_{A1} + T_{A2}$$

which permits us to place customer 2 in the event file. The matter of a
customer's departure requires a little more consideration for now before
we can do anything about his departure we must first ascertain when his
service starts. In this instance, since he is the first customer, we can
assume that the server is not preoccupied in which case service starts upon
arrival. After generating his service time we have

$$t_{D1} = t_{A1} + T_{S1}$$

which now permits us to place customer 1 back in the event file. At this point we must introduce another concept in our simulation. Since one of the matters we must be able to ascertain is whether or not the server is busy, we can introduce the notion of a counter with values of either 0 or 1 to indicate the server's status. Letting 1 denote that he is busy, we would set the counter to 1 after placing the end of service event for customer 1 in the event file. Our simulation has now progressed from time t_0 to t_{A1} and we have two future events in our event file:

1. The arrival of the second customer to occur at t_{A2}.
2. The departure of the first customer to occur at t_{D1} and the counter showing the server busy because of customer 1. When will the server counter go to 0 showing that the server is idle?

Since we now wish to advance time to that specific instance at which the next event takes place it is a simple matter to look at our event file and select that event that has the earlier time. To facilitate this selection we could, and should, file events chronologically by time; if this practice is followed the next event will always be the first event in our file. First let us assume that $t_{D1} < t_{A2}$.

In that circumstance we advance time to t_{D1}, we gather such data as we need on customer 1, set the server counter to 0 to show that he is idle and permit the customer to happily pass from our system whose state is now essentially what it was at t_0. The simulation would proceed to the next event, which from our event file would be the arrival of customer 2. To proceed with the simulation the process described on the arrival of customer 1 can be repeated; that is, generate the arrival of customer 3 and the departure of customer 2, and so on. Let us now replay the last sequence of events in our simulation with the assumption that $t_{D1} > t_{A2}$.

Had that been the case, the next event to occur would have been the arrival of customer 2. There is no problem in generating the arrival of customer 3 and placing that event into the event file just as we did before, but how about the departure of customer 2? Here we have the case where the server counter $= 1$, showing us that he is occupied with customer 1 and he cannot begin serving customer 2 until t_{D1}, an event that has yet to occur. There are a number of ways this situation can be handled, and we describe one of them in the following simulation. In the real system, customer 2 gets in line and waits his turn, and that's what we will do with our simulation model. To do so we establish another file that we will call the queue file and because the server is busy with customer 1, we place the event embracing the arrival of customer 2 into that second file. Having done so, our files at time t_{A2} would look like this:

Event File	Queue File
t_{D1}	t_{A2}
t_{A3}	

where $t_{A2} < t_{D1} < t_{A3}$

We are now ready for our next event, which we obtain from the head of the event file. We treat the departure of the first customer as we did before, set the server counter at 0 and we are now ready to serve the next customer. With the simulation model we have, it is necessary on the departure of a customer to check the queue file to determine if a customer is waiting for service before retrieving the next event from the event file. In the instance in hand such a check would reveal that on the departure of customer 1, customer 2 is indeed waiting and that is our next event. When does customer 2's service start? Not at t_{A2} when he arrived because at that time he joined the queue but rather at t_{D1}, the time our first customer departed, which also happens to be the current time of our simulation. Thus after generating the service time for customer 2, we can compute his departure time since we can reason

$$t_{D2} = t_{D1} + T_{S2}$$

and we can place customer 2 with t_{D2} into the appropriate spot in the event file. Since the server is again busy, we set the counter to 1.

What would happen in our simulation sequence if when we check the queue file we find it empty instead of occupied as it was with customer 2? Simple enough; if no one was in the queue then no one was waiting to be served; the next event to occur, whatever it may be, must be at the head of the event file and we would proceed from there using the applicable process.

The simulation just described may sound complex to you at first reading but its principal features are relatively simple as shown in Figure 8.7. You should study that figure carefully for it will help crystallize the concepts of an event oriented simulation for you. Admittedly the illustrative flowchart in Figure 8.7 does not depict all the details such as the clock to keep track of time or the counter to keep track of whether or not the server is busy, but such omissions were deliberate to better highlight the event oriented simulation concept. You should note that the flowchart does contain a decision concerning ending the simulation run for without it, the run would never end. This is not always a simple matter and now that we understand the basic concepts behind making the model run we should address the topics of starting and ending the run.

**8.6
LENGTH OF
SIMULATION
RUNS**

The first consideration in deciding how long a simulation run should be is the question of when to start the run. For example, the Chuck-A-Luck game has no transient state. Aside from the fact that the random number we use to start the random number generator may influence the data we obtain from a run, the model and simulation of the game is essentially in the steady state from the moment the simulation starts. Is the same thing true about the gas station simulation? The fact of the matter in the latter

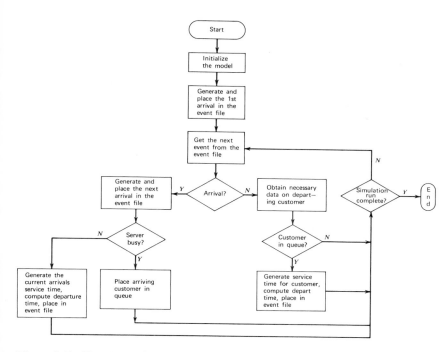

Figure 8.7 Simulation flow chart of single-server gasoline station.

case is that we don't know whether or not the simulation is in the steady state from the outset. Certainly if customers are going to arrive faster than they can be served on the average, the queue will build up as the simulation proceeds since the simulation started with an empty queue. If we were interested in obtaining data on customer waiting time, the early portion of the simulation would not reflect accurate waiting times as the system passed through the transient state. To overcome this we could run the simulation until the system reaches steady state, discard the observations made during the transient state, reset the time to $t_0 = 0$ but leave the system in the steady state and then start the simulation run for the record.

As a general rule, we will rarely know enough about a system at the outset to know when it will reach steady state. An analyst could simply rely on his judgement and permit the simulation to run "long enough" to get the system sufficiently removed from the initial conditions before starting the run for the record. With little information about the system at the outset, however, this judgmental approach may not provide much confidence that the transient state has been passed. This insecurity may be appreciably lessened by making a number of runs from the same starting point and comparing the observed state of the system at various run lengths. The knowledge thus gained can be used to get a feel for how quickly the system approaches steady state and can be used to reinforce judgmental decisions on how long the simulation should be permitted to run before starting a run for the record.

The question of how many observations we should produce in our simulation run can be approached more precisely assuming the run will contain only steady-state data. Let us use our game to examine this question. For the sake of clarity during the examination we shall look only at the bet-on-one-number-at-a-time strategy; the principles discussed are applicable to simulation experiments in general.

Suppose after 20 plays our simulation has produced the data shown in Table 8.4. We could say, based on our first 10 plays, that we could

Table 8.4 Outcome Summary of 20 Plays

	Payoffs per Play				Net	Fund
Play Sequence	− $1	$1	$2	$3	Earnings	Status
First 10 Plays	6	3	1	0	− $1	$49
Second 10 Plays	5	4	1	0	$1	$50
Totals	11	7	2	0	0	

expect the game to be over in 500 plays whereas the second 10 plays would lead us to the conclusion that the game would go on as long as we wanted to play since those plays produced a net gain of $1. The estimate of the winnings per game, $\bar{x}$, for the first series would be

$$\bar{x}_{1,10} = \frac{-1}{10} = -.1 \text{ while for the second series}$$

$$\bar{x}_{11,20} = \frac{1}{10} = .1$$

What is the true mean winnings per game? While we don't know the answer from the data we have, intuitively we would say that by considering all 20 games we should produce a better estimate of the true mean than either series did. With that reasoning

$$\bar{x}_{1,20} = \frac{\bar{x}_{1,10} + \bar{x}_{11,20}}{2} = 0$$

Carried further, our reasoning would lead us to the conclusion that as we increased the number of 10 play series, n, we would get better estimates and that as $n \to \infty$, $\bar{x}_{1,\infty} \to \mu$, where μ is the true mean. This reasoning is correct* and it remains for the analyst to decide how large n should be in order to produce an estimate of the desired accuracy.

The relationship between the parameters in question can be stated mathematically in terms of probabilities since we desire

$$P(\mu - d \leq \bar{x} \leq \mu + d) = 1 - \alpha \qquad 0 < \alpha < 1 \qquad (8.5)$$

where d is the tolerance on either side of the mean within which we desire our estimate to fall with a probability of $1 - \alpha$. Since $\bar{x}$ is approximately normally distributed, its relationship to the unit normal distribution could be stated as

$$\bar{x} = z\sigma_{\bar{x}} + \mu$$

then

$$P(\mu - d \leq \bar{x} \leq \mu + d) = P(\mu - d \leq z\sigma_{\bar{x}} + \mu \leq \mu + d)$$
$$= P(-d \leq z\sigma_{\bar{x}} \leq d)$$
$$= P\left(\frac{-d}{\sigma_{\bar{x}}} \leq z \leq \frac{d}{\sigma_{\bar{x}}}\right)$$

and an examination of the area under the curve shows this to be equivalent to

$$= 2P\left(z \leq \frac{d}{\sigma_{\bar{x}}}\right) - 1 \qquad (8.6)$$

From (8.5) and (8.6) we can write

$$2P\left(z \leq \frac{d}{\sigma_{\bar{x}}}\right) - 1 = 1 - \alpha$$

$$P\left(z \leq \frac{d}{\sigma_{\bar{x}}}\right) = 1 - \frac{\alpha}{2} \qquad (8.7)$$

Then if we let the value of the unit normal random variable, $z_{1-(\alpha/2)}$, be such that

$$P\left(z \leq \frac{d}{\sigma_{\bar{x}}}\right) = P[z \leq z_{1-(\alpha/2)}] = 1 - \frac{\alpha}{2}$$

then

$$\frac{d}{\sigma_{\bar{x}}} = z_{1-(\alpha/2)}$$

---

* It can be shown that the distribution of the sample mean, $\bar{x}_{i,i+10}$, is approximately normally distributed about the true mean, μ, with a variance of σ^2/n where $n > 5$ and σ^2 is the true variance. The variance of the sample mean, $\sigma_{\bar{x}}^2 = \sigma^2/n$, and therefore decreases as n increases and we can expect $\bar{x} \to \mu$ as $n \to \infty$.

and since

$$\sigma_{\bar{x}}^2 = \frac{\sigma^2}{n}$$

$$\frac{d\sqrt{n}}{\sigma} = z_{1-(\alpha/2)} \qquad (8.8)$$

or

$$n = \left[\frac{\sigma z_{1-(\alpha/2)}}{d}\right]^2 \qquad (8.9)$$

EXAMPLE   In other words we can determine how many observations we want in our simulation if we specify the acceptable tolerances and the probability that our experimental mean will fall within those tolerances provided that we know the true variance. One of the problems frequently encountered is that we do not know the true variance when we are designing our simulation experiment and we shall look at that contingency in a moment. Despite the artificiality of knowing σ for our game, let's assume we do know that it is equal to .5 to see how (8.9) could be used in those cases where it is known. Let us specify that we would like our experimental mean of the winnings per play to be accurate within $\pm$ five cents with a probability of 95 percent.

Then

$$1 - \alpha = .95$$

$$d = .05$$

and from a unit normal distribution table, Appendix B,

$$z_{1-(\alpha/2)} = 1.96$$

Then

$$n = \left[\frac{(.5 \times 1.96)}{.05}\right]^2 = 384.16$$

and it would require 385 simulated plays of the game to provide us with an experimental mean of the winnings per game, which would be within the limits prescribed. The method is general and direct when we know σ but, more often than not, we will not know it. This problem is not particularly troublesome in a computer simulation since the generation of additional data when it is required is simply a matter of continued exercise of the model. Let us look at our game again and remove the assumption that we know $\sigma = .5$ but retain our specifications for d and α.

To handle this situation we can utilize the notion of upper and lower
limits, U and L, respectively, which are defined as

$$U = \bar{x} + z_{1-(\alpha/2)}\frac{\sigma}{\sqrt{n}}$$

$$L = \bar{x} - z_{1-(\alpha/2)}\frac{\sigma}{\sqrt{n}}$$

That is, U and L define an interval about $\bar{x}$ such that the interval will
contain the true mean with a confidence level of $1-\alpha$. In this event $\bar{x}$
becomes the best point estimator of the true mean. Although we still do
not know σ we can compute a good approximation of L and U by
substituting the sample standard deviation, s, for the true standard
deviation, σ, provided that $n \geq 100$.*
     Now our problem is reduced to running the simulation for 100 plays,
obtaining $\bar{x}$ and s from the 100 observations and then computing U and L
from the values obtained for $\bar{x}$ and s. If L and U fall within the specified
tolerances we then know that interval defined by L and U will contain the
true mean $(1-\alpha)$ percent of the time and that $\bar{x}$ is the best point estimate
of that true mean. If L and U do not fall within the specified tolerances we
continue the simulation for 100 more plays and obtain a new $\bar{x}$, s, L, and
U. The process is repeated until L and U do fall within specified
tolerances and, once they do, the simulation is stopped. These computations can be programmed into the simulation model so that the computer
will automatically terminate the simulation after the proper number of
plays. Table 8.5 illustrates a summary of these computations as they
might appear in a simulation of our game. Note that for $n = 100$ plays that
$U - L = .176$, which exceeds our specification of .1, and the simulation is
continued until $n = 400$. The simulation is terminated at that point since
$U - L$ has now fallen inside our specification. Our conclusion at this point
would be that the true mean of our winnings per play lies in the interval
$U = -.034$ and $L = -.124$ with a confidence level of 95 percent. Our
best point estimate, $\bar{x}$, of the true mean would be $-.079$ and we conclude
that the strategy of playing one number at a time would result in an
expected loss of $\$.079$ per play of the game.

---

* When $n < 100$ the t distribution should be used to compute L and U by utilizing the
expressions

$$L = \bar{x} - t_{1-(\alpha/2)}(n-1)\frac{s}{\sqrt{n}}$$

$$U = \bar{x} + t_{1-(\alpha/2)}(n-1)\frac{s}{\sqrt{n}}$$

Table 8.5 Confidence Interval Computations for Simulation Results

n	$\bar{x}$	s	U	L	$U-L$
100	−.072	.449	.016	−.16	.176
200	−.074	.426	−.015	−.133	.118
300	−.080	.459	−.028	−.132	.104
400	−.079	.459	−.034	−.124	.090
Terminate the simulation					

$d = \pm.05; 1 - \alpha = 95$ percent.

Somewhere during the chapter the thought probably occurred to you that the computer programs to conduct simulations require a great deal of overhead in the way of clocks, file maintenance, statistical computations, and the like. You would, of course, be right but the task has been considerably simplified by the development and availability of simulation languages. Now that we understand the general theory behind simulation experiments, we conclude this chapter with a brief examination of simulation languages and what they can do for us.

**8.7
SIMULATION
LANGUAGES**

**8.7.1
General**

Computer programs for simulation experiments can be written in a general purpose, problem-oriented language such as FORTRAN IV without resorting to a special purpose simulation language. To do so, however, requires that the programmer expend a great deal of effort in devising routines and instructions to carry out housekeeping and administrative tasks some of which are, at best, only a means to an end. Furthermore, many of these tasks recur from time to time in different simulation experiments, and reinvention of the wheel each time it is needed can prove to be quite costly. While it is true that learning yet another language also takes time, once a special purpose simulation language is learned (and most of them can be learned relatively quickly) its power is available to reduce the time required to program simulation experiments repetitively and drastically.

Let us examine some of the more important features that should be considered in selecting such a language:

1. Fundamental to the usability of any such language is the requirement that it provide the modeler a means whereby the system being modeled can be described effectively. A language that can only handle continuous type simulations would not ordinarily be a good choice for conducting an event-oriented simulation.

2. It is a rare occasion when a complex system can be modeled, programmed, and run the first time it is passed to the computer. Thus a good language will contain a set of diagnostic routines that can be

invoked simply and that permit internal examination of the various parts of the simulation model at will as well as automatic meaningful diagnostic messages. A language that has already been extensively used has already encountered many of the types of problems each of us are apt to make at one time or another; automatic messages with substantive diagnostic content are invaluable to the modeler.

3. Experiments are conducted in order to gather statistics and a simulation language worthy of its name has the capability of collecting a wide variety of statistics in various forms with a modicum of effort on the part of the modeler. Equally important is the facility the language provides for report generation so that the information resulting from the experiment is readily made available for the decision process to follow.

4. The capability the language presents to the modeler for varying parameters from one experiment to another as well as the flexibility of altering parts of the model itself without extensive overhauling of the remainder of the model are important aspects which a modeler should consider. These capabilities play a particularly important role with respect to any model that is apt to lead to "what if" questions as the experiment unfolds.

5. As mentioned earlier simulation experiments are fairly expensive. Aside from the construction of the model itself one should consider the costs connected with acquiring the language, training costs associated with learning to use the language, and finally the costs connected with operating the language in simulation experiments.

It is not the intent of this section to compare the capabilities of the various simulation languages available today but to make the reader aware of the major considerations that should be examined in the selection of a language. The reader who desires to pursue language comparisons can use reference [15] at the end of this chapter, and we shall only look at some representative examples of the various types of languages available.

8.7.2 Discrete Languages

Two of the most widely used event-oriented languages are GPSS and SIMSCRIPT. The former was developed at the International Business Machine Corporation while the latter was developed at the Rand Corporation. Both have been in use for a number of years but differ from each other in some respects.

In a broad and general sense, SIMSCRIPT views the world to be simulated as being composed of entities that can be described in terms of their attributes, and events that are points in time when the status of the system being modeled changes. Thus in the gas station model we have been examining, the server or attendant would be an entity; one of his attributes would be his service time; an event would be the completion of service to a customer, which is the time that the server goes from a status of being busy to idle. Entities are related through membership in sets, a rather more general notion than that described earlier for the files we established in our discussion of the gas station model. SIMSCRIPT deals conceptually with the generation and scheduling of events in much the same way as we did earlier in the chapter.

In general the programming language of SIMSCRIPT can be said to be FORTRAN based and provides a powerful yet easy to use language. It includes provisions for report generation which the user will find to be flexible, powerful, and relatively easy to use.

GPSS is very much like SIMSCRIPT in its conceptualization of the statistics of the system to be modeled. Although terminology differs, it too views the system in general as being composed of entities of various types, their attributes, which are called parameters, and the file or set relationship, which is called a user chain. However, instead of viewing the arrival of a customer at the gas station as an event that leads to a series of events changing the status of the system until the customer departs the system, it views his arrival as a transaction that then flows through system, which is processed at the various entities in the system until it finally departs the system. Thus instead of perceiving the simulation as a series of events which take place, GPSS perceives the simulation as a number of transaction flows that take place.

In general the programming language of GPSS is a special language built around a fairly comprehensive list of simulation functions each of which is labeled and can be represented by a block in a block diagram. Because of this construction, the analyst models the system to be simulated by means of a block diagram, utilizing the GPSS defined simulation functions (blocks), by visualizing how the "transactions" flow through the system. Once this has been done, the GPSS program falls directly out of the block diagram by specification in the program of the block titles. GPSS also includes provisions for a large variety of statistical output, some automatically and others optionally.

8.7.3
Continuous
Languages

One of the best known continuous languages is DYNAMO, developed at M.I.T. It is often used in simulations of systems that contain flows, rates of flow, feedback loops, and delays all of which are continuously interrelated to some degree. Businesses as a whole are such systems and are frequently concerned with questions such as "what effects will changes in sales have in receivables and raw material status given that a firm operates in a certain way?" and "given that certain effects would occur when sales change what will be the effect of various policy or decision rule changes in the operation of the business?" Because of the feedback loops and delays in such systems, they frequently react to changes quite differently than we expect.

In general such systems can be modeled mathematically in terms of differential or difference equations once the system has been described in terms of its flows, rates, delays, and their interrelationships as described by Forrester [2].

The programming language of DYNAMO is a special language built to facilitate the simulation of such systems as was discussed above. Although the language itself is fairly straightforward and easy to learn, the concepts embodied in modeling such systems are fairly complex and require considerable learning time unless the user is already familiar with the field of servomechanisms and feedback theory. The language has a report generator that facilitates analysis.

8.7.4
Hybrid
Languages

To be considered a hybrid language, a simulation language must provide the user with a capability to deal with discrete and/or continuous simulation models. Many systems contain elements or subsystems of each kind and the language's capability to deal with such systems in a single simulation model can not be turned aside lightly. GASPIV is a well-documented, readily available, hybrid-simulation language. The discrete capability contained within GASPIV is constructed around the concepts of entities, attributes, and events much the same as SIMSCRIPT and the description of the gas station in this chapter. It also contains a file relationship that is very much like that described for the gas station simulation. Indeed if GASPIV were used to simulate the gas station as described, it would view the system very much as we did. However, the language refers to the type of event invoked in our description as a time event, that is, it is an event that will occur at a specific point in time. GASPIV also makes provision for another type of event, one that occurs when the system or some part thereof reaches a particular state and thus can not be prescheduled on the basis of the time at which it will occur. For example, suppose in our gas station model we have two attendants, one for serving the gas pumps and one for serving the lubrication racks where the lubrication rack attendant only serves gas when the pumps have a queue of three customers or more. The event where the second server starts serving gasoline can be thought of as the second type of event and is called a state event, that is, the second attendant becomes operative when the gas customer queue reaches the state of population ≥ 3. Finally GASPIV provides the capability to keep track of state variables where they are continuous variables rather than discrete. To accomplish this the language provides the facility for expressing state variables in terms of difference and differential equations in much the same fashion as is done in DYNAMO. Since GASPIV permits either type of event to initiate the other type, the language provides for continuous, discrete, or hybrid simulations.

GASPIV is FORTRAN based thus making it quite transportable and fairly easy to learn. It also provides a powerful, flexible report generator.

**8.8
APPLICATION
STUDIES**

8.8.1
Cutting Quality
Control Costs*

Application Study

Should individual telephone wires be repaired before being bundled into cable units or afterwards? The answer might seem obvious, but simulation of cable manufacture at the Hawthorne Works of the Western Electric Company showed that costs could actually be reduced by allowing defects to pass into the stranding operation.

The Hawthorne cable plant produces approximately 50 billion conductor feet of copper wire each year. The bare wire is pulp-insulated and twisted into pairs of various twist lengths that are identified by color coding. After twisting, the pairs are stranded or bundled into units varying from 25 to 100 pairs. These units are grouped together to form complete cables which are enclosed with metallic and polyethylene sheaths.

Two cabling machines handle the entire 50 billion conductor feet of cable. It is essential that these two machines be kept in operation and any changes to the operations preceding cabling have a reasonable chance of success. The twisting and stranding operations are done prior to cabling. Although twisted pairs are 100 percent detailed, up to 80 percent of the stranded units still have to be repaired. Since the major portion of repair time is rewinding, it was proposed to allow the defective pairs to pass through twisting and be repaired in the stranded stage only. Because of the interrelation of defects from one stage to the next and the difficulties of analyzing the sensitivity to change in various defect levels, the complete operation was simulated to determine the relative merits of repairing defects before and after stranding.

The distributions of one or more types of defects in individual wire pairs may be obtained from routine inspection results or from specially collected data. The problem considered here is to determine defect distributions for units of 25, 50, or 100 pairs when the individual pairs, some of which are defective, are allowed to pass into stranding without repair and may be cut into two or three lengths.

Simple situations can be handled by direct calculation, but the tendency to use direct calculation must be balanced against the danger that fitting the real problem into a theoretical model will reduce the usefulness of the ultimate solutions. In real-life situations a theoretical approach may not even produce useful insights regarding the true nature

* Reprinted with permission from *Industrial Engineering*, Vol. 3, No. 5, May 1971. Copyright © American Institute of Industrial Engineers, Inc., 25 Technology Park/Atlanta, Norcross, Ga. 30071.

of the problem. The power of simulation is its ability to approach reality and, thus, reduce the danger of problem distortion.

The first step in setting up the simulation model was to obtain an understanding of the elements that have an effect on the process to be simulated. It was then necessary to collect data that represented these elements and alternatives. To simulate the twisting and stranding operations of pulp-insulated wire, the following information was needed:

- A distribution of defective reels and defects within a reel of paired wire by gauge for shorts, opens, and chips.

- Machine time per reel and repair time per defect by gage for shorts, opens, and chips.

- Test time per reel of paired wire.

- A distribution of defective units; defective pairs per unit; and defects per pair by gage and unit size for shorts, opens, and crosses.

- Machine time per unit and repair time per defect by gage and unit size for shorts, opens, and crosses.

Using GPSS/360 language to model the process, functions were set up based on the distribution of defective reels of paired wire and stranded units, the type and number of defects per defective reel, the number of defective pairs per unit, and the type and number of defects per defective pair in a unit. The data was based on shop records and work sampling done in the test and repair areas for paired wire and stranded units.

Having obtained the data required for the model selected, the sequence of steps in the process was then modeled with variables set up to compute the various test and repair times and associated costs based on present piece-rates data. With the necessary elements of the process specified in proper sequence, the computer goes ahead and creates an image of an individual reel of wire of a particular gage, randomly assigning various defects according to the functions associated with the stranding operation. Here again, the defective pairs and defects remain identified with that particular unit until it is terminated as a good, stranded unit ready for cabling.

A simulated run of 6000 reels was used as representative of the process for a particular gage and stranded unit size. As each reel of paired wire and unit generated in the model passed through the simulated operations, computations were made on the number of particular defects assigned to individual reels and units, the test time and cost, and the repair time and cost. As these computations were made, they were accumulated in a defect time and cost matrix that was printed out at the end of a simulated run of 6000 reels.

From other data printed out, information on maximum queue lengths ahead of the twisted pair or unit repair facilities, waiting time, and utilization of facilities was gathered that reflects the dynamics of the process. This was done first for the present method of operation and, subsequently, for the alternative method.

A simulation run for the different alternatives was made for each gage and unit size. From information in the matrices and tables printed out at the end of each run, a comparison of costs between alternatives was made; a comparison of facilities and personnel required to handle the repairs was also made.

The simulation showed that it is feasible to allow defective paired wire to pass into the stranding operation without repair and then do all the repairing in the stranded unit stage. Although the advantages seem apparent, there are several reasons why this alternative may not be successfully implemented.

There is no assurance that twisted pair quality can be maintained on a sampling basis; there is no way of knowing, except by actual trial, what effect the so-called defective pairs may have on cable quality further along in the process; and additional unit repair facilities are necessary.

This particular application reveals a number of reasons to justify the simulation of a process. It is possible to study a complex system without the expenditure and risk of making the changes in the real system. At the same time, new policies for operating a complex system may be tested. Simulation also provides the ability to model a dynamic situation. An intangible effect of the simulation is a better understanding of present operations, and it may bring to light other areas for improvement in the process.

**8.8.2
A Corporate
Financial
Model***

Application Study

The Sun Oil model projects the financial performance of the company by simulating the operating procedures and the accounting system in terms of mathematical equations. Figure 8.8 indicates, in a general way, the flow of crude oil and refined products in an integrated oil company. To represent the company, the equations in the model simulate the barrel flow from the oil well to the service station, the revenues and expenses associated with it, and the impact of capital investments.

The model makes a projection based on certain assumptions. Values that must be specified are called inputs. They include:

● Product prices and volumes.

---

* This problem has been adapted from G. W. Gershefski, *The Development and Application of a Corporate Financial Model*, The Planning Executives Institute, Oxford, Ohio, 1968. Used with the permission of Sun Ventures, Inc., 680E. Swedesford Road, Wayne, Pa. 19087.

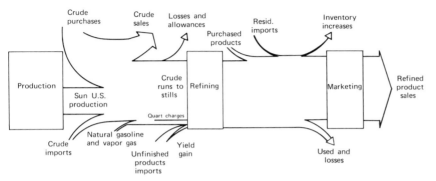

Figure 8.8 The Sun Oil Company crude oil and refined product flows.

- Raw material costs.
- General economic conditions.
- Investments.
- Subsidiary company incomes.
- Discretionary expense items.

The general economic conditions specified as inputs are important restrictions, the rates for U.S. taxes and mineral depletion allowance, and the allowable levels of crude oil production as set by state regulatory agencies. Although most investments must be specified before running the model, it can determine the investment requirements in the marketing and production areas. Subsidiary companies have not been modeled yet so that all projections regarding income have to be input to the model. Discretionary expense items include, for example, research and development, the sale of securities, writeoffs, and advertising. Generally, management has a great deal of control over these and can carefully plan strategies to increase or decrease them.

This is a very general description of the type of information required to make a projection. Actually 1500 items of input are required to simulate a year. These inputs can be divided into two large categories: 500 inputs that are based on past averages, statistical relationships, or historic fact and 1000 inputs or forecasts that must come from the operating departments. It is estimated that 50 inputs are of major importance in their effect on net income.

The large number of inputs is due to the philosophy that was used when designing the model. When a statistical relationship was found that provided a reasonably accurate projection, then the equation was used in the model. When it was not possible to find a good relationship, the variable was specified as an input. An alternative would have been to construct the model based on the average value over the last several years and to use this as the best forecast of future conditions. However, by specifying the item as input, the user is reminded that it might be appropriate to change the value based on specific knowledge of future plans.

Based on the values of the inputs, the model simulates the operations of the company and provides these key reports:

- Income statement.
- Capital investment schedule.
- Source and use of funds statement.
- Statement of earnings employed and stockholders' equity.
- Tax report.
- Rate of return analysis.
- Financial and operating summary.

The income statement indicates revenues, operating expenses, non-cash charges, foreign and federal taxes, and net income after tax for Sun Oil and each of the subsidiary companies. The capital investment schedule shows the capital expenditures to be made by each department. Based on these schedules, the source and use of funds statement equates the sources and uses of funds. Sources consist of net income, recovery of capital, deferred taxes, borrowings, or a reduction in working capital. Uses entail funds required for capital expenditures, cash dividends, the purchases of treasury stock, repayment of prior borrowing, or increases in working capital. The statement of earnings employed and stockholders' equity indicates the number of shares outstanding, stock and cash dividends payments, earnings employed, stockholders' equity, earnings per share, stock price, and the total common stock market value. The tax report details the adjustment required to reconcile book income with taxable income, special deductions, handling of foreign taxes as credits or deductions against U.S. taxes, the investment credit, and the tax to be accrued. The rate of return analysis indicates the return on both gross and net operating investment, and it provides an analysis in terms of profit margin and asset turnover. The financial and operating summary highlights financial items such as net income, revenue, total assets, long-term debt, the return on stockholders' equity, and the return on total assets employed; operations are highlighted in terms of the amount of crude oil produced, the crude oil to be run in the refineries, the level of crude oil reserves, gasoline sales, and market share. A balance sheet will be prepared when working capital has been modeled in more detail. In total,

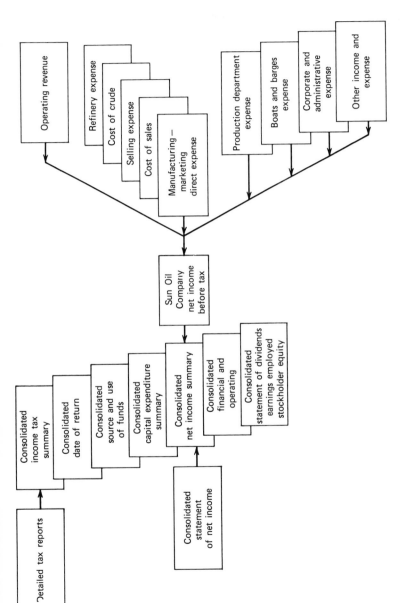

Figure 8.9 Reports generated by the financial model.

these reports provide management with a comprehensive overview of the company's operations.

In addition, the model generates a number of supporting statements. The organization of the output reports is shown in Figure 8.9. The reports are arranged so that summary information is shown first and supporting detail follows. In all cases, the reports are based on the same accounting definitions as are currently used by the company. This was done so that it would not be necessary to sell both the model and new reporting concepts at the same time. A sample output page is shown in Figure 8.10.

Approximately 5200 items of data are generated and stored for each year being simulated. All of this information can be retrieved easily to develop reports for management.

Physically, the corporate financial model is a computer program consisting of a series of equations that represent the company. The

	Actual			Estimate				
	1963	1964	1965	1966	1967	1968	1969	1970
Revenue	900	925	950	975	1000	1025	1050	1075
Cost and expenses	800	820	840	860	880	900	920	940
Net income	100	105	110	115	120	125	130	135
Cash income	150	160	170	180	190	200	210	220
Long-term debt	10	15	10	15	5	10	15	200
Stockholders' equity— Dec. 31	700	720	730	740	750	760	770	780
Net income per dollar of stockholders' equity (percent)	14.3	14.6	15.1	15.5	16.0	16.4	16.9	17.3
Net income per dollar of revenue—percent	11.1	11.4	11.6	11.8	12.0	12.2	12.4	12.6
Percent long-term debt	1.4	2.1	1.4	2.0	6.7	1.3	1.9	25.6
Max. stock dividend allowable (percent)	10	9	8	8	9	10	10	9
U.S. crude production	10	20	30	40	45	50	55	60
U.S. crude runs to stills	60	61	61	62	62	63	63	64
U.S. crude reserves	100	220	360	440	450	550	660	660
U.S. self-sufficiency (percent)	60	60	61	61	62	62	63	63
U.S. reserves/production ratio	10	11	12	11	10	11	12	11
Gasoline sales—BSL	30	35	40	45	50	55	60	65
Gasoline market share (percent)	8.1	8.2	8.3	8.4	8.5	8.6	8.7	8.8

Figure 8.10 The financial and operating summary (in millions).

equations are grouped to form a series of blocks, or subroutines. Each block represents a specific aspect of company operations and considers the physical operations performed, operating alternatives available, the relationship between costs and volumes, and the accounting procedure followed. The blocks are interrelated to determine consolidated net income as shown in Figure 8.11.

The model is to be used on a case-study basis. It does not have an automatic capability of searching through a large number of alternatives and choosing the best set, nor does it automatically consider variations in the forecasts submitted as inputs to the model. The sensitivity to any changes must be determined by running a series of cases. Technically, the model does have the capability of projecting for 40 years into the future. However, when developing the equations and the procedures to be used within the model, a 5- to 10-year period was considered most useful; these equations might be simplified if a longer-run forecast were required.

Provisions for flexibility and ease of use were made. For example, the model was developed by building a separate block or subroutine for each area of the company. This was done to enable construction of several blocks concurrently as well as to simplify model modification and extension. Thus, each area of the company can now be examined independently.

A number of predictive equations have been built into the model. The constants for all regression equations are specified as inputs. This enables cost structures to be changed easily without the need for reprogramming. It is standard practice to review the coefficients of the regression equations as the actual data for each new year becomes available to determine if changes are required. Even though predictive equations have been built into the model, the design of the model enables one to override any of these with a desired value. A particular group may feel that future conditions or policies are to be significantly different from those which existed in the past. Because of this override provision, they can input the values that they feel are most appropriate.

The model design enables one to make several multiple-year runs or several sensitivity analyses at one submittal of the program. This provision was made to simplify the case study approach. If an identical value is to be used for input for successive years, it is only necessary to specify the value for the first year. The program will continue to use this value for each remaining year until another input is specified for a particular year. This provision reduces the input cards required for running multiple-year cases.

The model was originally designed for use by executive management; summary reporting was used throughout. As the model gradually gained acceptance, it became necessary to include more detail concerning

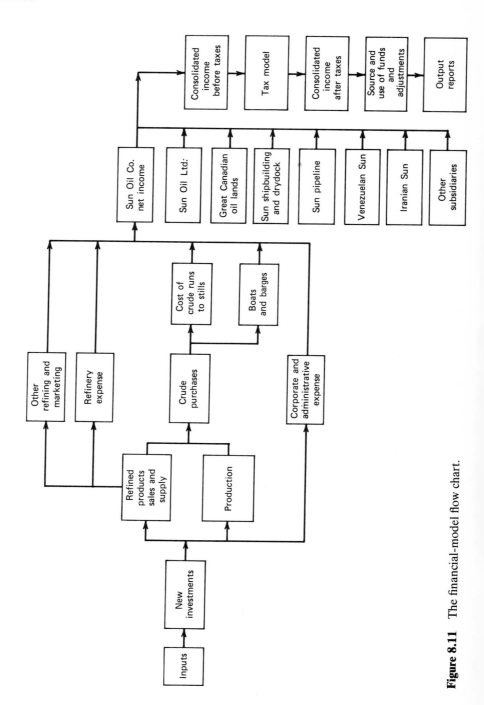

Figure 8.11 The financial-model flow chart.

the operating departments. It was obvious that the program system needed the flexibility to change the content or arrangement of reports very easily. This requirement led to the development of the report writing program. In addition to retrieving information from computer storage and specifying the format statements required for a report, the report writing program also performs calculations such as determining percent change or calculating the difference from one year to another.

A number of programs, information libraries, and temporary storage facilities are required to make a case study with the model. These constitute the computer system, which is shown in Figure 8.12.

The corporate financial model computer program consists of program blocks or subroutines that are stored on a permanent disc file. The blocks are also maintained in card form. During a model run, the blocks are selected from the permanent disc file and loaded into the memory of the computer for execution. When a block is to be modified, a programmer changes the card form of the block. The block is then loaded into computer memory from cards rather than from the permanent disc file. After changes have been tested, the updated blocks are incorporated into the program library file on permanent disc. The current operating version of the model consists of a combination of program blocks selected from the program library file and program blocks in card form where changes have been made.

Once the program has been loaded into the computer, the input data library is read. If there are data changes, the input data library is read from permanent disc onto a temporary file. This file is updated by data changes read from cards to form the current input data file. Changes are incorporated into the input data library on permanent disc only after they have been tested.

The output from the model consists of the tax and consolidation reports and the input–output data library. The input–output data library contains all the data input to the program and all the data calculated by the model.

A report selection program reads report identifications from cards, extracts the information for each requested report from the report specifications library on permanent disc, and creates a temporary file of these specifications. Each report specification gives the title of the report, the variable and caption desired for each row, and the year or case for each column. Based on this input, the report writing program retrieves information from the input–output data library, constructs the format statements required for each report, and writes the reports onto a temporary report library from which copies can be produced.

Because the corporate financial model program, the input data libraries, the report writer program, and the report specification libraries are stored on permanent disc files, independent studies and program

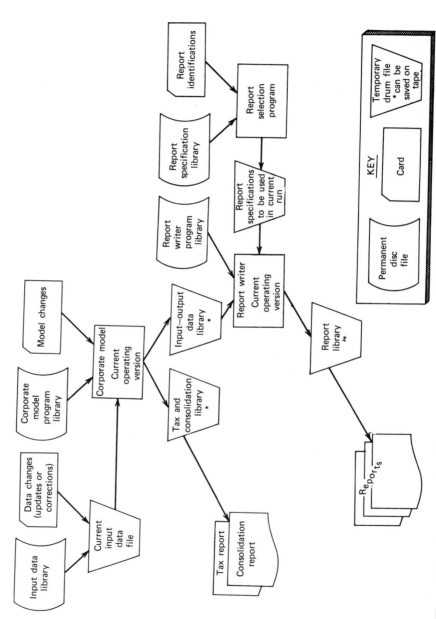

Figure 8.12 The financial-model computer system.

modifications proceed without disrupting regular operation of the model. The program blocks and data blocks that are unchanged in a particular study are taken from the permanent libraries. All changes are input on cards. After testing, the program or data changes can be incorporated into the permanent libraries if desired. This arrangement enables computer program development to proceed and yet insures that an operable production version of the model is available at all times.

The model was originally programmed in FORTRAN IV to run on the GE 635 computer. A core of approximately 38,000 words of 36 bits each is required. Fourteen seconds of processor time are required to simulate one year of company operations, and seven seconds of processor time are required to produce one page of output. This amazingly short time stems, in part, from the fact that the equations within the model are relatively simple and there is very little internal looping.

The problem was to determine the optimum number of patrol operators for servicing several hundred identical production machines operating on a 24-hour-a-day basis. The standards that were in existence at the time had been established on the basis of maintaining waste at a very low level, without considering the total economic situation.

8.8.3 Developing Manning Standards*

Application Study

Patrol-type jobs are characterized by having some work elements occurring randomly, as well as some predictable sequences of work elements of a repetitive nature. These jobs are also usually characterized by having both nondeferrable and deferrable duties, where there is a time-related cost occurring as a consequence of delayed action on the deferrable duties. For example, the longer a necessary action is delayed, the higher the resulting cost (downtime, waste production, etc.). Some examples of such jobs include patrolling mechanics, machine servicing operators, and miscellaneous types of trouble shooters. There is often a lack of comprehensive labor control standards that were developed on the basis of waste production and nonproductive machine downtime costs as well as labor costs available for application in this type of work.

The patrol operators worked in one of two physically distinct areas representing sequential processing steps as shown in Figure 8.13. Each was assigned a specific number of machines to service. When a machine interruption occurred, an operator was required to return the machine to productivity either working alone or in conjunction with another operator from the other area.

As shown in Figure 8.14, the production set-up for an individual machine has a wall physically separating it into two processing areas. On

* Reprinted with permission from *Industrial Engineering*, Vol. 6, No. 3, March 1974. Copyright © American Institute of Industrial Engineers, Inc., 25 Technology Park/Atlanta, Norcross, Ga. 30071.

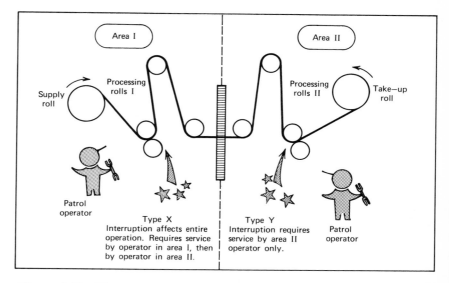

Figure 8.13 The production setup for an individual machine has a wall physically separating it into two processing areas.

each machine, material is pulled from a supply package through the set of processing rolls in area I. Then the material is passed through the wall and the set of processing rolls in area II, and finally onto the take-up package. The operator in area I is responsible for:

- Replacing empty supply packages with full ones.

- Monitoring and recording conditions related to the processing rolls in area I.

- Correcting malfunctions in feed through the rolls such as roll wraps and jammed rolls. Similarly, the operator in area II must correct similar malfunctions in the processing rolls in his area and replace full take-up packages with empty ones. A full supply package will last several hours and the repetitive duties related to monitoring and recording conditions do not require much time. Thus, the major portion of operator time is spent in locating and correcting malfunctions that cause interruptions in production. Since operators in each area have a number of machines to patrol, an interruption can occur while the operator is doing something else (such as correcting another interruption), so that a machine cannot be serviced immediately.

A type Y interruption in area II causes material to wind around the processing rolls, creating a certain amount of waste product. However,

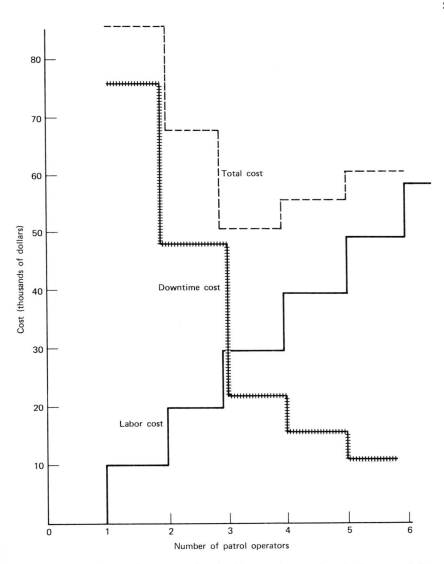

Figure 8.14 The total cost associated with patrol operations is the sum of the labor costs and the costs of machine downtime.

the operator in area I notices no change since material continues to be pulled through the wall. An interruption in area II is corrected by the operator in area II with no assistance from the operator in area I.

On the other hand, a type-X interruption in area I also stops the operation in area II. In order to correct the situation, the operator in area

I must rethread his processing rolls, then notify the operator in area II that he is ready to pass the material through the wall. The operator in area II must then rethread his rolls. In this case, area I and area II operators work as a team but do not leave their respective areas.

If the machine cannot be serviced immediately, then costs are accumulated due to the production of waste material as well as the loss of salable product which could have been produced. The total cost associated with patrol is the sum of the labor costs and the costs of machine downtime, Figure 8.14. The operators were also assigned to regular repetitive duties not directly related to servicing machine interruptions, some of which were deferrable and others nondeferrable. The deferrable, nonmachine service tasks were done during the operators' slack time when possible. The nondeferrable nonmachine service tasks were done whenever required and the machine servicing duties were subsequently delayed.

The machine interruptions are related to a number of factors, such as product mix and the level of production. Their occurrence is random. The operators have no control over preventing them. Servicing interruptions can be delayed with the result of incurring downtime and waste production costs.

Jobs that have significant patrol content are difficult to quantify by traditional work measurement techniques. Furthermore, even if the data are collected to compute patrol operator work load from task frequencies and task times, the results do not take into account the queueing effects of the situation where servicing tasks can accumulate and the total economics of the work assignment. Thus, it is possible to assign patrol responsibilities to an operator that would insure that the operator has a full work load on the average. However, the queueing nature of servicing needs in the problem are such that once the operator has a queue of patrol duties waiting, the consequences can be severe enough to warrant assigning extra operators to the operation. Thus, the most efficient operation from an overall cost viewpoint may be one in which the individual operators do not have a "full" work load (of course, an effort should be made to find constructive uses for this nonproductive operator time that would not interfere with the patrol duties).

A number of techniques other than simulation might have been used to develop the required labor standards. Simulation was chosen because it allows quantitative evaluation to be made of total cost considerations for a complex problem. Furthermore, simulation offers the advantage of not disrupting the production operation while "experimentation" is carried out in an "off-the-job" environment.

Once the scope of the problem was defined as involving only the patrol phase of production, the level of detail of the model needed to be determined. In order to do this, the modeler became intimately familiar with the operation. Only then could a set of logic and task priority rules be developed that would allow the model to duplicate the operation and generate information for the total cost evaluation without omitting any essential details or restrictions.

Production records provided the necessary information on interruption history. Interruptions were categorized by type or cause, and a distribution of time between interruptions was tabulated for each category. The machine interruption categories correspond to the service time classification previously prepared. Logic rules were developed that related the occurrence of interruptions in one of the two separate patrol areas with subsequent occurrence in the other area.

Cumulative frequency distributions were prepared for both service time and time between interruptions (Figure 8.15). The simulation

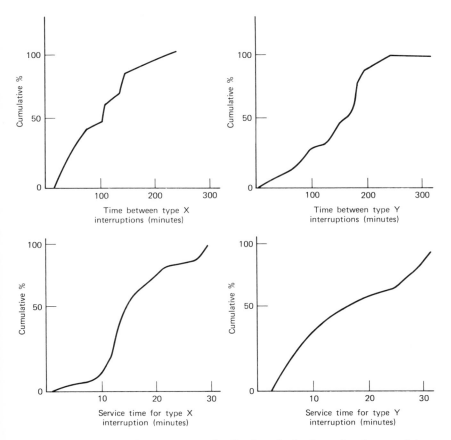

Figure 8.15 Cumulative frequency distributions for both service times and time between X- and Y-type interruptions.

package system used, IBM GPSS/360, required that distributions be in cumulative form. However, no assumptions had to be made to attempt to fit observed distributions with theoretical curves such as Poisson or exponential—the observed data were input directly. This avoided confusing production supervision with assumptions made on input data and allowed the logic of the model itself to be the primary interest.

The basic logic shown in Figure 8.16 was used in constructing the model. The individual steps shown represent a number of GPSS logic

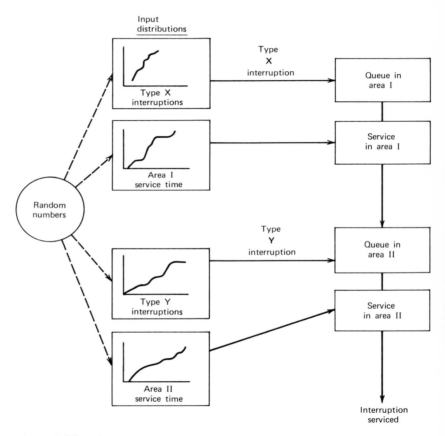

Figure 8.16   The basic logic used in constructing the simulation model.

blocks. Interesting statistics were operator utilization, average and maximum queue length in both areas, total downtime, and maximum downtime for individual breakdowns. The cost of waste was calculated from total downtime using production rate conversion and the unit cost of waste (assuming linearity). In like manner, the cost of machine downtime was calculated by multiplying total downtime by the cost of lost potential capacity per unit time.

Results of trial simulation runs and the basic model logic were reviewed with production supervision to establish the validity of the model. Then, the model was run with a fixed number of machines and operators in area I and area II, generating several months of simulated data. The number of operators in one or both areas was then varied and the model rerun to generate another set of simulated data. This process was repeated until the lowest total cost was determined for the machine level in question. Then, the number of machines was changed and the entire process repeated. At each machine level, the required labor standard corresponded to the lowest total cost situation (see Table 8.6) unless overridden by another factor, such as excessive downtime for individual breakdowns that might lead to machine damage or safety hazards.

The simulation model resulted in a 20-percent reduction in the standard labor requirements and an annual saving of $190,000. The simulation showed that the operation could be staffed with fewer patrol operators, reducing total costs despite an increase in downtime and waste production. However, any significant change in cost of labor, downtime, or waste would indicate the need to reevaluate the standards by simulation, which could be easily done by changing the appropriate model input parameters.

8.9 PROBLEMS

1. A gasoline station has two attendants. The primary work station of one attendant is at the gasoline pumps; the primary work station of the second is at the lubrication rack. The lubrication rack attendant only works at the pumps when there are three or more customers wanting gasoline. Only one customer can be serviced at the pumps at a time by one attendant because each customer automatically gets full service. Develop a systems flow chart of:

(a) The gasoline station system.

(b) A simulation model of the gasoline station system.

2. Go to the library and verify that the 20 random numbers from reference [12] at the end of this chapter, starting at the top of page 182 are 90500, 96657, 64842, 49222, 49506, 10145, 48455, 23505, 90430, 04180, 24712, 55799, 60857, 73479, 33581, 17360, 30406, 05842, 72044, 90764.

3. Assuming a game that utilizes two dice that are fair, and are thrown from a cup to determine how many squares a marker can be moved, construct a probability distribution table as illustrated in Table 8.1 showing the probability distribution and the cumulative distribution for moving from 2 through 12 squares on each throw of the dice. Using

Table 8.6 Simulation Results Show Operator Utilization and Total Annual Costs for Varying Numbers of Machines and Operators

| Machines | Operators | | Operator utilization | | Annual cost | | | *Indicates |
	Area I	Area II	Area I	Area II	Downtime	Labor	Total	level chosen
15	2	5			Continuous queue building			
15	3	4	.82	.97	$36,300	$52,500	$88,800	
15	3	5	.82	.77	15,800	60,000	75,800	*
15	2	6			Continuous queue building			
10	2	2			Continuous queue building			
10	2	3	.82	.86	$13,800	$37,500	$51,300	*
10	2	4	.81	.65	12,100	45,000	57,100	
10	3	3	.55	.86	13,600	45,000	58,600	
10	3	4	.54	.65	8,700	52,500	61,200	
8	2	2	.65	.99	$241,200	$30,000	$271,200	
8	2	3	.65	.68	8,100	37,500	45,600	*
8	2	4	.65	.51	7,400	45,000	52,400	
8	1	4			Continuous queue building			

the 20 random numbers in problem 2, how many squares would be traversed in a simulation of each of 20 dice throws in the game?

4. The sales records of a newsstand reveal that the daily sales (exclusive of weekends) of a certain newspaper occur with the frequencies shown:

No. of sales per day	97	98	99	100	101	102	103	104	105	106	107	108	109
No. of days occurring	11	14	15	22	26	28	29	27	24	21	16	14	13

Using the 20 random numbers of problem 2, generate the simulated sales for 20 days of operation of the newsstand. Plot the cumulative distribution curve of the historical records and the simulated sales. How do you explain the differences between the two curves? What would you do to get a closer fit of the curves?

5. Generate two random variables for each set of conditions shown below. In each case use the random numbers of problem 2 starting with the first and use as many random numbers as required to obtain the two random variables requested.

Distribution	Parameters
(a) Uniform, continuous	Over the range 2–8
(b) Uniform, discrete	Over the range 2–8
(c) Binomial	$n = 10$, probability of success of a Bernoulli trial, $p = .4$
(d) Normal	Over the range 60–100 with a mean of 75 and a standard deviation of 8.

6. For the distribution of daily sales of the newsstand in problem 4, the true mean is 103 and the standard deviation is 3.25. How many daily sales would you have to generate in a simulation in order to produce an experimental mean within ± 2 of the true mean with a probability of 95 percent.

7. Assume you do not know the mean and standard deviation of the daily sales distribution in problem 6. How many daily sales would you generate in a simulation to produce a mean of the daily sales that would fall within upper and lower limits of ± 2 with a 95 percent confidence level?

8. Consider the following system description containing an airport that is serviced by two crossing runways:

(a) Aircraft departure schedule—bunch aircraft to depart shortly after the hour and half hour.

(b) Aircraft ground servicing—during the busy hours of the day maximum time for an aircraft on the ground is 1.5 hours with .75 hours as the average. There is a minimum time interval between flights, however, of .33 hours.

(c) Runway scheduling—both runways are used when wind conditions permit; otherwise one runway is used for both takeoff and landing.

(d) Aircraft landing—under visual flight rules (VFR) the interval between aircraft ranges from 60 to 75 seconds. Landings under instrument flight rules (IFR) require 75 to 110 seconds. Weather conditions determine VFR and IFR.

(e) Crossing runway scheduling—when both runways are in use one is used only for landings and the other for takeoffs. At least 20 seconds must pass from the time the landing aircraft has touched down and passed the runway intersection point and the time the aircraft taking off will reach the intersection. Once the aircraft taking off has passed the intersection, 40 seconds are required until the landing aircraft can touch down.

You have been asked to develop a simulation model of the system. Specify:

(a) The events and attributes you would require in the model.

(b) The files you would establish for the conduct of the simulation.

(c) The statistics you would want to collect from the simulation experiment.

9. Prepare a review of between 400–500 words on a published report covering the use of simulation to solve a problem.

10. Conduct a simulation of the Chuck-A-Luck game to ascertain the expected winnings per game for each betting combination strategy described in Section 8.5. Which strategy would you follow to make your entertainment fund last the longest?

11. Esto Oil Company is considering bidding on a contract to supply fuel oil to a port in the United Kingdom. Esto's plan is to tap its production facilities in Africa and transport the oil in its own tankers. The fuel is to be delivered to the customer's tank facilities in port at the United Kingdom. The capacity of these facilities is 1250 units of oil and the customer's invitation to bid specifies that the supply must not be less than 250 units more than 5 percent of the time.

Demand on the tank facilities in the United Kingdom is uniformly distributed over the interval from 65 to 135 units, inclusive.

Esto management wants to know how many of its standard 625 unit tankers it must employ on a full-time basis to maintain the required service level.

Management also wants to know by what amount the demand in the United Kingdom could increase (assuming uniformly distributed demand

over a 71-unit level) before the customer's indicated "5 percent specification" could no longer be met without adding another ship to the run.

System constraints are:

(a) *Berth Facilities.* There is one berth in the United Kingdom and
two berths in Africa. 24 ± 6 hours and 20 ± 6 hours are required
to load a ship berthed in Africa and the United Kingdom,
respectively.

(b) *Travel Time.* 8 ± 2 days are required for a ship to make the trip
from Africa to Britain and 7 ± 2 days are required for the return
trip.

(c) *Weather.* A ship cannot enter or leave a berth during a storm.
Storms are seasonal with this pattern:

	Probability of a Storm	
	April 1 to Sept. 30	Rest of Year
Africa	.2	.1
United Kingdom	.1	.2

If a storm is in progress when a ship arrives at the United Kingdom,
its remaining duration can be approximated to be 4 ± 3 hours. If a storm is
in progress when a ship arrives at the African facility, its remaining
duration is approximately 5 ± 2 hours.

Esto's production facilities in Africa do not pose a constraint.

Construct and run a model for simulating Esto's situation for the
purpose of providing management with the requested information. What
additional information would be useful?

12. Air Manufacturer, Inc. has contracted with Crunchy Chips to
build an on-site nitrogen plant that will generate gaseous nitrogen that
will be bubbled through CC's potato chip vats. The nitrogen will reduce
the probability of the potato chip vats turning rancid. Simulation has been
suggested as an appropriate means of evaluating various designs for the
plant. Flow chart the system for the following conditions:

The Contract. AM, Inc. will provide CC with gaseous nitrogen for the
next 20 years at the rate of 350 mcf (thousand cubic feet) per hour around
the clock. Usage may vary ±10 percent from hour to hour. AM, Inc. will
be paid \$2,300,000 per year plus any incremental operating costs caused
by inflation. Product generated by the plant and not used by CC belongs
to AM, Inc. and may be sold to other customers. These sales are limited to
1.5 million cubic feet in any day. If CC has to shut down its equipment
because there is no nitrogen, AM, Inc. must pay 200 percent of all
shutdown costs to CC. The shutdown cost to CC is estimated to be
$\$5000+1000\times$ hours of shutdown.

Alternatives. AM, Inc. is considering the use of parallel medium size on-sites plus a buffer storage of liquid nitrogen. The buffer storage will be filled by liquefying excess nitrogen generated by the on-sites or with liquid nitrogen brought from other AM, Inc. plants. AM, Inc. considers an attractive rate of return to be 10 percent.

Equipment. The on-sites being considered cost $4,000,000 each and will have no salvage value at the end of the contract. They cost $25 per hour to operate. If the on-site is shut down for any reason, it costs $150 to restart the equipment and takes 4 hours. The equipment does not deteriorate significantly as long as the on-site is taken down for a preventive maintenance each year. There is some latitude about when the on-sites will be taken down but in no case can there be more than 14 months between maintenance. The on-sites may be taken down individually and the maintenance is equally likely to take any time between 30 and 60 hours. Table 8.7 shows a history of breakdowns on this equipment. Each on-site produces 200 mcf per hour of gaseous nitrogen. Excess nitrogen is either vented or it is liquefied and placed in the buffer tank.

Table 8.7 History of Breakdowns

Date	Hours Down
1/17/69	10
1/18/69	15
6/9/69	7
12/11/69	8
12/14/69	15
4/3/70	4
5/17/70	9
10/11/70	6
10/13/70	16
2/22/71	11
4/1/71	25
11/4/71	7
11/7/71	17
4/9/72	6
7/4/72	12
11/24/72	9
11/26/72	19
8/13/73	4
9/12/73	12
11/6/73	19
6/4/74	9
6/6/74	12
11/23/74	19

The costs to liquefy nitrogen are negligible but the efficiency of the process is only 50 percent.

The Buffer Tank. There is room for only one buffer tank. There are three tank sizes being considered:

$$5,000,000 \text{ cubic feet @ } \$500,000$$
$$10,000,000 \text{ cubic feet @ } \$1,500,000$$
$$20,000,000 \text{ cubic feet @ } \$4,000,000$$

The product is stored as a liquefied nitrogen and is evaporated as needed. The efficiency of the evaporation process is 100 percent and the cost is negligible. Trucks holding 750 mcf are available to supplement the storage. The cost of the first truck in a day is $500 and cost of the second truck is $1000. A maximum of two truckloads per day are available. Product sold out of the tank to other customers is valued at $350 per truckload.

Power Failures. Power failures are common during the months of June, July, and August. The interruptions occur at random and average one per month. The duration of the power failure can be described by an exponential distribution with a mean of five hours. During a power failure all on-sites are down but product must still be supplied to CC.

13. Develop a simulation program that will provide a risk profile on the investment in a new venture.

The user is expected to input information about (a) purchase price, (b) annual revenue, (c) annual expenses, (d) salvage value, and (e) service life. Each of these values will be input as risk variables having one of two distributions (a) uniform distribution or (b) triangular distribution defined by three estimates $(X, Y, \text{ and } Z)$ as indicated

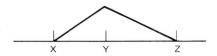

In addition the user will be required to supply deterministic inputs for (a) annual rate of return, (b) simulation seed, and (c) number of simulation runs (it is suggested that this be multiples of 100).

As an output the program should provide a risk profile of the present worth of the venture. The output should also include an estimate of the mean and standard deviation of the present worth of the project. You may ignore income tax considerations.

14. Prepare a report of between 750–1000 words highlighting the main features of one of the simulation languages listed below and be prepared to make a 10–15 minute oral presentation on that language to the remainder of the class.

(a) SIMSCRIPT II
(b) GPSS/360
(c) DYNAMO II
(d) GASPIV

REFERENCES

1. Box, G. E. P. and M. E. Muller, "A Note on the Generation of Random Normal Deviates," Annuals of Mathematical Statistics, XXIX, 1958.
2. Forrester, J. W., *Industrial Dynamics*, The M.I.T. Press, Cambridge, Mass., 1961.
3. General Purpose Simulation System/360, Introductory User's Manual, Program Library, Ref H20-0304-1, IBM Corp.
4. Gershefski, G. W., *The Development and Application of a Corporate Financial Model*, The Planning Executives Institute, Oxford, Ohio, 1968.
5. Hillier, F. S. and G. J. Lieberman, *Operations Research*, second edition, Holden-Day, Inc., San Francisco, Cal., 1974.
6. Hatsell, W. R. and D. E. Pendelton, "Standards for Patrolling Operations," *Industrial Engineering*, Vol. 6, No. 3, March 1974.
7. Kiviat, P. J., R. Villanueva and H. M. Markowitz, *The SIMSCRIPT II Programming Language*, Prentice-Hall, Englewood Cliffs, N.J., 1969.
8. Maisel, H. and G. Gnugnoli, *Simulation of Discrete Stochastic Systems*, Science Research Associates, Inc., Chicago, 1972.
9. Pritsker, A. A. B., *The GASPIV Simulation Language*, Wiley, New York, 1974.
10. Pugh, A. L., *DYNAMO User's Manual*, second edition, The M.I.T. Press, Cambridge, Mass., 1963.
11. Przybylski, E., "Simulation of Production Process Cuts Quality Control Costs," *Industrial Engineering*, Vol. 3, No. 5, May 1971.
12. Rand Corporation, *A Million Random Digits with 1,000,000 Normal Deviates*, The Free Press, New York, 1955.
13. Schmidt, J. W. and R. E. Taylor, *Simulation and Analysis of Industrial Systems*, Richard D. Irwin, Inc., Homewood, Ill., 1970.
14. Shannon, R. E., *Systems Simulation: The Art and Science*, Prentice-Hall, Englewood Cliffs, N.J., 1975.
15. Teichrow, D., J. Lubin and T. Truitt, "Discussion of Computer Simulation Techniques and Comparison of Languages," *Simulation*, Vol. 9, No. 4, October, 1967.

Appendix A
random numbers*

52065 08853	30104 79937	66913 53200	84570 78079	28970 53859
37632 80274	35240 32960	74859 07359	55176 03930	38984 35151
82576 82805	94031 12779	90879 24109	25367 77861	09541 85739
69023 64971	99321 07521	95909 43897	71724 92581	05471 64337
98949 03606	78236 78985	29212 57369	34857 67757	58019 58872
96526 28749	56592 37871	72905 70198	57319 54116	47014 18285
33692 72111	60958 96848	17893 40993	50445 14186	76877 87867
50335 09513	44346 26439	55293 06449	44301 63740	40158 72703
88321 85062	57345 66231	15409 03451	95261 43561	15673 28956
90303 62469	82517 43035	36850 15592	64098 59022	31752 04370
50486 11885	23085 41712	80692 48492	16495 99721	36912 28267
27882 16269	64483 11273	02680 01616	46138 54606	14761 05134
45144 63213	49666 27441	86989 29884	54334 06740	08368 80051
81020 17882	74973 74531	94994 24927	64894 22667	20466 82948
66831 47427	76033 31197	59817 20064	61135 28556	29695 80179
74058 18293	09963 35278	13062 83094	23373 90287	33477 48865
30348 70174	11468 25994	25343 22317	01587 30682	00001 67814
59557 23362	13746 82244	42093 24671	79458 93730	45488 60234
67098 09899	25775 00332	36636 57594	19958 85564	58977 12247
60774 66371	69442 20385	14486 91330	50332 46023	75768 59877
60081 92936	72302 75064	85727 52987	05750 19384	33684 78859
80458 69902	34870 88684	49762 40801	86291 18194	90366 82639
53844 96326	65728 48563	26027 52692	62406 76294	41848 63010
69841 29451	36170 21529	16525 64326	22086 24469	57407 96033
37771 31002	18311 93285	31948 14331	58335 15977	80336 81667

* Reproduced from page 7, *A Million Random Digits with* 1,000,000 *Normal Deviates*, The Free Press, 1955, with permission of the Rand Corporation.

27286	24361	61638	57580	95270	46180	76990	53031	94366	02727
49944	19278	05756	51875	53445	33342	01965	07937	10054	97712
87693	58124	46064	39133	77385	09605	65359	70113	90563	86637
94282	12025	31926	24541	23854	58407	32131	92845	20714	27898
26917	50326	35145	50859	72119	95094	29441	42301	62460	75252
94267	38422	73047	24200	85349	72049	91723	97802	98496	12734
73432	10371	57213	53300	80847	46229	07099	72961	13767	65654
31102	82119	96946	65919	81083	03819	57888	57908	16849	77111
41429	92261	45263	01172	55926	78835	27697	48420	58865	41207
21406	08582	10785	36233	12237	07866	13706	92551	11021	63813
71512	65206	37768	94325	14721	20990	54235	71986	05345	56239
52028	01419	07215	55067	11669	21738	66605	69621	69827	08537
18638	60982	28151	98885	76431	25566	03085	23639	30849	63986
73287	26201	36174	14106	54102	57041	16141	64174	03591	90024
73332	31254	17288	59809	25061	51612	47951	16570	43330	79213
11354	55585	19646	99246	37564	32660	20632	21124	60597	69315
31312	57741	85108	21615	24365	27684	16124	33888	14966	35303
69921	15795	04020	67672	86816	63027	84470	45605	44887	26222
79888	58982	22466	98844	48353	60666	58256	31140	93507	69561
06256	88526	18655	00865	75247	00264	65957	98261	72706	36396
46065	85700	32121	99975	73627	78812	89638	86602	96758	65099
52777	46792	13790	55240	52002	10313	91933	71231	10053	78416
54563	96004	42215	30094	45958	48437	49591	50483	13422	69108
59952	27896	40450	79327	31962	46456	39260	51479	61882	48181
50691	64709	32902	10676	12083	35771	79656	56667	76783	03937

Appendix B
cumulative normal
distribution*

$$F(x) = \int_{-\infty}^{x} \frac{1}{\sqrt{2\pi}} e^{-\frac{t^2}{2}} dt$$

x	.00	.01	.02	.03	.04	.05	.06	.07	.08	.09
.0	.5000	.5040	.5080	.5120	.5160	.5199	.5239	.5279	.5319	.5359
.1	.5398	.5438	.5478	.5517	.5557	.5596	.5636	.5675	.5714	.5753
.2	.5793	.5832	.5871	.5910	.5948	.5987	.6026	.6064	.6103	.6141
.3	.6179	.6217	.6255	.6293	.6331	.6368	.6406	.6443	.6480	.6517
.4	.6554	.6591	.6628	.6664	.6700	.6736	.6772	.6808	.6844	.6879
.5	.6915	.6950	.6985	.7019	.7054	.7088	.7123	.7157	.7190	.7224
.6	.7257	.7291	.7324	.7357	.7389	.7422	.7454	.7486	.7517	.7549
.7	.7580	.7611	.7642	.7673	.7704	.7734	.7764	.7794	.7823	.7852
.8	.7881	.7910	.7939	.7967	.7995	.8023	.8051	.8078	.8106	.8133
.9	.8159	.8186	.8212	.8238	.8264	.8289	.8315	.8340	.8365	.8389
1.0	.8413	.8438	.8461	.8485	.8508	.8531	.8554	.8577	.8599	.8621
1.1	.8643	.8665	.8686	.8708	.8729	.8749	.8770	.8790	.8810	.8830
1.2	.8849	.8869	.8888	.8907	.8925	.8944	.8962	.8980	.8997	.9015
1.3	.9032	.9049	.9066	.9082	.9099	.9115	.9131	.9147	.9162	.9177
1.4	.9192	.9207	.9222	.9236	.9251	.9265	.9279	.9292	.9306	.9319
1.5	.9332	.9345	.9357	.9370	.9382	.9394	.9406	.9418	.9429	.9441
1.6	.9452	.9463	.9474	.9484	.9495	.9505	.9515	.9525	.9535	.9545
1.7	.9554	.9564	.9573	.9582	.9591	.9599	.9608	.9616	.9625	.9633
1.8	.9641	.9649	.9656	.9664	.9671	.9678	.9686	.9693	.9699	.9706
1.9	.9713	.9719	.9726	.9732	.9738	.9744	.9750	.9756	.9761	.9767

* From A. M. Mood, *Introduction to the Theory of Statistics*. Copyright © 1950, McGraw-Hill. Used with permission of McGraw-Hill.

x	.00	.01	.02	.03	.04	.05	.06	.07	.08	.09
2.0	.9772	.9778	.9783	.9788	.9793	.9798	.9803	.9808	.9812	.9817
2.1	.9821	.9826	.9830	.9834	.9838	.9842	.9846	.9850	.9854	.9857
2.2	.9861	.9864	.9868	.9871	.9875	.9878	.9881	.9884	.9887	.9890
2.3	.9893	.9896	.9898	.9901	.9904	.9906	.9909	.9911	.9913	.9916
2.4	.9918	.9920	.9922	.9925	.9927	.9929	.9931	.9932	.9934	.9936
2.5	.9938	.9940	.9941	.9943	.9945	.9946	.9948	.9949	.9951	.9952
2.6	.9953	.9955	.9956	.9957	.9959	.9960	.9961	.9962	.9963	.9964
2.7	.9965	.9966	.9967	.9968	.9969	.9970	.9971	.9972	.9973	.9974
2.8	.9974	.9975	.9976	.9977	.9977	.9978	.9979	.9979	.9980	.9981
2.9	.9981	.9982	.9982	.9983	.9984	.9984	.9985	.9985	.9986	.9986
3.0	.9987	.9987	.9987	.9988	.9988	.9989	.9989	.9989	.9990	.9990
3.1	.9990	.9991	.9991	.9991	.9992	.9992	.9992	.9992	.9993	.9993
3.2	.9993	.9993	.9994	.9994	.9994	.9994	.9994	.9995	.9995	.9995
3.3	.9995	.9995	.9995	.9996	.9996	.9996	.9996	.9996	.9996	.9997
3.4	.9997	.9997	.9997	.9997	.9997	.9997	.9997	.9997	.9997	.9998

z	1.282	1.645	1.960	2.326	2.576	3.090	3.291	3.891	4.417
$F(z)$	.90	.95	.975	.99	.995	.999	.9995	.99995	.999995
$2(1-F(z))$		.20	.10	.05	.02	.01	.002	.001	.0001	.00001

index